CHURCH DOGMATICS
INDEX VOLUME

CHURCH DOGMATICS

BY

KARL BARTH

INDEX VOLUME
WITH
AIDS FOR THE PREACHER

EDITORS
THE REV. PROF. G. W. BROMILEY, D.LITT., PH.D., D.D.
THE VERY REV. PROF. T. F. TORRANCE, D.LITT., D.D., D.THEOL.

EDINBURGH: T. & T. CLARK LTD., 38 GEORGE STREET

Original German Edition

Published by

EVZ–VERLAG—ZÜRICH, 1970

Authorised English Translation

Copyright © T. & T. CLARK LTD., 1977

PRINTED IN SCOTLAND BY

MORRISON AND GIBB LIMITED

EDINBURGH AND LONDON

FOR

T. & T. CLARK LTD., EDINBURGH

0 567 09046 9

FIRST PRINTED 1977

EDITORS' PREFACE

PUBLICATION of the General Index brings to an end a work which began some forty years ago when Professor G. T. Thomson translated Volume 1, 1 of the Church Dogmatics. After the interruption of the second world war and its aftermath translation began again as a team project and once publication resumed the available volumes came out in rapid succession. Barth himself did not live to complete the projected series but an index volume was compiled with his approval. It is with the translation of this volume that we now complete the English version.

Attentive readers will quickly see that the General Index is essentially a compilation of the indexes to the individual volumes. It would have been an almost intolerable burden to have started again from the beginning but because the original indexes vary in quality and classification, at least in relation to subjects, a certain unevenness arises. If anything, this is compounded in the English by the inevitable change in the order of concepts and the related difficulties of cross-reference to the German. A useful innovation is the differentiation of type in biblical quotations and names which makes it easy to distinguish the more significant from the more incidental references. As regards the subjects we have attempted in this version some improvement in the grouping of concepts but these have been kept to a minimum so as not to complicate unduly the task of relating the English and the German. Incidentally readers who wish to find their way more readily from the translation to the original, or *vice versa*, might find it helpful to know that throughout the series 90 pages of English text correspond on a rough average to 100 pages of German, with some variation according to the amount of fine print.

As the original editors planned it, the General Index was to have included a series of essays on the significance of Barth's theology. In the event only one of these found its way into the German edition. As it seems to us, the inclusion of a single essay of this kind serves little useful purpose. Indeed, it is not obvious why Barth's own work should be padded out by evaluations that properly belong to another context. We have thus thought it better to abandon this part of the project and to add to the references only the preceding sectional theses and the ensuing selections from the different volumes presented in the Preachers' Aids.

The Preachers' Aids present problems of their own because of different versions of the Christian Year and the different readings which different churches assign for the individual days. Yet the difficulties are not insuperable. The structure of the Christian Year is basically the same and one can easily make the necessary adjustments, e.g., between Epiphany and Lent or Trinity and Pentecost. Enough readings are also given to cover varying situations or to open up new preaching possibilities for those who follow an alternative set of lections. In any case, Barth's theology stands in so integral a relation to the pulpit, and offers such enrichment in biblical exposition, reflection, and application, that even if some difficulties arise over the wider ecumenical area, the inclusion of the aids is, we think, abundantly worthwhile. Needless to say, the selections from Barth are not meant to replace the scriptural passages.

With the conclusion of the official series we wish to thank all those who have contributed to it in different ways. Translators, assistant editors, publishers and printers have all played their part magnificently in the formidable task of making this work available to English readers who cannot make use of the original German. For this Index volume we are particularly indebted to the Rev. Iain R. Torrance for considerable help with the proofs at every stage. Barth would have been the last to claim that wisdom either began or died with him. Nevertheless, there are in the Church Dogmatics rich stores of learning and understanding from which all of us can and ought to profit. To have helped to open up these stores to a broader range of readers is no little reward for the time and effort expended in the task.

PASADENA AND EDINBURGH, *Christmas* 1976

PREFACE

BETWEEN 1932 and 1967 Karl Barth published thirteen part-volumes of his *Church Dogmatics* with a total of more than 9000 pages. The larger the series grew, the more insistent became the demand for a comprehensive index. Not every reader found himself in a position to read through every part-volume from beginning to end. Many wanted to be able to use the part-volumes of the *Church Dogmatics* as a special kind of theological encyclopedia from some specific angle. When Barth decided to call a halt to the series, and to publish the fragment on baptism (IV, 4) as the final part, the preparation of a General Index seemed to him to be a worthwhile project, to which he gave immediate assent.

From the very outset it has obviously been necessary to think of the projected General Index not simply as a new arrangement of the indexes of Scripture References, Names and Subjects in the individual part-volumes. These indexes are undoubtedly of great assistance to readers of the parts concerned. But they also have some basic weaknesses. In particular there is no clear indication, in relation to the Scripture References and Names, whether the passage listed contains an express discussion or merely a bare mention. Preparation of a new index has had to seek essential improvements. This has posed a gigantic task, for at essential points the index has had to be reconstructed from the very foundation. The present work can meet much more exacting demands than the individual indexes. The indexes of Scripture References, Names and Subjects have been improved and integrated. Furthermore, the first two have been provided with a system of differentiation. The type enables the reader to see at a glance whether there is an express treatment of the reference or name in the body of the *Church Dogmatics* or whether there is only more or less incidental reference. Barth's theological work is thus opened up in a way which many will find helpful and which will make the use of the volumes easier.

But there is another aspect of the reconstruction. From the publication of the first part-volumes many pastors and church workers have consulted the *Church Dogmatics* as an exegetical, theological and practical aid in the preparation of sermons and other forms of Gospel proclamation. Previously this has involved various technical problems. To find in the *Church Dogmatics* the crucial expositions of specific passages or of theological questions relating to the message of Advent, Christmas, Easter, or Pentecost was time-consuming. One has only to try to do this to realise what laborious research is needed. The General Index is designed to offer alleviation in this respect too. It contains exegetical and theological extracts assembled from the whole set of the *Church Dogmatics* and arranged in six series (I–VI) as preachers' aids for the Christian year, so that some 400 meditations are provided based on Old or New Testament passages. Shortly before his death, in the radio broadcast " Music for a Guest," Barth himself said: " My whole theology, you see, is fundamentally a theology for parsons. It grew out of my own situation when I had to teach and preach and counsel a little " (*Letzte Zeugnisse*, Zürich, 1969, p. 19). This self-interpretation of Barth's theology shows how appropriate it is to provide these preachers' aids in the General Index.

Another proposal in the reconstruction of the indexes has also been considered but then dropped. The question arose whether the General Index should not contain a series of essays on the established influence of the *Church Dogmatics* in the various churches and branches of the Christian world. Such a series, however, would have changed the character of the General Index as a working volume and unduly extended its size.

The EVZ-Verlag has been fortunate to be able to entrust the preparation of the General Index to several scholars who by reason of their exactness and expertise have been in a position to complete the work in a comparatively short space of time. Professors Ernst Wolf and Helmut Gollwitzer offered valuable advice in the preliminary discussions. Richard Grunow, known as an outstanding Barth scholar from his *Barth Brevier* (Zürich, 1966), was chosen as the first editor, but in October, 1968, when in Zürich for discussions, he died tragically in a hotel fire. We lost in him a capable and willing helper. His place was taken by Pastor Helmut Krause (Basthorst), who has been aided by his wife, by Wolfgang Erk (Hamburg), by Marcel and Marianne Pfändler (Hombrechtikon-Zürich), and by a host of younger assistants. It is hard to convey how much editorial labour was involved in preparing this volume. While expressing our sincere thanks to all who had a hand in it, we express the hope that the General Index will make access to the *Church Dogmatics* much easier and thus further in its totality the theological work and the theological knowledge of our day.

Tenniken (Baselland) and Zürich,   For the EVZ-Verlag
        May, 1970   MAX GEIGER

CONTENTS

CONTENTS OF THE
CHURCH DOGMATICS

PART III   THE OUTPOURING OF THE HOLY SPIRIT

Chapter III   Holy Scripture

another in expounding and applying it. By the authority of Holy Scripture on which it is founded, authority in the Church is restricted to an indirect and relative and formal authority.

§21   FREEDOM IN THE CHURCH   I, 2, p. 661
A member of the Church claims direct, absolute and material freedom not for himself, but only for Holy Scripture as the Word of God. But obedience to the free Word of God in Holy Scripture is subjectively conditioned by the fact that each individual who confesses his acceptance of the testimony of Scripture must be willing and prepared to undertake the responsibility for its interpretation and application. Freedom in the Church is limited as an indirect, relative and formal freedom by the freedom of Holy Scripture in which it is grounded.

Chapter IV   The Proclamation of the Church

§22   THE MISSION OF THE CHURCH   I, 2, p. 743
The Word of God is God Himself in the proclamation of the Church of Jesus Christ. In so far as God gives the Church the commission to speak about Him, and the Church discharges this commission, it is God Himself who declares His revelation in His witnesses. The proclamation of the Church is pure doctrine when the human word spoken in it in confirmation of the biblical witness to revelation offers and creates obedience to the Word of God. Because this is its essential character, function and duty, the word of the Church preacher is the special and immediate object of dogmatic activity.

§23   DOGMATICS AS A FUNCTION OF THE HEARING CHURCH I, 2, p. 797
Dogmatics invites the teaching Church to listen again to the Word of God in the revelation to which Scripture testifies. It can do this only if for its part it adopts the attitude of the hearing Church and therefore itself listens to the Word of God as the norm to which the hearing Church knows itself to be subject.

§24   DOGMATICS AS A FUNCTION OF THE TEACHING CHURCH I, 2, p. 844
Dogmatics summons the listening Church to address itself anew to the task of teaching the Word of God in the revelation attested in Scripture. It can do this only as it accepts itself the position of the teaching Church and is therefore claimed by the Word of God as the object to which the teaching Church as such has devoted itself.

VOLUME II   THE DOCTRINE OF GOD

Chapter V   The Knowledge of God

§25   THE FULFILMENT OF THE KNOWLEDGE OF GOD   II, 1, p. 3
The knowledge of God occurs in the fulfilment of the revelation of His Word by the Holy Spirit, and therefore in the reality and with the necessity of faith and its obedience. Its content is the existence of Him whom we must fear above all things because we may love Him above all things; who remains a mystery to us because He Himself has made Himself so clear and certain to us.

Chapter VI   The Reality of God

Chapter VII   The Election of God

man is a predestination not merely of man but of Himself. Its function is to bear basic testimony to eternal, free and unchanging grace as the beginning of all the ways and works of God.

§33 THE ELECTION OF JESUS CHRIST   II, 2, p. 94
The election of grace is the eternal beginning of all the ways and works of God in Jesus Christ. In Jesus Christ God in His free grace determines Himself for sinful man and sinful man for Himself. He therefore takes upon Himself the rejection of man with all its consequences, and elects man to participation in His own glory.

§34 THE ELECTION OF THE COMMUNITY   II, 2, p. 195
The election of grace, as the election of Jesus Christ, is simultaneously the eternal election of the one community of God by the existence of which Jesus Christ is to be attested to the whole world and the whole world summoned to faith in Jesus Christ. This one community of God in its form as Israel has to serve the representation of the divine judgment, in its form as the Church the representation of the divine mercy. In its form as Israel it is determined for hearing, and in its form as the Church for believing the promise sent forth to man. To the one elected community of God is given in the one case its passing, and in the other case its coming form.

§35 THE ELECTION OF THE INDIVIDUAL   II, 2, p. 306
The man who is isolated over against God is as such rejected by God. But to be this man can only be by the godless man's own choice. The witness of the community of God to every individual man consists in this: that this choice of the godless man is void; that he belongs eternally to Jesus Christ and therefore is not rejected, but elected by God in Jesus Christ; that the rejection which he deserves on account of his perverse choice is borne and cancelled by Jesus Christ; and that he is appointed to eternal life with God on the basis of the righteous, divine decision. The promise of his election determines that as a member of the community he himself shall be a bearer of its witness to the whole world. And the revelation of his rejection can only determine him to believe in Jesus Christ as the One by whom it has been borne and cancelled.

Chapter VIII   The Command of God

§36 ETHICS AS A TASK OF THE DOCTRINE OF GOD   II, 2, p. 509
As the doctrine of God's command, ethics interprets the Law as the form of the Gospel, i.e., as the sanctification which comes to man through the electing God. Because Jesus Christ is the Holy God and sanctified man in One, it has its basis in the knowledge of Jesus Christ. Because the God who claims man for Himself makes Himself originally responsible for him, it forms part of the doctrine of God. Its function is to bear primary witness to the grace of God in so far as this is the saving engagement and commitment of man.

§37 THE COMMAND AS THE CLAIM OF GOD   II, 2, p. 552
As God is gracious to us in Jesus Christ, His command is the claim which, when it is made, has power over us, demanding that in all we do we admit that what God does is right, and requiring that we give our free obedience to this demand.

VOLUME III   THE DOCTRINE OF CREATION

Chapter IX   The Work of Creation

Chapter X   The Creature

Chapter XI   The Creator and His Creature

the angels, who precede the revelation and doing of His will on earth as objective and authentic witnesses, who accompany it as faithful servants of God and man, and who victoriously ward off the opposing forms and forces of chaos.

Chapter XII   The Command of God the Creator

VOLUME IV
THE DOCTRINE OF RECONCILIATION

Chapter XIII
The Subject-Matter and Problems of the Doctrine of Reconciliation

Chapter XIV   Jesus Christ, the Lord as Servant

Chapter XV   Jesus Christ, the Servant as Lord

sinful man in His community and thus gives him the freedom, in active
self-giving to God and his fellows as God's witness, to correspond to the
love of God in which God has drawn him to Himself and raised him up,
overcoming his sloth and misery.

Chapter XVI   Jesus Christ, The True Witness

§69   THE GLORY OF THE MEDIATOR   IV, 3, i, p. 3
" Jesus Christ as attested to us in Holy Scripture is the one Word of God
whom we must hear and whom we must trust and obey in life and in death."

§70   THE FALSEHOOD AND CONDEMNATION OF MAN   IV, 3, i, p. 368
As the effective promise of God encounters man in the power of the resurrection of Jesus Christ, man proves himself to be a liar in whose thinking, speech
and conduct his liberation by and for the free God transforms itself into an
attempt to claim God by and for himself as the man who is bound in his
self-assertion—a perversion in which he can only destroy himself and finally
perish.

§71   THE VOCATION OF MAN   IV, 3, ii, p. 481
The Word of the living Jesus Christ is the creative call by which He awakens
man to an active knowledge of the truth and thus receives him into the new
standing of the Christian, namely, into a particular fellowship with Himself,
thrusting him as His afflicted but well-equipped witness into the service of
His prophetic work.

§72   THE HOLY SPIRIT AND THE SENDING OF THE CHRISTIAN COMMUNITY
                                                IV, 3, ii, p. 681
The Holy Spirit is the enlightening power of the living Lord Jesus Christ
in which He confesses the community called by Him as His body, i.e., as
His own earthly-historical form of existence, by entrusting to it the ministry
of His prophetic Word and therefore the provisional representation of the
calling of all humanity and indeed of all creatures as it has taken place in
Him. He does this by sending it among the peoples as His own people,
ordained for its part to confess Him before all men, to call them to Him and
thus to make known to the whole world that the covenant between God and
man concluded in Him is the first and final meaning of its history, and that
His future manifestation is already here and now its great, effective and
living hope.

§73   THE HOLY SPIRIT AND CHRISTIAN HOPE   IV, 3, ii, p. 903
The Holy Spirit is the enlightening power in which Jesus Christ, overcoming the falsehood and condemnation of sinful man, causes him as a
member of His community to become one who may move towards his final
and yet also his immediate future in hope in Him, i.e., in confident, patient
and cheerful expectation of His new coming to consummate the revelation
of the will of God fulfilled in Him.

THE FOUNDATION OF THE CHRISTIAN LIFE   IV, 4, p. 2
A man's turning to faithfulness to God, and consequently to calling upon
Him, is the work of this faithful God which, perfectly accomplished in the
history of Jesus Christ, in virtue of the awakening, quickening and illuminat-

ing power of this history, becomes a new beginning of life as his baptism with the Holy Spirit.

The first step of this life of faithfulness to God, the Christian life, is a man's baptism with water, which by his own decision is requested of the community and which is administered by the community, as the binding confession of his obedience, conversion and hope, made in prayer for God's grace, wherein he honours the freedom of this grace.

SCRIPTURE REFERENCES

The General Index contains approximately 15,000 references from all the volumes of C.D. An eclectic procedure is followed here. There are two main groups (in heavy type and italics) in the left column and two subsidiary groups (one marked by *) in the right column. The references in the left column relate to particularly important expositions (e.g., I, 1: 472) and to others slightly less important, often philological exegesis (e.g., *I, 1: 495*). The passages marked by * in the other column often bear no direct relation to the biblical passage, but should not be disregarded in view of their significance in respect of other (e.g., historical, and usually longer) contexts. Passages which were previously provided with ff. have often been given more exactly. Finally in Synoptic references the parallels are given (though only in the main column). Thus a reference to Mark or Luke marked in the body of the text by " par." will correspond to a new reference to Matthew. This added feature arose out of the preparation of the Preachers' Aids and should reduce the burden of independent research. It should be noted that in the case of I, 1 the references are given from the second edition, with the corresponding pages from the first edition following in parentheses.

GENESIS

14

CHAP.

14¹¹			III, 1: 155
14¹⁵			II, 2: 673
14²⁰	III, 3: 487		
15			I, 2: 253
15²ᶠ·			II, 1: 601
15⁸, ¹⁰			III, 1: 107
15⁹ᶠ·	II, 1: 601		
15¹¹	II, 1: 361		II, 1: 339
15¹⁸			III, 3: 155
15²⁶	**III, 4: 369**		
16			I, 1: 237 (272)
16²ᶠᶠ·			III, 3: 435
16⁴			III, 1: 141
16²⁹	**III, 1: 221**		
17²ᶠ·			III, 1: 279
17⁵ᶠ·			II, 2: 674
17⁸ᶠ·			II, 2: 375
17⁸⁻¹⁶	IV, 3: 63		
17¹⁰ᶠ·			IV, 1: 428
18¹ᶠ·			II, 2: 356; IV, 1: 28; IV, 3: 690
19–20	I, 1: 180 (205)		
19³⁻⁶	**IV, 1: 423**		
19⁵			II, 2: 683; III, 1: 151; IV, 3: 692
19⁶	IV, 2: 512		
19⁸	**IV, 1: 424**		
19¹²			I, 2: 154
19¹²ᶠ·			II, 2: 674
19¹⁴ᶠ·			IV, 1: 628*
19¹⁷			IV, 4: 94
19²⁰			IV, 1: 424
19²¹ᶠ·			II, 2: 674
19²⁴			IV, 1: 428
20			II, 1: 451
20 f.			II, 2: 674
20¹ᶠ·			II, 2: 674
20²	**II, 2: 572**		I, 2: 274; II, 1: 302, 588*; III, 3: 178*
	IV, 1: 424		
	I, 2: 585		
20³	**IV, 3: 101**		
20³, ⁵	**II, 1: 452**		
20⁴			IV, 3: 255*
20⁵	**IV, 3: 101**		II, 2: 378
20⁶	IV, 2: 799		II, 1: 372
20⁷			IV, 4: 94
20⁸ᶠ·			III, 1: 221
20⁸⁻¹¹	**III, 4: 50, 53**		
20¹¹			III, 1: 19, 100; III, 2: 579
20¹²	**III, 4: 242 f.**		
	I, 2: 585		
	III, 4: 243		
20¹³	**III, 4: 344 ff., 397 ff.**		
20¹³ᶠ·			IV, 2: 466
20¹⁴	**III, 4: 232**		

CHAP.
40³⁵ . . . . I, 2: 201

JOSHUA

CHAP.

1-11	*IV, 3 : 578*	
1^{13}	. . . .	IV, 1: 179
2	. . . .	I, 2: 212; IV, 1: 28
$2^{1f.}$	. . . .	II, 2: 356
2^{1-20}	. . . .	IV, 3: 691
2^{12}	. . . .	I, 2: 425*
3	. . . .	IV, 4: 45
$3^{15f.}$	. . . .	III, 1: 147
4^6	. . . .	III, 4: 244
4^{24}	. . . .	IV, 3: 184
5^{13-15}	*III, 3 : 456 f.*	
5^{14}	. . . .	IV, 2: 429
6^{23}	. . . .	II, 2: 356
7^6	. . . .	IV, 2: 429
$7^{25f.}$	. . . .	III, 4: 437
$8^{34f.}$	. . . .	II, 2: 573
9^{27}	. . . .	II, 2: 357, 519*
10^{11}	. . . .	III, 3: 435
10^{12}	. . . .	III, 1: 159
10^{28}	. . . .	III, 2: 379
14^{13}	. . . .	III, 2: 580
20^6	. . . .	III, 4: 399
21^{45}	. . . .	IV, 3: 62
22^5	. . . .	I, 2: 385; IV, 2: 799
22^{31}	. . . .	IV, 3: 184
23^{14}	**IV, 3: 62**	
24	**IV, 1: 23**	III, 4: 476
24^{15}	. . . .	IV, 2: 781
$24^{15f.}$	**I, 2: 351**	

JUDGES

2^1	. . . .	III, 3: 488
$2^{11f.}$	. . . .	II, 1: 415
3^{10}	. . . .	III, 2: 357
$4^{17f.}$	. . . .	IV, 3: 691
5^{17}	. . . .	III, 1: 149
5^{20}	. . . .	III, 1: 159; III, 3: 449
5^{31}	. . . .	III, 1: 164; IV, 1: 566; IV, 2: 791 f.
$6^{11f.}$	. . . .	III, 3: 487
6^{11-24}	. . . .	IV, 3: 578
6^{12}	. . . .	III, 3: 503
6^{15}	. . . .	IV, 1: 440
6^{24}	. . . .	IV, 1: 25
8^{23}	*IV, 1: 438*	
9	. . . .	IV, 1: 437
$9^{1f.}$	. . . .	II, 2: 386
11^{15}	. . . .	II, 2: 356
13-16	. . . .	III, 4: 391
13^{2-23}	**III, 3: 487 ff.** . . .	III, 3: 504
13^{18}	. . . .	I, 1: 322 (370)

CHAP.

21^5		III, 2: 365
21^{15}		IV, 1: 457
21^{20}		IV, 1: 454
$21^{25f.}$		IV, 1: 454
22^{1-40}	**IV, 1: 458**	IV, 1: 454
22^{16}		IV, 1: 454
22^{19}	*III, 3: 448 f.*	II, 1: 474; III, 1: 191
$22^{21f.}$	*III, 2: 358*	
22^{24}		III, 2: 357
$22^{26f.}$		IV, 1: 454
22^{33}		II, 2: 381
22^{39}		IV, 2: 449
$22^{49f.}$		III, 1: 149

2 KINGS

$1^{10ff.}$		III, 3: 435
2^{1-18}	**III, 2: 636 f.**	
$2^{9, 15}$		III, 2: 357
4^{40}		IV, 3: 531
$5^{1f.}$		I, 2: 425; IV, 1: 28; IV, 3: 482, 488
5^7		III, 2: 616
5^{15}		IV, 3: 691
6^{16}	*III, 3: 395*	
$7^{2, 19}$		III, 1: 137
9^{30-37}	**IV, 1: 455**	
13^{23}		IV, 1: 24
$14^{23f.}$		IV, 2: 448
17^{16}		III, 1: 165; III, 3: 420
$17^{29f.}$		IV, 2: 450
19^7		III, 2: 358
19^{15}		II, 1: 302
$19^{15f.}$		III, 1: 40
$19^{16f.}$		II, 1: 452
19^{25}		III, 1: 12
19^{35}		III, 3: 487
$20^{1f.}$	**III, 4: 369 f.**	
$21^{3f.}$		III, 1: 165
$23^{2f.}$		II, 2: 573
$23^{5, 12}$		III, 1: 165
23^{15-20}	**II, 2: 397**	
23^{27}		II, 2: 376
23^{34}	*III, 1: 124*	
24^{16}		II, 2: 270
24^{17}		III, 1: 124; IV, 1: 469
25^{1-21}	**IV, 1: 471**	
$25^{27f.}$		II, 2: 57, 385

1 CHRONICLES

1		II, 2: 217
3^1		IV, 2: 432
5^{26}		III, 2: 365

CHAP.

$6^{9f.}$	. . . .	IV, 3: 399 f.
6^{12}	. . . .	IV, 3: 403
$6^{15f.}$	. . . .	IV, 3: 455, 459 f.
$7^{1f., 4f.}$	. . . . . .	IV, 3: 399
7^6	. . . .	IV, 3: 400
$7^{9f.}$	. . . .	III, 2: 589; IV, 3: 400
7^{12}	. . . .	III, 1: 172; IV, 3: 403
$7^{15f.}$	. . . .	III, 3: 599; IV, 3: 400
$7^{17f., 20}$	. . . . . .	IV, 3: 403
8^8	. . . .	I, 2: 585*; IV, 3: 456
$8^{8f.}$ **III, 2: 578**		
9	. . . . . .	II, 1: 388*
9^3	. . . . . .	III, 2: 617
9^6	. . . . . .	III, 1: 150
$9^{11f.}$	. . . . . .	IV, 3: 404
$9^{17f.}$	. . . . . .	IV, 3: 403
$9^{19, 22f.}$	. . . . .	IV, 3: 404
$9^{25f.}$	. . . . . .	IV, 3: 400
$9^{30f.}$	. . . . . .	IV, 3: 404
9^{33}	. . . . . .	IV, 3: 407
$9^{34f.}$	. . . . . .	IV, 3: 403
10^{1-3}	. . . . . .	IV, 3: 403
$10^{4f.}$	. . . . . .	I, 2: 51
10^8	. . . . . .	III, 1: 21
$10^{8f.}$	. . . . . .	III, 1: 245; IV, 3: 403
10^9	. . . . . .	III, 1: 150
10^{12}	. . . . . .	III, 3: 10*
$10^{16f.}$	. . . . . .	IV, 3: 404
$10^{18f.}$	. . . . . .	IV, 3: 399
$10^{20f.}$	. . . . . .	IV, 3: 403
$10^{21f.}$	. . . . . .	IV, 3: 400
$11^{7f.}$	. . . . . .	II, 1: 469
11^8	. . . . . .	III, 1: 140; III, 2: 590; III, 3: 420
12^2	. . . . . .	IV, 3: 455
$12^{3, 12}$	. . . . .	IV, 3: 456
$13^{1f.}$	. . . . . .	IV, 3: 456
13^4	. . . . . .	IV, 3: 456
13^5	. . . . . .	IV, 3: 455
$13^{7f., 9f.}$	. . . .	IV, 3: 455
13^{12}	. . . . . .	IV, 3: 455, 460
13^{15}	. . . . . .	IV, 3: 403
$13^{18f.}$	. . . . . .	II, 1: 388; IV, 3: 403
13^{22-25}	. . . . .	IV, 3: 403
$14^{1f.}$	. . . . . .	II, 1: 388; IV, 3: 400
14^2	. . . . . .	III, 2: 559
14^5	. . . . . .	III, 3: 228*
14^6	. . . . . .	IV, 3: 403
14^7	. . . . . .	IV, 3: 400
14^{7-12} *III, 1: 246*		
$14^{10, 12}$	. . . . .	IV, 3: 400
14^{13-17}	. . . . .	IV, 3: 400, 423 f.
14^{22}	. . . . . .	IV, 3: 399
15^8	. . . . . .	II, 1: 50

CHAP.

34^{16}	**II, 1: 392**	IV, 1: 535
34^{20}		III, 3: 174
35^{28}		II, 1: 385
36^{5}		III, 1: 140; III, 3: 426
$36^{5f.}$		II, 1: 107 f.
36^{6}		II, 1: 385; III, 1: 151, 181; III, 3: 174*; IV, 1: 531
$36^{6f.}$		III, 3: 60
36^{7}		II, 1: 594
36^{9}	**II, 1: 111** **IV, 3: 509**	I, 1: 465* (532*); II, 1: 108, 121, 263; III, 1: 120, 283; III, 2: 590; IV, 2: 122*
37^{4}		II, 1: 654; II, 2: 650*
37^{6}		III, 1: 164
37^{20}		IV, 1: 535
38		I, 2: 29
$38^{2f.}$		IV, 1: 536
39		I, 2: 29
39^{3}		III, 1: 245
39^{4}		I, 1: 387 (445)
$39^{4f.}$	**III, 4: 373**	
39^{5}		III, 2: 559
$39^{5f.}$		III, 2: 362
39^{12}		IV, 2: 628
$40^{7f.}$		IV, 1: 278, 281 f.
40^{7-9}		IV, 2: 518
40^{8}		II, 2: 604*
$40^{8f.}$		I, 2: 489; II, 2: 605*
$40^{12f.}$		II, 2: 604*
40^{16}		IV, 2: 792
40^{18}		II, 2: 604*
41^{5}		III, 2: 634
42		I, 2: 29; III, 2: 412*
42^{1}	*IV, 3: 534*	
42^{5}	**III, 2: 593** *III, 2: 328 f.*	
42^{10}	**III, 2: 592** **IV, 2: 665**	
42^{11}	**III, 2: 593** *III, 2: 328 f.*	
43		III, 2: 412*
43^{5}	**III, 2: 593** *III, 2: 328 f.*	
44		I, 2: 29
$44^{2f.}$		III, 2: 579
44^{4}		III, 3: 35*
$44^{7f.}$		IV, 3: 838
44^{23}		IV, 3: 717
45^{2}		I, 1: 122 (137)
45^{3}		I, 2: 153; II, 1: 653
45^{7}		II, 2: 344
46^{1-3}		III, 1: 148
46^{4}		III, 1: 280
$46^{4f.}$		II, 1: 480

CHAP.

89³		. . . . . .	II, 2: 342
89⁵	**III, 3: 446**	. . .	III, 1: 191; III, 3: 454; IV, 2: 512
89⁶		. . . . .	II, 1: 302; III, 3: 455 f.*
89⁷		. . . . .	III, 1: 191; III, 3: 454
89⁸ᶠ.	**III, 3: 456**		
89⁹ᶠ.		. . . . .	III, 1: 147
89¹¹ᶠ.		. . . . .	III, 1: 37
89¹⁴		. . . . .	I, 1: 191 (217); II, 1: 207
89²⁴		. . . . .	I, 1: 191 (217)
89²⁶ᶠ.		. . . . .	IV, 1: 169
89²⁷		. . . . .	IV, 3: 64
89³²ᶠ.		. . . . .	IV, 1: 169
89⁴⁸	**III, 2: 590**	. . .	III, 2: 591
90¹		. . . . .	II, 1: 108
90¹ᶠ.	*III, 2: 578*	. .	III, 2: 581
90²		. . . . .	III, 1: 146
90²ᶠ.	**II, 1: 609**		
90³		. . . . .	III, 1: 245; III, 2: 362; III, 3: 144
90⁴	**I, 2: 66**	. . .	III, 1: 125; III, 2: 510
90⁵		. . . . .	III, 2: 559
90⁷		. . . . .	I, 2: 262
90⁷ᶠ.		. . . . .	IV, 1: 536
90⁸		. . . . .	II, 1: 554
90⁹		. . . . .	III, 2: 559
90¹⁰	**III, 4: 570**	. .	III, 2: 362; IV, 3: 674
	III, 4: 473		
90¹²	**III, 2: 588**	. . .	I, 1: 387 (445); III, 2: 634; III, 4: 373
	III, 4: 589		
90¹³ᶠ.	*II, 1: 108*		
91¹ᶠ.	**II, 2: 559**		
91⁴		. . . . .	II, 1: 207
91⁵		. . . . .	III, 1: 128
91⁹⁻¹²	**III, 3: 517**		
91¹⁰ᶠ.		. . . . .	IV, 3: 811*
91¹¹ᶠ.	**III, 3: 518**		
91¹⁴ᶠ.		. . . . .	III, 4: 106
92¹²ᶠ.		. . . . .	III, 1: 155; IV, 1: 570
93¹		. . . . .	III, 1: 149; IV, 3: 57
93¹ᶠ.		. . . . .	II, 1: 108
93²		. . . . .	II, 1: 474
93²ᶠ.		. . . . .	III, 1: 148
93⁴ᶠ.		. . . . .	II, 1: 108
94⁵ᶠ.		. . . . .	II, 1: 555
94⁹		. . . . .	II, 1: 230*
94¹⁴		. . . . .	II, 2: 268, 276 f.*
94¹⁷		. . . . .	III, 2: 590
95¹⁸		. . . . .	IV, 3: 731
95³		. . . . .	III, 3: 155
95⁴		. . . . .	III, 2: 616
95⁴ᶠ.		. . . . .	II, 1: 107; III, 1: 37
95⁵		. . . . .	III, 1: 145
95⁶ᶠ.		. . . . .	IV, 3: 731
96		. . . . .	II, 1: 107

CHAP.

III, 4: 74

104	*II, 1: 108*	II, 1: 114*; III, 1: 21*
104¹ᶠ.	. . . . .	II, 1: 653*; III, 1: 119*
104³	. . . . .	III, 1: 137
104⁴	. . . . .	III, 3: 408*
104⁵	. . . . .	III, 1: 101
104⁵ᶠ.	. . . . .	III, 1: 146
104⁶	. . . . .	III, 1: 105
104¹⁴ᶠ.	. . . .	III, 1: 21
104¹⁹	. . . . .	III, 1: 163
104²⁰⁻²³	*III, 4: 527*	
104²³	. . . . .	III, 1: 20; III, 4: 472 f.
104²³ᶠ.	**III, 3: 87**	
104²⁴	. . . . .	II, 1: 114; IV, 3: 698*
104²⁷	**III, 1: 152** . .	III, 1: 245; IV, 3: 687
104²⁷ᶠ.	. . . . .	II, 1: 114
104²⁷ᶠᶠ.	. . . . .	III, 3: 59
104²⁹	**III, 2: 362** . .	I, 2: 262
104²⁹ᶠ.	*III, 1: 57* . . .	I, 1: 472 (539); III, 1: 107
104³⁰	. . . . .	I, 1: 472 (539); III, 1: 246
104³²	. . . . .	III, 1: 150
104³³	. . . . .	III, 3: 81
104³³ᶠ.	. . . . .	II, 1: 114
104³⁵	. . . . .	II, 1: 108
105	. . . . .	II, 1: 601; IV, 3: 55
105⁸	. . . . .	IV, 2: 774
105²⁶	. . . . .	II, 2: 342
105³¹	. . . . .	III, 3: 144
106	. . . . .	II, 1: 611; IV, 1: 571, 605; IV, 2: 774; IV, 3: 55
106⁴	. . . . .	II, 1: 354
106⁹	. . . . .	III, 1: 146
106¹⁶	*IV, 2: 512*	
106²³	. . . . .	II, 2: 342
107	. . . . .	IV, 2: 774; IV, 3: 55
107¹ᶠ.	. . . . .	III, 1: 155
107⁹	. . . . .	III, 2: 379
107¹⁷ᶠ.	. . . . .	III, 4: 369
107²³ᶠ.	. . . . .	III, 1: 149
107²⁴ᶠ.	. . . . .	IV, 2: 590
108⁴	. . . . .	IV, 3: 63
108⁵	. . . . .	II, 1: 353; III, 1: 140
109⁸	. -	II, 2: 469
109¹³ᶠ.	. . . .	III, 2: 634
109²⁶	*II, 1: 354*	
110	. . . . .	I, 2: 99
110¹ᶠ.	**III, 3: 439 f.**	
110⁴	. . . . .	I, 2: 426*; II, 2: 604; IV, 1: 276
111³	. . . . .	II, 1: 385
111⁷ᶠ.	. . . . .	IV, 2: 589
111⁹ᶠ.	**II, 1: 430**	
111¹⁰	. . . . .	IV, 3: 426
112¹	. . . . .	II, 1: 737

CHAP.

124^1f.		IV, 1: 733; IV, 3: 732
124^2		IV, 2: 222*
124^2f.		III, 1: 148
124^6		IV, 3: 732
124^6f.		IV, 2: 222*
124^7		III, 1: 176
124^8		IV, 1: 733
127^1		III, 3: 95; III, 4: 316; IV, 3: 732
127^1f.		II, 1: 6
127^2		II, 2: 344
127^3f.		III, 4: 266
130		I, 2: 29; IV, 1: 606
132^13		II, 1: 480
135^1f.	**II, 1: 479 f.**	
135^4		IV, 2: 768
135^5f.		II, 1: 558
135^19		III, 4: 74
135^21	**II, 1: 480**	
136		III, 3: 90; IV, 1: 605; IV, 3: 55
136^2f.		III, 1: 162
136^5		III, 1: 52
136^6		III, 1: 146
136^26		III, 3: 438
138^1f.		III, 4: 95
139		I, 2: 29, 274
139^1f.	**IV, 1: 482** .	I, 2: 271; II, 1: 228, 554; III, 3: 135
	II, 2: 636	
139^2	**II, 1, 228**	
139^5		I, 1: 445 (510); IV, 1: 327; IV, 4: 36
139^5-10	**II, 1: 469** .	II, 1: 476, 478
139^5-12	**III, 2: 141**	
139^6		II, 1: 184*
139^7	*II, 2: 636* .	I, 1: 472 (539); II, 1: 57; III, 2: 356
139^8		III, 2: 590, 616; III, 3: 425
139^8ff.	**III, 3: 437**	
139^9		III, 1: 145
139^10		III, 3: 35*
139^11f.		II, 1: 555
139^12	**III, 1: 106**	
139^14		III, 2: 172
139^14f.		III, 1: 20 f.
139^16	**III, 2: 537** .	I, 2: 67; III, 3: 228
139^19f.		II, 1: 108
139^23f.	*II, 2: 636* .	II, 1: 558*
141^2		III, 3: 471
142		I, 2: 29
142^3		III, 2: 365
142^5f.		IV, 1: 607
143		I, 2: 29; II, 1: 388
143^1		II, 1: 385
143^1f.		IV, 1: 607
143^2		II, 1: 387*
143^4		III, 2: 365

PROVERBS

CHAP.

$3^{11f.}$	. . . . .	IV, 1: 537
3^{12}	*III, 4: 281* . . .	II, 1: 361
3^{14-26}	. . . . .	II, 1: 428 f.*
3^{18}	. . . . .	III, 1: 155, 275, 282 f.
3^{19}	. . . . .	III, 1: 52*
3^{34}	*IV, 1: 189*	
6^{6-11}	**III, 4: 472**	
$6^{20f.}$	. . . . .	III, 4: 244
6^{23}	. . . . .	III, 1: 105
7^{23}	. . . . .	III, 2: 435
8	. . . . .	I, 2: 144*; II, 1: 429–431; III, 1: 52,* 57
8^{17}	. . . . .	II, 1: 279, 429
$8^{22f.}$	. . . . .	III, 1: 52*
$8^{27f.}$	. . . . .	III, 1: 145
$8^{30f.}$	**III, 3: 86**	
8^{31}	. . . . .	II, 1: 666*
8^{35}	. . . . .	II, 1: 429*
9^{1}	. . . . .	I, 1: 64* (71)*
9^{10}	**IV, 3: 184** . .	IV, 3: 426
$9^{10f.}$	. . . . .	II, 1: 429 f.*
$9^{16, 18}$	. . . . .	II, 1: 429*
10^{1}	. . . . .	III, 4: 244
10^{2}	. . . . .	II, 1: 385
10^{7}	. . . . .	III, 2: 634
$10^{11, 14, 21}$	. . . .	IV, 2: 424 f.*
$11^{5, 18}$	. . . . .	II, 1: 385
12^{1}	. . . . .	IV, 2: 425*
12^{10}	**III, 4: 352** . . .	I, 2: 387; III, 1: 180
$12^{15, 23}$	. . . . .	IV, 2: 424*
13^{6}	. . . . .	II, 1: 385
13^{20}	. . . . .	IV, 2: 424*
13^{24}	. . . . .	III, 4: 281
$14^{8, 16, 24}$	. . . . .	IV, 2: 424*
14^{30}	. . . . .	III, 1: 245
14^{34}	**III, 1: 272** . . .	II, 1: 385
15^{7}	. . . . .	IV, 2: 425*
15^{20}	. . . . .	III, 4: 244
15^{21}	. . . . .	IV, 2: 424*
15^{29}	**II, 1: 511**	
16^{1}	**III, 4: 632** . .	III, 3: 95
16^{2}	. . . . .	III, 2: 365
16^{4}	. . . . .	II, 2: 129*
16^{9}	**III, 4: 632** . .	III, 3: 95
16^{33}	. . . . .	III, 3: 95
17^{12}	. . . . .	IV, 2: 424*
17^{25}	**III, 4: 244**	
17^{28}	. . . . .	IV, 2: 424*
18^{6}	. . . . .	IV, 2: 424*
18^{10}	**IV, 4: 94** . .	III, 4: 314*
18^{22}	*III, 1: 326*	
19^{14}	**III, 4: 227**	
19^{18}	. . . . .	III, 4: 281

CHAP.

14^{4-21}	*III, 2: 634*	
14^{10}		III, 2: 589
14^{12}		III, 1: 167; III, 3: 530
14^{13}	*III, 1: 101*	
$14^{14f.}$		III, 1: 140
14^{18}		III, 2: 634
14^{20}		III, 2: 634
17^{7}		III, 1: 12*
$17^{12f.}$		III, 1: 148
18^{4}		II, 1: 505
$19^{18f.}$		IV, 1: 28
19^{18-25}		IV, 3: 59*
19^{21}	**III, 4: 476**	
$20^{2f.}$		III, 1: 329
$21^{1f.}$		III, 1: 155
$21^{11f.}$	**III, 1: 128**	
$22^{9f.}$		III, 1: 40
22^{11}		III, 1: 12
24^{1}		III, 1: 155
$24^{1f.}$	*III, 1: 159*	
24^{4}		III, 1: 167
24^{23}		III, 1: 151; III, 3: 155, 464
25^{6}		II, 2: 279
$25^{6f.}$		IV, 1: 28
25^{7}		IV, 2: 160
25^{8}	**III, 2: 617**	
$26^{2f.}$		IV, 1: 606
$26^{8f.}$		II, 1: 654
26^{9}		III, 2: 365
26^{12}		III, 3: 133*
26^{16}		III, 3: 95
26^{19}	*III, 2: 619*	III, 2: 590
27^{1}	*III, 1: 172*	III, 1: 142
28^{16}		II, 1: 390; II, 2: 241, 248
29^{9-12}		II, 2: 277
29^{10}		III, 1: 325
29^{13}		II, 2: 482; III, 2: 504*; III, 4: 251
$29^{13f.}$	**III, 4: 113**	
29^{14}		II, 1: 435
29^{18}		III, 1: 127
29^{19}		II, 1: 654
29^{23}		II, 1: 361
29^{24}		III, 2: 358
30^{1}		IV, 1: 171
30^{7}		III, 2: 358
30^{9}		IV, 1: 171
$30^{15f.}$		IV, 2: 562
$30^{18f.}$		II, 1: 381
$30^{20f.}$	*IV, 2: 562*	
30^{25}		III, 1: 280
30^{26}		III, 1: 165
30^{27}		IV, 4: 94
31^{4}		III, 1: 151

EZEKIEL

CHAP.

32²⁷	. . . . . .	III, 2: 589
33¹¹	. . . . . .	III, 2: 617; III, 4: 400
34²⁻⁶	**IV, 2: 186 f.**	
34²⁵, ²⁸	. . . . . .	III, 1: 280
36²³	. . . . . .	IV, 2: 501
36²⁵	. . . . . .	I, 2: 242; IV, 4: 115
36²⁵ᶠ.	. . . . . .	I, 2: 222
36²⁶	. . . . . .	II, 2: 604; IV, 2: 780
36²⁶ᶠ.	. . . . . .	IV, 1: 32; IV, 2: 561; IV, 4: 8
36²⁸	. . . . . .	IV, 1: 22–34*
36²⁹	. . . . . .	III, 3: 144
36³⁵	. . . . . .	III, 1: 277
37	. . . . . .	IV, 1: 325, 468
37¹⁻¹¹	**III, 1: 247 f.**	
37¹⁻¹⁴	. . . . . .	III, 2: 361, 619
37¹⁴	. . . . . .	III, 3: 143
37²⁶	. . . . . .	II, 2: 102
37²⁸	. . . . . .	IV, 2: 501
38²⁰	. . . . . .	III, 1: 171, 181
47¹ᶠ.	. . . . . .	IV, 1: 31
47¹⁻¹²	. . . . . .	III, 1: 280*; IV, 3: 57
47⁸ᶠ.	. . . . . .	III, 1: 176

DANIEL

2¹⁸ᶠ.	. . . . . .	III, 1: 140
2¹⁹	. . . . . .	III, 3: 438
2²¹	. . . . . .	I, 2: 67
2²²	. . . . . .	III, 1: 120
3²⁵ᶠ.	. . . . . .	IV, 2: 831
4⁷ᶠ.	. . . . . .	III, 1: 154 f.; III, 3: 426
4¹⁰	. . . . . .	III, 3: 454
4¹⁴	. . . . . .	III, 1: 154, 191; III, 3: 454
4¹⁷	. . . . . .	IV, 3: 184
4²⁰	. . . . . .	III, 3: 454
4³⁴	. . . . . .	III, 3: 155
5¹²	. . . . . .	III, 2: 365
5²³	. . . . . .	III, 2: 362
6¹⁶	. . . . . .	I, 1: 265 (305)
7	**I, 2: 99**	III, 2: 45 f., 209; III, 4: 476; IV, 1: 16 ;
7¹ᶠ.	. . . . . .	III, 1: 206
7¹⁰	. . . . . .	III, 1: 191; III, 3: 456; IV, 1: 332
7¹³	**III, 2: 45**	IV, 3: 292
7¹³ᶠ.	. . . . . .	II, 2: 102; III, 3: 436
7¹⁴	. . . . . .	III, 3: 440
7²⁷	. . . . . .	IV, 2: 512
8¹⁰	. . . . . .	III, 3: 426
8¹⁴	. . . . . .	III, 1: 130
8¹⁶	. . . . . .	III, 3: 455, 457
8¹⁸	. . . . . .	III, 1: 325
9⁴	. . . . . .	II, 1: 354; IV, 2: 799
9⁴ᶠ.	. . . . . .	II, 1: 389
9²¹	. . . . . .	III, 3: 455, 457

CHAP.

11⁴	**II, 1: 453**	.	.	.	I, 2: 377; IV, 2: 758
11⁸ᶠ.	**IV, 2: 758**				
11⁹	.	.	.	.	.	.	IV, 2: 500
11¹¹	.	.	.	.	.	.	III, 1: 176
13⁵	.	.	.	.	.	.	III, 1: 155
13¹⁴	**III, 2: 616**				
14⁴	.	.	.	.	.	.	IV, 2: 761

JOEL

1¹²	.	.	.	.	.	.	III, 1: 155
2¹⁰	.	.	.	.	.	.	III, 1: 166; III, 3: 420
2¹¹	.	.	.	.	.	.	II, 1: 390
2¹³	.	.	.	.	.	.	I, 2: 68; II, 1: 381, 407, 498
2²²	.	.	.	.	.	.	III, 1: 155, 180
2²⁸	**IV, 4: 77**	.	.	.	I, 1: 455 (521); IV, 2: 332
2³²	.	.	.	.	.	.	II, 2: 249*; III, 1: 151; IV, 4: 77, 94
3¹⁵	.	.	.	.	.	.	III, 1: 166
3¹⁶	.	.	.	.	.	.	III, 3: 445
3¹⁸	.	.	.	.	.	.	III, 1: 280

AMOS

1¹	**IV, 2: 445–452**				
1²	.	.	.	.	.	II, 2: 397; IV 2: 446, 448
1³ᶠ., ⁶ᶠ., ¹¹ᶠ., ¹³ᶠ.	.	.	.	IV, 2: 447
2¹ᶠ.	.	.	.	.	.	IV, 2: 447
2⁶	.	.	.	.	.	.	IV, 2: 449
2⁶ᶠ.	.	.	.	.	.	IV, 2: 449
2⁷	.	.	.	.	.	.	IV, 2: 449 f.
2⁸	.	.	.	.	.	.	IV, 2: 449
2¹¹ᶠ.	.	.	.	.	.	IV, 2: 450
2¹³ᶠ.	.	.	.	.	.	IV, 2: 446
2¹⁶	.	.	.	.	.	III, 1: 329
3¹	.	.	.	.	.	.	IV, 2: 451
3²	**IV, 2: 768**	.	.	.	IV, 2: 451; IV, 3: 725
3⁶	.	.	.	.	.	.	III, 1: 106
3⁷	**I, 2: 490**	.	.	.	III, 3: 24, 143
3⁸	.	.	.	.	.	.	II, 2: 397; IV, 2: 446
3⁹ᶠ.	.	.	.	.	.	IV, 2: 450
3¹⁰, ¹², ¹⁵	.	.	.	.	IV, 2: 449
4¹	.	.	.	.	.	.	IV, 2: 449
4⁴	.	.	.	.	.	.	I, 2: 328*
4⁴ᶠ.	.	.	.	.	.	IV, 2: 551
4⁶ᶠ.	.	.	.	.	.	IV, 2: 446
4¹¹	.	.	.	.	.	.	II, 2: 232
4¹³	.	.	.	.	.	.	III, 1: 106
5²	.	.	.	.	.	.	IV, 2: 447
5⁴	.	.	.	.	.	.	IV, 2: 451, 562
5⁴ᶠ.	.	.	.	.	.	IV, 2: 451
5⁵	.	.	.	.	.	.	I, 2: 328
5⁷	.	.	.	.	.	.	IV, 2: 450
5⁸ᶠ.	.	.	.	.	.	III, 1: 164

OBADIAH

JONAH

CHAP.

3^4 . . . . . . III, 2: 452
$3^{5f.}$ *IV, 3: 691*
3^8 . . . . . . III, 1: 181; IV, 2: 565
4 . . . . . . III, 1: 399*
4^2 . . . . . . II, 1: 407, 414, 498
$4^{5f.}$ . . . . . . II, 1: 414
4^8 *III, 2: 598*
4^{11} . . . . . . III, 1: 180, 286

MICAH

1^8 *III, 1: 329*
3^6 . . . . . . I, 1: 158 (180)
3^8 . . . . . . III, 2: 257
$4^{1f.}$ . . . . . . IV, 1: 28; IV, 3: 58
4^7 . . . . . . III, 1: 151
5^3 . . . . . . II, 2: 102
6^8 **II, 2: 572 f., 704** . II, 2: 537–551*; IV, 3: 193
7^6 *III, 4: 261* . . II, 2: 158
$7^{7f.}$ . . . . . . II, 1: 388*
$7^{18f.}$ . . . . . . III, 2: 579 f.*

NAHUM

1^3 . . . . . . III, 1: 147

HABAKKUK

1^1 . . . . . . III, 3: 24
2^3 **IV, 3: 913**
2^4 **II, 1: 390**
2^5 **III, 2: 591**
2^{14} . . . . . . III, 1: 151; IV, 3: 59
3^3 . . . . . . III, 1: 150
3^8 . . . . . . III, 1: 147
3^{10} . . . . . . III, 1: 151

ZEPHANIAH

1^5 . . . . . . III, 1: 165
1^{14} . . . . . . II, 1: 390
1^{15} . . . . . . III, 1: 127
3^9 . . . . . . III, 4: 476; IV, 3: 59

HAGGAI

1^{13} *III, 3: 513*
$2^{6, 21}$ . . . . . . III, 3: 445
2^{23} . . . . . . II, 2: 342; IV, 2: 762

ZECHARIAH

MALACHI

ECCLESIASTICUS

SONG OF THE THREE CHILDREN

MATTHEW

CHAP.

5¹⁴ᶠ·	**IV, 1: 776** . . .	I, 2: 414; II, 2: 429, 695; IV, 2: 157, 326 f.
5¹⁴⁻¹⁶	**I, 1: 50 (54)**	
5¹⁵	. . . . .	III, 2: 506; IV, 1: 724*
5¹⁶	. . . . .	II, 2: 692; III, 3: 433; IV, 1: 690*; IV, 2: 804; IV, 3: 510
5¹⁶ᶠ·	. . . . .	IV, 2: 593
5¹⁷	**I, 2: 489** . . .	II, 2: 245, 691, 696; III, 2: 60, 460; IV, 2: 199 f.
5¹⁷ᶠ·	**IV, 2: 551** . . .	I, 2: 72, 514, 517*; II, 2: 563, 690, 696; IV, 2: 173, 177, 200
5¹⁷⁻²⁰	**II, 1: 384**	
5¹⁸	. . . . .	III, 1: 141
5¹⁹	. . . . .	III, 3: 434
5²⁰	**IV, 2: 200, 551** . .	II, 2: 689, 690 f.; III, 3: 434
5²¹ᶠ·	. . . . .	II, 2: 689, 690 f.; III, 4: 399
5²¹⁻²⁶	**III, 4: 413**	
5²¹⁻⁴⁸	. . . . .	II, 2: 696; IV, 2: 174, 199, 549, 551
5²²	. . . . .	IV, 2: 426 f.*
5²³ᶠ·	. . . . .	IV, 2: 173 f.
5²⁵	*II, 2: 480*	
5²⁵ᶠ·	. . . . .	IV, 2: 174
5²⁶	. . . . .	II, 2: 486
5²⁷	. . . . .	III, 2: 415
5²⁷⁻³¹	. . . . .	III, 4: 144
5²⁸	**III, 4: 233** . .	IV, 2: 466
5²⁹	. . . . .	II, 2: 696; III, 1: 30
5³¹	*III, 4: 204*	
5³¹ᶠ·	**III, 4: 233**	
5³²	. . . . .	III, 4: 205*
5³³ᶠ·	. . . . .	II, 2: 691; III, 4: 206
5³⁴	. . . . .	II, 1: 474; III, 3: 438
5³⁵	. . . . .	III, 1: 150; III, 3: 155
5³⁸ᶠ·	. . . . .	II, 2: 691; III, 4: 206; IV, 2: 179, 549
5³⁸⁻⁴²	. . . . .	III, 4: 429 f.
5³⁸⁻⁴⁴	**IV, 2: 179**	
5³⁹	**IV, 2: 548** . . .	II, 2: 696
5³⁹ᶠ·	**III, 4: 679** . . .	IV, 1: 190, 243
5⁴⁰, ⁴²	. . . . .	IV, 2: 548
5⁴³ᶠ·	. . . . .	I, 2: 419; IV, 1: 190, 243
5⁴³⁻⁴⁸	**IV, 2: 550** . . .	IV, 2: 805*
5⁴⁴	**IV, 3: 625** *III, 2: 582*	
5⁴⁴ᶠ·	. . . . .	III, 4: 111*
5⁴⁴⁻⁴⁸	**II, 2: 567**	
5⁴⁵	**IV, 1: 210** . . .	II, 1: 508; III, 1: 164; III, 3: 67; IV, 1: 191; IV, 2: 223, 764, 775; IV, 3: 336, 789; IV, 4: 98
5⁴⁵ᶠ·	. . . . .	IV, 2: 764
5⁴⁸	**I, 2: 396** . . . **II, 2: 512, 567**	III, 4: 649; IV, 1: 190; IV, 2: 167
6¹ᶠ·	. . . . .	II, 2: 689; IV, 2: 174
6¹⁻¹⁸	**III, 4: 667** . . .	II, 2: 694; IV, 2: 552*

CHAP.

10^{20}	. . . . . .	III, 4: 90; IV, 3: 646; IV, 4: 31
10^{21}	. . . . .	III, 4: 261
10^{22}	**IV, 3: 624 f.**	
$10^{22f.}$	**III, 2: 500**	
10^{23}	**IV, 3: 626** . . .	IV, 3: 295
10^{24}	. . . . .	I, 2: 678; IV, 3: 180*
$10^{24f.}$	**II, 2: 499** . . .	II, 2: 448; III, 2: 500; IV, 1: 244
	III, 4: 662	
	IV, 3: 640	
10^{25}	. . . . .	IV, 2: 203, 208, 548
$10^{26f.}$	*II, 2: 448* . . .	II, 2: 597; IV, 2: 181
10^{26-28}	. . . .	IV, 3: 647*
10^{26-34}	**IV, 1: 776–779**	
10^{27}	**IV, 3: 844** . . .	IV, 2: 264, 552*
	IV, 4: 147	
10^{28}	**III, 2: 379** . . .	III, 2: 354
$10^{28f.}$	. . . . .	IV, 2: 181, 549 f*
10^{29}	. . . . .	III, 3: 95
$10^{29f.}$	**III, 3: 174** . . .	II, 1: 554; III, 1: 39
10^{31}	**IV, 3: 645** . . .	III, 1: 175; IV, 2: 181
10^{32}	**IV, 1: 777**	
	IV, 3: 642, 789	
$10^{32f.}$	**III, 4: 76** . . .	I, 2: 415; IV, 1: 218
10^{33}	. . . . .	IV, 2: 539; IV, 3: 640
10^{34}	**III, 4: 263** . . .	I, 2: 680; IV, 1: 218; IV, 2: 419; IV, 3: 237, 899*
	IV, 1: 777	
	IV, 3: 625	
$10^{34f.}$	. . . . .	III, 2: 60; IV, 2: 559
10^{34-37}	**III, 4: 261 f.**	
	IV, 2: 158	
10^{36}	. . . . .	IV, 3: 625
10^{38}	. . . . .	I, 2: 277, 678; II, 2: 569; IV, 3: 647
$10^{38f.}$	. . . . .	IV, 1: 218
10^{39}	. . . . .	III, 2: 354; IV, 3: 627, 640, 652
10^{40}	**I, 2: 487** . . .	I, 2: 211
10^{42}	**I, 2: 447**	
11^{2}	**I, 1: 102 (115)** . .	III, 2: 460, 498; IV, 4: 63
$11^{2f.}$	. . . .	III, 2: 331, 460
11^{2-6}	**I, 2: 57 f.** . .	I, 2: 27
11^{2-15}	**IV, 2: 206**	
11^{3}	. . . . .	I, 2: 22, 120; IV, 2: 206
$11^{3f.}$	. . . . .	IV, 2: 197
11^{4}	. . . . .	II, 2: 674
$11^{4f.}$	. . . . .	IV, 1: 127; IV, 2: 196
11^{5}	. . . . .	IV, 2: 191
$11^{5f.}$	**III, 2: 600**	
11^{6}	. . . . .	I, 2: 62; IV, 2: 168, 189, 206
11^{9}	. . . . .	I, 2: 120, 675
11^{10}	*III, 3: 513* . .	IV, 2: 160
11^{11}	. . . . .	I, 2: 120; IV, 2: 160, 206; IV, 4: 55
11^{12}	. . . . .	III, 2: 460; III, 3: 434; IV, 2: 160; IV, 3: 406; IV, 4: 55

CHAP.

$6^{30f.}$	**II, 2: 447**	
6^{37}	. . . . . .	IV, 3: 778*
6^{46}	. . . . . .	III, 4: 49; IV, 2: 185
6^{50}	. . . . . .	II, 2: 597; IV, 2: 181
$6^{51f.}$	. . . . . .	II, 2: 447
6^{56}	. . . . . .	IV, 2: 216
$7^{1f.}$	. . . . . .	IV, 2: 175
7^{4}	. . . . . .	IV, 4: 45
$7^{6f.}$	*II, 2: 482* . . .	II, 2: 499*
7^{6-13}	*III, 4: 251* . .	III, 4: 259
$7^{8f.}$	*II, 2: 482*	
$7^{11f.}$	*IV, 2: 173*	
7^{13}	*II, 2: 482*	
7^{14}	. . . . . .	IV, 2: 185
$7^{14f.}$	. . . . . .	IV, 2: 175
7^{24}	. . . . . .	IV, 2: 170
$7^{24f.}$	. . . . . .	I, 2: 425
7^{24-30}	**I, 1: 177 (202)**	
7^{27}	. . . . . .	IV, 2: 170, 769; IV, 3: 50
$7^{31f.}$	. **I, 1: 151 f. (171 f.)**	
7^{33}	. . . . . .	IV, 2: 216
7^{34}	. . . . . .	IV, 2: 195
7^{36}	. . . . . .	IV, 2: 137
8^{2}	. . . . . .	III, 2: 211
8^{11}	. . . . . .	IV, 1: 260
$8^{11f.}$	**IV, 2: 217** . . .	IV, 2: 239*
8^{12}	. . . . . .	III, 2: 328, 365; IV, 2: 137
8^{23}	. . . . . .	IV, 2: 216
8^{27}	. . . . . .	IV, 1: 127
8^{27-30}	**II, 2: 437**	
	IV, 2: 91	
	IV, 3: 50	
8^{28}	. . . . . .	IV, 4: 55
8^{29}	**III, 4: 79**	
8^{31}	. . . . . .	II, 2: 640; IV, 2: 599
$8^{31f.}$	. . . . . .	IV, 2: 253
8^{33}	. . . . . .	IV, 2: 387
8^{34}	**IV, 2: 539**	
$8^{34f.}$	**IV, 2: 264** . . .	I, 1: 387 (445); IV, 2: 599*
8^{34-37}	**III, 4: 387**	
8^{35}	**IV, 1: 421** . . .	I, 2: 157*; III, 4: 335; IV, 1: 744*;
	IV, 2: 751	IV, 2: 159, 197, 264, 467, 600; IV, 4: 122
	IV, 3: 442	
	IV, 4: 15	
	IV, 3: 652	
8^{38}	. . . . . .	III, 3: 501 f.; III, 4: 233; IV, 2: 264, 539
9	. . . . . .	III, 2: 500
9^{1}	*III, 2: 499* . . .	IV, 2: 138, 198; IV, 3: 302
$9^{1f.}$	. . . . . .	IV, 3: 294
9^{2}	. . . . . .	III, 2: 478; IV, 4: 64
$9^{2f.}$	*II, 1: 643* . . .	I, 1: 452 (518); IV, 2: 137 f.*
9^{2-8}	*III, 2: 478*	
9^{3}	. . . . . .	III, 3: 465

CHAP.

12^{42}	. . . . .	.	II, 2: 468
13	*III, 2: 501*	. .	I, 2: 11; II, 2: 438
$13^{1f.}$	. . . . .	.	IV, 2: 177
13^{4}	*III, 2: 501*		
13^{5}	. . . . .	.	II, 2: 578
13^{6}	. . . . .	.	IV, 3: 95
13^{7}	. . . . .	.	II, 2: 597; IV, 2: 181
13^{11}	**I, 1: 455 (521)**		
13^{13}	**IV, 3: 624 f.** .	.	IV, 4: 93
13^{24}	. . . . .	.	III, 1: 121,* 167*
$13^{24f.}$	*III, 2: 500 f.*		
13^{30}	*III, 2: 500 f.* .	.	IV, 3: 295*
13^{31}	. . . . .	.	III, 1: 17; III, 2: 470; III, 3: 420; IV, 2: 107, 164
13^{32}	**III, 2: 498** .	.	III, 4: 582; IV, 2: 95
13^{37}	. . . . .	.	II, 2: 439
14 f.	**II, 2: 449–506**		
14^{1}	. . . . .	.	III, 2: 501
$14^{1f.}$	. . . . .	.	IV, 2: 262
14^{3-9}	**IV, 2: 796–798**		
14^{4}	. . . . .	.	II, 2: 471*
$14^{4ff.}$	**II, 2: 449–506**		
14^{7}	. . . . .	.	II, 2: 472*; IV, 2: 174
14^{8}	. . . . .	.	IV, 2: 259
14^{9}	. . . . .	.	IV, 2: 163
14^{10}	. . . . .	.	II, 2: 549
$14^{10f.}$	. . . . .	.	II, 2: 463
14^{18}	. . . . .	.	II, 2: 471, 549
14^{19}	. . . . .	.	II, 2: 471
14^{21}	. . . . .	.	II, 2: 461
$14^{22f.}$	. . . . .	.	IV, 2: 258
14^{24}	**III, 2: 214**		
14^{26}	**IV, 3: 866**		
14^{29}	. . . . .	.	IV, 2: 168
$14^{30f.}$	. . . . .	.	IV, 2: 388 f.
$14^{32f.}$	. . . . .	.	III, 4: 401
14^{33-42}	**IV, 1: 265–272**		
14^{34}	. . . . .	.	I, 2: 158; IV, 1: 267
14^{35}	. . . . .	.	IV, 1: 264, 267
14^{36}	**IV, 1: 238** .	.	I, 1: 385, 458 (442, 524); IV, 1: 264, 269 f.; IV, 4: 60
14^{37}	. . . . .	.	IV, 1: 267; IV, 2: 388
$14^{37f.}$	. . . . .	.	I, 2: 330
14^{38}	**III, 4: 95** .	.	IV, 1: 267, 733
14^{40}	. . . . .	.	IV, 1: 267; IV, 2: 554
14^{41}	. . . . .	.	IV, 2: 253; IV, 3: 413
$14^{41f.}$	. . . . .	.	IV, 1: 264
14^{47}	. . . . .	.	II, 2: 459
$14^{47f.}$	. . . . .	.	IV, 3: 632
14^{49}	. . . . .	.	IV, 2: 253
14^{50}	. . . . .	.	IV, 1: 267
$14^{50f.}$	. . . . .	.	IV, 2: 250; IV, 3: 627
$14^{53f.}$	. . . . .	.	IV, 2: 263

CHAP.

$13^{31f.}$		IV, 3: 626
13^{32}		IV, 2: 176
$13^{32f.}$		IV, 2: 259
13^{34}	**IV, 2: 261**	
14^{1}		I, 2: 264
$14^{1f.}$		IV, 2: 226
14^{7}		IV, 3: 851
$14^{7f.}$		III, 4: 667; IV, 2: 548
14^{8}		IV, 1: 235
14^{10}		III, 4: 668; IV, 1: 164, 684
14^{11}		IV, 1: 190
14^{14}		IV, 2: 189
14^{16-24}	**II, 2: 588**	
14^{19}	**IV, 3: 851**	
14^{20}		IV, 2: 550
14^{23}		IV, 3: 528 f.
$14^{25f.}$		II, 2: 438
14^{26}	**III, 4: 262**	III, 4: 162*; IV, 3: 625
	IV, 2: 625	
14^{27}		I, 2: 277; IV, 2: 264
$14^{28f.}$		IV, 3: 779
15		II, 1: 278
$15^{1f.}$		IV, 2: 21
15^{2}		III, 2: 330; IV, 1: 83,* 244
$15^{3f.}$		IV, 1: 259
15^{7}		II, 1: 454; II, 2: 124; III, 3: 500; IV, 2: 182
15^{10}		II, 1: 454; III, 3: 500; IV, 2: 182
$15^{11f.}$		III, 1: 36; IV, 1: 392, 772
15^{11-32}	**IV, 2: 21 ff.**	IV, 4: 98
15^{16}		III, 2: 412
15^{18}	**I, 1: 407 (466)**	III, 3: 424; IV, 2: 312*
15^{20}		III, 2: 211
15^{23}		IV, 3: 572*
15^{24}		III, 2: 27*
15^{25}		IV, 2: 23
$15^{28f.}$		IV, 2: 24
15^{29}		I, 1: 387 (445); IV, 2: 22
15^{30}		IV, 2: 23
15^{32}	**III, 2: 601**	I, 2: 261; II, 2: 124; IV, 1: 544; IV, 2: 556
$16^{1f.}$	**IV, 2: 174**	I, 1: 246 (282); III, 1: 37; IV, 1: 525
16^{8}	**III, 4: 529**	III, 2: 276*; III, 4: 419*; IV, 2: 725*; IV, 3: 467
	IV, 2: 417	
16^{9}	**IV, 2: 174**	IV, 2: 544, 548, 629
$16^{10f.}$		III, 4: 628
16^{11}	**IV, 2: 174**	
16^{15}		I, 2: 311
16^{16}		IV, 2: 160; IV, 4: 55
$16^{19f.}$		III, 4: 361; IV, 2: 169; IV, 3: 112
16^{20}		IV, 3: 339*
16^{21}		III, 2: 412

CHAP.

20^{19}	**III, 2: 462**			
20^{27-38}	**III, 2: 462**			
20^{35}				III, 4: 240
20^{36}				III, 2: 295; IV, 1: 210; IV, 3: 534
$20^{37f.}$				I, 2: 66
20^{38}	**IV, 1: 669**			III, 2: 295, 620
21^{14}				IV, 3: 631
$21^{14f.}$	**I, 1: 455 (521)**			
21^{17}				IV, 3: 624 f.
21^{24}				II, 2: 300
21^{25}				III, 1: 167
21^{28}	**IV, 2: 527**			I, 1: 409 (469)
21^{36}				II, 2: 439
22 f.	**II, 2: 458–506**			
22^{3}				II, 2: 461, 482
$22^{3f.}$				II, 2: 463
22^{15}				III, 2: 412
22^{19}	*III, 2: 328*			III, 2: 469; IV, 2: 163
22^{20}				IV, 1: 252
22^{22}				II, 2: 459
22^{23}				II, 2: 461
22^{25}				IV, 2: 170
22^{27}				III, 4: 476, 662; IV, 1: 164; IV, 3: 601
22^{30}				IV, 2: 197
22^{31}	*IV, 1: 268*			
$22^{31f.}$				II, 2: 439
22^{32}	**IV, 2: 565**			I, 2: 330, 427; III, 4: 111; IV, 2: 387
22^{33}				IV, 3: 639
22^{35}	**IV, 2: 178**			
22^{35-37}				IV, 3: 639
22^{36-38}	**IV, 3: 631**			
22^{37}				IV, 3: 395
22^{41}				IV, 1: 267
22^{42}				I, 2: 187
22^{42-44}	**IV, 1: 269 f.**			
22^{43}	**III, 3: 501**			IV, 4: 64
22^{44}	**III, 4: 401**			III, 2: 329 f.; IV, 1: 265,* 268
22^{46}				II, 2: 436
$22^{50f.}$	**IV, 3: 632**			
$22^{52f.}$				III, 2: 462
22^{53}				III, 1: 127; III, 2: 462
22^{61}				IV, 1: 392*
$22^{61f.}$				IV, 2: 388, 392
$22^{67f.}$				III, 2: 503*
23^{2}				IV, 2: 168; IV, 3: 395
23^{5}				IV, 2: 168
$23^{6f.}$				IV, 2: 263
$23^{7f.}$				III, 4: 80
23^{12}				IV, 2: 418*
23^{14}				IV, 2: 168
23^{24}				III, 1: 167
23^{25}				IV, 2: 445
23^{26}				IV, 1: 226, 239

CHAP.

24⁴⁹	.	II, 2: 435; IV, 2: 322, 325, 330
24⁵⁰	.	III, 2: 582
24⁵⁰⁻⁵³ **III, 2: 452**		
24⁵¹ **IV, 2: 153** . .	.	III, 1: 141; IV, 2: 144
24⁵³	.	IV, 2: 173

JOHN

1 . . . . III, 2: 137, 166

1–2 . . . . . . I, 1: 173 (197)

1¹ *I, 1: 137 (155)* . . I, 1: 173*, 419, 435 (197,* 459, 499); I, 2: 159; III, 1: 14,* 51,* 113; III, 2: 65, 221, 483 f.; IV, 1: 71; IV, 2: 101; IV, 3: 9, 685*

1¹ᶠ. **II, 2: 95–99** . . . I, 1: 425 (479); I, 2: 18, 32, 37, 133,* 149;
IV, 2: 33 II, 1: 481, 607; II, 2: 101, 104,* 108, 117, 145; IV, 2: 44; IV, 3: 13, 232

1¹⁻¹⁸ *I, 1: 380 (436)*

1² **III, 2: 66** . . . . III, 2: 483*; IV, 3: 232, 611

1²ᶠ. . . . . . . III, 1: 54*

1²⁻³⁶ *IV, 4: 61*

1³ **III, 1: 116** . . . . I, 1: 401, 441 f.* (459, 506*); I, 2: 159; II, 1: 317, 432 f.; II, 2: 97, 99, 490; III, 1: 14, 29 f.,* 51*; III, 2: 153, 157, 483 f.; IV, 1: 44; IV, 3: 9

1³ᶠ. . . . . . . III, 1: 53*

1⁴ . . . . . . III, 2: 153, 335; IV, 2: 226; IV, 3: 50; IV, 4: 125

1⁴ᶠ. . . . . . . I, 1: 401 (459); II, 1: 42; II, 2: 97; IV, 2: 134; IV, 3: 9*

1⁵ **I, 1: 49 (53)** . . . I, 1: 408 (468); I, 2: 61, 151, 222; IV, 1:
IV, 3: 232 71f.; IV, 2: 382, 621; IV, 3: 167,* 232, 236, 239, 267

IV, 2: 424

1⁶ . . . . . . IV, 4: 54 f.

1⁶ᶠ. *IV, 3: 611* . . I, 2: 120, 159, 222

1⁶⁻⁸ **I, 1: 112 (126)**

1⁷ᶠ. *IV, 2: 161* . . II, 2: 425

1⁸ . . . . . . I, 2: 120*; IV, 3: 239, 611, 835*

1⁹ . . . . . . I, 1: 158 (180); I, 2: 148; II, 1: 42; II, 2: 97, 422, 539*; III, 1: 14; IV, 1: 57,* 70; IV, 2: 382; IV, 3: 9, 49; IV, 4: 25

1⁹ᶠ. . . . . . . II, 1: 459, 626

1⁹⁻¹³ . . . . . . IV, 4: 15

1¹⁰ . . . . . . II, 1: 317; II, 2: 97 f.; III, 1: 19, 51*; III, 2: 487; IV, 2: 33; IV, 3: 232

1¹⁰ᶠ. . . . . . . III, 1: 19, 51

1¹¹ . . . . . . I, 1: 408, 443 (468, 508); II, 2: 461, 482; III, 1: 51, 67; III, 2: 487; IV, 1: 70 ff., 402, 670; IV, 2: 36, 261; IV, 3: 182, 526, 532, 537

1¹¹ᶠ. . . . . . . III, 2: 585*

CHAP.

7⁴¹	. . . . . .	III, 3: 180
7⁴²	. . . . . .	I, 2: 175
7⁴⁴ᶠ·	. . . . . .	IV, 2: 262
7⁴⁶	. . . . . .	II, 1: 606
7⁵²	. . . . . .	III, 3: 180; IV, 3: 49
8²⁻¹¹	. . . . . .	III, 4: 232
8³⁻¹¹	**III, 4: 234**	
8⁴⁻⁶	. . . . . .	III, 4: 234
8⁷⁻¹¹	. . . . . .	III, 4: 233–235
8¹²	. . . . . .	I, 2: 18; II, 1: 42; II, 2: 422, 429, 569; III, 1: 120; IV, 1: 668; IV, 2: 226, 537; IV, 3: 9, 50, 80, 231 f., 236, 510,* 584, 612, 902
8¹²⁻¹⁴	*IV, 3: 612*	
8¹⁴	. . . . . .	IV, 3: 234
8¹⁵	. . . . . .	IV, 3: 237
8¹⁶	. . . . . .	III, 2: 63*; IV, 1: 218; IV, 3: 234, 237
8¹⁸	. . . . . .	IV, 3: 234
8¹⁹	. . . . . .	I, 1: 390 (448); II, 1: 50
8²³	. . . . . .	III, 3: 436
8²⁴	. . . . . .	III, 2: 63; IV, 1: 392
8²⁶	. . . . . .	III, 2: 63; IV, 3: 234, 236
8²⁸	. . . . . .	IV, 1: 166; IV, 2: 200,* 255; IV, 3: 185,* 187,* 234
8²⁹	. . . . . .	III, 2: 63; IV, 1: 164
8³⁰⁻⁵⁹	**I, 1: 456 (522)**	
8³¹⁻³⁶	. . . . . .	II, 2: 589–593*
8³²	**IV, 3: 476** .	II, 1: 208
8³⁴	. . . . . .	IV, 2: 495*
8³⁵	. . . . . .	I, 1: 458 (524)
8³⁶	**IV, 1: 745** .	IV, 2: 129, 496*
	IV, 2: 633	
8⁴⁰	. . . . . .	IV, 3: 234
8⁴²	. . . . . .	III, 2: 63; IV, 2: 793
8⁴³ᶠ·	**IV, 3: 260**	
8⁴⁴	. . . . . .	III, 3: 531; III, 4: 400
8⁴⁵	. . . . . .	I, 1: 176 (201)
8⁴⁶	. . . . . .	I, 2: 156; II, 1: 397
8⁴⁶ᶠ·	. . . . . .	I, 1: 138, 151 (157, 172)
8⁴⁸	. . . . . .	IV, 2: 231
8⁴⁹	. . . . . .	I, 1: 176 (201)
8⁵⁰	. . . . . .	III, 2: 65; IV, 1: 164; IV, 3: 234
8⁵¹	*I, 2: 278* .	III, 2: 621
8⁵⁴	. . . . . .	III, 2: 65
8⁵⁶	**I, 2: 75** .	I, 1: 145 (164); I, 2: 73; III, 2: 481; IV, 2: 182; IV, 3: 233
8⁵⁶ᶠ·	. . . . . .	II, 2: 102
8⁵⁸	**II, 1: 622** .	I, 1: 401 (460); III, 2: 63; IV, 2: 33; IV, 3: 232
9	. . . . . .	III, 2: 63
9¹ᶠ·	**IV, 2: 236 ff.**	IV, 2: 175, 239
9²ᶠ·	**IV, 2: 223**	
9³	. . . . . .	IV, 2: 226

CHAP.

11⁴		III, 2: 65
11⁵		III, 2: 329; IV, 2: 765
11⁹		II, 2: 422; IV, 3: 50
11¹¹	**III, 2: 638**	
11²⁰⁻⁴⁵	**IV, 2: 227**	
11²⁵	**III, 4: 594** . . .	I, 2: 18; III, 2: 335; IV, 2: 139*; IV, 3:
	IV, 1: 303	9, 231, 233, 645; IV, 4: 121
11²⁶		III, 2: 621
11²⁷		I, 2: 18
11²⁸		IV, 3: 486*
11³³	*III, 2: 328, 365*	
11³⁴	*III, 2: 329*	
11³⁵	~~O for 11.35.~~ . .	IV, 2: 765
11³⁸	*III, 2: 328*	
11⁴⁰		II, 1: 625; III, 2: 63; IV, 2: 241
11⁴³		IV, 3: 512; IV, 4: 126
11⁴⁷ᶠ.		IV, 2: 238, 262
11⁵⁰		II, 2: 479*; III, 4: 437; IV, 1: 231
11⁵¹		III, 2: 503
11⁵¹ᶠ.		III, 2: 213*
12		II, 2: 471 f., 500
12¹⁻⁸	**II, 2: 462**	
12³⁻⁸	*IV, 2: 796 f.*	
12¹⁶		III, 2: 65; IV, 2: 163
12²³		III, 2: 65; IV, 3: 234
12²⁴		I, 1: 387 (444); I, 2: 23; III, 2: 639;
		IV, 2: 256
12²⁵		III, 2: 639; III, 4: 387; IV, 3: 652
12²⁶		I, 1: 176 (201); II, 2: 569*; III, 2: 211;
		III, 4: 477, 661 f.*; IV, 2: 264; IV, 3:
		587, 603
12²⁷	**IV, 1: 272** . . .	III, 2: 462; IV, 1: 265*; IV, 2: 250
12²⁸		III, 2: 65, 221
12²⁹		III, 3: 501
12³¹		IV, 1: 265, 272; IV, 3: 268
12³¹ᶠ.	*IV, 2: 256*	
12³²		IV, 1: 166; IV, 2: 529; IV, 3: 278,*
		487; IV, 4: 17
12³⁴		II, 2: 102; III, 2: 337
12³⁵		III, 4: 582
12³⁵ᶠ.		III, 4: 583
12³⁶	**IV, 3: 510** . . .	III, 1: 120; IV, 1: 210; IV, 3: 236, 534,
		902*
12³⁷ᶠ.		I, 2: 73
12³⁸		IV, 4: 64
12⁴¹		III, 2: 481
12⁴⁴		III, 2: 63
12⁴⁵		III, 1: 202; III, 2: 63
12⁴⁶		II, 1: 42; II, 2: 422; III, 2: 60; IV, 3:
		50, 486, 510
12⁴⁷	**III, 2: 60** . . .	IV, 3: 236
12⁴⁸		IV, 1: 218, 392, 415; IV, 3: 236
12⁴⁹		III, 2: 63; IV, 3: 234

CHAP.

4¹²	. . . . . .	I, 2: 659; II, 2: 99; IV, 2: 274 f.*; IV, 3: 95; IV, 4: 67
4¹⁸	. . . . . .	IV, 2: 210*
4¹⁸ᶠ·	. . . . . .	III, 4: 76
4²⁴	. . . . . .	III, 1: 19, 100
4²⁷	. . . . . .	I, 1: 385 (442); II, 2: 102, 117; IV, 1: 194; IV, 3: 601; IV, 4: 98
4²⁷ᶠ·	. . . . . .	IV, 2: 326, 515
4²⁸	. . . . . .	IV, 1: 239
4²⁹	**I, 2: 711**	
4³⁰	. . . . . .	I, 1: 385 (442); IV, 1: 194; IV, 3: 601; IV, 4: 93, 98
4³²	**IV, 3: 888**	
4³³	. . . . . .	I, 2: 114; IV, 1: 299; IV, 3: 613
5	. . . . . .	I, 2: 109*
5¹ᶠ·	**I, 2: 330** . . .	III, 2: 601; IV, 2: 178
5¹⁻¹¹	. . . . . .	III, 4: 225,* 399,* 627
5³ᶠ·	. . . . . .	I, 1: 460 (526)
5⁵	*III, 1: 249*	
5¹⁴	. . . . . .	II, 2: 271
5¹⁹ᶠ·	. . . . . .	III, 3: 487
5²⁸	. . . . . .	IV, 4: 93
5²⁹	**III, 4: 250** .	. . . II, 2: 609
5²⁹⁻³²	**III, 4: 85**	
5³¹	**IV, 4: 81 f.**	III, 3: 439 f.; IV, 2: 183, 201
5³²	. . . . . .	IV, 2: 322
5⁴¹	. . . . . .	IV, 4: 93
5⁴²	. . . . . .	IV, 2: 197, 201
6¹	. . . . . .	IV, 2: 646
6¹ᶠᶠ·	**IV, 3: 890**	
6²	*IV, 3: 602*	
6⁴	**I, 1: 53 (58)**	
6⁴ᶠᶠ·	**IV, 3: 610**	
6⁵	. . . . . .	IV, 3: 872
6⁷	. . . . . .	II, 1: 29*; IV, 2: 646
6⁸⁻¹⁰, ¹²	. . . . . .	IV, 3: 610
6¹⁵	. . . . . .	III, 3: 513*
7	. . . . . .	I, 2: 108; II, 2: 478, 487
7¹ᶠ·	. . . . . .	II, 2: 204; IV, 3: 890
7²ᶠ·	. . . . . .	I, 2: 311*
7¹⁷	. . . . . .	IV, 2: 646
7²²	. . . . . .	II, 1: 605
7³⁹ᶠ·	. . . . . .	II, 2: 485
7⁴²	*II, 2: 484*	
7⁴⁹	. . . . . .	II, 1: 474; III, 1: 150
7⁵⁴ᶠ·	**III, 4: 437**	
7⁵⁵	. . . . . .	II, 2: 487*; III, 1: 141
7⁵⁶	. . . . . .	III, 3: 436, 439
7⁵⁹	*III, 2: 638* .	. . II, 2: 487*; III, 1: 249; IV, 1: 160
8¹	. . . . . .	IV, 3: 199
8³	. . . . . .	II, 2: 478
8⁴	. . . . . .	IV, 4: 83, 85
8⁵ᶠ·	. . . . . .	IV, 3: 890

CHAP.

16¹⁵			IV, 1: 749; IV, 4: 83, 180

CHAP.

20⁷	**III, 2: 458**	III, 1: 228*
	III, 4: 53	
20²⁷ᶠ.	. . . . . .	III, 1: 149*
20²⁸	. . . . . .	IV, 1: 255
20³²	*IV, 2: 633* . . .	II, 1: 354
20³³	. . . . . .	III, 2: 413
20³⁵	**IV, 2: 786**	IV, 2: 189
21⁸	. . . . . .	IV, 3: 872, 890
22¹⁻²¹	**III, 2: 471**	
22³ᶠᶠ.	**IV, 3: 198–211**	
22⁴	. . . . . .	II, 1: 29
22⁵	. . . . . .	IV, 3: 199
22⁶⁻²²	. . . . . .	IV, 3: 198
22⁷	. . . . . .	IV, 3: 204
22⁸	. . . . . .	IV, 3: 198, 204
22⁹	. . . . . .	IV, 3: 203
22¹⁰	. . . . . .	IV, 3: 204
22¹²⁻²¹	. . . . . .	IV, 3: 205, 207
22¹³	. . . . . .	IV, 3: 209
22¹⁴	. . . . . .	III, 2: 481; IV, 3: 201, 203
22¹⁴⁻¹⁶	**IV, 4: 112**	
22¹⁵	. . . . . .	IV, 3: 198, 209
22¹⁶	**IV, 4: 210, 213** . .	IV, 1: 160; IV, 4: 46, 112, 127, 179
22²¹	. . . . . .	IV, 3: 209
22²²	. . . . . .	III, 2: 471
23⁸	. . . . . .	III, 3: 393*
24¹⁴	. . . . . .	II, 1: 29
26²	*IV, 2: 188*	
26²⁻²³	. . . . . .	III, 2: 471
26⁵ᶠᶠ.	**IV, 3: 198–211**	
26¹¹	. . . . . .	IV, 3: 199
26¹²	. . . . . .	IV, 3: 199
26¹²⁻²⁰	. . . . . .	IV, 3: 204, 206
26¹⁴	. . . . . .	IV, 3: 200, 205
26¹⁶	. . . . . .	IV, 3: 198, 209
26¹⁶ᶠ.	. . . . . .	IV, 3: 203
26¹⁷ᶠ.	. . . . . .	IV, 3: 209, 505
26¹⁸	. . . . . .	IV, 3: 509
26¹⁹	. . . . . .	I, 1: 18* (19*); III, 3: 436; III, 4: 605
26¹⁹ᶠ.	. . . . . .	IV, 3: 203
26²⁰	. . . . . .	IV, 2: 595
26²²	. . . . . .	I, 2: 73, 489; III, 2: 481
26²⁴	. . . . . .	III, 2: 471
26²⁸	. . . . . .	IV, 1: 749; IV, 3: 509
27²³	. . . . . .	III, 3: 487
27²⁴	. . . . . .	IV, 2: 181
27³¹	. . . . . .	IV, 2: 198, 201

ROMANS

1	. . . . . .	II, 2: 485, 487; III, 4: 166
1 f.	. . . . . .	I, 2: 110; II, 1: 104, 107, 109, 123

CHAP.

4¹ᶠ·	· · · · ·	I, 2: 331; III, 2: 581
4³ ·	· · · · ·	II, 2: 215; IV, 3: 577
4³ᶠ·	· · · · ·	IV, 1: 615
4⁵ ·	· · · · ·	II, 1: 279, 383
4⁶ ·	· · · · ·	I, 2: 220
4⁹⁻²⁵	*II, 2: 215 f.*	
4¹¹ ·	· · · · ·	IV, 1: 614
4¹³	*IV, 1: 614*	
4¹⁴ ·	· · · · ·	I, 1: 233* (266*)
4¹⁵ ·	· · · · ·	I, 2: 311; III, 2: 604; III, 4: 282; IV, 1: 451,* 585
4¹⁶ ·	· · · · ·	II, 2: 216
4¹⁷	**IV, 1: 301** · · ·	I, 1: 389 (447); II, 1: 279; III, 1: 17, 113, 244; III, 2: 153 ff.*
	IV, 3: 530	
4¹⁸ ·	· · · · ·	I, 1: 225 (257); III, 2: 156; IV, 1: 454
4¹⁹ ·	· · · · ·	II, 2: 215, 228
4¹⁹ᶠ·	· · · · ·	I, 1: 463 (530)
4²⁰ ·	· · · · ·	III, 4: 393
4²³ᶠ·	· · · · ·	I, 2: 489
4²⁴ ·	· · · · ·	I, 1: 387 (444)
4²⁴ᶠ·	· · · · ·	II, 1: 404*
4²⁵ ·	· · · · ·	I, 1: 387 (444); I, 2: 57, 110; II, 2: 223, 365,* 489, 759*; III, 2: 214; III, 4: 240; IV, 1: 255, 305 f., 307, 310, 555
5–8		IV, 2: 273; IV, 3: 210
5¹	**IV, 1: 83, 538** · ·	II, 1: 161; II, 2: 720; IV, 1: 252, 277; IV, 2: 790
	IV, 2: 273	
	IV, 1: 74	
5²	**II, 2: 600**	
5²ᶠ·	· · · · ·	IV, 3: 644
5³	**III, 4: 676** · · ·	IV, 3: 641, 647
5³ᶠ·	· · · · ·	II, 2: 638
5⁴ᶠ·	· · · · ·	II, 1: 277
5⁵ ·	· · · · ·	I, 1: 453 (519); I, 2: 241, 248, 373; III, 2: 275*; IV, 1: 74, 308, 531; IV, 2: 780, 835; IV, 3: 210, 538, 916; IV, 4: 76
5⁶ ·	· · · · ·	II, 1: 398
5⁶ᶠ·	**IV, 1: 229 f.** · ·	IV, 1: 74, 224; IV, 2: 329, 771
5⁷ᶠ·	· · · · ·	I, 2: 373
5⁸	**IV, 1: 295** · · ·	II, 1: 278, 398; IV, 1: 72, 224; IV, 2: 766
5⁹ ·	· · · · ·	II, 1: 398; IV, 1: 255
5¹⁰	**IV, 1: 244** · · ·	I, 1: 408, 409 (468, 469); II, 1: 398; III, 2: 335; IV, 1: 72, 224, 252; IV, 3: 365; IV, 4: 17
	IV, 2: 580	
5¹¹ ·	· · · · ·	I, 1: 409 (468)
5¹²	**IV, 1: 139, 586** ·	I, 2: 110; IV, 1: 253,* 500,* 505, 507; IV, 4: 16
	I, 2: 193	
5¹²ᶠ·	· · · · ·	IV, 3: 859
5¹²⁻¹⁸	**III, 2: 600 f., 616** ·	IV, 3: 109*
5¹²⁻¹⁹	**I, 2: 157**	
5¹²⁻²¹	**IV, 1: 507, 512** · ·	III, 2: 46*
	II, 1: 456	

CHAP.

5[13]	. . . . . .	IV, 1: 585 f.
5[14]	. . . . . .	III, 1: 203; III, 2: 600; IV, 1: 513, 756*; IV, 2: 23
5[15]	. . . . . .	II, 1: 355
5[15f.]	. . . . . .	IV, 1: 513
5[17]	. . . . . .	II, 1: 355; II, 2: 344; III, 2: 600; IV, 4: 16
5[18]	. . . . . .	IV, 1: 273, 511 f.; IV, 3: 487
5[19]	. . . . . .	II, 2: 561; IV, 1: 194, 196,* 257, 511 f.
5[20]	**IV, 1: 68** . . . . *IV, 1: 82*	I, 2: 310; II, 1: 153; II, 2: 502; IV, 1: 488, 586
5[21]	. . . . . .	II, 1: 355; IV, 4: 16
6	*IV, 2: 371* . .	II, 2: 591 f.
6–8	**II, 2: 589–593**	
6[1]	**IV, 1: 627** . .	IV, 1: 82
6[1f.]	. . . . . .	II, 1: 361; II, 2: 591
6[1-11]	**IV, 4: 79, 196 f.** .	III, 2: 469; IV, 4: 91
6[2-8]	**IV, 1: 295** . . .	IV, 1: 254 f.
6[2-10]	. . . . . .	IV, 4: 117 f.
6[3]	**IV, 4: 91** . .	IV, 3: 639; IV, 4: 47,* 127
6[3f.]	**I, 1: 240 (275)** . . **IV, 4: 117 f.**	I, 1: 387 (445); I, 2: 261; III, 2: 304; IV, 4: 120
6[4]	**IV, 1: 321** . . **IV, 4: 160** *IV, 1: 323*	I, 1: 323, 387 (371, 444); II, 1: 606, 642; III, 1: 52, 280; III, 2: 470, 606,* 621,* 624*; IV, 1: 303, 308 f., 555; IV, 2: 277, 365, 563; IV, 4: 9, 45, 69, 118
6[5]	*IV, 3: 639* . .	I, 1: 458 (525); I, 2: 278; IV, 1: 295; IV, 3: 641; IV, 4: 9, 17
6[5f.]	. . . . . .	II, 2: 591
6[6]	. . . . . .	I, 1: 387 (445); III, 2: 621*; IV, 1: 295 f., 582, 663; IV, 2: 365, 601; IV, 3: 603, 639; IV, 4: 9, 16, 69, 119
6[8]	. . . . . .	III, 2: 621,* 623*; IV, 1: 295, 329, 582; IV, 2: 277, 375; IV, 3: 639; IV, 4: 9
6[9]	. . . . . .	II, 2: 482; IV, 1: 313, 503
6[9f.]	. . . . . .	III, 2: 470; IV, 2: 164
6[10]	**III, 2: 441, 470** .	I, 2: 13; II, 1: 398; IV, 1: 224, 255, 307, 316, 503*; IV, 2: 257
6[11]	. . . . . .	IV, 1: 321, 582; IV, 2: 365, 377; IV, 4: 9, 69
6[12f.]	. . . . . .	II, 2: 592
6[13]	**IV, 4: 28** . .	IV, 1: 321
6[14]	. . . . . .	I, 1: 239 (274); I, 2: 398; II, 2: 591 f.; IV, 1: 582
6[15]	. . . . . .	II, 1: 361
6[16f.]	. . . . . .	II, 1: 398
6[17]	**I, 2: 619 f.** . .	II, 1: 37; II, 2: 483, 587; IV, 3: 603
6[18]	*I, 2: 273* . . .	II, 1: 361; II, 2: 590
6[19]	**IV, 4: 28** . .	IV, 1: 321
6[20]	. . . . . .	II, 2: 589; IV, 3: 603
6[21]	. . . . . .	IV, 1: 367
6[21-23]	. . . . . .	II, 2: 590
6[22]	. . . . . .	I, 2: 273; IV, 3: 603

CHAP.

8⁴	. . . . .	IV, 1: 312, 583; IV, 2: 257
8⁴ᶠ·	. . . . .	IV, 3: 210
8⁶	. . . . .	III, 2: 600; IV, 4: 16
8⁷	. . . . .	I, 1: 408 (468)
8⁹	I, 2: 249 f. . .	I, 1: 450, 453 (515, 518); II, 1: 483; II, 2: 731; IV, 1: 695; IV, 2: 321, 323, 332, 377; IV, 3: 538
8¹⁰	. . . . .	I, 2: 261; II, 1: 422; IV, 1: 311; IV, 3: 543
8¹⁰ᶠ·	III, 2: 360 . .	II, 2: 728
8¹¹	. . . . .	I, 1: 453 (519); IV, 1: 308, 312, 329, 666; IV, 2: 332; IV, 4: 100
8¹³	. . . . .	I, 2: 261; III, 2: 601; III, 4: 347; IV, 1: 295
8¹⁴	IV, 2: 570 . .	I, 1: 454, 458 (520, 524); III, 2: 358;
	I, 2: 273	IV, 1: 312, 531; IV, 2: 129, 322, 332
8¹⁴⁻¹⁶	. . . . .	IV, 3: 532
8¹⁴⁻²⁷	IV, 2: 328 f.	
8¹⁵	I, 1: 458 (524) . .	I, 1: 387 (444); I, 2: 241, 397; II, 2: 592,
	II, 2: 604	597; III, 2: 358; IV, 1: 600; IV, 4: 28
8¹⁵ᶠ·	. . . . .	III, 4: 94; IV, 1: 733
8¹⁶	I, 1: 453 f. (519–521)	I, 1: 458 (524); III, 2: 366; IV, 1: 308,
	IV, 4: 28	321, 600; IV, 2: 322, 328, 826*; IV, 3:
	IV, 2: 320	942; IV, 4: 77, 99
8¹⁷	IV, 1: 604 . .	I, 1: 458, 463 (524, 530); III, 2: 623; IV, 1: 330, 600
8¹⁷ᶠ·	. . . . .	II, 1: 422; II, 2: 592
8¹⁸	. . . . .	II, 1: 642; III, 4: 676; IV, 1: 330; IV, 3: 358
8¹⁹	III, 4: 355 . .	III, 2: 494, 505; III, 3: 184
	IV, 3: 210	
	II, 1: 649	
8¹⁹ᶠ·	IV, 2: 611 . .	III, 2: 622 f.; IV, 1: 331, 733; IV, 4: 199
8¹⁹⁻²³	IV, 3: 532 . .	IV, 3: 302, 358
8²⁰	. . . . .	III, 1: 181; III, 4: 172
8²¹	I, 1: 457 f. (523 f.) .	III, 2: 494; IV, 3: 603
8²²ᶠ·	. . . . .	II, 2: 495; III, 1: 473*
8²³	IV, 3: 916 . .	I, 1: 409, 453, 463 (469, 519, 530); III, 1: 249; III, 2: 358, 494; IV, 1: 330; IV, 2: 322; IV, 3: 674; IV, 4: 77
8²⁴	II, 1: 633 . .	III, 2: 494; IV, 1: 331; IV, 3: 911
	IV, 3: 913 f.	
8²⁶	III, 2: 360 . .	I, 2: 263; IV, 1: 308; IV, 4: 100
	III, 4: 100	
8²⁶ᶠ·	I, 1: 23 (25) . .	I, 1: 453 (519); III, 4: 94; IV, 1: 733
	I, 2: 698	
	III, 1: 181	
	III, 4: 90	
8²⁷	I, 1: 456 (522) . .	III, 3: 472
8²⁸	II, 1: 422 . .	I, 2: 263, 379; II, 2: 426, 592; III, 1:
	II, 2: 16	135, 142; III, 3: 39 f.*; III, 4: 667;
	III, 3: 368	IV, 2: 280, 770, 792 f.; IV, 3: 485, 593, 600, 646

CHAP.

12¹⁵	**IV, 3: 774 f.**	. . .	III, 2: 284; IV, 1: 724*; IV, 2: 227, 667
12¹⁶	. . . . .	III, 4: 668; IV, 1: 189; IV, 2: 636; IV, 3: 858
12¹⁷	. . . . .	III, 4: 681; IV, 1: 243; IV, 2: 805
12¹⁷⁻²⁰	. . . . .	III, 4: 429
12¹⁸ᶠ·	**III, 4: 434**	
12¹⁹ᶠ·	. . . . .	IV, 1: 243
12²⁰	. . . . .	IV, 2: 804
12²¹	. . . . .	IV, 2: 805
13	**II, 2: 717–732**	
13¹	. . . . .	II, 1: 526; III, 3: 458*
13¹ᶠ·	. . . . .	III, 4: 172; IV, 1: 189
13³	. . . . .	II, 2: 597
13⁴	. . . . .	III, 4: 399; IV, 3: 603
13⁶	**IV, 2: 687** .	. . IV, 2: 640
13⁷	. . . . .	III, 4: 685
13⁸	**IV, 2: 732** .	. . IV, 1: 583; IV, 2: 810
13⁸ᶠ·	. . . . .	I, 2: 407
13⁹	. . . . .	III, 2: 412
13¹⁰	**IV, 2: 732** .	. . I, 2: 372; IV, 1: 107,* 583; IV, 2: 784, 810; IV, 3: 210
13¹¹	**IV, 2: 554** .	. . I, 1: 409 (469); I, 2: 76 f.; III, 2: 505; IV, 3: 511*
13¹¹ᶠ·	. . . . .	III, 4: 583
13¹²	**III, 4: 581 f.**	. . IV, 3: 510
13¹⁴	. . . . .	III, 4: 347; IV, 2: 277; IV, 3: 546; IV, 4: 14
14¹ᶠ·	. . . . .	IV, 2: 13
14²ᶠ·	. . . . .	IV, 1: 295
14⁴	. . . . .	IV, 1: 235; IV, 2: 718*
14⁷	. . . . .	IV, 3: 537
14⁷ᶠ·	. . . . .	III, 2: 638
14⁸	**IV, 2: 602 f.**	. . I, 1: 388 (446); II, 1: 526; III, 2: 620
14⁸ᶠ·	. . . . .	IV, 1: 321; IV, 3: 925
14⁹	. . . . .	II, 2: 205
14¹⁰	. . . . .	II, 1: 381; IV, 3: 921
14¹¹ᶠ·	. . . . .	IV, 1: 235
14¹⁴	. . . . .	IV, 3: 546
14¹⁵	. . . . .	III, 2: 223; IV, 1: 250; IV, 2: 784
14¹⁷	. . . . .	IV, 2: 182, 657
14¹⁸	. . . . .	III, 4: 477; IV, 3: 603
14²²	. . . . .	IV, 2: 718
14²³	. . . . .	III, 1: 211; IV, 1: 392, 758; IV, 2: 595
15²	. . . . .	I, 2: 387; II, 2: 577
15⁴	. . . . .	I, 2: 489, 737
15⁴ᶠ·	**I, 2: 492–495** .	. I, 2: 215
15⁵ᶠ·	. . . . .	II, 1: 455
15⁶	. . . . .	IV, 3: 866
15⁷	. . . . .	IV, 2: 637, 822; IV, 3: 546
15⁸	. . . . .	I, 2: 73 f.; IV, 3: 601, 890
15⁸ᶠ·	. . . . .	II, 2: 296
15⁸⁻¹²	. . . . .	IV, 3: 487
15⁹	. . . . .	II, 1: 375; II, 2: 298

1 CORINTHIANS

CHAP.

7^{40}	. . . . . .	III, 4: 146
8^1	. . . . . .	I, 2: 372; IV, 2: 635, 799, 833
$8^{1f.}$	II, 1: *42 f.*	
$8^{2f.}$	. . . . . .	I, 1: 244 (279)
8^3	. . . . . .	IV, 2: 754, 792; IV, 3: 185
8^{4-6}	II, 1: *454*	
8^5	I, 2: *390* . . .	IV, 1: 646; IV, 2: 214, 279 f.
8^6	IV, 3: *99* . . .	I, 1: 385, 402, 442* (443, 460, 506*); II, 2: 248; III, 1: 20, 51, 53; III, 2: 483; III, 3: 59
8^{10-13}	IV, 2: *637*	
8^{11}	. . . . . .	III, 2: 223
9^1	. . . . . .	IV, 3: 198, 203, 546
9^2	. . . . . .	IV, 3: 546
9^5	. . . . . .	III, 4: 144
9^6	. . . . . .	III, 4: 472
9^9	. . . . . .	III, 3: 174*
9^{10}	. . . . . .	I, 2: 489
9^{16}	I, 2: **273, 491** III, 2: **607** III, 4: **76**	
9^{18}	. . . . . .	IV, 2: 203
9^{19}	. . . . . .	IV, 3: 603
9^{20}	. . . . . .	IV, 3: 774, 877*
9^{21}	. . . . . .	II, 2: 563; IV, 1: 583
9^{22}	IV, 3: **774**	
$9^{24f.}$	IV, 2: **376 f.**	
9^{27}	. . . . . .	II, 2: 430, 637; IV, 3: 658
10^1	. . . . . .	IV, 4: 45
10^{1-4}	I, 2: *74*	
10^2	IV, 4: *90*	
10^4	IV, 4: *90* . .	III, 2: 481
10^{11}	. . . . . .	I, 2: 489; III, 4: 582
10^{14}	. . . . . .	IV, 2: 370
$10^{15f.}$	. . . . . .	I, 2: 412
10^{16}	IV, 2: **657** IV, 3: **758**	
$10^{16f.}$	IV, 1: **665** . .	I, 2: 215
10^{17}	. . . . . .	II, 1: 454
$10^{20f.}$	. . . . . .	IV, 2: 230
$10^{21f.}$	. . . . . .	IV, 2: 370
10^{23}	III, 2: **305** . .	IV, 2: 635
10^{24}	. . . . . .	III, 4: 536
10^{31}	III, 2: **410** . .	III, 4: 326*
10^{32}	. . . . . .	IV, 3: 774
$10^{32f.}$	. . . . . .	III, 4: 681*
11	. . . . . .	III, 1: 205; III, 2: 313; III, 4: 155 f., 174
11^1	. . . . . .	II, 2: 576; III, 2: 313
$11^{1f.}$	. . . . . .	III, 2: 312*
11^{1-16}	III, 2: **309** . .	III, 4: 155 f.*
$11^{2f.}$	II, 2: *483*	
11^3	III, 4: **173** . .	I, 1: 386 (443); III, 2: 310 f., 314; III, 4:

CHAP.

11⁷		III, 1: 203,* 303*
11⁸		III, 1: 326
11⁸ᶠ·		I, 2: 194*
11¹⁰	**III, 3: 472**	III, 3: 500; III, 4: 156, 174
11¹¹	**III, 4: 163**	III, 4: 144 f.*
11¹⁹		II, 2: 638
11²⁰		III, 2: 502; IV, 3: 758
11²³	*II, 2: 483*	I, 2: 552; II, 2: 461
11²⁴	**III, 2: 214**	IV, 1: 231
11²⁴ᶠ·	**IV, 2: 704 f.**	III, 2: 469; IV, 2: 163
11²⁵		IV, 1: 252
11²⁶	**III, 2: 214**	I, 2: 227; III, 2: 502; IV, 1: 250, 299, 665; IV, 2: 164, 658; IV, 3: 758
11²⁶ᶠ·		IV, 2: 267 f.
11²⁸	**II, 2: 640**	
11³⁰		III, 2: 601, 638
11³⁴		I, 2: 552
12		I, 1: 455 (521); III, 4: 603, 627; IV, 1: 717; IV, 2: 826; IV, 4: 38, 49
12–14		III, 4: 114*
12³		I, 1: 450 (515); I, 2: 10, 19; IV, 2: 328; IV, 3: 538, 859
12³ᶠ·		IV, 1: 666 f.
12⁴ᶠ·	*III, 4: 603*	I, 1: 313, 348,* 451 (360, 401,* 517); I, 2: 212, 704; III, 2: 358
12⁴⁻¹¹	**IV, 2: 321**	
12⁴⁻¹⁹	**IV, 3: 856–858**	
12⁴⁻³¹	*IV, 1: 663–669*	IV, 2: 660
12⁶		III, 3: 34, 95; IV, 1: 668; IV, 2: 593
12⁷		IV, 1: 667
12⁷⁻⁹	*III, 4: 603*	
12⁸	**IV, 3: 879**	
12⁸ᶠ·		IV, 3: 857, 863, 890
12⁹	**III, 4: 368**	IV, 1: 615; IV, 3: 110, 887*
12¹⁰		IV, 2: 320; IV, 3: 871, 895
12¹¹	*III, 4: 603*	III, 4: 606; IV, 2: 324; IV, 3: 110, 857
12¹¹ᶠ·		II, 1: 454 f.
12¹²		IV, 1: 663, 665
12¹²ᶠ·	*III, 4: 603*	I, 2: 215*
12¹³		IV, 1: 312, 666; IV, 3: 110; IV, 4: 30, 31, 83, 91
12¹⁴⁻²⁶		III, 3: 193*
12¹⁸		IV, 1: 667
12²⁰		IV, 1: 707; IV, 3: 110
12²⁴		IV, 1: 667
12²⁶⁻³⁰	**IV, 3: 857–863**	
12²⁷		IV, 1: 663 f.; IV, 2: 365; IV, 3: 758; IV, 4: 84, 97
12²⁸		IV, 3: 863
12²⁸ᶠ·	*III, 4: 603*	IV, 2: 201, 827; IV, 3: 890
12²⁹		III, 2: 309; IV, 2: 827, 830
12³¹	**I, 2: 372** *IV, 2: 732*	IV, 2: 826 f., 830, 839 f.

CHAP.

13	**IV, 2: 826–840** .	.	III, 2: 284*; III, 4: 128*; IV, 2: 784,
	I, 2: 332		788*
	IV, 2: 732		
13^1	**IV, 3: 658**		
13^2	. . . .	.	IV, 4: 108
13^3	. . . .	.	I, 2: 447
13^4	. . . .	.	IV, 2: 746, 832
13^{4-6}	. . . .	.	III, 2: 284*
$13^{6f.}$	. . . .	.	I, 2: 372
13^8	**III, 2: 276** .	.	I, 2: 398; II, 2: 719; IV, 1: 33, 331;
	IV, 2: 748		IV, 2: 732
$13^{8f.}$	*II, 1: 52*		
13^9	. . . .	.	II, 1: 187
$13^{9f.}$	. . . .	.	IV, 1: 520
13^{11}	. . . .	.	III, 4: 615*
$13^{11f.}$	**IV, 3: 389**		
13^{12}	**II, 1: 42** .	.	I, 1: 14, 244 (13, 279); I, 2: 360, 495;
	III, 3: 49		II, 1: 56; II, 2: 608; III, 2: 295; IV, 1:
	I, 1: 166 (189)		331, 730*; IV, 2: 621*; IV, 3: 185, 210,
			923, 926
13^{13}	*IV, 2: 731 f.*	.	I, 1: 229 (262); IV, 3: 912
14	. . . .	.	I, 1: 455 (521); III, 4: 156; IV, 2: 639,
			695,* 830
14^1	*IV, 3: 895* .	.	IV, 2: 799, 826
14^2	. . . .	.	IV, 4: 108
14^3	. . . .	.	IV, 2: 636, 830
$14^{3f.}$	. . . .	.	IV, 2: 634 f.
$14^{4f.}$	*IV, 3: 895*		
$14^{5, 7f.}$	. . . .	.	IV, 2: 829
14^{12}	. . . .	.	IV, 2: 635
14^{15}	. . . .	.	III, 4: 91
14^{17}	. . . .	.	IV, 2: 637
14^{18}	. . . .	.	IV, 2: 829
14^{24}	*IV, 3: 895*		
$14^{24f.}$	**IV, 3: 898**		
14^{29}	*IV, 3: 895*		
$14^{31f.}$	**IV, 3: 895**		
14^{32}	. . . .	.	IV, 2: 320
$14^{32f.}$	. . . .	.	III, 3: 161
14^{33}	**IV, 1: 186, 529**	.	II, 1: 353; II, 2: 606; III, 2: 310; IV, 1:
			186, 529
$14^{33f.}$	**IV, 2: 513** .	.	III, 4: 156*; IV, 2: 461*
14^{33-38}	. . . .	.	III, 2: 309
14^{34}	*III, 4: 172* .	.	III, 1: 327
14^{37}	*IV, 3: 895*	.	III, 4: 156*
15	. . . .	.	I, 1: 144 (163); I, 2: 114; IV, 1: 329;
			IV, 2: 143
15^1	. . . .	.	II, 2: 600
15^3	*II, 2: 483* .	.	III, 2: 213; IV, 1: 255, 295, 299; IV, 4: 16
$15^{3f.}$	. . . .	.	I, 2: 489; III, 2: 481
15^{3-8}	. . . .	.	III, 2: 452*
15^4	. . . .	.	IV, 1: 304
15^{4-8}	. . . .	.	IV, 1: 335*

CHAP.

5⁷			II, 1: 496; IV, 1: 639
5¹⁰			IV, 3: 546
5¹³	**III, 4: 606**		I, 1: 457 (523); II, 2: 589; III, 4: 477, 604; IV, 2: 817; IV, 3: 573, 603
5¹³⁻¹⁸			IV, 2: 370
5¹⁴			I, 2: 388, 401, 415; II, 1: 454; IV, 1: 583
5¹⁶			I, 2: 262; III, 2: 358, 509; IV, 1: 312, 640; IV, 3: 310
5¹⁶ᶠ·			II, 2: 730
5¹⁷	**IV, 2: 496, 533**		III, 2: 413
5¹⁸			I, 1: 454 (520); III, 2: 358, 509; IV, 1: 312; IV, 2: 129
5²¹			IV, 1: 330
5²²	**IV, 4: 39**		
5²²ᶠ·			III, 2: 358
5²⁴			I, 1: 387 (445); III, 4: 347; IV, 1: 295, 638; IV, 2: 365, 601; IV, 4: 17
5²⁵			II, 2: 730; III, 2: 358, 509; IV, 1: 321
5²⁶	**III, 4: 666**		
6¹			II, 2: 577; IV, 1: 639; IV, 2: 321
6²			I, 2: 407; III, 4: 536; IV, 1: 189, 583; IV, 2: 637; IV, 4: 14
6³ᶠ·			I, 2: 366
6⁴			II, 2: 640; III, 4: 644
6⁶			IV, 4: 152
6⁷	**IV, 3: 700**		III, 1: 284; III, 3: 151, 167
6⁷ᶠ·	**II, 1: 405**		II, 2: 590
6⁸			III, 2: 601; IV, 1: 329; IV, 2: 366; IV, 3: 210; IV, 4: 16
6¹⁰	**IV, 2: 806**		IV, 2: 805
6¹²			IV, 1: 642
6¹³			IV, 1: 640
6¹⁴			IV, 1: 295, 638; IV, 2: 277; IV, 3: 639
6¹⁴ᶠ·	*III, 1: 33 f.*		IV, 2: 601
6¹⁵			III, 3: 6; IV, 1: 49, 321, 640 f., 749; IV, 2: 45; IV, 4: 9
6¹⁶			II, 2: 274; IV, 1: 640, 671; IV, 2: 769
6¹⁷			III, 2: 621; IV, 1: 189, 638; IV, 2: 601; IV, 3: 638
6¹⁸			III, 2: 365

EPHESIANS

1			II, 2: 334; III, 2: 461
1¹			IV, 1: 749
1³			III, 2: 582; III, 3: 435 f.
1³ᶠ·			II, 2: 15, 21, 102, 426, 429
1³⁻⁶	**IV, 3: 731**		
1⁴	**IV, 2: 517**		II, 1: 279; III, 1: 17; III, 2: 210, 484*; IV, 1: 664, 667; IV, 2: 34, 520, 624; IV, 3: 483, 546, 753
1⁴ᶠ·			II, 1: 505, 622; II, 2: 60–76,* 88, 110 f., 114, 148, 154, 334; IV, 1: 44

158 Church Dogmatics Index

CHAP.

4^4		I, 1: 313, 348 (360, 401); III, 4: 600; IV, 1: 707*
$4^{4f.}$		II, 1: 445; III, 4: 602; IV, 3: 110
4^5		IV, 4: 85
4^7		IV, 2: 623
$4^{7f.}$		I, 2: 704
4^9		I, 1: 115 (130); IV, 1: 187
$4^{9f.}$		IV, 2: 21, 110
4^{10}		I, 2: 16; II, 1: 488 f.; III, 3: 420, 441; IV, 2: 625
4^{11}		I, 2: 487; IV, 2: 201, 623, 830; IV, 3: 863, 872, 895
$4^{11f.}$		IV, 2: 595, 634
4^{11-16}	**IV, 2: 659 ff.**	
4^{12}		I, 2: 215; IV, 1: 663
4^{12-15}	**IV, 2: 623 ff.**	
4^{13}		III, 2: 296; IV, 2: 629; IV, 3: 184
$4^{13f.}$		IV, 1: 711
4^{14}		I, 2: 484; III, 4: 615
4^{15}	**IV, 2: 799, 834**	I, 2: 216, 241, 372; II, 1: 208; IV, 2: 799
$4^{15f.}$		IV, 2: 660
4^{16}	*IV, 2: 635 f.*	I, 1: 64 (71); I, 2: 372; IV, 1: 663; IV, 2: 799
$4^{17f.}$	**IV, 2: 371**	
4^{19}		II, 2: 485
4^{22}		I, 1: 387 (445); III, 2: 601
$4^{22f.}$		IV, 1: 310; IV, 2: 366
4^{24}	**IV, 2: 166**	III, 1: 34; IV, 1: 49, 321; IV, 4: 7
4^{28}		III, 4: 472, 526*
4^{29}		I, 2: 704
4^{30}		I, 1: 409, 464 (469, 530); IV, 2: 322; IV, 3: 505
$4^{31f.}$		II, 2: 516
5		III, 1: 326 ff.; III, 2: 312 f., 318, 323
5^1	**IV, 1: 190**	III, 4: 477, 649; IV, 1: 634; IV, 2: 780
$5^{1f.}$	**II, 1: 673 f.** **II, 2: 576**	II, 2: 490*; IV, 2: 822
5^2		I, 2: 378; II, 2: 106, 488 ff.; III, 2: 214, 328 f.; IV, 1: 166, 277; IV, 2: 766, 822
5^5		IV, 2: 197
5^8		I, 2: 54; III, 1: 127; III, 2: 469; III, 4: 681; IV, 3: 546; IV, 4: 199
$5^{8f.}$	**IV, 3: 510**	II, 2: 639
5^9		III, 1: 120
5^{11}		IV, 2: 590; IV, 1: 210; IV, 3: 513*
$5^{11f.}$		IV, 3: 510
5^{12}		I, 1: 162 (184)
$5^{12f.}$		IV, 1: 392
5^{13}		IV, 2: 158
5^{14}	**IV, 3: 509, 511 f.**	II, 2: 602; IV, 2: 366, 382, 554, 556
5^{15}		II, 1: 439; III, 1: 53; III, 4: 682
$5^{15f.}$		III, 4: 583
5^{16}		III, 2: 507; IV, 1: 733*

CHAP.

2^{12}	. . . . . .	I, 1: 408 (469); I, 2: 387; II, 1: 37; IV, 2: 377; IV, 4: 122
$2^{12f.}$	**IV, 3: 940**	I, 2: 366; II, 1: 381*; IV, 2: 593; IV, 3: 654, 680
2^{13}	. . . . . .	III, 3: 95; IV, 2: 366
2^{15}	. . . . . .	III, 4: 682; IV, 1: 750; IV, 3: 510, 763
$2^{15f.}$	. . . . . .	IV, 2: 366
2^{17}	. . . . . .	III, 4: 476; IV, 1: 759; IV, 2: 640; IV, 3: 592
2^{18}	. . . . . .	II, 2: 588
2^{22}	. . . . . .	II, 2: 638
2^{27}	. . . . . .	II, 1: 371
2^{30}	. . . . . .	III, 4: 476
3	. . . . . .	IV, 1: 605
3^1	. . . . . .	II, 2: 588; IV, 3: 546
3^2	. . . . . .	II, 2: 280
3^5	. . . . . .	II, 2: 228
$3^{5f.}$	. . . . . .	IV, 3: 199
3^8	. . . . . .	IV, 3: 185
3^9	. . . . . .	IV, 1: 531, 614 f.
$3^{9f.}$	. . . . . .	II, 1: 14
3^{10}	. . . . . .	I, 1: 387, 458 (445, 525); III, 2: 622; IV, 1: 299; IV, 2: 365; IV, 3: 184 f., 638 f.
$3^{10f.}$	. . . . . .	I, 2: 261; IV, 1: 329
3^{12}	. . . . . .	I, 2: 273; IV, 1: 603,* 752; IV, 3: 543
$3^{12f.}$	. . . . . .	II, 1: 25*; IV, 2: 376 f.*; IV, 3: 210, 646
3^{12-14}		III, 4: 613*
3^{13}	**IV, 2: 578** . . .	II, 1: 170,* 628; III, 2: 156; IV, 1: 503
$3^{13f.}$		I, 2: 119*
3^{14}	*III, 4: 600*	IV, 3: 546, 573
3^{20}	**II, 2: 723** . . .	III, 2: 156; IV, 2: 183, 277
	III, 3: 435	
	IV, 2: 628 f.	
3^{21}	. . . . . .	II, 1: 525; III, 2: 331, 494
4^1	. . . . . .	IV, 2: 366; IV, 3: 547
4^3	. . . . . .	II, 2: 16
4^4	**II, 2: 588** . . .	I, 1: 219 (251); II, 1: 654*; IV, 2: 182; IV, 3: 546
4^5	**III, 4: 504** . .	III, 2: 284, 505 f.; III, 4: 681; IV, 2: 805
$4^{5f.}$	. . . . . .	IV, 2: 478*
4^6	. . . . . .	II, 2: 597; III, 4: 93, 95
4^7	. . . . . .	I, 1: 222 (254 f.); II, 1: 42; III, 3: 83; IV, 3: 546, 594, 764
$4^{7f.}$	**IV, 2: 417**	
	III, 2: 284	
4^8	. . . . . .	IV, 2: 417, 805
4^{10}	. . . . . .	IV, 3: 546
4^{12}	. . . . . .	IV, 1: 189
4^{13}	*III, 4: 393* . .	I, 2: 674
4^{21}	. . . . . .	IV, 3: 546

COLOSSIANS

CHAP.

1²⁴	**IV, 2: 601** . . .	I, 2: 215; II, 2: 499; IV, 1: 666; IV, 3:
	III, 2: 622	644 f.
	IV, 1: 190, 295	
1²⁴⁻²⁶	**IV, 3: 638**	
1²⁵	. . . . .	IV, 3: 603
1²⁶	. . . . .	I, 1: 119* (133*); I, 2: 215; III, 2: 469
1²⁷	. . . . .	IV, 3: 543, 911; IV, 4: 108
1²⁸	. . . . .	I, 2: 415, 695; II, 1: 439
1²⁹	. . . . .	IV, 2: 591
2²	. . . . .	I, 2: 695; IV, 3: 184 f.
2²ᶠ·	. . . . .	II, 1: 40; IV, 2: 269; IV, 4: 108
2³	**I, 2: 11** . . .	I, 2: 695; II, 1: 432; IV, 1: 527*;
	II, 1: 252	IV, 3: 13, 185
	IV, 1: 81	
2⁶	. . . . .	IV, 3: 546
2⁷	. . . . .	III, 3: 83; IV, 2: 650
2⁸	**I, 2: 617, 731 f.**	
2⁹	**II, 1: 401** . . .	I, 1: 401 (459); I, 2: 55, 166, 169,* 215*;
	IV, 1: 160	II, 1: 483 f.; IV, 1: 187*; IV, 2: 77,
		86, 88*; IV, 3: 13
2⁹ᶠ·	. . . . .	II, 2: 99
2⁹⁻¹²	**IV, 4: 118**	
2¹⁰	. . . . .	III, 1: 51; III, 2: 311, 483; III, 3: 458,
		500; III, 4: 173
2¹¹	*IV, 4: 14* . . .	IV, 1: 255,* 295 f., 663
2¹¹ᶠ·	*III, 2: 585*	
2¹²	**IV, 4: 160** . . .	III, 2: 621; IV, 1: 308, 321, 324; IV, 3:
		282; IV, 4: 91, 118 ff., 127
2¹²ᶠ·	. . . . .	III, 2: 622; IV, 2: 277, 365
2¹³	. . . . .	IV, 1: 256, 296; IV, 2: 277, 365, 496
2¹³⁻¹⁶	. . . . .	IV, 4: 118 f.
2¹⁴	. . . . .	I, 1: 265 (305); IV, 1: 255
2¹⁴ᶠ·	**I, 2: 107** . . .	IV, 2: 277
2¹⁵	*IV, 3: 168 f.* . .	I, 1: 155 (177); III, 3: 458
2¹⁷	*III, 2: 331* . . .	IV, 1: 663
2¹⁸	*III, 3: 421* . . .	III, 3: 483*
2¹⁹	*IV, 2: 660* . . .	IV, 1: 663
2²⁰	. . . . .	III, 2: 621; IV, 1: 295, 322; IV, 2: 277
2²⁰ᶠ·	**I, 2: 617**	
2²³	**IV, 1: 619** . . .	III, 4: 347; IV, 4: 119
3¹	**III, 3: 438, 441** . .	II, 1: 490*; III, 2: 622; III, 3: 473;
		IV, 1: 315, 321; IV, 2: 154; IV, 3: 357
3¹ᶠ·	**I, 1: 219 (251)** . .	IV, 2: 277, 576; IV, 4: 119
	I, 2: 370	
	II, 1: 475	
	II, 2: 580	
	IV, 1: 743	
	IV, 2: 103	
3¹⁻³	**IV, 2: 375**	
3²	**III, 3: 436** . .	II, 1: 159; III, 1: 150; IV, 4: 9
	III, 4: 347	
3²ᶠ·	. . . . .	III, 2: 156 f.
3³	**II, 1: 149** . . .	I, 1: 387 (445); I, 2: 118,* 782 f., 786*;

2 THESSALONIANS

1 TIMOTHY

CHAP.

1¹⁵	.	.	.	.	.	.	.	IV, 2: 491
2²	.	.	.	.	.	.	.	IV, 2: 731
2³	.	.	.	.	.	.	.	IV, 3: 603
2⁵	.	.	.	.	.	.	.	III, 4: 172
2¹¹	**IV, 3: 173**	.	.	.	.	.	II, 2: 108; IV, 3: 487
2¹¹ᶠ.	**II, 1: 361**	.	.	.	.	.	IV, 2: 563
2¹¹⁻¹⁴	**II, 2: 606 f.**						
2¹²ᶠ.	**III, 4: 263**						
2¹³	.	.	.	.	.	.	.	I, 1: 401 (460)
2¹⁴	**IV, 2: 590**	.	.	.	.	.	II, 1: 397 f.; IV, 1: 255, 274; IV, 4: 120
	IV, 4: 115						
3¹	.	.	.	.	.	.	.	III, 3: 458; IV, 4: 114
3²	.	.	.	.	.	.	.	III, 2: 284; III, 4: 681; IV, 3: 487
3⁴	**IV, 1: 35**	.	.	.	.	.	II, 1: 665; IV, 1: 738
	IV, 3: 667						
	III, 2: 218						
3⁴⁻⁷	.	.	.	.	.	.	.	IV, 4: 114
3⁵	*IV, 4: 9*	.	.	.	.	.	I, 2: 222, 231; II, 1: 372; IV, 2: 322,
							563; IV, 4: 9, 15, 47, 94 f., 114 f., 120,
							122, 127
3⁶	.	.	.	.	.	.	.	IV, 2: 332 f.
3⁷	.	.	.	.	.	.	.	I, 1: 463 (530)
3⁸	.	.	.	.	.	.	.	IV, 4: 114

PHILEMON

v. 1	.	.	.	.	.	.	.	I, 2: 273
v. 2	.	.	.	.	.	.	.	III, 4: 228
v. 8	.	.	.	.	.	.	.	IV, 3: 546
v. 9	*IV, 3: 591*						
v. 10	.	.	.	.	.	.	.	III, 4: 244
v. 23	.	.	.	.	.	.	.	IV, 3: 546

HEBREWS

1	.	.	.	.	.	.	.	III, 2: 137, 166
1 f.	.	.	.	.	.	.	.	II, 2: 578
1¹	**I, 2: 84**	.	.	.	.	.	I, 2: 13; III, 1: 115*
1¹ᶠ.	**IV, 3: 584**	.	.	.	.	.	I, 1: 411 (471); III, 2: 462
	IV, 3: 93 f.						
1¹⁻⁶	*IV, 2: 34*						
1²	.	.	.	.	.	.	.	I, 1: 442 (506); I, 2: 148; III, 1: 51;
							III, 2: 483
1²ᶠ.	**II, 1: 420**	.	.	.	.	.	I, 1: 401 (460); II, 2: 99
	III, 1: 53						
1³	*I, 1: 386 (443)*	.	.	.	.	I, 1: 402 (460); II, 1: 416, 606, 661; III, 1:
							51, 54; III, 2: 466; III, 3: 10, 35, 59,
							430 ff.; IV, 1: 44; IV, 3: 195, 767
1³ᶠ.	.	.	.	.	.	.	.	I, 2: 379
1⁴	*III, 3: 452 f.*						
1⁴ᶠ.	.	.	.	.	.	.	.	III, 2: 14*
1⁵	.	.	.	.	.	.	.	I, 2: 52; III, 2: 469
1⁵ᶠ.	.	.	.	.	.	.	.	I, 1: 401 (459)
1⁵⁻¹⁴	.	.	.	.	.	.	.	III, 3: 500*

CHAP.

1^6	. . . . . .	III, 2: 210; III, 3: 500
1^7	. . . . .	IV, 2: 320
1^8	. . . . .	I, 1: 402 (460)
1^{10}	*III, 1: 51–53* . .	III, 2: 483
1^{13}	. . . .	III, 3: 439
1^{14}	*III, 3: 453* .	I, 1: 409 (469); III, 3: 384, 483; IV, 2: 320
2	. . . . .	III, 1: 55
2^5	. . . . .	III, 2: 46
$2^{5f.}$	. . . .	II, 1: 113; III, 1: 206; III, 2: 20*
2^8	. . . . .	II, 1: 113
2^9	**III, 3: 501** . .	III, 2: 213; IV, 1: 250; IV, 4: 16
2^{10}	. . . .	I, 2: 33; III, 2: 449
2^{11}	**IV, 2: 515** .	I, 2: 422*; II, 2: 114, 118 f.; IV, 1: 106*
	IV, 4: 59	
	IV. 1: 259	
2^{14}	*IV, 1: 259* .	III, 2: 209; IV, 1: 165, 255; IV, 2: 37, 42; IV, 3: 169
$2^{14f.}$	. . . .	I, 2: 19, 147
2^{15}	. . . .	III, 2: 495, 601; IV, 2: 181
2^{16}	*IV, 1: 259* .	I, 2: 160; IV, 2: 42
2^{17}	**IV, 4: 21** . .	I, 2: 33, 422*; II, 1: 460; IV, 1: 165
	IV, 1: 259	
2^{18}	*IV, 1: 259* .	IV, 1: 165, 194
3^1	. . . .	II, 2: 432; III, 4: 600; IV, 3: 12 f., 583
3^2	. . . .	I, 1: 386 (443); IV, 4: 21
3^6	. . . .	IV, 4: 21
3^7	*III, 2: 469* .	III, 4: 583; IV, 1: 314
$3^{7f.}$	. . . .	I, 2: 52
$3^{12f.}$	. . . .	III, 4: 583*; IV, 2: 569
3^{13}	*III, 2: 469* .	I, 1: 239 (274); I, 2: 52
3^{14}	**IV, 3: 526**	
3^{15}	. . . .	I, 2: 52; III, 4: 583*; IV, 1: 314
$4^{1f.}$	. . . .	I, 2: 52
4^{1-8}	*III, 2: 469*	
4^{1-11}	**III, 2: 458**	
4^3	**III, 1: 227**	
4^4	. . . .	III, 3: 70
4^7	. . . .	I, 2: 52; III, 4: 583*
$4^{9f.}$	**III, 1: 227**	
4^{12}	**III, 2: 355** .	I, 1: 150, 181 (170, 206); II, 2: 636; IV, 1: 772*; IV, 2: 370; IV, 3: 238
	IV, 3: 627	
$4^{12f.}$	**I, 2: 676** .	IV, 2: 158*
4^{13}	. . . .	II, 1: 477 f., 554
4^{14}	. . . .	III, 2: 466; III, 3: 436, 441; IV, 1: 275 f., 314
$4^{14f.}$	. . . .	II, 1: 157
4^{15}	**I, 2: 152** .	I, 2: 157; II, 1: 398; III, 2: 210; IV, 1: 165, 282
	IV, 3: 395	
	IV, 1: 259	
$4^{15f.}$	. . . .	I, 2: 19
5^2	. . . .	IV, 1: 282
$5^{2f.}$	. . . .	I, 2: 152

CHAP.

5⁴		IV, 3: 503*
5⁵		I, 2: 52; III, 2: 469
5⁶	**I, 2: 421**	III, 2: 469; IV, 1: 314
5⁶ᶠ·		II, 2: 562
5⁷		III, 2: 329, 462; IV, 1: 260, 265; IV, 2: 95; IV, 3: 395
5⁷ᶠ·	**I, 2: 158**	I, 1: 386 (443); III, 2: 337, 462; IV, 2: 250; IV, 4: 70
5⁸	**IV, 1: 165**	I, 1: 387 (444); I, 2: 157; II, 2: 106, 606; III, 2: 329; IV, 1: 193, 260, 282; IV, 2: 607*
5¹⁰	**I, 2: 158**	IV, 1: 303
6¹		IV, 2: 590,* 633
6¹ᶠ·		IV, 4: 113
6¹⁻¹⁰	*IV, 2: 568 f.*	
6¹⁻²⁰	*I, 2: 399 f.*	
6²		IV, 1: 717; IV, 4: 45
6⁴	**IV, 3: 509**	I, 2: 13; III, 3: 435; IV, 2: 321
6⁵	**IV, 3: 644**	II, 1: 606; IV, 2: 219
6⁵ᶠ·		I, 1: 453 (519)
6⁷		III, 1: 150
6¹⁰		IV, 2: 595
6¹¹		III, 2: 413
6¹¹ᶠ·		IV, 2: 569
6¹³		II, 2: 102
6¹³ᶠ·		II, 1: 492
6¹⁷⁻²⁰		IV, 2: 275 f.
6¹⁹		IV, 3: 911
6²⁰		I, 2: 421*; III, 2: 214; IV, 1: 314
7¹		I, 1: 239 (274)
7¹ᶠ·		I, 2: 421*; IV, 1: 276
7³	**III, 4: 261**	I, 2: 181, 193; III, 2: 335, 469; IV, 4: 178
7¹¹ᶠ·		IV, 1: 275
7¹⁶		II, 1: 606; III, 2: 335; IV, 1: 275
7¹⁶ᶠ·		II, 2: 102
7¹⁷		III, 2: 469; IV, 1: 314; IV, 3: 397*
7²⁰ᶠ·		IV, 1: 276
7²¹		III, 2: 469
7²⁴		IV, 1: 314
7²⁴ᶠ·		IV, 3: 397*
7²⁵		II, 1: 390; III, 2: 214; IV, 1: 299, 314
7²⁶		I, 2: 157; III, 3: 441; IV, 1: 299
7²⁷	**IV, 1: 274 ff.**	I, 2: 13; II, 2: 106; III, 2: 441; IV, 1: 224
8¹	**III, 3: 439**	III, 2: 466; IV, 1: 276, 314
8⁵	**IV, 1: 276**	
9¹ᶠ·		IV, 1: 276
9⁷	**IV, 1: 275**	
9¹⁰		IV, 4: 45
9¹²		I, 2: 13; III, 2: 441; IV, 1: 274 ff., 314
9¹⁴	**IV, 1: 276 f.**	I, 1: 386 (443); II, 2: 102, 106, 117; III, 2: 601; IV, 1: 255, 309; IV, 2: 324, 590; IV, 4: 29, 113

CHAP.

4^{14} . . . . III, 2: 559
4^{17} **III, 4: 539**
$5^{1f.}$ . . . . IV, 2: 169
5^{4} . . . . III, 4: 536
5^{8} *III, 2: 505*
5^{11} . . . . IV, 2: 189; IV, 3: 643
$5^{11f.}$ . . . . III, 4: 676
$5^{14f.}$ . . . . III, 4: 370
$5^{16f.}$ **II, 1: 511** . . . III, 4: 111
5^{20} . . . . IV, 4: 122

1 PETER

1^{1} . . . . IV, 2: 628
$1^{1f.}$ *II, 2: 427* . . . II, 1: 37
1^{2} . . . . I, 1: 313, 451 (360, 517); I, 2: 241*;
        IV, 2: 321, 650; IV, 4: 113
1^{3} **II, 1: 406** . . . I, 1: 463 (530); II, 1: 373, 510; III, 2:
  IV, 1: 600   449, 490, 622; IV, 1: 604, 749; IV, 2:
  IV, 3: 643   365; IV, 3: 282, 929*; IV, 4: 15
  IV, 4: 197
$1^{3f.}$ **IV, 1: 330** . . . IV, 4: 9
  IV, 3: 911
1^{3-13} *III, 2: 496*
1^{4} . . . . III, 3: 435
1^{5} . . . . III, 3: 83
1^{6} . . . . IV, 3: 643
$1^{6f.}$ **II, 2: 638**
1^{7} . . . . III, 4: 581; IV, 3: 646
1^{8} . . . . IV, 2: 655, 793
1^{10-12} *I, 2: 74*
1^{11} . . . . I. 1: 453 (518); IV, 3: 67*
$1^{11f.}$ . . . . IV, 2: 197
1^{12} **III, 1: 441** . . . III, 2: 413; III, 3: 436, 500; IV, 3: 732 f.
  II, 2: 588
1^{13} . . . . I, 2: 250; III, 4: 581; IV, 3: 911
1^{14} *II, 1: 37*
1^{15} **IV, 2: 515**
$1^{15f.}$ **II, 1: 364**
1^{16} **IV, 2: 501**
$1^{16f.}$ . . . . II, 2: 427
1^{17} . . . . II, 1: 381; III, 4: 604; IV, 2: 628
1^{18} . . . . II, 2: 304; IV, 1: 274
$1^{18f.}$ . . . . I, 2: 300*; II, 1: 622; IV, 2: 34
1^{19} . . . . I, 2: 156
$1^{19f.}$ . . . . II, 2: 365; IV, 1: 166, 277, 280
1^{20} **III, 2: 484** . . . II, 1: 505; II, 2: 102, 117; III, 2: 462;
        IV, 2: 35
1^{21} . . . . IV, 1: 299, 749
1^{22} . . . . II, 1: 385; IV, 2: 639, 799, 817
1^{23} . . . . I, 1: 150, 153 (170, 174); III, 4: 247*;
        IV, 1: 749; IV, 2: 365; IV, 4: 9
1^{24} . . . . I, 1: 153 (174)
1^{25} . . . . I, 2: 754; IV, 4: 180

CHAP.

2^{19}		IV, 3: 603
3$^{1-10}$	III, 2: 509 f.	
3^{2}		I, 2: 692 f.
3^{3}		III, 2: 412
3^{4}	IV, 3: 913 f.	III, 2: 509, 638
3^{8}		I, 2: 692 f.; II, 1: 609
3^{9}		I, 2: 68; II, 1: 415; II, 2: 71*
3^{10}		III, 1: 141; III, 2: 499
3^{12}	I, 2: 70 IV, 2: 606 IV, 3: 940	III, 2: 497; III, 4: 581; IV, 3: 331
3^{13}		III, 1: 17; III, 4: 582; IV, 1: 49, 257; IV, 3: 661; IV, 4: 199
3^{15}		I, 2: 68
3^{18}		IV, 2: 650

1 JOHN

1^{1}	III, 2: 444–448 IV, 1: 341	I, 1: 401 (459); II, 2: 95 f.; III, 1: 51; III, 2: 329, 483; III, 4: 581; IV, 1: 70, 305; IV, 3: 47
1$^{1f.}$	III, 2: 483	I, 1: 454 (514); IV, 2: 143
1$^{1-4}$	I, 2: 490 *I, 2: 16*	I, 2: 587
1^{2}		I, 2: 18; II, 1: 263; II, 2: 431; III, 2: 335, 442; IV, 1: 665; IV, 2: 144
1^{5}	II, 1: 555	III, 3: 464; IV, 3: 510
1^{7}		IV, 1: 255; IV, 3: 510; IV, 4: 112
1$^{8f.}$		I, 2: 395; IV, 1: 316*
1^{9}		II, 1: 389, 459
2^{1}		II, 1: 157, 390; IV, 1: 314; IV, 2: 326
2^{2}		II, 2: 422*; III, 2: 213; IV, 1: 282; IV, 3: 487; IV, 4: 99
2^{3}		II, 1: 28
2$^{4f.}$	II, 2: 563	
2^{5}		IV, 3: 546
2^{6}	*II, 2: 600*	IV, 2: 276
2$^{7f.}$	II, 2: 574 IV, 2: 810 f.	
2^{8}		III, 1: 127
2$^{8-11}$	I, 2: 407	
2^{10}	*II, 2: 600*	
2^{12}		IV, 4: 93
2$^{12-14}$		III, 4: 615
2^{13}		III, 1: 51; III, 4: 393
2$^{13f.}$	III, 4: 281 f.	III, 2: 483
2^{14}		I, 1: 153 (174); I, 2: 271
2$^{14f.}$		IV, 2: 371
2$^{15-17}$		III, 2: 412
2^{17}	*II, 2: 600*	III, 4: 582; IV, 2: 15
2^{18}		I, 2: 52; III, 4: 494, 581
2^{20}	IV, 2: 322	I, 1: 454 (520); II, 1: 364; II, 2: 432

NAMES

The General Index contains almost all the 1000 or so names in the various volumes of C.D. There are here two groups. Entries in italics indicate more explicit discussion of the relevant names, while the others denote for the most part only a reference.

In the case of I, 1 the page numbers are those of the revised edition with references from the first edition following in parentheses.

Abelard, Peter, I, 2: 284; III, 3: 377 f.
Abraham of Santa Clara, II, 2: 502
Abramowski, Rudolf, II, 2: 191
Adam, Karl, I, 1: 105 (118); I, 2: 142, *145 f.*, 564
"Ad Diem," Encycl., I, 2: 142
Adenauer, Konrad, IV, 3: 694
Adler, Alfred, III, 4: *136*
Æsop, I, 2: 475
"Æterni Pacis," Encycl., II, 1: 582
Athelstani Psalterium, I, 2: 174
Alacoque, Maria Margarete, I, 2: 137
Aland, Kurt, IV, 4: 164
Albert, H., III, 1: *129*
Alexander VI, IV, 1: *707*
Alstedt, H., I, 1: 303 (348); I, 2: 537; II, 1: 574
Allmen, J.-J. von, IV, 4: 107
Altdorfer, Albrecht, III, 3: *492*
Althaus, Paul, I, 1: 22, *83 f.*, 237, 253, 335 (23, *93, 271*, 290, *385*); I, 2: 57, 180 f., 189, 793 f., 795; III, 3: *408*; III, 4: 20, 22, *141, 457*; IV, 3: 370
Althusius, Johannes, IV, 1: 55
Althing, Johann Heinrich, I, 2: 285, 839; II, 2: 77
Ambrose of Milan, I, 1: 87, 95, 266, 349 (97, 107, 305, 401); I, 2: 140, 604, 783; IV, 2: 23
Amesius, Wilhelm, II, 2: 338; III, 4: 8, *66*, 186; IV, 1: 54
Amida-Buddha, I, 2: *340 f.*
Ammonius, III, 3: 163
Amsdorf, Nikolaus, I, 2: *604*; IV, 2: 362
Aner, Karl, I, 1: 146, 234 (166, 268)
Angelus Silesius *v.* Scheffler, J.

Anglican (Thirty-Nine) Articles, II, 2: 86
Anselm of Canterbury, I, 1: 14, 16, *18 f.*, 20, 21, *84*, 114, *234, 236*, 240, 242, 246, 276, *336*, 338, 350, 356, 365, *370*, 413, 435, 443, 469 (14, 17, *19*, 23, 25, *94*, 128, *263, 270*, 275, 277, 282, 317, *386*, 388, 402, 409 f., 419, *425*, 473, 498, 507, 537 f.); I, 2: *8 f., 135*, 141, 148, 166, 604, 608, 614; II, 1: 4, *92 f., 185, 191*, 195, 302, 305, 323, 379 f., 444, *446 f.*, 608, 610, 614, 656 f.; III, 1: 29 f., 116, 126, *360*; III, 2: 153 f.; III, 3: *71*, 383; IV, 1: 253, *407, 412, 485 ff.*, 493, 499; IV, 2: 412, *415*; IV, 3: 32, 85 f., 802
Anthony (St.), IV, 2: 13
Apelles, III, 1: 338
Apollinaris of Laodicea, III, 2: 355
Apollonius of Tyana, IV, 2: *212 f.*
Apophis, Book of, III, 1: *112*
Apostles' Creed, I, 2: 51, 89, 118, *174*, *196 f.*, 626, 629, 631, 650, 655; II, 1: *14*, 525, 677; IV, 3: 90, 925
Arausicanum, Council of, I, 2: 373, 626
Aretius, Benedict, I, 2: 65
Aristides, II, 2: *617*; III, 1: *12*; III, 2: 153
Aristotle, I, 1: *8 f. (10 f.)*; I, 2: 484, 554, *728*, 783, 791, *874*; II, 1: 84, *127*, 265, 305, *382*; III, 1: 103, *414*; III, 2: 7, 10, 15, 81, 279, *380*; III, 3: 11, 31, *98 ff., 100, 103*, 107, 174, *334*, 400, 404; III, 4: 20, 406; IV, 2: 737, *739, 758 f.*; IV, 3: *524*
Arius, I, 1: *310 f., 352*, 438, 442 (*356*,

Doumergue, Emile, I, 2: 837
Drews, Arthur, I, 2: 17, 350
Drey, Johann Sebastian von, I, 2: *560,*
564
Driesch, Hans, III, 2: 428
Dubois-Reymond, III, 2: 81, *386*
Duhm, Bernard, III, 4: *74;* IV, 1:
468, 471, 474 ff.; IV, 2: 449, 451
Dulles, John Foster, IV, 3: 694
Duns Scotus, I, 1: 85, 191 (95, 218);
I, 2: 134, *141;* II, 1: 237; II, 2: 191
Duraeus, Johannes, IV, 3: 24, 36
Dürer, Albrecht, I, 2: 496; IV, 3: 615,
917
Düsseldorf Theses (1933), I, 2: 460

Ebeling, Gerhard, IV, 2: 82
Eck, John, I, 2: 475, 557
Eckhardt, Meister, I, 2: 496; II, 1:
327; IV, 1: 386
Egede, Hans, IV, 3: *24*
Eichrodt, Walther, I, 2: 79, 95, *99;* III,
1: 87, 137; IV, 1: 22 f., 24, 26; IV,
2: 763
Eisenhuth, H. E., I, 1: 161 (183)
Elert, Werner, I, 2: 837; IV, 3: 370
Eliot, John, IV, 3: *24*
Elizabeth of Dijon, IV, 1: 768
Ellul, Jacques, IV, 1: 25
Emmerich, Kurt, III, 3: 211
Empedocles, IV, 1: *263*
Engelland, Hans, I, 1: 23 (24)
Enoch, I, 2: 99
Enuma elish, III, 1: *83 f., 112 f.,* 163,
243
Ephesinum Conc., I, 1: 426 (488); I,
2: 139, 141, *626;* IV, 2: *71;* IV, 3:
13
Ephraem, I, 1: 477 (546); II, 1: 200
Epicurus, III, 2: 383; III, 3: *10,* 12,
174
Epiphanius, I, 1: 477 (546); I, 2: 135,
548; III, 3: 382
Erasmus of Rotterdam, I, 2: 137, 378,
476, 540, *668;* IV, 2: 506; IV, 3: *36*
Ernesti, Johann Augustus, IV, 3: 6
Essenes, IV, 2: *18*
Eugenius III, II, 1: 331
Eunomius, I, 1: 352 (405); II, 1: 327
Euripides, III, 2: 279
Eusebius of Caesarea, I, 1: 104, 270
(118, 310); I, 2: 477, 600; II, 1:
185; III, 3: 25, 381; III, 4: 412;
IV, 3: 13; IV, 4: 95

Eusebius of Emesa, IV, 1: 211
Eutyches, I, 2: *24;* IV, 2: 67 f.

Fabricius, Andreas, I, 2: 604
Farel, William, I, 1: 417 (478); I, 2:
637
Fechner, Gustav Theodor, III, 2: 428
Fehr, Jakob, II, 1: 81 ff.
Feuerbach, Ludwig, I, 1: 128, 211, 343
(145, 241, 394); I, 2: 6, *41 f., 290;*
II, 1: *292 f., 449, 467,* 613; II, 2:
514; III, 2: 21, *240 f., 277 f.,* 385 *ff.;*
IV, 2: *83;* IV, 3: *72–85,* 564
Feuling, Daniel, II, 1: 81 ff.
Fezer, Karl, I, 1: *56 (61)*
Fichte, Johann Gottlieb, I, 2: 20, *41;*
III, 2: *96 ff., 113, 240;* III, 3: *111*
Fides Damasi, I, 1: 354 (407); I, 2: 38
Flacius Illyricus, IV, 1: 481
Flacius, Matthias, III, 2: 27 f.
Florentinum, Conc. (1438–1445), I, 1:
69, 353, 364, 375, 487 (76, 406, 419,
431, 557); I, 2: 476, 478, 568; III,
4: 123
Florenz, Karl, I, 2: 340 f.
Flückiger, Felix, IV, 2: *380,* 561
Foerster, Werner, III, 1: 16 f., 46,
114
Fontane, Theodore, II, 2: *542*
Formula Concordiae, IV, 2: *66,* 82
Fouillée, Alfred, III, 4: 326
Francis of Assisi, I, 2: 250, 340, 496;
III, 4: 349; IV, 1: *190;* IV, 2: *12,*
14; IV, 3: *514*
Francis Xavier, I, 2: 341; IV, 3: *23*
Franck, Johann, I, 2: *253*
Franck, Sebastian, I, 2: *668*
Francke, August Hermann, I, 1: 20, 23
(21, 25); IV, 3: 25, 33, *568 f.*
Francois de Sales, II, 1: 573
Frank, Franz Hermann Reinhold, I, 2:
616; II, 1: *330,* 341, 344; III, 2: 5;
IV, 1: 125; IV, 2: 77, 83; IV, 3: 6
Franklin, Benjamin, II, 2: 113
Frederick, William I, III, 1: 412
Frederick William IV of Prussia, I, 1:
252 (289)
Freethinkers Congress of Naples (1869),
I, 2: 571
Freud, Sigmund, III, 1: 334; III, 4:
135, 159
Friedrich, Gerhard, IV, 2: 202, 204
Fritzsche, Herbert, III, 4: 352
Frommel, Gaston, IV, 3: 569

SUBJECTS

In the use of this index it will be noted that many terms are also listed in other places as sub-headings. Since the meaning may vary according to the main term, it has not always been possible to assemble these. This makes it necessary to make many references to other places. Those which may be consulted to advantage are marked by " cf." It should be noted that sub-headings in these references are separated from the main headings by a comma. Thus " *v.* Ethics, Man " means that " Man " is to be sought under " Ethics," whereas in the case of " *v.* Ethics! Man! " the main headings " Ethics " and " Man " are both to be consulted. When " *q.v.*" is used the reference is to the main heading, but " *v. supra* " or " *v. infra* " refers to another sub-heading under the same chief head.

calling, I, 1: 19, 286 (20, 238)

Christology, I, 2: 122 f., 871, 882

Church, I, 1: 17, 75, 273 (18, 84, 314); I, 2: 770 f., 775 ff., 797 ff., 806 ff., 839 ff.

Church proclamation, I, 1: 71, 249, 280 (79 f., 286 f., 321 f.); I, 2: 770 ff., 798 f., 812 f., 852 ff.

content, I, 2: 366, 881 ff.

dangers, I, 2: 860 ff., 882 ff.

dogma, I, 1: 273, 310 (313, 356)

education, I, 1: 283 (325 f.)

end, I, 2: 800

ethics, I, 2: 239, 782 ff., 881 ff.; II, 2: 12, 512 f., 539 f., 543 f., 548 ff., 603

exegesis, II, 2: 35

extra-church proclamation, I, 1: 81 (91)

faith, I, 1: 17, 83, 273 (17, 93, 314); I, 2: 809, 823, 855, 868

Glaubenslehre?, I, 1: 265 (304)

heteronomy, I, 2: 815, 857 ff.

irregular, I, 1: 277 (318)

justification, I, 1: 285 (327 f.)

knowledge of truth, I, 1: 12 (12)

laymen, I, 1: 77 (86)

material, I, 2: 779 f.

method, I, 2: 583 ff.

need, I, 1: 25 (26)

norm, I, 2: 812 ff.

path to knowledge, I, 1: 287 (330)

possibility, I, 1: 36 (38)

prayer, I, 1: 23 (25); I, 2: 776, 840, 843

problem, I, 1: 266 (305)

prolegomena, I, 2: 3, 124, 870 f.

regular, I, 1: 275, 278 (316, 320)

relevance, I, 2: 843

results, I, 2: 769

revelation, I, 1: 84 f. (94 f.)

as school, I, 1: 79 (88)

science, I, 1: 5, 275, 279, 286, 308 (3, 315 f., 321, 329)

system, II, 2: 861 ff.

task, I, 1: 3, 71, 265, 279 (1, 79 f., 304, 321, 354); I, 2: 766 ff., 775 ff., 781 ff., 804 ff.

theonomy, II, 2: 815, 857 ff., 866

traditional, IV, 1: 139, 149 f., 359, 765

truth of revelation, I, 1: 15, 86, 269 (15, 96, 309)

unity, I, 2: 877

Dualism, II, 1: 501, 562

Duelling, III, 4: 450

Duty, III, 2: 100 f.

Early Communion, IV, 4: 190

Earth, the, III, 1: 17 f., 27 f., 63, 99 f., 103 f., 141 ff., 241; III, 3: 431

desert, III, 1: 155

fertility, III, 1: 153, 179, 207, 241, 248

mother earth, III, 1: 244

land and sea, III, 1: 141 ff.

mountains, III, 1: 151

world of animals, III, 1: 152, 156 f.

world of plants, III, 1: 143, 152, 207, 241

Earthliness, IV, 2: 318 f.

Easter,

faith, IV, 3: 288, 290 ff., 317

festival, IV, 3: 283 f., 290 f., 317

hymns, IV, 3: 302 f., 305

stories, IV, 3: 283, 308 ff.

Eastern Church, III, 3: 311; IV, 1: 527, 559

Ebionitism, I, 2: 19 f., 136, 163, 375, 526

Ecclesiology, II, 1: 144 f., 148 f., 155 ff.; IV, 1: 124, 149 f.

Economic Order, III, 4: 452, 532, 543

Ecumenical Church, III, 4: 110

Ecumenicism, IV, 1: 527, 683, 703; IV, 2: 7 f.; IV, 3: 36 f., 736 f.

Education, III, 4: 280, 622

discipline, III, 4: 280 f.

limit, III, 4: 284

Elect, the,

blessedness, II, 2: 412

calling, II, 2: 345, 348, 351, 410, 510

Church, II, 2: 426

determination, II, 2: 410 ff., 449, 510

distinction, II, 2: 340 f.

elect and rejected?, II, 2: 351 ff., 428, 451 f.

individual, II, 2: 427

life, II, 2: 321

ministry, II, 2: 345, 412 ff., 511

office, II, 2: 414

secret, II, 2: 341 ff., 413

sign, II, 2: 418

sin, II, 2: 347 f.

witness, II, 2: 345 ff., 413 ff., 423 ff., 510

Election (of Grace), the, I, 1: 48, 56,

ascension, I, 2: 413, 421, 424, 433, 692 f.; II, 1: 540; II, 2: 173, 412; III, 4: 439; IV, 2: 100, 107, 132 ff.; IV, 3: 356; IV, 4: 25 51

assumptio carnis, I, 2: 147 f., 163 ff., 198; II, 1: 151, 252 f., 316 ff., 662; III, 1: 26, 73, 380 ff.

baptiser, with the Holy Spirit, IV, 4: 33, 61, 70, 74 ff., 80, 83, 90 f.

baptism, I 2: 199; III 2: 57, 459, 479, 484

basis of baptism, IV, 4: 52 ff., 67 f., 89, 91, 195 f.

beneficia, I, 1: 416, 419 f., 422 (476, 480, 484)

birth, III, 3: 504 f.

blood, IV, 4: 111 f., 124

Brother, III, 2: 53, 223, 508

Christomonism?, IV, 4: 19, 207 f.

Christus solus, IV, 4: 32 f., 86, 89 f., 150, 159 f.

Church, I, 1: 4, 12, 15, 41, 49, 57, 95, 100, 206, 261, 330, 376 (3, 11, 16, 44, 53, 62, 106, 113, 235, 299, 380, 432); I, 2: 146, 198, 213 ff., 247, 270 ff., 355 ff., 383, 412, 424, 576 ff., 670, 748, 847 ff.; II, 1: 154, 160 f., 163 f., 319 f., 373, 405

community, III, 1: 190, 203 f., 320 ff., 328; IV, 2: 285 ff., 304 ff.

confession of sin, IV, 4: 57 ff.

conflict, IV, 3: 238, 328 ff.

concealment, IV, 2: 285 ff., 304 ff.

creation, II, 2: 99, 116, 195

creature, III, 1: 332, 376 ff.

creatureliness, IV, 2: 37 f., 165

cross, I, 2: 36, 54, 56, 61 f., 86 ff., 100 ff., 151, 156 f., 679, 749, 751, 756 f.; II, 1: 56, 151, 154, 279, 394 ff., 422, 511 f., 607, 626 f., 665; II, 2: 117, 120 ff., 161, 167 f., 172, 174, 179, 198, 206 ff., 211 f., 261, 266, 282, 438 ff., 492, 563; III, 1: 386; III, 2: 443 f., 523, 531, 544, 549; III, 3: 305, 312, 360, 471; III, 4: 42, 263, 383, 401; IV, 1: 178 f., 192, 208, 244 f., 250, 262, 299 ff., 309, 334, 343 ff., 350, 392, 411; IV, 2: 95, 140 f., 163, 249 ff., 354 f., 399, 519, 599,

622; IV, 3: 378, 397, 442 f., 638; IV, 4: 16, 59 f., 78 ff., 84, 98 f., 119 f., 158 ff.

Crucified, the, IV, 3: 408 ff., 411, 638

dead and raised in Him, IV, 4: 14 ff., 116 ff., 158 ff., 196 f.

death, II, 2: 229, 235, 318, 453, 558 f., 607, 748 ff.; III, 2: 205, 304, 327, 441, 450, 498, 602, 623, 628 f.; IV, 2: 140 f., 143, 257, 290 ff., 381, 389 f., 487

deity, I, 1: 289 f., 323, 384, 401, 402, 409, 414 (332 f., 371, 442 f., 460, 462 f., 469 f., 474 f.); I, 2: 21, 33, 37 ff., 132 ff., 155, 159; II, 1: 318, 486, 514, 606 f.; II, 2: 7, 26, 59, 95 f., 103 f., 116 f., 125, 157, 165, 176, 247, 490 f., 605; III, 2: 27, 42 f., 49, 65 f., 149 f., 207, 220 f., 262, 332, 341, 439 f., 448, 516, 601 f.; IV, 2: 3, 25 f., 73 f., 86 f., 100, 113, 295 f., 336; IV, 3: 39 ff., 79, 98, 225, 533 f.

begotten of the Father, I, 1: 425 (487)

begotten not created, I, 1: 430 (492)

Creator, I, 1: 442, cf. 389 (506 f., cf. 447)

one Lord, I, 1: 424 (485)

only-begotten, I, 1: 424 (486)

stipulations of the Nicene Creed, I, 1: 423 (484)

of one substance with the Father, I, 1: 438 (501 f.)

Very God of Very God, I, 1: 428 (491)

direction, IV, 2: 118, 265 ff., 361 f., 452, 523, 527 ff.

correction, IV, 2: 367 f., 523, 527

indication, IV, 2: 363 f., 523, 527

instruction, IV, 2: 372 f., 523, 527

divine humanity, I, 2: 14, 122 ff., 499; II, 1: 19, 150 f., 317 355 400, 485 f., 514 ff., 665, 667; II, 2: 7, 95, 103, 116, 145, 150, 154, 157, 162 173 f. 199 f., 509, 777; III, 2: 53, 83; IV, 1: 126 ff., 135 ff., 170, 177, 183, 185, 550 f.

divinity *v.* deity

Elect, the, II, 2: 6 f., 25 f., 52 ff., 94 ff., 116 ff., 145, 148, 153, 157, 174, 333, 351, 412, 421; III, 2:

impartation, I, 1: 324 f. (372 f.); I,
2: 236 f.
incarnation, I, 2: 1 ff., 698 f., 712,
717 f.; II, 1: 151, 253, 265, 274,
317, 418, 446, 515 ff.
Israel, I, 2: 70 f., 79 f., 85 ff., 96, 111,
124, 328, 381, 383, 510
limit, IV, 1: 325
miracle, I, 2: 63 f., 147, 160 f., 181 f.,
187, 196 f., 201 f., 244 f., 258,
266 ff., 392, 450, 507, 516, 528,
532, 553, 700, 712, 756; II, 2:
19, 22, 228, 232, 257 f., 273, 296,
748, 757
   sign, II, 2: 55, 226, 297
mystery, I, 2: 84, 101 f., 124 ff.,
172 ff., 233, 268, 470 ff., 516,
532, 700, 712; II, 1: 40 ff.,
56 f., 151, 210 f., 283 f., 348 f.,
357 f., 423 ff., 546, 591, 603 f.;
II, 2: 104, 151, 157 f., 185 f.,
257, 273, 296, 748, 757; IV, 1:
81, 83, 134, 163, 176 ff., 192 ff.,
207, 211, 213, 246, 296, 302, 519,
644, 656; IV, 2: 32, 42, 252,
292, 297, 335
necessity, I, 2: 32, 34, 135; II, 1:
206, 402, 518
in the New Testament, I, 2: 14 f.,
23 f., 72 ff., 101 ff., 486 ff.
offence, II, 1: 55 f., 146
in the Old Testament, I, 2: 70 ff.,
486 ff., 489 ff.
order, II, 1: 317 f., 348 f., 352, 375 f.,
540, 603; II, 2: 8, 12, 22, 33,
151, 157, 174 f., 193, 219, 223,
244, 254, 589, 600, 739
original, IV, 1: 45
outpouring of the Holy Spirit, I, 2:
203 ff.
possession of?, I, 2: 556 f., 688
possibility, I, 2: 26 ff., 242 ff.
proclamation, I, 1: 99, 120 f., 148 f.,
304 (111, 136, 169, 349)
prophecy, I, 2: 93 ff.; II, 2: 252,
258 f., 271, 276 ff., 505
reality, II, 1: 210 ff.
revelations?, I, 1: 291, 320, 324,
331 f., 424 (334, 367, 372, 381 f.,
486); I, 2: 28 f., 239 f., 496 f.
scandal, I, 2: 61, 189 f., 508 ff.
secret reality, III, 4: 23 f.
self-revelation of Jesus Christ, IV, 1:
163, 177 f., 356; IV, 2: 122,

125 ff., 144 ff., 156, 160, 299,
307, 330 ff., 350
signs, II, 1: 17, 51 f., 198, 395 ff.,
412 f., 419 f., 539
simplicity, I, 2: 10
time, III, 2: 445
truth, IV, 2: 5, 36, 126, 296 ff., 388,
561
" truths of," I, 1: 15, 86, 266 ff., (15,
96, 306 ff.)
uniqueness, I, 2: 12, 80, 483 f., 489,
500, 543 ff., 671
unity, I, 1: 318 f. (366); I, 2: 56 f.,
72 ff., 103, 310 ff., 482 ff.; II, 1:
364 ff., 381 f.; II, 2: 150 f.,
197 f., 200 ff., 419 f.; III, 1:
63 f., 202 f., 369 ff.; III, 3:
179 f., 216
veiling and unveiling, I, 1: 169, 174,
299, 320 f., 363 (192, 198, 344,
368 f., 417); I, 2: 28 ff., 40 f.,
61 f., 84 ff., 106 ff., 280 ff.; II,
1: 37 ff., 54 ff., 193 f., 210 f.
death and resurrection, I, 1: 337 f.
(444)
form of a servant, I, 2: 62 ff.
God in Himself and for us, I, 1:
170, 409 (194 f., 476 f.)
mystery, I, 1: 118 f., 165, 174, 303,
409 (133, 188, 199, 348, 468)
veracity, II, 1: 209 ff., 223 f., 341
world history, I, 2: 63, 68, 422; II,
2: 7 f., 47, 55, 136, 185
v. Church! Holy Scripture! Holy
Spirit! Jesus Christ! Sacrament!
Triunity! Word of God
Revolution, II, 1: 468; III, 4: 545;
IV, 2: 544
Righteousness, II, 1: 375 ff.
alien, IV, 1: 83, 97 ff., 219, 555, 575
decision, II, 1: 390 ff.
faithfulness, II, 1: 385 ff.
of God, II, 1: 375 ff.; IV, 1: 188,
219 f., 237, 256 f., 518, 531 ff.,
555
human, IV, 1: 95 ff., 219, 555, 575
iustitia distributiva, II, 1: 381
judgment, II, 1: 393 ff.
simul iustus et peccator, IV, 1: 517,
567 ff., 596, 602
Righteousness of Works, II, 2: 236,
273 f.
Roman Catholicism, I, 1: 34, 36 (36,
38); II, 2: 528 ff.; III, 2: 10,

244 (29, 271, 273, 280); I, 2:
180, 264 f., 280; II, 1: 88 f.,
131 f.
preliminary understanding, I, 1:
36, 129 (39, 146)
primal revelation, I, 1: 335 (385)
proofs of God, III, 1: 6, 357 f.;
III, 2: 79 f.
provisional understanding, II, 1:
230 f.
rationalisation, I, 2: 9 f., 27
religion, I, 2: 284 f.
religious *a priori*, I, 1: 193 (220)
religio-psychological circle, I, 1:
131, 422 (148, 483)
respectability, II, 1: 141, 164
Scriptural basis?, II, 1: 97 ff.
speculation, I, 2: 246
vitality, II, 1: 165
Neo-Protestantism, *q.v.*
object, II, 2: 59 f.
Older Protestant, IV, 2: 19, 104 ff.,
156, 502; IV, 3: 505, 783 f.,
870 f. *q.v.*
orders, III, 4: 22 f., 28, 306
order of cognition, I, 2: 4 ff., 43 f.,
172 f., 204, 232 f., 295 f.
and philosophy, I, 1: 39, 84, 114,
126 ff., 165, 197, 200, 204,
220, 256, 283 f., 296, 340, 368,
378, 481 (42, 94, 128 f., 143 f.,
188, 225, 229, 252, 294, 325 f.,
340, 391, 422, 434, 448 f., 551);
I, 2: 483, 728 ff., 750 f., 836 f.,
841, 874; III, 3: 389 f., 403,
410; IV, 1: 757; IV, 2: 668
politics, I, 1: 256 (294)
positive, I, 1: 162 f., 253 (185, 290 f.)
practical, IV, 3: 881
as proclamation, I, 1: 51 (55)
Protestant, II, 1: 584 f.
rationalising, I, 1: 296, 368 (340,
422)
Reformation, III, 3: 14, 32, 116 f.,
209, 390, 402; IV, 2: 19, 233,
380, 498
Reformed, IV, 1: 108, 132, 180, 525;
IV, 2: 19, 51 ff., 66 ff., 75 ff.,
79, 89 f., 104 ff.; IV, 3: 553
of revelation, I, 1: 253, 422 f. (290,
483 f.)
scientia practica, I, 1: 192 (219)
self-consciousness, I, 2: 772
speech, IV, 1: 209 f.

summum bonum?, III, 2: 209 f.
symbolics, I, 2: 827 f.
systematic, IV, 3: 881
theocentric, I, 1: 213 (243)
theologia crucis, I, 1: 14, 167, 179 (15,
190, 204); IV, 1: 250, 273, 304,
526, 558 ff.; IV, 2: 9, 29, 355;
IV, 3: 409
theologia gloriae, I, 1: 167, 178 f., 262
(190, 203 f., 300); IV, 1: 526,
558; IV, 2: 9, 29, 355
theologia viatorum, II, 1: 209
truth, question of, III, 3: 376
unbelief, I, 2: 293 f.
Western, IV, 1: 524, 527, 558; IV,
2: 69, 222 f., 233, 247
Theonomy, II, 2: 177 ff., 184
Time, I, 2: 45 ff.; II, 1: 61, 409 ff.,
417 ff., 465 ff., 592 ff.; II, 2: 95,
151, 155, 159, 183, 185, 188, 219,
236 f., 662 f.; III, 1: 71 ff.;
III, 3: 87 f.; III, 4: 56, 329,
372 f., 569 ff., 577, 580 ff., 685;
IV, 1: 117, 188, 286 ff., 333, 337,
348, 353; IV, 1: 31, 107, 110,
422 ff., 444 ff., 462 ff., 467 ff.
allotted, III, 2: 553 ff., 594, 627 f.
beginning, III, 2: 511, 514, 572 ff.,
595
centre, III, 2: 439, 462
of the Church, I, 2: 413, 423, 676,
692
of the community, IV, 1: 318 ff., 327,
349, 725 ff.; IV, 2: 617 f., 621
contemporaneity, III, 2: 481 f.
created, III, 2: 438, 518 ff., 526, 551
of creation, III, 1: 67 ff.
differentiation, IV, 1: 322
end, III, 2: 511, 568, 587 ff., 596,
622; IV, 1: 324, 334, 349, 731
end-time, IV, 1: 531, 734 ff.
endlessness, III, 2: 515, 551, 560
eternity, III, 2: 526 ff.
expectation, I, 2: 53 f., 70 ff., 481;
II, 1: 616 f.; III, 2: 475 f., 485
form of existence, III, 2: 520, 524 f.,
551
forty days, I, 2: 122, 424, 543 f.
fulfilment, I, 2: 48 ff., 58, 66 ff., 106,
114, 118, 481; II, 1: 625 ff.;
III, 2: 441, 458 f., 545 f.
future, II, 1: 626 ff.
past, II, 1: 626 ff.
present, II, 1: 611, 617 f., 624 f.

the Lord's, I, 1: 141, 273, 445 (160, 314, 510)

and man, I, 1: 190 ff., 445, 448 (217 f., 509, 514)

mystery, I, 1: 162 ff., 436 (184 f., 500)

one-sidedness, I, 1: 174 ff., 181, 207 (198 f., 207, 236)

personality, I, 1: 136 ff. (155 f.)

power, I, 1: 149 ff., 206, 445 (170, 235, 510)

as proclamation, I, 1: 88 ff., 117, 250, 289 f. (98 f., 131 f., 286 f., 332 f.); I, 2: 743 ff.

purposiveness, I, 1: 139 ff., 205 (158 ff., 234)

reality, I, 1: 157 f. (179 f.)

the Reconciler's, I, 1: 142, 445 (161, 510)

the Redeemer's, I, 1: 142 f. (162)

as revelation, I, 1: 117 f., 289 f., 304, 469 (131 f., 332 f., 349, 468, 497)

and sacrament, IV, 4: 103 f., 113 f

secularity, I, 1: 165 f., 267 (188 f., 236)

as speech, I, 1: 132 ff. (149 f.)

spirituality, I, 1: 133 ff., 208 (151 f., 237)

temporal manifestation, I, 2: 241 f.

three forms, I, 2: 497, 573, 699, 742 ff., 768, 802 f., 806, 870

truth, I, 1: 136, 214 f., 305 (154, 245 f., 350)

and work of God, IV, 4: 48 f., 74, 80, 96 ff.

worldliness, I, 1: 165 f., 267 (188 f., 236)

Work,

basis, ethical, III, 4: 522 f.

contract, III, 4: 541

dignity, III, 4: 536

employee-employer, III, 4: 532 f.

enthusiasm, III, 4: 537

fever, III, 4: 539 f., 552 ff.

humanity, III, 4: 535

inner, III, 4: 549

limit, III, 4: 551 ff., 560

mask of God, III, 4: 520

objectivity, III, 4: 528

praise of God, III, 4: 535

social character, III, 4: 528 f.

time, III, 4: 60 f., 558 ff.

v. God, work

Working Day, III, 4: 56, 64, 71 f.

Works, Good, IV, 1: 621 ff.; IV, 2: 584 ff.

World, II, 1: 124, 211, 261, 280, 304 f., 315 ff., 427, 446, 499 ff., 532, 536 f., 562, 593; II, 2: 7 f., 26 f., 89, 94, 159, 170, 173, 420, 429, 571, 724, 731; III, 1: 1 f., 19, 102 ff., 107, 114, 167 f.; III, 3: 195, 279, 419 f., 430 f.; III, 4: 146, 263, 443, 501 ff., 509 ff., 682; IV, 1: 168 f., 179 f., 280, 511, 524, 545, 663 f., 666 f., 686, 697 f., 724, 779, 808; IV, 3: 40, 97, 116, 154 f., 166, 185 f., 239 f., 280 f., 557 f., 598, 620 ff., 769 f., 826 f., 844, 847

determination, IV, 3: 301 ff.

end, IV, 1: 296

essence, II, 2: 26

Christian?, III, 4: 504

goal, IV, 1: 310, 661

mystery, II, 2: 185

mythological understanding, IV, 2: 228 f.

new, IV, 3: 713 ff.

passing, III, 4: 263

redeemed, IV, 3: 327 ff.

worldly wisdom, IV, 2: 410 f.

World History, II, 1: 395, 399, 405, 625; III, 3: 24, 49, 54 f., 159, 186, 191, 233 f., 280, 515; III, 4: 17, 52, 309 f., 458, 485, 492, 510, 574; IV, 1: 215, 257, 311, 505 ff., 612, 643, 649, 734 ff., 776; IV, 2: 269, 334, 423, 444 f.; IV, 3: 64, 191 f., 321, 685 ff., 693 ff., 701 ff.

goal, III, 3: 159 f., 187, 195

meaning, III, 3: 170 f.

nexus, III, 3: 195

order, III, 3: 164 f.

theme, III, 3: 218

World-picture, III, 2: 4 f., 445, 447; III, 3: 193, 250

World-view, III, 1: 160, 340 ff.; III, 2: 5, 22, 386, 578; III, 3: 11, 20 f., 54 f., 111, 139 f., 516; IV, 3: 255 ff., 269 f., 703 f., 721, 771

Christian, III, 3: 18, 55 f.

World Improvement?, III, 4: 507

World Judgment, III, 4: 56

World Occurrence, III, 4: 622

AIDS FOR THE PREACHER

The biblical passages for the 394 preachers' aids with some 800 extracts from all the volumes of C.D. are taken from the Lutheran *Ordnung der Predigttexte* published by the Lutheran Liturgical Conference of Germany, Lutherisches Verlagshaus, Berlin, 1958. These are passages which are recommended to pastors of the Evangelische Kirche for Sunday preaching in six series. The 467 passages of the order, with a further 185 passages in the margin and 90 extracts from the Psalms, form a selection from the Bible which is the main basis of preaching.

The first two series (I and II), with the occasional addition of Ib or IIb, consist of the ancient Gospels or Epistles of the Early Church. Series III and V are Gospels and IV and VI Epistles apart from some Old Testament passages. The six readings for each Sunday or Feast Day are grouped around a common theme so that all the extracts may be read in amplification. This is especially true in the case of the (73) Sunday readings which are not dealt with in C.D. When the basic series are not in use, the Index added at the end of the preachers' aids provides an opportunity to use the extracts in the present form even apart from this order, e.g., for sermon series or Bible studies.

It should be noted expressly that usually only the references are given here for passages quoted in full in C.D., so that a Bible is needed for a proper understanding of the context. (H.K.)

In the case of extracts from Vol. I, 1 the text of the second edition is used but the page references for the first edition follow in parentheses. (G.W.B. and T.F.T.)

FIRST SUNDAY IN ADVENT

MATTHEW 21$^{1-9}$ (I)

ROMANS 13$^{11-14}$ (II)

Christians . . . are those who waken up. This . . . biblical picture (v. 11) tells us more clearly than any abstract term that we might substitute what is really at issue. As they awake they look up, and rise, thus making the counter-movement to the downward drag of their sinfully slothful being. They are those who waken up, however, because they are awakened. They do not waken of themselves and get up. They are roused, and they are thus caused to get up and set in this counter-movement. Thus strictly and finally this awakening as such is in every sense the source in whose irresistible flow they are set in the obedience of discipleship . . . Where someone is awakened and therefore wakes and rises, he has previously been asleep, and has been lying asleep. Christians have indeed been lying asleep like others. What distinguishes them from others is that this is now past; that they have been awakened and are awake. Or is it not the case that they are still asleep, or fall asleep again? Is there not still a Christianity which sleeps with the world and like it? (IV, 2, p. 554. The Awakening to Conversion.)

The New Testament witnesses have a specific consciousness of time. What do they know and say of time? Obviously not just that it is limited, unique and finite, i.e., that it has the peculiarity that one day it must end and then be past, but rather that it is the last time, that it is time really coming to an end, that its ending is already an event and in process of completion. These men are still in time, but in a time which already bears its end in itself, so that, to the degree that it still continues, it hastens towards birth—this image is actually used in 1 Thess. 5³—and therefore the revelation and realisation of its end. (III, 4, p. 581. The Unique Opportunity.)

LUKE 1⁶⁷⁻⁷⁹   (III)

The origin of the *Magnificat* and *Benedictus* is obscure. It seems likely that they come from a very early period of the Church, possibly from its early worship, or as private compositions of one or more of its members. For can we really explain v. 48 and v. 76 except against a Christian background? On the other hand, it may well be that Christians have worked over hymns which originally came from the parallel movement of awakening and reform which we have learned to know much better through recent discoveries by the Dead Sea . . . What we can say is that Luke thought them sufficiently true and important to use them at this point as a kind of introduction to his account of the " things delivered unto us, " ascribing them to such exalted personages as the mother of Jesus and the father of the Baptist. (IV, 2, p. 183. The Royal Man.)

Nowhere in the New Testament is knowledge merely intellectual or contemplative, having its theme and content in abstractly objective things or essences. Here, too, since everything characterised and described as an object of knowledge is to be understood as a description of the divine action and therefore historically, it is a matter of the salvation which comes to man (v. 77), of the truth which discloses itself to him (1 Tim. 2⁴), of the grace of God directed toward him (Col. 1⁶), of the love which He has for us (1 Jn. 4¹⁶), of His legal decision which alters our whole situation (Rom. 10³), of what is given us in him (1 Cor. 2¹²). The contexts show . . . that is a matter of the knowledge of the Son of God (Eph. 4¹³). (IV, 3, p. 211. Jesus is Victor.)

But what does it mean to praise God's mercy (v. 50, 54, 72, 78)? The hymns as such are only an expression of the praise, not merely verbal and mental, but existential and actual, to which the earthly creation is stirred by the heavenly. It consists in the fact that men look and move willingly and ready to the One who comes, as earthly creatures who have appropriated what is said to them even though they know that they are in no position for what is said to come to them and actually to happen ... They have appropriated it because it is a matter of the helping and saving presence of God, of the mystery of His grace. (III, 3, p. 504. The Ambassadors of God and Their Opponents.)

Cf. also II, 1, p. 371 f.

1 THESSALONIANS 5[1-11]   (IV)

New Testament expectation is always characterised as imminent expectation. It is primarily the expectation of the man Jesus Himself (in the subjective sense): the expectation in which He Himself lived and went to His death; the expectation of what He saw before Him as the goal of His life and death. It is the expectation of His own resurrection from the dead, Mk. 8[31]; 9[31]; 10[34]. Yet the Gospels obviously rule out the imminent expectation which is expectation of a definite date. Jesus Himself admitted that He shared the human uncertainty understandable in this respect, Mk. 13[32]. Even after the resurrection He can still say: Acts 1[7]. The revelation of the kingdom is linked with the consummation of the life of Jesus in His death. And this fulfilment of His life in His death, which will be followed by His revelation, is accomplished by the incarnate Son in obedience to the will of His Father and therefore in acceptance of the right point of time appointed not by Himself but by the Father. What He does know and teach, because His disciples are always to know it too, is that the kingdom of God, the revelation of its hidden reality, will come soon and suddenly like a thief in the night, v. 2; Mt. 24[43]; 2 Pet. 3[10]; Rev. 16[15]. Its coming will be soon because it is the goal of the limited life in time of Jesus of Nazareth and will follow hard on His death and therefore in the foreseeable future. And it will come suddenly because it is foreordained and foreknown by God alone, and will occur when men are least expecting it, beneficially if terrifying upsetting all their expectations and plans, and thus their anxieties and hopes, as actually happened in the first instance with the resurrection of Jesus. (III, 2, p. 498 f. Jesus, Lord of Time.)

It is clear that all these (vv. 6–10) are not demands to give ourselves a new life and resurrection and glory by the fulfilment of a new law. Those who are dead in Christ (Col. 2[20]) and therefore liberated (Gal. 5[1]) are expressly warned against such dangerous and futile undertakings. It is equally clear that these are consequences which we have necessarily to draw from the alteration of our situation. If we come from this point and stand in this place, this is again the acknowledgment and affirmation which has become inevitable, the grateful praise of God for what He has done for us and to us.

Walking worthy of the Gospel does not work the work of God. God Himself does that and only God, the God who calls Himself our Father and us His children in Jesus Christ. Nor does our walk guarantee the work of God. The Holy Spirit alone does that, dwelling in us and constraining us as such. But where the work of the Father who alone can do it is done, it is inevitable that it should be honoured and attested by the walk of Christians. This is the intention and the demand of the imperatives addressed to them. (IV, 1, p. 322. The Verdict of the Father.)

ISAIAH 63¹⁵–64⁴

By the name " father " we do, of course, denote the natural human author of our existence. But our natural human father is not our Creator. He is not the lord of our existence, not even the lord of our life, let alone our death. When Scripture calls God our Father it adopts an analogy only to transcend it at once.

Hence we must not measure by natural human fatherhood what it means that God is our Father (v. 16). It is from God's fatherhood that out natural human fatherhood acquires any meaning and dignity it has (Eph. 3¹⁵).

God our Father means God our Creator (cf. for this Deut. 32⁶ and Is. 64⁷). And it should be clear by now that it is specifically in Christ, as the Father of Jesus Christ, that God is called our Creator. That God is our Creator is not a general truth that we can know in advance or acquire on our own; it is a truth of revelation. Only as that which we know elsewhere as the father-son relation is transcended by the Word of Christ, the Crucified and Risen, only as it is interpreted by this Word, which means, in this case, only as it acquires from this Word a meaning which it cannot have of itself, only in this way may we see what creation means. But in this way we can see. The Father of Jesus Christ who according to the witness of Scripture is revealed in Jesus His Servant has the qualities of a Lord of our existence. The witness to Him leads us to the place where the miracle of creation can be seen. It bears witness to the holy God who alone is God, the free God. (I, 1, p. 389 [447]. God the Father/God as Creator.)

HEBREWS 10¹⁹⁻²⁵ (VI)

The eternal action of Jesus Christ grounded in His resurrection is itself the true and direct bridge from once to always, from Himself in His time to us in our time. Because as crucified and dead He is risen and lives, the fact of His death on the cross can never be past, it can never cease to be His action, the decision which God makes *hic et nunc* to His own glory and in our favour, summoning us on our part to responsibility, as is brought out so impressively and in a way to stir the conscience in vv. 19 ff. (v. 22 f). Jesus Christ Himself lives, His obedience pleading for our disobedience. His blood shed in obedience speaks against us and for us to-day as it did on the day of Golgotha. He receives for us to-day as on Easter Day the grace of God which we have not deserved. For this reason the judgment fulfilled by Him, the sacrifice offered by Him, is effective for us. Not therefore in some answer of ours to our questions: What are we going to make of it? How can we bring home this matter to ourselves and other men? Or how can we bring ourselves and other men to this matter? Where and how do we experience and prove its efficacy? There is a relative place for these questions and answers, but only in the light and in strict explanation of the one question and answer which God Himself has put and given in Jesus Christ, which indeed He does put in eternity and therefore to-day, and which He answers in the antithesis of the obedient Son and the gracious Father. Our answer and our question have to be sought (Col. 3^1) " above, where Christ is seated at the right hand of God. " But this means in prayer, prayer in the name of Jesus. (IV, 1, p. 315. The Verdict of the Father.)

The context here (10^{22}) is that of exhortation to make undeviating use of the entry into the sanctuary of God which has been opened and assured by the blood of Jesus Christ (v. 19). It is the context of exhortation, then, to make an unwavering confession of hope (v. 23). The relevant verse runs: " Let us draw near with a true heart in full assurance of faith, having our hearts sprinkled from an evil conscience, and our bodies washed with pure water. " It will be seen that there is no express reference to baptism. The final clause is so vivid, however, that one can hardly deny that there is actual allusion to water baptism ... One thing that is not so clear in baptism, however, is that with the washing of the body there has also taken place the sprinkling of the hearts of the readers, so that in virtue of the washing of the body they are capable of drawing near with a true heart ... Unless appearances deceive, one can hardly ascribe sacramental significance to baptism on the occasion of its mention in Heb. 10^{22}. (IV, 4, p. 112 f. The Foundation of the Christian Life.)

SECOND SUNDAY IN ADVENT

LUKE 21$^{25-36}$ (I)

" Lift up your heads " is the call. What is meant is that they should look to Him, the exalted, royal man, who has come to them as their own, their Brother, and will come again, and is now present with them below even though He is above; that they should look to Him, the Holy One, and in this looking to him as their Lord and Representative be His saints. This looking to Him, now with bowed but uplifted head, is the setting up of these men. It is their positive sanctification ... " Looking unto Jesus, the author and finisher of our faith " (Heb. 12^2), they live. This looking is their sanctification *de facto*. As they are called by Him, and look to Him and therefore lift up themselves, they have a part here below in the holiness in which He is the One who alone is holy. (IV, 2, p. 527. The Holy One and the Saints.)

ROMANS 15⁴⁻¹³ (II)

ROMANS 15$^{4\text{-}13}$ (II)

The man who hopes in the Old Testament sense does not await the fulfilment of his own comforting or comfortless prognoses and dreams, and therefore he need not be on guard against threats to his expectation. He looks to that which in virtue of His self-declaration the God of Israel was and is and will be and mean and do in the history of this people both for Israel and for himself as a man united with it as a member ... New Testament hope ... is also exclusive hope in God Himself as the one source and sum of all expected blessing and salvation. The only point is that God Himself, the " God of hope " (v. 13), in the glory still to be manifested, is not an abstraction but bears the features of a specific human countenance well known to the one who hopes, namely, the countenance of the One who has come already in the event which fulfils the hope of Israel, and who will Himself come again in that future event in full revelation of His salvation and glory. It is to be noted further that the hope of New Testament man, too, is upheld and guaranteed and ordered as his personal fulfilment of the hope of the community of which he is a member. The only point is that the hoping community and he who hopes in and with it already exist in virtue of the first event in direct fellowship with the One for whose new coming they may hope, and that they have received, and must continually pray for and receive again, directly from Him the freedom to hope for His future coming. (IV, 3, p. 908 f. The Subject of Hope and Hope.)

Cf. also I, 2, pp. 492–495. Scripture as the Word of God.

1 TIMOTHY 6¹¹ᵇ⁻¹⁶ (IIb)

1 TIMOTHY 6$^{11\text{b-}16}$ (IIb)

Since the reference is to a definite and highly important event in his life, it is most natural to follow Chrysostom, J. A. Bengel, and in recent times Schlatter and M. Dibelius, who all speak of his baptism before the assembled congregation, of this basic event at the beginning of his Christian life. In this he himself, not of himself but in answer to the call issued to him, declared once and for all that he would follow the way of flight from temptation and pursuit after righteousness. In what follows (v. 13 f) he can be reminded of this in solemn and categorical tones. When he professed his calling, he submitted unconditionally to the command issued to him. This is the basis of the exhortation. It is expected and very definitely required of him that in his life even to the final horizon in the appearing of Jesus Christ he should not sully the purity of this command but display it as "an example of the believers " (4¹²). Significant here is the distinctive form in which the command is given. The apostle entreats his reader to come with him into the presence of God and Jesus Christ. He addresses him before the face of the life-giving God. This means, more precisely that he addresses him before the face of the Witness whose confession (before Pontius Pilate) Timothy can only follow in the confession which he himself makes in and with his baptism, whose confession he can and must endorse and appropriate as one which is binding for him too. This is what he had already done in his baptism before the eyes and ears of many witnesses, the whole congregation . . . The apostle can now remind him of this, and in thus reminding him of his once-for-all answer to the call issued to him in the confession of Jesus Christ, he can summon him to fight the good fight of faith, ordering him to honour and not to dishonour the command which is well known to him as a soldier of Jesus Christ. (IV, 4, p. 148 f. The Foundation of the Christian Life.)

MALACHI 3^{1-3b}, 4   (III)

V. 1 refers to the coming to the temple of a preceding messenger, of the Lord Himself, and of the angel of the covenant . . . He is identical with the angel who elsewhere is called the angel of Yahweh and who in Jud. 2^1 is expressly said to be concerned with the covenant of Yahweh with Israel . . . This conception was taken up by the authors of the New Testament (Lk. 2^9) . . . *The* angel is *the* witness of God. With his appearance, words and acts he attests the work of God as such in the history of salvation and therefore in primal and eschatological history. He attests the election of Israel, the election of the Church, the election of the covenanted community. (III, 3, p. 487 f. The Ambassadors of God and Their Opponents.)

Now Jesus Christ, (like the Old Testament prophets), is also a witness of the covenant. But what distinguishes Him from them is that He stands on the basis of the fulfilment of the covenant. The abyss of the contradiction is no longer before but behind them. The " sun of righteousness " (4^2), the light of the glory of God and salvation of men, has risen and is shining. The kingdom of God on earth, which is the goal of the covenant, is no longer an indicated future. It is the present in and from which He speaks. What He attests is the peace made in the co-existence of God with His people. (IV, 3, p. 51. The Glory of the Mediator.)

There have to be in the world (according to God's will) men who even in the night, perhaps only at midnight or before, look forward to the morning, to the rising sooner or later of the Sun of righteousness, to the end and goal of all things and therefore to their new beginning in light, which no further end can follow. There have to be men by whose irrepressible and constant unrest at least a few and even perhaps quite a number of their fellows are prevented from falling asleep as though nothing had happened and nothing out of the ordinary could happen in the future. In so doing, they do provisionally, and in great weakness and frailty, as God's representatives, that which He Himself will finally do with unequivocal and irresistible power when His day comes. (IV, 3, p. 933. Life in Hope.)

Cf. IV, 3, p. 165.

REVELATION 3^{1-6} (IV)

The figure of the new garment which is given to the Christian and which he has to put on and wear does not mean that man himself can adopt the distinctive being of a Christian, dressing up as it were in it. Nor does it mean that what is given him is no true Christian being but only something external, not to speak of a mere Christian appearance, a hood which is pulled over him and under the concealment of which he can be the same as he always was ... The elect and called are not arbitrarily or autonomously clothed in the white robes which they are said to wear in Revelation ($3^{4,5}$; 6^{11}; 7^9). These white garments are the official robes along with which—clothes make the man—they receive a new being and are both empowered for and engaged to a corresponding new activity. (IV, 4, p. 6 f. The Foundation of the Christian Life.)

In the New Testament election is the divine ordination to discipleship, to the apostolate, to the community ... the divine ordination to participation in the salvation of the Messianic future. The " book " spoken of by God in Ex. 32^{32} has always, and quite rightly, been connected with the election of grace. In Ps. 69^{29} it is called unequivocally the " book of the living " (Prayer Book Version), and it is described as the " book of life " in the New Testament (Phil. 4^3; Rev. 3^5, 17^8, $20^{12, 15}$). One's name may not be in this book. It can be blotted out from it. And yet there are not two columns, but only one. Similarly, the concept of the divine " purpose " used in Rom. 8^{28} and 9^{11} and Eph. 1^{11} etc. relates to the divine election to salvation, but only to that election as such, and not to the accompanying non-election, or rejection. The problem began to be obscured when the " book of life " came to be spoken of as though it had in it a death-column; when the divine election and the divine rejection came to be spoken of as inter-connected divine acts similar in character and determination; when they came to be regarded and understood as if they could both be grouped under the one over-ruling concept. (II, 2, p. 15 f. The Problem of a Correct Doctrine of the Election of Grace.)

MATTHEW 24^{1-4} (V)

Note that in the series of historical signs listed in vv. 6–14 the last and culminating sign is the work of the community: v. 14. Whether this sign is set up or not, is the question of its present existence, addressed to it in the parable of the talents (25^{14-30}) in relation to the end of time which will decide concerning it too. (III, 2, p. 507. Jesus, Lord of Time.)

Against the fact that love cannot be lost (p. 397), the text in Mt. 24^{12} has been alleged, in which we are told that in times of persecution the increase of " lawlessness " will mean that the love of many will grow cold. But does this really refer to those who are genuinely obedient to Jesus' commandment to love? There are, of course, all kinds of other love: the love of relatives and friends, which, according to the sayings of Jesus, can in time of temptation turn not only into indifference but even into hate. It is impossible that Jesus should have meant and said the same thing about the love to God and neighbour of the commandment. (I, 2, p. 398. The Life of the Children of God.)

The Christian's love for God, which is identical with his love for Jesus, consists in the fact (if we may be permitted an expression which sounds banal but in the strict sense is full of content) that he is a man who is *interested* in God, i.e., in " God in Christ. " God has him, and therefore for good or evil he must have God. God is for him, and so he has no option but to be for God. He is this not merely peripherally but centrally; not merely momentarily but—no matter how often he may, like Peter, forget or deny it, in the continuity of his existence, his life-act. He does not cease to confess that he is a great sinner. But like Jeremiah (1^5) and Paul (Gal. 1^{15}) he will think of himself as predestinated to love, and therefore, although his love may and will grow cold, there can be no question of its complete extinction . . . He is God's prisoner, and therefore stands strongly on this rock and is solidly at home in this fortress. (IV, 2, p. 793 f. The Act of Love.)

2 THESSALONIANS 3^{1-5} (VI)

True private and public prayer will always have this particularly in common, that as petition they will have the character of intercession. This follows both from the nature of the individual praying man as a member of the community, from that of each assembled congregation as a single form of the one ecumenical Church in the narrower and wider sense of the term, and also from its task in relation to the world, especially the world outside. We have seen that one cannot plead one's own cause before God without first and foremost pleading His, which is also the cause of the whole community, of the ecumenical Church and indeed of all creation. The individual will plead his own cause legitimately, joy-fully and effectually when he does so in this greater context. (III, 4, p. 111. Prayer.)

Is not 2 Thess. 3^2 putting it very mildly when it says that not all have faith? Not all? Who, then, can and will have faith and be faithful to God? According to Mk. 10^{24} Jesus says very generally that it is hard to enter the kingdom of God. So great is the difficulty that of the rich, though obviously not of them alone, it may be said (v. 25) that a camel will go more easily through a needle's eye than they into the kingdom of God. The disciples of Jesus undoubtedly took the saying thus (v. 26), and they were " astonished out of measure, saying among themselves, Who then can be saved? " The answer of Jesus is again very general (v. 27): " With men it is impossible, but not with God: for with God all things are possible. " (IV, 4, p. 3 f. The Foundation of the Christ Life.)

Cf. on Matthew 16²¹⁻²⁷ First Sunday in Lent (Invocavit).

THIRD SUNDAY IN ADVENT

MATTHEW 11²⁻¹⁰ (I)

... as viewed by the synoptic tradition the Baptist belongs to the history of the fulfilment of the Old Testament promise even in his Old Testament character, even as the last and greatest bearer of pure promise. Even as he promised, he was himself promised—not the promised One, but promised (v. 13 f). Thus, while he is still outside, he is already inside. And to the extent that he is also inside, he can and must be called the first whose speech is described as " preaching " in the Gospel story. (IV, 2, p. 206. The Royal Man.)

The Messiah is the Representative of the positive will of God who engages the advance posts of the underworld (i.e., demons) in victorious combat. In His environment the blind necessarily see, the lame walk, the deaf hear, the dead are raised, and the Gospel is preached to the poor, i.e., the oppressed of the Old Testament Psalms (v. 5 f). Surely this can only mean that the signs of divine grace and assistance are provisionally set up against the signs of divine judgment. All the miracles of Jesus ... are countersigns of this nature. God will not chide for ever. He will not always allow death, which has broken loose, to run its course. (III, 2, p. 600. Ending Time.)

Cf. also I, 2, pp. 56–58. God's Time and Our Time.

1 CORINTHIANS 4¹⁻⁵ (II)

" I know nothing by myself—an unbroken self-consciousness indeed! But—" I am not hereby justified: but he that judgeth me is the Lord. " Christian faith does not live by the self-consciousness with which the Christian man can differentiate himself from the non-Christian. There is such a self-consciousness, and in its own place it, of course, is both right and necessary. But this self-consciousness has its natural limitations. It cannot possibly mean that the Christian would try to assert himself before God in a righteousness and holiness of his own. Unbroken in relation to man, it is broken in relation to God. It is because it is broken in the one case that it is unbroken in the other ... The apostolic self-consciousness which is unbroken in relation to man is therefore breached in this way. (I, 2, p. 331. True Religion.)

The Christian may and should have a thick skin so far as his own honour is concerned. Not by a long way need he take to heart all the distorted accounts given of him, all that is said or written or especially printed about him. Experience shows us that most lies are short-lived. In particular, what is written in the press is quickly forgotten and is of no lasting significance. In more recent theological history there is at least one instance of a man who is supposed to have died of a review written against him. But he had no business to do this. If he did, it is more to his own shame than that of the reviewer. What a pity that we do not realise or make better use of the wide measure of immunity in which we may always rejoice in respect of our honour! No, we do not always have to repay in kind when something unkind is said about us. We do not need to go grey because of all the misunderstandings and misinterpretations of which we may become the victims. Above all, it should always be regarded only as an *ultima ratio* to allow ourselves to become entangled in judical proceedings in respect of the so-called wounding of our honour. From these, as from the various feuds in newspapers and books, there seldom accrues any unequivocal gain to the honour of the one under attack. (III, 4, p. 679. Honour.)

Cf. IV, 3, p. 920 f.

LUKE 3$^{1-9}$ (III)

The readiness demanded by the future event proclaimed by John, and therewith his baptism, had, however, a special character. When the kingdom of heaven is set up as God's rule on earth, a strict subordination of all independent human sovereignties and claims to dominion is demanded. When God's judgment falls, the recognition that it is just and merited, and that it must be accepted without murmuring, is unavoidable. When the good news of God's rectifying righteousness, and consequently of the remission of sins, proves true, then nothing remains for man but the astonished joy of faith. But who is ready for this subordination, this recognition, this joy of faith? For whom does it not go against the grain? Who is capable of it? If there is to be readiness for this new thing, if justice is to be done to it, a new man is needed, a man who is radically changed in mind and thought and aspiration and will, a man who is adequate for this new thing and open to it. Whether among the publicans and harlots or among the scribes and Pharisees, there can be no readiness for the coming act of God along the familiar lines of human thought and desire. For all of them readiness for it can only mean renewal. Renewal, however, can only mean conversion. (IV, 4, p. 56 f. Baptism with Water.)

We cannot try to see and realise the conversion of man in a new movement and activity (whether purely inward or purely outward). Because God is for him, and he for God, it is a matter of his heart, his thinking, his will, his disposition and also of his consequent action and abstention on the same ultimate basis. It is a matter of his disposition and action together; of the two as a totality. Conversion in a separate inner or

religious sphere, or conversion in a purely cultic or moral, political or
ecclesiastical sphere, is not the conversion of man as it is set in motion by
God. Peace with God is indivisible. The conversion in which he returns
to this peace embraces in this sense too the whole man. (IV, 2, p. 564 and
p. 566. The Awakening to Conversion.)

ISAIAH 40$^{1-11}$ (IV)

God also lives in His time. But His time is eternity, which has no fixed
span, no margins, no other measure but Himself ... Man on the other
hand lives in the time created and given him by God. If he were God
and not man, the allotment of his time would not be a problem, for his
time would not be alloted. For he would be eternal. But that is a dream,
and a bad one at that. Since man is man and not God, and he is not
therefore eternal, the dimension which he is left, and over which he has
no control (as God has over His, because He is His own dimension), is
created time, which in distinction from the eternity of the Creator has a
beginning, middle and end which are not simultaneous but separate,
distinct and successive, so that it has margins and a measure in its beginning and end, and is thus allotted time, the time between its beginning and
end. But these boundaries are necessarily the boundaries of human life.
This brings us to that narrow gorge with precipitous walls on either side.
Where does our life come from? From its beginning, i.e., the beginning
of its time, before which it did not exist. Where is it going? Towards its
end, i.e., the end of its time, after which it will be no longer. Why not?
Because it is creaturely life in this its creaturely dimension. Because by
acquiring creaturely time it acquires as its time the dimension appropriate
to it as a creaturely life. The life of God requires and has a different
dimension. For the life of God is not only unfathomable and inexhaustible, but self-grounded and self-creative, welling up from within itself.
That is why it is eternal life, and why eternity is its dimension. In clear
distinction from His, our life too acquires the dimension it needs, a
dimension which fits and suits it like a tailor-made garment. To each his
own! The proper dimension for the life of the creature which is not self-
grounded or self-creative, welling up from within itself, but has its basis
in the life of God, is the time in which beginning and end are distinct, and
therefore constitute its boundaries. Human life as created by the eternal
God has its proper boundaries in respect of which we must speak as the
Bible does in relation to man: Ps. 90$^{5,\ 9f}$; 102^{12}; Isa. 40^6; Jas. 4^{14}. (III,
2, p. 558 f. Allotted Time.)

LUKE 3$^{7-20}$ (V)

To convert in the sense of the Baptist and the synoptic Jesus does, of
course, include the new beginning of human life at a particular time. It
also includes all kinds of action commanded at a particular time (vv. 10–14).

But New Testament *metanoein* is differentiated from the well-known and highly estimated " penitential " (*t'shubah*) of current Jewish theology and piety, which consisted essentially in a once-for-all or repeated human movement, by the fact that it is " a radical change in the relationship of God to man and man to God " (J. Behm in TWNT, IV, p. 995, cf. TDNT, IV, p. 1000), of which it is a distinctive feature that it is not in the background as something which has to be repeated from time to time, but it controls and characterises the whole life of man from this beginning. In New Testament *metanoia* man moves forward steadily to continually new things in the same movement. " Though our outward man perish, yet the inward man is renewed day by day " (2 Cor. 4^{16}). (IV, 2, p. 567. The Awakening to Conversion.)

According to Lk. 3$^{10f.}$ the people, the publicans and the soldiers asked: " What shall we do? ", and the directions given obviously illustrate the fact that *metanoein*, far from being an abstract generality, touches the sorest practical point in the life of every man. Materially, however, only one thing is at issue: " they justified God, " they admitted He was right, they gave Him the right which is His due. According to Lk. 7$^{29f.}$ this is to the credit of the people and publicans who accepted John's baptism, in contrast to the scribes and Pharisees who did not do this, and who thereby rejected the counsel of God which applied to them as well as to all the rest. (IV, 4, p. 57. The Foundation of the Christian Life.)

REVELATION 3$^{7-13}$ (VI)

FOURTH SUNDAY IN ADVENT

JOHN 1$^{19-28}$ (I)

The priests and Levites who opposed the work of John the Baptist from Jerusalem, the Pharisees and Sadducees who visited him personally at the Jordan (Mt. 3$^{7f.}$), were in their own way awakened and even aroused and startled people, but they were so aroused and startled that they never even thought of submitting to the baptism of John. From the standpoint of the meaning of his baptism, they were so well armed morally that they actually stood in need of supreme moral disarmament. But what help would this have been to them? Moral disarmament is also commended to us to-day, not without striking a sympathetic chord, and sometimes very instructively, through such varied media as journalism, literature, drama and cabaret. The possibility is held out before us that the Pharisee can be turned into a publican, a rigid ethical idealist into a cheerful man of the world. But this kind of thing, too, has nothing whatever to do with the conversion which is at issue in baptism. It can even work against it just as powerfully as the corresponding rearmament. There are Pharisaic publicans, and these might well be the worst of all Pharisees. (IV, 4, p. 139. The Foundation of the Christian Life.)

LUKE 1²⁶⁻³⁸   (Ib)

The description of Mary as the " mother of God " was and is sensible and permissible and necessary as an auxiliary christological proposition . . . But the use of this biblically grounded proposition . . . as the basis of an independent Mariology (as it is called) was and is one of those characteristically Roman Catholic enterprises against which there has to be an Evangelical protest not only for their arbitrariness in form but also for the precariousness of their content. The content of the biblical attestation of revelation does not give us any cause to acknowledge that the person of Mary in the event of revelation possesses even relatively such an independent and emphatic position as to render it necessary or justifiable to make it the object of a theological doctrine that goes beyond the one statement made, or even of a mariological dogma. Nor can we conclude otherwise from the most earnest interpretations of the dogma which have arisen than that in this case we are dealing essentially, not with an illumination, but with an obscuring of revealed truth, in other words, with a false doctrine. Mariology is an excrescence, i.e., a diseased construct of theological thought. Excrescences must be excised . . . The greatness of the New Testament figure of Mary consists in the fact that all the interest is directed away from herself to the Lord. It is her " low estate " (v. 48), and the glory of God which encounters her, not her own person, which can properly be made the object of a special consideration, doctrine and veneration. Along with John the Baptist Mary is at once the personal climax of the Old Testament penetrating to the New Testament, and the first man of the New Testament (v. 38). She is simply man to whom the miracle of revelation happens. (I, 2, pp. 138–140. Very God and Very Man; cf. also pp. 172–202. The Miracle of Christmas.)

These passages (v. 35; Mt. 1¹⁸, ²⁰) do not say that the man Jesus is the Son of the Holy Spirit and that the Holy Spirit is thus His Father, but simply that this conception—which is no miracle as conception in the womb of a woman—is nevertheless a pure miracle in so far as this man has no physical father, and that in the event of His conception God deals with His mother as Creator to the exclusion of male volition and action. The relationship of this man to the Holy Spirit is so close and special that He owes no more and no less than His existence itself and as such to the Holy Spirit. But in the Old and New Testaments the Holy Spirit is God Himself in His creative movement to His creation. (III, 2, p. 333. Jesus, Whole Man.)

Cf. also III, 3, p. 503 ff.; IV, 2, p. 45.

PHILIPPIANS 4⁴⁻⁹   (II)

What the community owes to the world, and each individual within it, is basically that in its life, and in the lives of all its members, there should be attempted an imitation and representation of the love with which God loved the world. But this means that the Christian community cannot be against the world; it can only be for it . . . Where Christians are unwilling to love men, how can they say that God loves them or that they are loved by God? They can only prove thereby that they are not too sure about this themselves, and perhaps that they are not even aware of it. For they themselves are only men, and they are always non-Christians as such. As the friends of God they are also His enemies, as believers godless. Their decisive presupposition in respect of every man can be only that Jesus Christ has died for his sin too, and for his salvation. They must regard and approach every man from this angle. Hence they can never be against men. They can only be for them, not just theoretically but practically, with their action or inaction, their speech or silence, their intervention or toleration, as these procure space and courage and joy for them simply as men. The whole credibility of the Christian service of witness as a human act depends on whether the work of active human love precedes and follows it, accompanying and sustaining it as the commentary and illustration of an eloquent parable (v. 5) . . . There can be nothing either before this or without it. (III, 4, pp. 502–504. The Active Life.)

The *chairete* (especially of Phil. 2^{18}; 3^1; 4^4) seems to epitomise, as it were, all apostolic exhortation. How can any part of what Paul demands of Christians be rightly done if in the first instance it is not done with joy, as an " ought " whose seriousness lies at bottom in the fact that it is a " may ", something permitted? (II, 2, p. 588. The Form of the Divine Claim.)

Cf. on Luke 1^{46-55} and also III, 2, p. 284; IV, 2, pp. 467–478 *infra*.

LUKE 1^{46-55} (III)

The God who stoops down to man . . . in judgment and mercy, slaying and making alive, is Himself supremely and most strictly an object of desire, joy, pleasure, yearning and enjoyment (v. 46 f.). (II, 1, p. 654. The Eternity and Glory of God.)

It is of a piece with this that—almost to the point of prejudice—He ignored all those who are high and mighty and wealthy in the world in favour of the weak and meek and lowly. He did this even in the moral sphere, ignoring the just for sinners, and in the spiritual sphere, finally ignoring Israel for the Gentiles. It was to the latter group and not the former that He found Himself called. It was among the latter and not the former that He expected to find the eyes and ears that God had opened, and therefore the men of good-pleasure of Lk. 2^{14}. It was in the latter and not the former that He saw His brethren. It was with the latter and not the former that His disciples were to range themselves according to His urgent counsel and command. Throughout the New Testament the kingdom of God, the Gospel and the man Jesus have a remarkable affinity, which is no mere egalitarianism, to all those who are in the shadows as far as concerns what men estimate to be fortune and possessions and success and even fellowship with God. Why is this the case? ... One reason is the distinctive solidarity of the man Jesus with the God who in the eyes of the world—and not merely the ordinary world, but the moral and spiritual as well—is also poor in this way, existing not only in fact and practice but even in theory, somewhere on the margin in its scale of values, as the mere content of a limiting concept. In fellowship and conformity with this God who is poor in the world the royal man Jesus is also poor, and fulfils this transvaluation of all values, acknowledging those who (without necessarily being better) are in different ways poor men as this world counts poverty. (IV, 2 p. 168 f. The Royal Man.)

Cf. III, 2, p. 365 and IV, 3, pp. 528–530.

ROMANS 5$^{12-21}$ (IV)

The Bible gives to all men the general title of Adam ... The meaning of Adam is simply man, and as the bearer of this name ... he appears in the Genesis story as the man who owes his existence directly to the creative will and Word and act of God without any human intervention, the man who is to that extent the first man ... There never was a golden age ... The first man was immediately the first sinner ... What is to Paul the relevant thing in this primitive representative of a humanity which moves in circles in abstraction from the divine will and Word and work? ... according to vv. 12–21 there is only one answer to this question. In that first and isolated figure, in that one who is created and exists by the will and Word and work of God, in that great and typical sinner and debtor at the head of the whole race, in that dark representative of all his successors who bear his name, he recognised quite a different figure. He, too, came directly from God, not as a creature only, but as the Son of God and Himself God by nature. He, too, was a sinner and debtor, but as the sinless and guiltless bearer of the sins of others, the sins of all other men. He, too, was the Representative of all others. The only difference is that He was not like them. He was not the *primus inter pares* in a sequence. He represented them as a genuine leader, making atonement by His obedience, covering their disobedience, justifying them before God. (IV, 1, pp. 507–512. The Fall of Man.)

Sin in all its fearful reality is at a disadvantage compared with even the most modest creature in that it has only " entered into " the world (v. 12). It does not belong to the creation of God. It can be present and active within it only as an alien. It has no appointed place, no place which belongs to it. If it has its place, it is that of an usurpation against the creative will of God, the place of an interloper. It is there where it has no business at all to be as that which God has not willed. It is there where it has nothing either to seek or to tell. (IV, 1, p. 139.)

All men are sinners (v. 12), but the only notorious sinners (with all that

that involves) are those to whom the will of God is revealed and proclaimed and known. (IV, 1, p. 586.)

Death is not a part of man's nature as God created it. But it entered into the world through sin as an alien lord (v. 12, 14, 17; 1 Cor. 15^{22}) . . . Death is the great mark of the unnatural state in which we exist. And it is this, not because of a chance fate, but because we exist under the thrall of the devil. It is this because we are sinners involved in guilt. It is this because our behaviour makes our life *eo ipso* a forfeited life given over to death. (III, 2, p. 600 f.)

Cf. also I, 2, p. 157; IV, 1, p. 68 f.

LUKE 1^{39-47} (V)

It was to safeguard this unity of the person of Jesus Christ as Son of God and Son of Man (as was necessary against Nestorius) that the title " Mother of God " (theotokos) was ascribed to Mary—not to her own honour, but to that of Jesus Christ—at the Council of Ephesus in 431. In practice, the Reformers could not make much of this title, and it seemed blasphemous in view of the current adoration of Mary. But even so, there was no question of changing it, and none of the Lutheran or Reformed orthodox of the following period disputed the necessity of the description (which had, of course, a biblical basis in v. 43) in elucidation of the unity of Christ's person. (IV, 2, p. 71. The Homecoming of the Son of Man.)

" Blessed is she that believed: for (as the translation must be in analogy to Mt. $5^{3f.}$ and Lk. $6^{20f.}$) there shall be a performance of those things which were told her from the Lord. "—It is obvious that Mary is blessed in the light of her faith, yet not because of her faith, but because of what was told her by the Lord and what she believed, and in relation to its accomplishment . . . For those who are pronounced blessed it is indeed a matter of their own being, but primarily it is a matter either of the fact that their own being is lit up in a new way by the kingdom of God which has come near to them in Jesus or of the fact that it is ordered by this in a new and very definite manner . . . and it is in this fact—this illumination or impression— that they are blessed in spite of all appearances to the contrary. This is what Jesus tells them about themselves. (IV, 2, p. 188. The Royal Man.)

Cf. IV, 3, p. 603.

ISAIAH 62^{1-12} (VI)

Men with their various (but by nature unanimously hostile) attitudes towards the Word of God come and go. Their political and spiritual systems (all of which to some extent have an anti-Christian character) stand and fall. The Church itself (in which somewhere the crucifixion of Christ is always being repeated) is to-day faithful and to-morrow unfaithful, to-day strong and to-morrow weak. But although Scripture may be rejected by its enemies and disowned and betrayed by its friends, it does not cease . . . to present the message that God so loved the world that He gave His only-begotten Son. If its voice is drowned to-day, it becomes audible again to-morrow. It it is misunderstood and distorted here, it again bears witness to its true meaning there. If it seems to lose its position, hearers and form in this locality or period, it acquires them afresh elsewhere. The promise is true, and it is fulfilled in the existence of the biblical prophets and apostles in virtue of what is said to them and what they have to say: v. 6 f. The maintaining of the Word of God against the attacks to which it is exposed cannot be our concern and therefore we do not need to worry about it. Watchmen are appointed and they wait in their office. The maintaining of the Word of God takes place as a self-affirmation which we can never do more than acknowledge to our own comfort and disquiet. We can be most seriously concerned about Christianity and Christians, about the future of the Church and theology, about the establishment in the world of the Christian outlook and Christian ethic. But there is nothing about whose solidity we need be less troubled than the testimonies of God in Holy Scripture. For a power which can annul these testimonies is quite unthinkable. Luke 19⁴⁰. (I, 2, p. 680 f. The Freedom of the Word.)

As God wills man to be free before Him, He always has in view the freedom of those who have something to relate about Him, the freedom of confessors who cannot keep silence but must speak of Him, their freedom to expose themselves to his glory, to commit themselves to His honour with clear and definite words, to be serviceable to Him in and with these words, to be His declared and decided partisans. (III, 4, p. 75. Confession.)

CHRISTMAS DAY

Luke 2¹⁻¹⁴   (I, III, V)

The angelic appearance and message are to those who are outside, to the shepherds in the fields who are the first to join those who are called and who with them become the first human witnesses of what has taken place. The angel of the Lord comes no less unexpectedly to the shepherds than to Zacharias, Mary and Joseph. When we are told that the glory of God, the revelation of His glory, majesty and power, shone round about them, this does not merely indicate the cosmic reality and perceptibility of the announcement made to them, nor does it merely denote that they have to do with a heavenly experience and therefore one which is new and strange to them as earthly creatures . . . It is the light of God which in this form breaks into the darkness of earth and illumines them. It is not to blind but to enlighten them, not to crush and destroy but to liberate, that the glory, power and majesty of God are revealed . . . And it is the clear intention of this heavenly witness that men as represented first by the shepherds should not be transfixed by amazement or terror at the revelation imparted to them, as later legends have usually depicted the matter, but that they should be moved to seek and find the child for themselves. The direction with which the angel sends the shepherds away from himself to the child in the manger is the decisive service which he can and must render as an angel. The radiance of God has shone round about them, and the great announcement of the event has been made, only in order that they may run—as they actually do—and see for themselves, thus becoming witnesses on their own account of what has taken place . . . It is to be noted again that the angels have no part in the event as such. They cannot anticipate it. They can only announce that it will take place. They neither see nor hear it taking place. When it has taken place, they can only point to God Himself and His completed act. When they have done this, they return to heaven, and for a long time we hear no more about them. Both before and after the event their function is merely to declare it. They do not issue any summons of their own. It is not they who awaken Zacharias and Mary to obedience. It is not they who set the shepherds on the way to Bethlehem. Indeed, it is particularly emphasised that the shepherds decided to go of themselves. But the angels drew attention to the fact that Christ would come and that He had come, and that it was necessary to be ready for the coming One and to seek in His lowliness the One who had come. Their activity acquires and has its substance in the fact that Christ actually will come and has come, and that the calling of His people—not by their power, but by the shining of that of God—will actually take place. Their ministry consists in making visible and audible on earth this whole happening whose subject and author is God Himself. As the heavenly creation, they are the medium in which this is possible . . . Luke's distinction of the beginning of the history of Jesus by the ministry of angels was intentional and is certainly instructive. Here at least in the New Testament we are made conscious by it of the distinctive atmosphere in which it became true and recognisable that " the word was made flesh ". But there are also good reasons why Luke should stand alone to the extent that this reference is not to be found in the Gospel tradition as a whole and does not seem to correspond to any principle. The angels demand our attention, but they refuse to be set systematically in the foreground of interest. (III, 3, p. 505 f. The Ambassadors of God.)

The name Jesus (Yahweh saves) implies salvation and life . . . " Unto you is born this day the *Soter*. " In the Pauline corpus this title, which was known at the time in other connexions, is applied to Jesus only in Phil. 3[20]; Eph. 5[23] and the Pastoral Epistles. It seems on the whole to belong to the later elements of New Testament witness. But it is easy to see that in a comprehensive retrospect it necessarily forced itself upon the community of the apostolic age, since everything that Jesus had done and effected could be compressed into the terms *sozein* and *soteria*, and finally into the personal name *Soter*. Only of this saving work can we say what must be said of Jesus—that His work itself is one with His active person, and therefore that He the doer and His deed are indissolubly one. Of Jesus this must be said. For the work of Jesus is the work of the Saviour. And the saving work which brings deliverance and life consists materially in the fact that He gives Himself. We may not and must not understand by the title Saviour only the death in which He consummates the self-devotion of His life, but His whole existence. He is the Saviour, and is born as such, in the fact that He is for the many, for the world. (III, 2, p. 61. Jesus, Man for God.)

Cf. III, 2, p. 309, 441, 469, 479.

TITUS 2[11-14]   (II, IV, VI)

" The grace of God hath appeared "—
the reference is to this person in whom God has concluded the eternal covenant with man; this text was rightly used by the Early Church as the Epistle for Christmas Day—
"bringing salvation to all men "—
the universal character ascribed to this person is to be noted: there is salvation for every man in this person—
" instructing us "—
it is therefore grace itself and as such (incorporated in this person), and not a factor which precedes or only follows grace (and therefore this person), that carries out our instruction, as the ethical principle which controls us and by which we must direct ourselves, as the command which sanctifies us—
" that, denying ungodliness and worldly lusts "—
there need be no fear that this instruction will not be radical and incisive; such anxiety would be in place only if we were entirely dependent on ourselves, and had to do with an abstract principle instead of the principle which encounters us in this all-powerful person and controls us in virtue of His authority; here, in Him, we have a true and overmastering *principium*, and therefore the effect of His instruction is a fundamental denial, renunciation and separation in face of the interposing false *principium* of the fall in its original form as our estrangement from God's grace and in its development as our domination by our own self-will; here in this *principium* there can be peace between God and us by the death of Adam on the cross of Golgotha—
" we should live soberly, righteously and godly, in this present world "—
grace, or this person, instructs us to do this, not only by taking from us what is ours, all the falsehood in which Adam tried to be free and suc- ceeded only in becoming a captive, but by giving us what belongs to God, all the wisdom and righteousness and holiness of the Son of God, every-

thing, as He is for us and represents us, everything, as we belong to Him and He treats us as His own, His members—

" looking for that blessed hope . . . " (v. 13 f.)—

It is surely clear that this conclusion does not speak of a further aim to which the grace that has appeared directs its instruction. Strictly, the passage speaks of only one such aim: " that . . . we live, " that we should be what we may and therefore ought to be in its sphere and under its order and authority. This is what it wills for us. This is what it accomplishes in us. In relation to this positive aim the preceding negative (" denying ") can have only a preliminary and subordinate position . . . Our instruction for that life still proceeds and is not, therefore, completed. Grace has still to be continually given and received by us. Therefore this life has still to be continually learned and exercised of and with grace. There is no one who can yet dispense with sanctification on the score that he is holy otherwise than by the fact that the command is holy and as such sanctifies him. The epiphany of Jesus Christ—the appearing of what has been done for us through Him, the disclosure of our life with Him as eternal life (1 Jn. 3[2])—has not yet taken place. In the words of 1 Cor. 13[12] we still see " through a mirror in a riddle. " For that reason and to that extent our life under instructing grace is a waiting. But its reality is not diminished by the fact that we wait for the epiphany of Jesus Christ and of our life with Him. We wait for the disclosure of that which here and now is veiled. But even here and now, in the concealment in which we now live it, this life does not lack anything of reality, and therefore of significance and power, of truth and force. What has happened—happened for us— has really happened. What is demanded of us is really demanded, and what is given us is really given. (II, 2, pp. 606–608. The Form of the Divine Claim.)

That God is gracious does not mean that He surrenders Himself to the one to whom He is gracious. He neither compromises with his resistance, nor ignores it, still less calls it good. But as the gracious God He affirms Himself over against the one to whom He is gracious by opposing and breaking down his resistance, and in some way causing His own good will to exert its effect upon him. Therefore the one to whom He is gracious comes to experience God's opposition to him . . . Grace " corrects us. " This is the holiness of God's grace. Just because God is gracious we must fear Him (cf. Hb. 10[26-31]) . . . The revelation of God, just because it is a revelation of His love and grace, means the revelation of His opposition to man, i.e., of His opposition to the opposition in which man exists over against Him. (II, 1, p. 361 f. The Grace and Holiness of God.)

Cf. IV, 3, pp. 185–196.

LUKE 2[15-21]

(I, 2)

Titus 3^{4-8a} (II, 2)

It is God's free decision and act to be " God our Saviour " and the Friend of man. But in this decision and act, in this self-determination to be our Saviour and Friend, we have an eternal presupposition of His creative work and therefore of all creatures. The One who came with the incarnation of His word could not be other than He was. In His majesty and freedom God wills from all eternity to be for men " God our Saviour. " The covenant fulfilled in time is a covenant resolved and established in God Himself before all time. There was no time when God was not the Covenant-partner of man. What appeared, therefore, in the epiphany of the man Jesus was not an accidental manner or disposition of this man, a moral disposition of this creature, but the kindness of the Creator, which is identical with His love for men. This is the inner necessity with which Jesus is at the same time both for God and for man. (III, 2, p. 218. Jesus, Man for Other Men.)

The liberation of the Christian is (3) his transition from the forcible dominion of things to the free territory of man and the human ... His personal existence has a definite and irresistible orientation. In this " humanistic " respect, too, he is fashioned by and made conformable to that which he is charged to attest, the loving-kindness of God for man. (IV, 3, p. 666 f. The Liberation of the Christian.)

Cf. IV, 4, p. 114 f.

Isaiah 9¹⁻⁶ (III, 2)

" Askest thou what the Christian Church is, or where the Christian Church is to be found? I will tell thee. The Christian Church thou must seek, not that it lies at Rome or at St. James or at Nuremberg or at Wittenberg, or among countryfolk, townsfolk or nobility, but it saith: ' the government shall be upon his shoulders '—that a right Christian and true member of the Churches is he who believeth that he sitteth upon Christ's shoulders, that is, that all his sins are hung on Christ's neck, so that his heart saith, I know no other comfort save that all my sins and misdeeds are laid upon His shoulders. Therefore those who lie on Christ's shoulders ... are called and are the Church and proper Christians " (Luther). (I, 2, p. 216 f. The Freedom of Man for God.)

1 Timothy 3¹⁶ (IV, 2)

" He was manifest in the flesh, justified in the Spirit, seen of angels, preached unto the Gentiles, believed on in the world, received up into glory. " The passage is introduced into the Epistle as a comprehensive definition of what is " by agreed confession " the one great " mystery of (Christian) godliness. " Its six clauses can hardly be understood as a list of successive saving events such as we have in the oldest versions of the Christian creed. They are rather six references from different standpoints

to a single event which can only be that of the resurrection or self-declaration of the living Jesus Christ as the divine act. All the references apply
to this. If the passage is really a hymn, it must surely be an Easter hymn,
or part of such a hymn ... The word *parousia* derives from Hellenistic
sources and originally means quite simply " effective presence. " A
parousia might be a military invasion, or the visitation of a city or district
by a high dignitary who, as in the case of the emperor, might sometimes
be treated so seriously that the local calendar would be dated afresh from
the occasion. The term was also applied sometimes to the helpful intervention of such figures as Dionysus or Aesculapius Soter. What is signified by
the term, if not the term itself, is familiar and important in the thinking
of the Old Testament. From His place, whether Sinai, Sion or heaven
Yahweh comes in the storm, or enthroned over the ark of the covenant, or
in His Word of Spirit, or in dreams or visions, or simply and especially in
the events of the history of Israel. To the men of His people He comes
finally as universal King in the unfolding of His power and glory. The
coming of " one like the Son of man with the clouds of heaven " (Da. 7^{13});
the coming of the righteous and victorious Messiah-King abolishing war
and establishing peace (Zech. $9^{9f.}$); above all the recurrent Old Testament
picture of the coming of the covenant Himself manifesting Himself in
movement from there to here—all these constitute materially the prepara-
tory form of what in the New Testament is called *parousia* in the pregnant
technical sense, namely, the effective presence of Jesus Christ. (IV, 3,
p. 291 f. The Glory of the Mediator.)

JOHN 3^{31-36} (V, 2)
    In the Old and New Testaments the Holy Spirit is God Himself in His
creative movement towards His creation. It is God who breathes specially
upon man (Gen. 2^7), thus living for him, allowing him to partake of His
own life, and therefore making him on his side a living being ... That this
Spirit rests on man, is laid on him and remains over him, that man is full
of the Spirit and his being and doing are consequently spiritual, and he
himself is spirit because created by the Spirit—these biblical statements
are not anthropological but exclusively Messianic. That man in general
lives, he owes of course to the Holy Ghost. Hence it can also be said of
man in general that the Holy Spirit is given to him, that he receives Him,
that he lives by and from the Spirit, that he has the Spirit and is of a
spiritual or intellectual nature. But there is this difference. Of man in
general, this can be said only in virtue of a special operation of God and of
specific events in which God turns towards him and enables him. From
the general anthropological standpoint, however, possession of the Spirit
is not a human state according to the Bible. In those events the Spirit is
imparted only " by measure " (v. 34). The events can cease ... Jesus
does not have the Holy Spirit in the way in which it can be said of any man

that he has the Spirit. He does not have Him only in virtue of an occasional transitory and partial bestowal. He could not be without Him, and would thus be subject to death and corruption. Jesus has the Holy Spirit lastingly and totally ... He breathes lastingly and totally in the air of the " life-giving Spirit ". He not only has the Spirit, but primarily and basically He is Spirit as He is soul and body. For this reason and in this way He lives. This is His absolutely unique relationship to the Holy Spirit. (III, 2, p. 333 f. Jesus, Whole Man.)

1 JOHN 3[1-6]   (VI, 2)

According to Holy Scripture the love of God has nothing to do with mere sentiment, opinion or feeling. On the contrary, it consists in a definite being, relationship and action. God is love in Himself. Being loved by Him we can, as it were, look into His " heart ". The fact that He loves us means that we can know Him as He is. This is all true. But if this picture-language of " the heart of God " is to have any validity, it can refer only to the being of God as Father, Son, and Holy Spirit. It reminds us that God's love for us is an overwhelming, overflowing, free love. It speaks to us of the miracle of this love. We cannot say anything higher or better of the " inwardness of God " than that God is Father, Son, and Holy Spirit, and therefore that He is love in Himself, without and before loving us, and without being forced to love us. (I, 2, p. 377. The Love of God.)

To what does Jesus Christ call those whom He calls? What kind of a being is that of the man called by Him, of the Christian? If, as we have laid down, it is the being of a man who by the call of God is called a child of God, and in the strength of this call really is a child of God (v. 1), then a second basic assertion is demanded ... The one who is called by Him, and thus called by Him a child of God and made a brother or sister, is set in fellowship with Him ... This is something which happens to him but not to all. All are elected and ordained for fellowship with Jesus Christ. All move towards it. It is waiting for all. But it is one thing to be elected for it and another to be set in it. (IV, 3, p. 534 f. The Goal of Vocation.)

Sin does not fit in anywhere and has no genuine potentiality and no right of actualisation. Sin is transgression (v. 4). In this respect the Old Testament is the best commentary on the New, and in the Old Testament where is sin anything else but transgression? Where is it judged in the light of a secret explicability and exculpability, of an ultimate compatibility with the will and work of God? And as transgression *sans phrase* it is not tolerated let alone accepted in the death of Jesus Christ. It is not even merely condemned, but broken and rejected. (IV, 1, p. 410. The Man of Sin.)

Cf. on Titus 2[11-14] Christmas Day; cf. also IV, 3, p. 319.

JOHN 1¹⁻¹⁴ (I, 3)

" The Word became Flesh "—this New Testament statement must guide us in our discussion of the dogmatic statement that Jesus Christ is very God and very Man.

The " Word " is the divine, creative, reconciling, redeeming Word which participates without restriction in the divine nature and existence, the eternal Son of God.

According to the whole content of John 1¹⁻¹², what is meant by Jn. 1¹⁴ is the Word that was in the beginning, that was with God and was indeed God Himself, by whom all things were made, the sum total of the life which shines as the light of revelation in man's darkness. His name is not John, but He is the object of John's witness. He begets children for God among men, not of their will or power, but completely and solely by His own might, whose glory is that of the only-begotten, of whose fulness His witnesses can only receive grace. The Logos is He who proclaims God, who is invisible for all others. He alone can proclaim Him, because He is Himself the only-begotten, in the bosom of His Father. (I, 2, p. 132. Very God and Very Man.)

" The Word became Flesh " (pp. 147–159)

" The Word became Flesh "—to this decisive factor in the whole christological question we must now turn. " The Word became "—that points to the centre, to the mystery of revelation, the happening of the inconceivable fact that God is among us and with us. If there is any synthetic judgment at all, it is this one, that " the Word became. " But can or will the Word of God become? Does He not surrender thereby His divinity? Or, if He does not surrender it, what does becoming mean? By what figures of speech or concepts is this becoming of the Word of God to be properly described? " The Word became "—if that is true, and true in such a way that a real becoming is thereby expressed without the slightest surrender of the divinity of the Word its truth is that of a miraculous act, an act of mercy on the part of God. (I, 2, p. 159. The Mystery of Revelation.)

. . . The Logos is where men are. He came to His own (v. 11) and His own—His own lieth in darkness—received Him not; nevertheless He came to His own. The true Light came into the world (v. 9), and it shineth in the darkness (v. 5). So to real men living in the world and in darkness there can be given power (*exousia*), which they do not possess of themselves, to be children of God. (v. 12f.) (I, 2, p. 151.)

The word " flesh " is frequently and primarily used in the Bible in the general and neutral sense of human existence or the human mode of being. It can often indicate man or mankind as such. But it undoubtedly has also an evil connotation. It indicates the condition of man in contradiction, in disorder and in consequent sickness, man after Adam's fall, the man who lives a fleeting life in the neighbourhood of death and corruption. Flesh is man, or soul and body, without the Logos. But the New Testament lays weight on the statement that the Logos became flesh. According to 1 Jn. 4[1f.] one recognises the Spirit of God in a Christian and therefore the authenticity of his Christian confession in the very fact that he confesses that Jesus Christ is come " in the flesh, " cf. 2 Jn. 7; 1 Tim. 3[16]; Rom. 8[3]; 1 Pet. 4[1]; Col. 1[22]; Eph. 2[14] etc . . . It is quite evident in all these passages that something happens to the flesh and therefore to the intrinsically more than dubious being of man when the Logos becomes flesh and the human person of Jesus is constituted in this way . . . In the flesh . . . something happens for and in the flesh. The flesh, which in itself is disobedient, becomes obedient. The flesh, which in itself profits nothing, becomes a purposeful instrument . . . In the flesh, victory is won, or in positive terms the transformation of the fleshly nature is achieved . . . In the flesh the reconciliation of the flesh is completed. (III, 2, p. 335 f. Jesus, Whole Man.)

The glory of the Word made flesh (v. 14), the kingdom of God which had drawn near to them in bodily form, the obedience of the Son of God, His death in our place and for our redemption, for the restoration of our peace with God—all this . . . was first revealed to them and perceived by them when the event was already past, when the man Jesus was dead and buried and had been taken from them and was no longer there, when all the bridges between Himself and them which had previously been available and passable had been broken. (IV, 1, p. 302. The Verdict of the Father.)

There are two elements in the event of the incarnation as it is attested in v. 14. If we put the accent on " flesh, " we make it a statement about God. We say . . . that without ceasing to be true God, in the full possession and exercise of His true deity, God went into the far country by becoming man in His second person or way of being as the Son—the far country not only of human creatureliness but also of human corruption and perdition. But if we put the accent on " Word, " we make it a statement about man. We say . . . that without ceasing to be man, but assumed and accepted in his creatureliness and corruption by the Son of God, man—this one Son of Man—returned home to where He belonged, to His place as true man . . . to the presence and enjoyment of the salvation for which he was destined. The atonement as it took place in Jesus Christ is the one inclusive event of the going out of the Son of God and coming in of the Son of Man. In its literal and original sense the word " to reconcile " means " to exchange. " The reconstitution and renewal of the covenant between God and man consists in this exchange—the abasement of God for the exaltation of man. It was God who went into the far country, and it is man who returns home. Both took place in the one Jesus Christ. (IV, 2, p. 20 f. The Homecoming of the Son of Man.)

" The Word became flesh " . . . *et homo factus est*. This is the beginning of all beginnings in Christian thinking and speaking, the presupposition of

all presuppositions with which the Christian community approaches the
world. When we say Jesus Christ, this is not a possibility which is somewhere ahead of us, but an actuality which is already behind us. With this
name in our hearts and on our lips, we are not laboriously toiling uphill,
but merrily coming down. This is where all Christian knowledge and life
derive their emphasis, or they are not what they give themselves out to be.
It is equally important to remember that this fact is an event . . . the act of
God in which it is a fact, and without which it would not be . . .: *et
homo factus est*. To celebrate Christmas is to think of the *perfectum* but
with a remembrance, and indeed in the face and presence, of the *perficere*
in which alone it is always actuality. To say Jesus Christ is to speak of
the *perficere* which creates the fact. (IV, 2, p. 45 f.)

Cf. on v. 1 f. II, 2, pp. 95–99; on v. 2 III, 2, p. 66; on v. 3. III, 1,
p. 116 f. (Luther); on vv. 6–8. I, 1, p. 112 [126]; on v. 14. I, 2, p. 222;
II, 2, p. 122.

HEBREWS 1¹⁻⁶ (II, 3)

Humanly God will be made manifest, when He is made manifest in
Jesus Christ. Man will have to do with one Man as God's representative,
as the upholder and proclaimer of the covenant; he will have to do with
a prophet, priest and king . . . The kings of Israel . . . the priests . . . the
prophets too . . . are all of them only instruments of divine action, not
themselves or of themselves divinely active. Obviously they all signify
the divine Agent, i.e., God Himself humanly present, God's own Son.
They do really signify Him. To that extent He is also manifest in them,
and to that extent men may already be called in the Old Testament " sons
of God, " even incidentally " gods. " But they signify Him in terms of
the infinite distance between the one who signifies and the One who is
signified. They all have to point beyond themselves, and with them we
have to look beyond themselves, in order to see the One who is signified.
Or rather we must regard them from the standpoint of the One who is
signified in order to realise that they do really signify Him. The covenant
of God with His people through the incarnation is in truth the mysterium,
the true mysterium, the mystery of the Old Testament. (I, 2, p. 83 f. The
Time of Expectation.)

The decisive moment of the biblical testimony to God's patience is that
according to v. 3 God upholds all things by the Word of His power. By
His Word! which means in any event that they are not occasioned by, and
dependent on, what becomes manifest and actual from our side as penitence
and faith. What is manifest and actual here is in point of fact the alternation of penitence and impenitence which is sufficiently clear in Israel's
example and the final outcome of which will be Israel's impenitence. To
this outcome in our experience there could correspond on God's part only
the judgment of wrath, and this is actually the case. God cannot sustain

all things or the sinful creature in his wretchedness by means of our final word. This word is definitely not effective to uphold all things. But God upholds them by His Word. And this Word as such is powerful. According to v. 2 it is the Word of the Son by whom He has spoken to us in these last days, i.e., at the end of the days of the fathers and the prophets, whom He has appointed heir of all things, by whom also He created the worlds, who is the brightness of His glory and the express image of His person. By this His Word in His Son Jesus Christ, He upholds all things and upholds them with power. (II, 1, p. 416 f. The Patience and Wisdom of God.)

Cf. also IV, 2, p. 34; IV, 3, p. 93 f., 584; III, 1, pp. 51–56.

JOHN 8[12-16]   (III, 3)

The Word of the living Jesus Christ is the creative call by which He awakens man to an active knowledge of the truth and thus receives him into the new standing of the Christian, namely, into a particular fellowship with Himself, thrusting him as His afflicted but well-equipped witness into the service of His prophetic work. (IV, 2, p. 510. Man in the Light of Life.)

His self-attestation " I am the light of the world " is said by the Pharisees to be witness to Himself which as such cannot be true (v. 13). They are told in reply that precisely as self-witness His witness is true because He knows what they do not know, namely, whence He comes and whither He goes (v. 14). Like all other men, they can attest only their existence as confined between beginning and end if they speak of themselves. Hence they certainly cannot speak the truth, as Jesus also says of Himself quite definitely in 5[31]. Yet when Jesus speaks of Himself, He speaks as well of the hidden whence and whither of His own and all human existence. Thus, speaking of Himself, He speaks the truth . . . As the one who comes from above He attests what He has seen and heard " above " (cf. also 3[11]). (IV, 3, p. 612. The Vocation of Man.)

I JOHN 1[1-4]   (IV, 3)

The history of the man Jesus, this salvation history, cannot be recounted without the story of Easter, the history of the forty days between His resurrection and ascension . . . For unless we wilfully ignore the clear indication of the New Testament sources, we are bound to recognise that this is a key position for our whole understanding of the man Jesus in His time. It shows us as nothing else can, according to the New Testament, that even as a man in His time Jesus is the Lord of all time. The Jesus whose life and time form the subject matter of the New Testament is the One whom at this time His disciples had heard, and seen with their eyes, and looked upon, and their hands had handled (v. 1); " that eternal life, which was with the Father, and was manifested unto us " (v. 2). It is impossible to read any text of the New Testament in the sense intended by its authors, by the apostles who stand behind them, or by the first communities, without an awareness that they either explicitly assert or at least tacitly assume that the Jesus of whom they speak and to whom they refer in some way is the One who appeared to His disciples at this particular time as the Resurrected from the dead. All the other things they know of Him, His words and acts, are irradiated by its light. Whatever they proclaim in His name, the power of their message, derives from the fact that it was conveyed and entrusted to them by the man Jesus after He was raised from the dead ... Whatever His being in time means for their being, and for that of all men in their time, derives from the fact that Jesus was among them even in this particular time, the Easter time. (III, 2, p. 441 f. Jesus, Lord of Time.)

According to the texts, and in spite of the obscurities and contradictions with which they speak of it, in spite of their legendary, their non-historical or pre-historical manner of statement, the Easter event is quite plainly one of an encounter, an encounter with God, an act of God to the disciples in which, as before and for the first time truly—revealed to them and recognised by them as such—God Himself confronted them and spoke with them in the person of Jesus Christ. (IV, 1, p. 341. The Verdict of the Father.)

Cf. I, 2, p. 18 and 490.

ISAIAH 11$^{1-5, \; 9}$ (V, 3)

We cannot impress upon ourselves too strongly that in the language of the Bible knowledge (yada, gignoskein) does not mean the acquisition of neutral information, which can be expressed in statements, principles and systems, concerning a being which confronts man, nor does it mean the entry into passive contemplation of a being which exists beyond the phenomenal world. What it really means is the process or history in which man, certainly observing and thinking, using his senses, intelligence and imagination, but also his will, action and " heart, " and therefore as whole man, becomes aware of another history which in the first instance encounters him as an alien history from without, and becomes aware of it in such a compelling way that he cannot be neutral towards it, but finds himself summoned to disclose and give himself to it in return, to direct himself according to the law which he encounters in it, to be taken up into its movement, in short, to demonstrate the acquaintance which he has been given with this other history in a corresponding alteration of his own being, action and conduct. We can and should say even more emphatically that knowledge in the biblical sense is the process in which the distant " object " dissolves as it were, overcoming both its distance and its objectivity and coming to man as acting Subject, entering into the man who knows and subjecting him to this transformation ... Note should be

taken of v. 9 . . . this is the alteration which the knowledge of God does
not merely entail but necessarily discloses. (IV, 3, p. 183 f. The Glory
of the Mediator.)

Cf. also III, 2, p. 333; III, 1, pp. 56ff.

COLOSSIANS 2³⁻¹⁰   (VI, 3)

Neither the ethics of the Sermon on the Mount nor the eschatology of
Mk. 13 and parallels, nor the healing of the blind, lame and possessed, nor
the statements of Pauline and Johannine metaphysics and mysticism (so
far as there are any), nor love to God nor love to neighbour, nor the passion
and death of Christ, nor the miraculous raising from the dead—nothing of
all that has any value, inner importance or abstract significance of its own
in the New Testament, apart from Jesus Christ being the Subject of it all.
His is the name in which it is all true and real, living and moving, by which
therefore everything must be attested. He is the mystery of God in which
all things are hidden . . . (v. 3). (I, 2, p. 10 f. Jesus Christ the Objective
Reality of Revelation.)

It is therefore true that Christ is the mystery of God, that all the
treasures of wisdom and knowledge are hidden in Him and not elsewhere,
and that they are to be acquired in Him and not elsewhere. Why?
Because He who has been appointed by God the beginning of all knowledge
is also the One who decides its total compass. It is, therefore, only at the
risk of immediate and total blindness that we separate ourselves from it,
trying to escape by discovering other depths and heights in other spheres.
(IV, 1, p. 81. The Grace of God in Jesus Christ.)

The use of a specific mode of thought and philosophy brought to the
task of scriptural exegesis can claim no independent interest in itself. It
cannot in any way become an end in itself. At this point we have to
remember the danger which philosophy has always involved, and always
can involve, in the matter of scriptural exegesis. (I, 2, p. 731. Freedom
in the Church.)

The New Testament tradition . . . is self-consistent in one great truth.
There can be no doubt about the full and genuine and individual humanity
of the man Jesus of Nazareth, but in that man there has entered in and there
must be recognised and respected One who is qualitatively different from
all other men. He is not simply a better man, a more gifted or a more wise
or noble or pious, in short a greater man. But as against all other men and
their differences we have in the person of this man One who is their Lord
and Lawgiver and Judge. He has full power to condemn them or to
pardon. He has full power to call them and bind them to Himself. He
has full power, as against their cosmic limitation, to pronounce in His
existence a final Word concerning them and all human history. He is the
Saviour before whom there was none other, neither shall be after. This
is the " act of God, " the " eschatological event of salvation, " to use our

modern jargon. In attestation of this understanding of the man Jesus the New Testament tradition calls Him the Messiah of Israel, the *Kyrios*, the second Adam come down from heaven, and, in a final approximation to what is meant by all this, the Son or the Word of God. It lifts Him right out of the list of other men, and as against this list (including Moses and the prophets, not to mention all the rest) it places Him at the side of God. The New Testament community does not merely think, but lives and acts in the knowledge and on the presupposition that in this man " dwells all the fulness of the Godhead bodily " (v. 9; Jn. 5^{23}; 14^9; Rom. 10^{12}; 1 Cor. 1^2; Acts $9^{14, 21}$; 22^{16}). The post-apostolic community was based on this knowledge of Jesus Christ and the corresponding confession. In this respect we have to note what is said and expounded with great theological naïveté but for that reason all the more clearly in the first Christian sermon known to us, the so-called 2 Clement: " Brethren, we must think of Jesus Christ as of God ... " And although the accounts are uncertain and primitive, it is noteworthy that what the governor Pliny had heard from lapsed Christians and reported to the emperor Trajan about 113 was this: They had confessed that the sum (*summa*) of their error or fault was that they used to meet before sunrise *carmenque Christo quasi Deo dicere secum in vicem* (and sing by turns a hymn to Christ as God) ... In the same connexion we might mention the caricature found in the Palatine at Rome, although it belongs to a later date. It depicts an ass fastened to a cross, and the form of a man worshipping it, with the inscription: " Alexamenos (obviously a Christian who is meant to be ridiculed) honours God. " It is quite clear from the impressions and reactions of these outsiders in what category the primitive Christians placed Christ. (IV, 1, p. 160 f. The Way of the Son of God into the Far Country.)

Cf. on Col. 1^{15-23} and the ascension I, 2, p. 617; and IV, 4, p. 118 f.

ST STEPHEN'S DAY (DECEMBER 26)

MATTHEW 23^{34-39} (I)

" Ye would not " ... This is the riddle of the existence of Israel in its relationship to Jesus. His will was to gather them ... For they were really His (Jn. 1^{11}). And He was theirs—the Son of David. The kingdom of God which had drawn near in Him was the fulfilment of their promise and hope. He would—but they would not. The whole history of Israel was repeated in concentrated form, in a single instant: the presence of Yahweh to the one elect people: the divine offer which is also the active and powerful work of His faithfulness and goodness; the prophetic man who could be claimed by no other people; and the prophetic word as no other people could perceive it. On God's part it was all as it had been before—but in a supreme climax and concretion. And on Israel's part, too, it was all as it had been before: its murmuring against Moses; its disobedience to Samuel; its secret and open fury against Elijah and Jeremiah; the obstinacy which answered faithfulness with unfaithfulness. This obstinacy later extended like a monstrous shadow to the Jewish colonies and synagogues of Syria and Asia Minor and Greece and Rome, constituting the problem to which Paul, who had met it in so many (even Christian) forms, devoted chapters 9–11 of the Epistle to the Romans. But now the shadow was only that of the event in which Jerusalem had opposed to the gathering of Jesus the oldest and thickest and most impregnable of all its walls, its own unwillingness: " Jerusalem, thou that killest the prophets, and stonest them which are sent unto thee. " Now more than ever it was quite impossible that the elect people of God should be neutral in face of what God Himself said and did. Its existence before God, or rather the existence of God as the God of this people, allowed it only this either-or. (IV, 2, p. 261. The Royal Man.)

Acts 6^{8}–$7^{2a, \ 51-59}$ (II)

From the historical standpoint capital punishment absorbs and transforms the act of self-defence and revenge formerly undertaken by the individual or his family. In the interests of general peace, but also of equity in individual cases, retribution is decided by the society which embraces individuals and families, and by the authority and power of its magistrates and officers. Cf. Ex. 21^{12}, then Lev. 20^2 . . . The next step is the judging of crimes which do not affect any particular individual but are aimed at society as such, at its constitution, laws and continued existence, so that society sees a direct threat to itself and must give itself wholeheartedly to self-defence. We remember Achan (Jos. 7^{25}): " And Joshua said, Why hast thou troubled us? the Lord shall trouble thee this day. And all Israel stoned him with stones. " We also remember that in the view of Caiaphas Jesus deserved to be put to death for a similar reason (Jn. 11^{50}). On the same assumption Stephen was stoned and the early Christians were both threatened and punished by death in the Roman Empire. For it was as a defensive act of the state against its enemies that capital punishment gained a new ascendance in imperial Rome. (III, 4, p. 437. The Protection of Life.)

Mark 13^{9-13} (III)

The Holy Spirit is the authorisation to speak about Christ; He is the equipment of the prophet and apostle; He is the summons to the Church to minister the Word. If we ask concerning the mind of the Spirit (Rom. 8^{27}), we must answer that it consists in the fact that He is the gift of speaking about the " wonderful works of God. " (I, 1, p. 455 f. [521].)

In the New Testament the word " hatred " nowhere seems to have, and does not have here, the sense of a personal emotion or personal aversion for the object of the hatred. The Christian is not hated as a human individual who is repulsive to the one who hates him on account of his personal being and action. He is hated as the bearer and representative of a specific claim and cause . . . It is thus that the disciples are hated by all men and the world . . . The Christian is accused of *odium humani generis*, and he is also the target of *odium humani generis*. As the witness of Christ he has only good things, indeed, the very best, to say to the world, and he finds himself regarded and treated not only as the bringer of bad news, of that No which is all the world can hear, but also . . . as a malicious disturber of the peace. In attesting Jesus Christ to the world, and therefore its reconciliation with God, he might well think that he is the best and most loyal and useful citizen, but to all his fellow-citizens he is necessarily an odious stranger and foreigner who is best expelled. He is their friend . . . and yet he must undergo the experience of being treated as their worst enemy . . . Thus the disciples are regarded and treated as outlaws—not because they are Peter, Paul or John, but because they represent to all men and to the world the alien and intolerable cause of the kingdom, the *coup d' état* of God. (IV, 3, p. 624 f. The Christian in Affliction.)

HEBREWS 10$^{32\text{-}39}$ (IV)

Illumination (v. 32) means that the light of life carries through its work in a particular man to its conclusion. It shines on all men. But in the event of vocation it shines for a man . . . in such a way that it illuminates this man. It does not now merely shine for him in general. It now shines for him in such a way that his closed eyes are opened by its shining, or rather his blind eyes are healed by its shining and made to see. This is the process of vocation. Man is called and becomes a Christian as he is illuminated. There is no question here of the flaring up of a light which has secretly been burning low in him already. We are confronted rather by the work of the wholly new and strange light of life shining on him wholly from without but now also lighting him within. This light imparts itself to him, making itself known in its newness, commending itself in its strangeness, becoming inward in its outwardness . . . Illumination . . . is his advancement to knowledge. That the revelation of God shines on and in him, takes place in such a way that he hears, receives, understands, grasps and appropriates what is said to him in it, not with new and special organs, but with the same organs of apperception with which he knows other things, yet not in virtue of his own capacity to use them, but in virtue of the missing capacity which he is now given by God's revelation. " Jesus, give me sound and serviceable eyes; touch Thou mine eyes. " . . . Christians are enlightened once and for all (6^4). This is their firm consolation and, of course, their immeasurable responsibility. (IV, 3, p. 508 f. The Event of Vocation.)

MARK 10$^{28\text{-}31}$ (V)

II, 2, pp. 627–630

JEREMIAH 1$^{17-19}$ (VI)
IV, 3, p. 581 f.

FIRST SUNDAY AFTER CHRISTMAS
December 27

JOHN 21^{19b-24} (I)
1 JOHN 1$^{5-10}$ (II)

" God is light, and in him is no darkness at all. " God's knowledge is a complete knowledge not only in the sense of a comprehensive but also in that of a penetrating knowledge. It is not merely an outer knowledge of its objects; it is also an inner knowledge. It is not partial; it is total. It not only knows them individually; it knows them in their inter-connexion. It knows the individual in the whole and the whole in each constituent individual. Only in this way can we say unreservedly what must be said about God—that nothing is hidden from Him. For His knowledge is exempt in every way from uncertainty, obscurity and error. Everything is open before Him not only in its existence but in all its limitations, possibilities and relationships. It is a knowledge which is absolutely clear, plain, definite, and intensive in its exhaustiveness. Everything which is in any way knowable is known by Him. " If I say, Surely the darkness shall cover me; even the night shall be light about me. Yea, the darkness hideth not from thee, but the night shineth as the day " (Ps. 139$^{11f.}$). (II, 1, p. 555. The Constancy and Omnipotence of God.)

FIRST SUNDAY AFTER CHRISTMAS
December 28

MATTHEW 2$^{13-18}$ (I)
REVELATION 12$^{1-6}$ (II)

FIRST SUNDAY AFTER CHRISTMAS
December 29–31

LUKE 2$^{22-40}$ (I)

Old Simeon and Anna, who waited for the consolation of Israel and the deliverance of Jerusalem, are now dismissed like faithful sentinels whose duty is done: " Lord, now lettest thou they servant depart in peace, according to thy word; for mine eyes have seen thy salvation " (v. 29 f.). This final word on this side of the turning-point in time becomes with its fulfilment the first and exclusively normative word for the future: Jn. 1^{45}. The apostles can only testify to this search and discovery. It is conclusive and final ... The Christian man looks back to this search and discovery and nothing else. He lives directly by the beginning made with it. The

Gospel story and the apostolic message mediate to him nothing but this beginning. And so the Church, whose life is sustained by the Gospel story and the apostolic message, can only mediate this beginning, testifying to the individual Christian that this beginning, Jesus Christ, is the beginning of his life too. It has, therefore, nothing else to offer him; nothing of its own, whether old or new. The historical existence of the Church is legitimate only in so far as it refrains from giving specific weight to its own possibilities, developments and achievements, from interesting its members in these things and therefore in itself instead of pointing simply to that beginning in direct and exclusive proclamation of Jesus Christ. The Christian Church exists only where it attests to its members and the outside world this beginning and nothing but this beginning. Only as it does this is it the " pillar and ground of the truth " (1 Tim. 3^{15}). It cannot, therefore, build itself on either its antiquity or its renewals. It cannot consolidate its life around its ministry or dogmas, its cultus or orders. It cannot place its confidence on its ministerial succession or on the religious, intellectual and political lustre of the fathers and saints and doctors and leaders with whom it has been blessed, on the certainty of its doctrinal and constitutional tradition, or on the progressive development of its preaching, institutions or activity. Nor can it insert all these things between that beginning and its contemporary present, between Jesus Christ and the men after His time, as though they had a special and independent value and authority and importance by the side of His. It can understand itself and its history in all its forms only as the context of a service which it has to perform. (III, 2, p. 583 f. Beginning Time.)

Cf. also I, 1, p. 154 [175]; III, 2, p. 479 f.

GALATIANS 4^{1-7} (II)

Pleroma (v. 4) is that which fulfils (fills full) a vessel, plan, concept or form. It is, therefore, the content, the meaning, the reality proclaimed as a possibility in this form. " Fulness of time " cannot, therefore, be regarded otherwise than as " real time. " In and with the incarnation of the Word, in and with the approach of the kingdom of God—we should perhaps say as its precursor or concomitant—it also happens that real time breaks in as new time, as the now and to-day of the Saviour (Eph. $1^{9f.}$) . . . In this context we might well pause to think of the fact that to have time for another, although in the abstract this says little, is in reality to manifest in essence all the benefits which one man can show to another. When I really give anyone my time, I thereby give him the last and most personal thing that I have to give at all, namely, myself. If I do not give him my time, I certainly continue to be his debtor in everything, even though in other ways I give him ever so much. The difference at once to be noted between our having time for others and God's having time for us is twofold, that if God gives us time, He who deals with us is He who alone has genuine, real time to give, and that He gives us this time not just partially, not with all sorts of reservations and qualifications, such as are habitual with us when giving to others, but entirely. The fulfilment of time that took place in Jesus is not just an alms from the divine riches; if, according to Gal. 4⁴, Jesus Christ is the " *pleroma* of the time, " we have to remember that, according to Col. 2⁹, " in him dwelleth all the *pleroma* of the Godhead bodily. " (I, 2, p. 53 and p. 55. God's Time and Our Time.)

He came under the Law, i.e., He stepped into the heart of the inevitable conflict between the faithfulness of God and the unfaithfulness of man. He bore it in Himself to the bitter end. He took part in it from both sides. He endured it from both sides. He was not only the God who is offended by man. He was also the man whom God threatens with death, who falls a victim to death in face of God's judgment. If He really entered into solidarity with us—and that is just what He did do—it meant necessarily that He took upon Himself, in likeness to us, the " flesh of sin " (Rom. 8³). He shared in the status, constitution and situation of man in which man resists God and cannot stand before Him but must die. (II, 1, p. 397. The Mercy and Righteousness of God.)

Cf. also I, 1, p. 458 f. [525] f., (Luther); I, 2, p. 138; III, 2, p. 360.

MATTHEW 2¹³⁻¹⁸   (III)
ISAIAH 63⁷⁻¹⁶   (IV)

If our own election is truly revealed to us in the election of the man Jesus—and that is the meaning of the New Testament when it speaks of this man's election as our Saviour, Head and Priest, and of the fore-ordination of His passion and death—it is because in Him we have to do not merely with elected man, but with the electing God, with the Word and decree which was in the beginning with God: not, then, with a messenger or angel (v. 9), but with God Himself, with our Saviour, with the One who alone can be a true and faithful witness to our election. (II, 2, p. 108. Jesus Christ, Electing and Elected.)

Cf. also on Isaiah 63¹⁵–64⁴ First Sunday in Advent.

JOHN 5³⁰⁻³⁸   (V)

God as the Father of Jesus Christ can be our Father because even apart from the fact that He reveals Himself as such He already is the One He reveals Himself to be, namely the Father of Jesus Christ, His Son, who as such is Himself God. God can be our Father because He is Father in Himself, because fatherhood is an eternal mode of being of the divine essence. In the One whose name, kingdom and will Jesus reveals, in dis-tinctive differentiation from the One who reveals Him and yet also in distinctive fellowship with Him, we have to do with God himself.

How is it that with the Church dogma we reach this understanding of the biblical witness to God the Father. The answer must simply be that we reach it as we accept the biblical witness and take it seriously to the degree that formally it absolutely conditions and binds the content of the revelation of the Father by its impartation in the person of the Revealer Jesus of Nazareth. Its content cannot be abstracted from this form. There can be no question here of distinguishing between content and form as though the content could be regarded as divine and necessary and the form as human and contingent, the former being the essence and the latter the historical manifestation of the revelation. The form here is essential to the content, i.e., God is unknown as our Father, as the Creator, to the degree that He is not made known by Jesus.

It is especially the Johannine tradition which expresses this exclusiveness with ever-renewed emphasis: Jn. 1^{18}; $5^{23, 37}$; 6^{46}; 8^{19}; 14^6; 17^{25}; 1 Jn. 2^{23} and 2 Jn. 9. But in the long run it is to be found with the same unmistakable clarity in the Synoptists too: Mt. 11^{27}. (I, 1, p. 390 [448]. The Eternal Father.)

JUDE 17–25 (VI)

The unequivocal reference of the term " upbuilding " is to the Christian community. It is not the Christian individual as such, but the community which, in its individual members and through their reciprocal ministry, is edified, and lets itself be edified, and edifies itself. In modern times, under the influence of Pietism, we have come to think in terms of the edification of individual Christians—in the sense of their inward inspiration and strengthening and encouragement and assurance. The cognate ideas has also arisen of that which is specifically edifying. Now all this is not denied. It is, indeed, included in a serious theological concept of up-building. But it is only included. In the abstract, it is quite impossible. Even in v. 20, which as far as I know is the only verse to which appeal may be made, *epoikodomein* cannot possibly mean private edification. No such thing is ever envisaged in the New Testament. The New Testament speaks always of the upbuilding of the community. I can edify myself only as I edify the community. (IV, 2, p. 627. The Holy Spirit and the Upbuilding of the Christian Community.)

NEW YEAR'S EVE

LUKE 12^{35-40} (I)

What do the New Testament witnesses know and say of time? Obviously not just that it is limited, unique and finite . . . but rather that it is the last time, that it is time really coming to an end, that its ending is already an event and in process of completion . . . It is a time (1) . . . (2) . . . (3) whose duration is unknown to those who live in it. They know indeed that it is His time and that it is therefore a short and limited time. They do not

know, however, at which point in time they will come up against its
frontier. They do not know where or when the decreed end of time will
be revealed and time, their time, will finally be at an end. The New
Testament witnesses regard as an unknown quantity the Where or When
of the frontier ahead. They even expressly make it an unknown quantity
for the man Jesus (Mk. 13[32]). This does not mean, however, that they
think of the future as empty or abstract. The purpose of all the passages
which touch on this (e.g., Mt. 24[43f.]; 24[45f.]; 25[1f.]) is not to impress upon
us that we are in darkness regarding the future but to make it plain that in
this interval we must orientate ourselves by the fact that time is expiring
quickly rather than by a known point when it will reach its end. Whether
used or misused, it will suddenly be gone. As the thief comes in the night
(1 Thess. 5[2]), as the lord returns to his house, as the bridegroom arrives
for the celebration, so at the hour chosen by the Lord but not previously
intimated, the end will be suddenly revealed to those who wait. They can
only wait for the One who will come suddenly and put an end to their time.
They cannot make special preparation for a known hour, for this would
mean that they need not wait for Him at other hours when He is not
expected, and they might thus spend these hours as if they did not form
part of the time which in its brevity belongs to Him. (III, 4, pp. 581–583.
The Unique Opportunity.)

ROMANS 8[31b-39]   (II)

It is indeed a hard and oppressive and humiliating thing to be a Christian,
and therefore with Jesus Christ and His Word in one's heart to have to be
against the whole world and oneself, but it is also an incomparably glorious,
comforting and proud thing to be a Christian and therefore to be at the
side of Jesus Christ, to be not merely an object in His work but a subject in
His service, to be not merely a hearer of His Word but a great or little,
skilful or unskilful witness of this Word. How can the difficulty of the
Christian way be avoided when the Jesus Christ who precedes on this way
is none other than He who bore the cross to Golgotha? But how can it
fail to be a glorious way when the power which sets the Christian on it is
that of the resurrection of Jesus Christ? God . . . is for him in either case,
on this way which is both difficult and glorious. This is what makes him
in all circumstances a positive man. His life is positive in the fact that
from the very first it is one long calling upon God. He calls upon God
representatively for those who do not yet do so, or do not seem to do so.
(IV, 3, p. 366 f. The Glory of the Mediator.)

It is true that God does not allow anything to be taken from Him. But
how if He gives Himself? If He does, it is even more true that He does
allow Himself to be taken . . . The Christian is able to take because God
gives him Himself and all that He possesses (v. 32). Thus the most
intimate thing in Christian prayer, and therefore in the whole Christian

attitude, is the fact that the Christian both may ask and actually does ask. In the praying of a Christian there is no impudence; no forgetting of distances; no arbitrary transcending of the antithesis between the one side and the other, between that which is above and that which is below; no self-seeking. On the contrary, he is doing that which corresponds and answers to the situation in which he finds himself placed by the Word of God. He does that which he is not merely permitted but commanded to do in this situation, seeing that he is obviously placed in this situation in order to do it. (III, 3, p. 269. The Christian under the Universal Lordship of God the Father.)

Cf. also III, 2, p. 213 f.; IV, 2, pp. 278–280, 285.

Isaiah 9[1-6]   (IIb)

Cf. on this Christmas Day.

Luke 12[32]   (III)

Certainly great membership rolls and good attendances and full churches and halls (and even lecture rooms) are facts which naturally impress us— who can fail to be impressed by them?—but what do they really have to do with the truth? . . . The Scribes and Pharisees were certainly in a majority against Jesus and His disciples, and yet they were wrong . . . The truth may undoubtedly lie with the minority . . . It may lie only with the two or three gathered together (Mt. 18[20]) in the name of Jesus Christ. That they number several millions is of no avail to those who are not gathered in His name. The whole legitimacy of the Reformation rests upon this possibility. There are some who go further and boldly affirm that the truth will very likely, indeed will fairly (or most) certainly, be found within the minority. An empty church is regarded as a comforting indication and prejudice in favour of the fact that the pure Gospel is proclaimed in it . . . In certain circumstances does it not involve a genuine pleasure and exaltation to be in a minority . . . the little flock to which it is the Father's good pleasure to give the kingdom, which is therefore a kind of advance guard of God? In Schiller's words: "What is majority? Majority is folly." Good sense is never found but with the few. But here again we must be careful. There have been minorities whose resistance to the majority has not been legitimate because their cause has had nothing whatever to do with the truth . . . In the history of the Church . . . there have been far too many little movements of reform instigated by men who appealed readily to the fact that a majority proves nothing, that truth and the good God are more likely to be on the side of the small and even the smallest battalions, and yet in the long run they proved to be no more lasting than a kind of carnival procession . . . There was something very far wrong when the little flock of Lk. 12 became the imperial world-Church of Constantine, and many a minority in the Church has lost more than it has gained by

becoming a majority, or a big Church instead of a small. But it is not
fundamentally the case that when the few become many the truth also
becomes error. (IV, 1, p. 709 f. The Holy Spirit and the Gathering of
the Christian Community.)

HEBREWS 13⁸, ⁹ᵇ   (IV)

The salvation addressed to man by God . . . is not a self-enclosed saving
fact either far behind us or high above us. It is a living redemptive happening which takes place. Or, more concretely, it is the saving operation
of the living Lord Jesus which did not conclude but began in His revelation on Easter Day. In its totality, in its movement to His final manifestation, it has the power of that which was once for all accomplished by Him
at Calvary. It is essential, and therefore necessary, to Him (v. 8), to be
not merely yesterday and for ever, but to-day—in the intervening time
which is our time. It would not be God's and therefore it would not be
our salvation if it did not create and maintain and continually renew the
provisional representation in which it is to-day. If we do not take it
seriously in this, we do not take it seriously at all. If we hold ourselves
aloof from this, we hold ourselves aloof from salvation and the Saviour . . .
He would not be a saint (sc. in the communion of saints) who tried to be so
in and for himself—apart from this provisional representation of the
sanctification which has taken place in Jesus Christ. *Extra ecclesiam nulla
salus.* (IV, 1, p. 621 f. The True Church.)

The Already and the Even Now are not less forms of the one *parousia,*
presence and action of Jesus Christ in His prophetic action than the Not
Yet. The commencement, continuation and consummation of His prophetic activity are all equal in this respect. Even if in a different manner, it
is the same person who was yesterday, is to-day, and will come to-morrow
and for ever. This means, however, that the One who rose from the dead
and came to His disciples on Easter Day was already, unrecognisably as
far as they were concerned, the same as He who then encountered them in
the outpouring of His Holy Spirit and who is present with His community
to this day in the power of the same Spirit. (IV, 3, p. 910. The Subject
of Hope and Hope.)

Cf. on Hebrews 13¹⁻⁹ᵇ Fourteenth Sunday After Trinity.

Cf. also IV, 1, p. 314 and IV, 3, p. 291.

JOHN 12⁴⁴⁻⁵⁰   (V)

What sin is, what the unbelief is which gives rise to disobedience, is
revealed in man's relationship, his confrontation with Jesus Christ. Man's
sin is unbelief in the God who was " in Christ " . . . The sin of man is the
human action which does not correspond to the divine action in Jesus
Christ but contradicts it. To that extent it is the action of unbelief and

therefore of disobedience. That unbelief, and particularly unbelief in Jesus Christ, is *the* sin, is in the New Testament a specific feature of the Johannine witness: v. 48; 3^{18}; 5^{23}; 8^{24}; 1 Jn. 5^{10} ... It was an insight of Luther, often expressed by him, especially when he was preaching on texts from John ... " Unbelief is the chief sin, and the source of all other sins. For where there is unbelief in the heart, so that we do not believe in Christ, the first result is that we do not receive his word, but either despise it or regard it as heresy and falsehood, persecuting it as though it had been spoken by the devil. A greater mischief then results, for we become disobedient to our fathers and mothers and the powers that be, not diligently pursuing our own office and calling, but living in all kinds of indiscipline and licence, except as restrained by fear and shame ... The fount and source of all evil is unbelief ... For what is sin? Is it not theft and murder and adultery and the like? Yes, these are sins, but they are not the chief sin. The chief sin ... is not to believe in Jesus Christ. The world knows nothing of this sin: it has to be taught it by the Holy Ghost. The world accepts as sin only that which is forbidden in the second table of Moses. It knows nothing of Christ, much less that it is sin not to believe in Him ... " (IV, 1, p. 415 f. The Pride and Fall of Man.)

That Jesus comes to bring about the ruin of any man is a thought which is wholly foreign to the New Testament. His coming brings destruction to the demons and only to the demons (Mk. 1^{24}). Salvation and life (Lk. 19^{10}; Jn. 10^{10}) is what Jesus effects by fulfilling the Law and giving His life for many. It is as he does this that He becomes the Judge; for His intervention on behalf of all exalts the lowly and humbles the proud. It is as He does this that He destroys the demons and becomes the promise of the world. And the promise which is the meaning of His whole action is salvation and life. " Unto you is born this day the Saviour " (Lk.2^{11}). (III, 2, p. 60 f. Jesus, Man for God.)

Cf. on Luke 2^{1-14} Christmas Day I, III, V

ISAIAH 51^{1-6} (VI)

NEW YEAR'S DAY

LUKE 2^{21} (I)

JOHN $16^{32b,\,33}$ (II)

Confidence in its cause and continuance and future and triumph depends absolutely upon the fact that it is always confidence in Him; that renouncing all other helpers it keeps only to Him who is not only a Helper but already the Conqueror, the Victor, the death of death, and who as such is not apart from but with His saints. For the community everything depends upon its readiness not to try to be anything more or better or surer than His people, His body, and to live and grow as such on earth. In every deviation from confidence in Him, it can only be deceived as to its preservation, and know that it is doomed and lost. There is no objective need, or even possibility, of concern and anxiety or despair concerning its preservation. This can arise only when there is deviation; when search is made for other helpers; when there is a desertion of the Victor by whom the community—even though it may be threatened on all sides, even though it may be under assault or the cross, even though it may be secularised or sacralised—is objectively victorious, and thus able at all times to throw off every fear. There is objective need to rejoice in its actual preservation. As the community does this, it is in a position to take up its human responsibilities with new thankfulness, seriousness and soberness, not folding its hands, but when it has prayed, and continuing to do so, going boldly to work as if it were not threatened by any dangers. *Fluctuat nec mergitur*. The One who is attested and attests Himself in the Bible will never have any other message for His threatened community than that it should be confident, not because it has no reason for anxiety as it exists in the world, but because of the counter-reason which radically removes this reason— that He has overcome the world (v. 33). (IV, 2, p. 675 f. The Upholding of the Community.)

GALATIANS 3[23-29]   (III)

This narrower context of v. 27 (vv. 26–29) stands for its part in the broader context of a demonstration that the Galatian Christians, by grasping in faith the promise fulfilled in Christ, are freed from the Mosaic Law which precedes this fulfilment, and especially from the requirement of circumcision, so that they do not have to become Jews first in order to become Christians. In both the narrower and the broader context, then, we obviously do not have in v. 27 a mere allusion to baptism but a statement about its meaning: believers are addressed as the baptised. In the light of their baptism it is said to them that their freedom when, grasping the promise, they received baptism, was grounded not only in their faith, but ontically. On the basis of a specific happening they are the children of God, they are all one as those who belong to Christ—not Hellenes as distinct from Jews, under no obligation to become Jews first just as slaves do not have to become free men or free women or *vice versa*. As those they are, they are all Abraham's seed, heirs of the promise given to them and now fulfilled. They believe as people who are all these things. They are all these things because they are in Christ Jesus (v. 26, 28). They are in Him as they have put Him on, as in virtue of His intercession for them they have been set directly in the sphere of His dominion, of the dynamically advancing law of His life, of His Spirit, as they have become new and different men. This is what is said to them in the light of the fact that they have had themselves baptised. Does this mean that the act with which they all began was itself their putting on of Christ, their ontic renewing? . . . If expounded sacramentally the saying in Gal. 3[27] is a foreign body in its narrower and wider context. (III, 4, pp. 115–117. Baptism with Water.)

Cf. also IV, 4, p. 16 and p. 91.

JAMES 4[13-17]   (IIb)

Cf. on Isaiah 40[1-11] Third Sunday in Advent.

JOHN 6[37-40]   (III)

Jesus Christ in His person . . . is the reality and revelation of the life-content of the elect man. For everything that He is . . . He is not for Himself, or for His own sake, but as the reality and the revelation of the will of God on behalf of an unlimited number of other men . . . For what many? . . . When we remember 2 Cor. 5[19]; Jn. 8[12]; 9[5]; 11[9]; 12[46]; 1[29]; 3[16]; 1 Jn. 2[2] etc. we cannot follow the classical doctrine and make the open number of those who are elect in Jesus Christ into a closed number to which all other men are opposed as the rejected. Such an assumption is shattered by the real and revealed will of God in Jesus Christ. It is shattered by the impossibility of reckoning with another divine rejection than the rejection whose subject was Jesus Christ, who bore it and triumphantly bore it away. It is shattered by the fact that Jesus Christ is the irreversible way from the depths to the heights, from death to life; and that as this way He is also the truth, the declaration of the heart of God, beside which there is no other and beside which we have no right to ask for any other. It is shattered by the fact that Jesus Christ will not reject any who come to Him. (v. 37) (II, 2, p. 421 f. The Election of the Individual.)

The "last day" (v. 39 f., 44, 54; 12[48]): Does this refer to the Easter event, or the return of Jesus Christ in the Holy Ghost, or His return at the end of the days? It is advisable not to solve the implied difficulty of interpretation by critical amputation. According to the New Testament, the return of Jesus Christ in the Easter event is not yet as such His return in the Holy Ghost and certainly not His return at the end of the days. Similarly, His return in the Easter event and at the end of the days cannot be dissolved into His return in the Holy Ghost, nor the Easter event and the outpouring of the Holy Spirit into His last coming. In all these we have to do with the one new coming of Him who came before. But if we are to be true to the New Testament, none of these three forms of His new coming, including the Easter event, may be regarded as its only form. The most that we can say is that a particular glory attaches to the Easter event because here it begins, the Easter event being the primal and basic form in which it comes to be seen and grasped in its totality. (III, 4, p. 294. The Glory of the Mediator.)

JOSHUA 1[1-9]   (IV)
IV, 3, p. 578.

LUKE 4$^{14\text{-}21}$ (V)

This day, then, the acceptable year of the Lord, has dawned. This day the message of peace sounds in your ears. This day there takes place the liberation which it proclaims. For I am present as the One who is anointed and sent, who has the authority to declare liberty with His Word and accomplish it with this act of His Word, to bring in the new age in His person ... There is a coincidence between the content of the news brought by Him and Jesus Himself who brings it ... We must now ask concerning the modern insistence on the coincidence and even identity of the New Testament *kerygma* with the event proclaimed in it. There is much to be said in favour of this, but we must be careful not to say too much, and to say the right things. G. Friedrich (TWNT, III, p. 702 f. [TDNT, III, p. 704]) states as a general rule that the action, the proclamation itself, is the new and decisive thing ... that it is by the proclamation itself that God assumes power and His kingdom comes. This is true enough in so far as we have to do with the *keryssein* of Jesus Himself. For here we have more than participation. We have coincidence and identity. The saying in Ps. 33^9 is relevant in the case of Jesus ... Jesus does not speak of someone or something that comes. He is Himself the One who comes, and with His coming there comes everything that is to come. It is as this Coming One that He speaks. He does not speak, therefore, of an assumption of power which has still to take place, or does so in some other way, but of that which is accomplished as He Himself comes. It is He who accomplishes it as He speaks. What He proclaims becomes actuality the moment He does so. His proclamation is the blast of the trumpet which not only indicates but inaugurates the new year of the Lord (v. 18 f.), allowing every man to return unto his own possession, and opening all prisons and remitting all debts, as in Lev. 25$^{8f\cdot}$. (IV, 2, p. 197 and 204 f. The Royal Man.)

The time we mean when we say Jesus Christ is not to be confused with any other time. Just as man's existence became something new and different altogether, because God's Son assumed it and took it over into unity with His God-existence, just as by the eternal Word becoming flesh the flesh was able not to repeat Adam's sin, so time, by becoming the time of Jesus Christ, although it belonged to our time, the lost time, became a different, a new time. (I, 2, p. 51. God's Time and Our Time.)

HEBREWS 13$^{20f\cdot}$. (VI)

SECOND SUNDAY AFTER CHRISTMAS

MATTHEW 2$^{13\text{-}23}$ (I)

1 PETER 4$^{12\text{-}19}$ (II)

The Roman Church is quite right when in its legends and teaching concerning the saints it understands and portrays them all as great sufferers

. . . When his own forces are reduced, when he is robbed of more than one of the aids which he values, when he is pushed into the corner and his back is against the wall, when he stands on unsafe and possibly crumbling ground and is thus thrown back with all the greater intensity on God and referred to the strength which comes from the covenant with Him, the Christian who takes up his cross and bears it will on this basis set his hand to the work with renewed willingness and energy, and although he may not do better or greater things, he will certainly do those which, since a limit has not yet been set, or is not yet felt or burdensome, will certainly be more tested and purified and substantial, and may indeed by better and greater, than ever before. There can be no doubt that every genuine good work of the Christian acquires finally the fiery glow mentioned in v. 12. (IV, 2, p. 609. The Dignity of the Cross.)

Thus those who, like Christians, suffer something corresponding in their little passions, as a reflection and likeness of His great passion, may rest assured that their suffering takes place (v. 13) in the light of the Easter revelation towards which He moved in His great passion. It thus has a goal and horizon in a future analogous to the Easter revelation of Jesus Christ. Hence they can and may expect no other than their existence in fellowship with the One who rose again and lives as the Crucified and Slain. They do not suffer absolutely, but in this expectation, in movement to this future, on the way to the revelation of their life with His, in participation in His life. This is the decisive reason why the Christian cannot be ashamed of the Gospel as the Word of the cross, why he may glory in afflictions, why he may rejoice in them, why he may know and experience them as a grace. Those who fight as witnesses of Jesus Christ and in fellowship with His suffering may fight under the promise of His resurrection and therefore in glorious hope. There fight becomes and is necessarily a good fight. (IV, 3, p. 642. The Christian in Affliction.)

Cf. also IV, 1, p. 616 f.; III, 4, p. 676, 681 f.

JOHN 12⁴⁴⁻⁵⁰ (III)

Cf. on John 12⁴⁴⁻⁵⁰ New Year's Eve.

ROMANS 8²⁴⁻³⁰ (IV)

Man might ask God for anything. The whole of human egoism, the whole of human anxiety, cupidity, desire and passion, or at least the whole of human short-sightedness, unreasonableness and stupidity, might flow into prayer, as the effluent from the chemical factories of Basel is discharged into the Rhine. What will be the result if it is this needy and doubtful asking of ours that constitutes the nature of prayer? But if God is not uneasy in this regard, we certainly need not be. We have already spoken of some of the smaller but undoubtedly effectual catalysts of human asking. To true prayer belong thanksgiving, repentance and worship.

Where these elements are at work, each will in its own way contribute to the purity of our asking, to the ordering and cleansing of our privation and desire. And the great catalyst in view of which we need have no anxiety about that danger is that this is not just any kind of asking but the asking addressed to God at His command. We may again think of the intervention of Jesus Christ and the Holy Spirit which makes our human asking a movement in the cycle which goes out from God and returns to God. (III, 4, p. 100 f. Prayer.)

Prayer can be the recognition that we accomplish nothing by our intentions, even though they be intentions to pray. Prayer can be the expression of our human willing of the will of God. Prayer can signify that for good or evil man justifies God and not himself. Prayer can be the human answer to the divine hearing already granted, the epitome of the true faith which we cannot assume of ourselves. We do not speak of true prayer if we say " must " instead of " can ". According to Rom. $8^{26f.}$ the way from " can " to " must " is wrapped in the mystery at the gates of which we here stand. With this reference we do not give anyone a means by which he can count on succeeding in his work. It must be said, however, that it is hard to see how else there can be successes in this work but on the basis of divine correspondence to this human attitude: "Lord, I believe; help thou mine unbelief." (I, 1, p. 23 f. [25]. Dogmatics as an Act of Faith.)

The relationship with Jesus Christ in which we must suffer is sufficient to overrule our suffering and the gift of our whole life for good (v. 28). In this relationship the worst and the harshest thing that we can encounter, and do encounter, is our inevitable death in time, with which we must finally profess this relationship. But even this, this imminent end of all things, is not only not unbearable—for in its unbearable reality it has all been borne for us by Jesus Christ—but is in fact the outwardly bitter, yet inwardly sweet, promise of the eternal life which has been won for us by Him. To grasp this promise, to be permitted to live with it already in this life as with the certainty in comparison with which everything else pales into uncertainty—this is what is meant be believing in God's Word. (II, 1 p. 421. The Patience and Wisdom of God.)

Finally . . . nothingness, even though it does not will to do so, is forced to serve God, to serve His Word and work, the honour of His Son, the proclamation of the Gospel, the faith of the community, and therefore the way which He Himself wills to go within and with His creation until its day is done. The defeated, captured and mastered enemy of God has as such become His servant. Good care is taken that he should always show himself to be a strange servant, and therefore that his existence should remind us who and what he used to be, and therefore that at the sight of him we can never cease to flee to the One who alone has conquered him and has the keys to his prison. Yet it is even more important to reflect that good care is taken by this One that even nothingness should be one of the things of which it is said that they must work together for good to them that love Him. (III, 3, p. 367 f. God and Nothingness.)

Cf. on Revelation 3$^{1\text{-}6}$ Second Sunday in Advent.

Cf. also II, 1, p. 634 f.; III, 4, p. 90.

MATTHEW 7$^{13,\ 14}$ (V)

The New Testament term *thlipsis* " affliction " signifies the experience of pressure which is exercised on a man from without by relationships or by a hostile and menacing environment, over the development, power and duration of which he has no control, which simply comes upon him as " tribulation, " and which he has simply to endure as long as it lasts. . . . For the most part the word signifies the external pressure to be endured by Christian existence as such. The Christian has to suffer under this pressure. He is assailed by it. It leads him into temptation. He can and should prove himself a Christian under it. His way is a narrow way (*hodos tethlimmene*). We are obviously reminded of Dürer's rider between death and the devil . . . " The Christian in Affliction. " Our present reference is to the additional, specific pressure to which he is exposed because he is a Christian . . . and which does not affect others, no matter how severely they may be afflicted in other respects. Even in the affliction which strikes the Christian as such we have . . . a matter of public and even universal interest. What is at issue in the existence of the Christian as such, in his witness, is the relationship between God and the world and the world and God. As the action in which, called by God, he must intercede for the world is one of ministry, so his passion or suffering under the affliction caused by the world must be one of ministry. Ultimately and basically, therefore, it does not concern himself alone but in a very real sense all other men, even those who cause it. Yet this is true only ultimately and basically, *sub specie aeternitatis*. In the first instance it is he and he alone who has to undergo and endure his affliction, whereas others, even though they do not in practice directly or indirectly cause it, can only be present as more or less sympathetic spectators, not suffering it themselves, but watching how he undergoes and wrestles with it. (IV, 3, p. 614 f. The Christian in Affliction.)

NUMBERS 13–14 (VI)

What follows in face of this situation is majestic: " Then Moses and Aaron fell on their faces before all the assembly of the congregation of the children of Israel " (v. 5). They did not try to contradict it. They did not speak any word of warning or exhortation. When the people of Yahweh holds back, the only hope for this people is Yahweh Himself: the absolute prostration of worship before Him; the intercession of those who know Him for those who do not, of those who persist in His calling and the certainty of His promise for those who forget and deny and surrender it. Yet in the first instance we are not told of any intercession, nor is there any express reference to Yahweh. We are simply told that they fell on their faces before this crowd in all the madness of its anxiety . . . The story ends on a dark and unconciliatory note (vv. 39–45). " The people mourned greatly " when Moses reported what had happened. They suddenly realise that they have sinned. But it does not appear . . . that their con-fession of sin goes so very deep, when early the following morning they come to Moses armed and ready to march northwards into the land: " Lo, we be here . . . " Has their fear of the death which they desired in the wilderness, and which has been ordained for them, suddenly become greater than their fear of the giants? At any rate, they are not ready to accept the destiny which now impends in consequence of their own guilt. They will march out and fight. ,But they can do this only in defiance of the command of Yahweh. The courage of those who are anxious is no more pleasing to Him than their cowardice . . . The only note of comfort at the end of the story—apart from the existence of the little ones about whom they have been so anxious (v. 31)—is that in this careless enterprise the care-ridden Israelites did not take with them the ark of God, and there-fore it was not involved in the catastrophe (v. 44). (IV, 2, pp. 578–583. The Sloth and Misery of Man.)

THE EPIPHANY

MATTHEW 2[1-12]   (I)

Astrology is almost universally condemned in the Bible. The only exception which calls for notice is the remarkable one of the story of the wise men from the East, of whom it is said uncritically that they . . . It can hardly be denied that the Evangelist presupposes a given reality of this occurrence and therefore of the whole possibility of astrology, and that he draws upon it as such in his presentation of the miraculous birth of Jesus Christ. But this does not mean that he justifies the action of the Magi or gives an invitation or even permission to imitate it and thus to make use of what is acknowledged to be a real possibility. The fact that some pagans are chosen, like the Magi, is not a vindication or commendation of their paganism. And when this story tells us that in the form of a comet, or (as it was later assumed) a conjunction of Jupiter and Saturn, there appeared a kind of holy star with this extraordinary function, the exception to the rule only confirms that it is not the normal function of the stars to give such signs . . . The Old Testament unquestionably reckons with the reality of these possibilities—but they are not to be used by the people of God . . . Why is it that this biblical rejection of astrology and star-worship is so necessary and so powerful? . . . The specific reason is obviously to be found in the fact that we have here a *corruptio optimi* which as such is *pessima.* The decisive fact is that the heavenly bodies are to " rule " in a way corresponding to the destiny given them in their creation, and that this is not the case when they are worshipped or even consulted by man. In both cases an objective order of God's creation is disturbed when man erroneously alienates the heavenly bodies from their specific destiny as images of the divine creation of light: ostensibly in their own favour, by exalting them to be lords and deities or at least teachers and counsellors; but in reality to the detriment of their real function, and for that reason to God's dishonour and man's destruction. They then cease to be signs and *media* of instruction for the history of the covenant. They lose their proper dignity when in their own fulness they take precedence of what they should depict, of what they should reveal in their transparency; or when what they should depict is not sought in the grace and judgment of the Word of God but in a supposed disclosure of other, arbitrarily invented necessities of human life. (III, 1, p. 165 f. Creation and Covenant.)

ISAIAH 60[1-6] (II)

It is particularly the teaching of the book of Isaiah which makes it clear that as such the last day which is the day of redemption for Israel will also be the day of redemption for the nations—the day of judgment, too, but, as the day of the last judgment, the day of redemption. It will then be revealed to the nations that it is not in vain and not for its own sake that Israel was and is, that its divine election and calling and all the history which followed in its brighter or darker aspects was no mere episode but an epoch, was not accidental but necessary, that its purpose was not a particular one, but the universal purpose of its mission, that its existence was the existence of a light for all men, a light which was once overlooked, but which then shone out unmistakably in the great darkness which covered the earth (v. 1—we may also recall the four rivers of Paradise in Gen. 2[19f.], and the river which flows out of the temple in Ezek. 47[1-12]). It will then be the case actually and visibly that " salvation is of the Jews " (Jn. 4[22]). All the texts quoted speak of this in their varied eschatological imagery. They make it plain that the race as a whole is not forgotten in the import- ance of those shattering events between Yahweh and Israel. . . . (IV, 1, p. 31. The Covenant as the Presupposition of Reconciliation.)

Cf. also IV, 3, pp. 56–60.

MATTHEW 3[13-17] (III)

To use for once the searching language of historical research and teaching, the story of the baptism of Jesus contains the aetiological " cult-legend " which creatively indicates the origin of Christian baptism. If·so desired, it might be stated thus. But perhaps instead of depositing it *ad acta* under this title, it might be more interesting to consider its significance in so far as there are legitimate grounds on which to do so. This is what we shall now attempt. (IV, 4, p. 52. The Foundation of the Christian Life.)

What John the Baptist " saw " by Jordan (and we have to remember that it is quite definitely a matter of vision according to the texts)—the heavens opened, and the descent of the Spirit like a dove upon Jesus as He came up from the waters of Jordan—was not just the individual event of that particular moment, as though Jesus had only now come to participate in the Spirit whom He had hitherto lacked. The voice which the Baptist hears from heaven says that this " is " (not " has now become ") my beloved Son . . . It is a matter of the revelation and knowledge of the man Jesus by John as the man who stands at the threshold between the old covenant and the new and is therefore the first to receive it. What we have here, in anticipation of the Easter revelation, is the first proclamation of the reality of Jesus before the eyes and ears of this man. Jesus is the beloved Son of God. (IV, 2, p. 324. The Exaltation of the Son of Man.)

As attested by His letting Himself be baptised with them and like them, Jesus thus entered on His Messianic office. Indeed, He here began the discharge of this office which was completed on the cross of Golgotha. In this office the main concern will be, and already is, the justification, sanctification and vocation of this whole wretched people. Already, then, those who with him and like Him are baptised by John are passive participants in His death, not in virtue of their own baptism, but in virtue of the fact that Jesus lets Himself be baptised with them and like them, and that He therewith enters upon, and begins to exercise, His saving office. (IV, 4, p. 15. Baptism with the Holy Spirit.)

Cf. also IV, 1, p. 259.

ISAIAH 2$^{1-5}$ (IV)
MARK 1$^{9-15}$ (V)

This saying (v. 10 f.) is not to the effect that an earthly man is approved and applauded from heaven, but that One has come from God and therefore from heaven, and has become man and earthly. (III, 3, p. 436. The Kingdom of Heaven.)

He " came, " bringing the " glad tidings " . . . (v. 14) . . . This is certainly more than a mere announcement. It is an actual irruption rather than mere imminence. If the kingdom could only be announced prior to its manifestation with the coming of Jesus as the Bearer of God's good news, in and with Him there also came, in hidden but very real form, the kingdom and therefore the fulness of time . . . When Jesus came, all the promises and prophecies of the Old Testament were fulfilled. No more was now needed than that this coming should run its course in time. The " year of grace, " the " great and glorious day of the Lord, " the true Sabbath of which the weekly Sabbath was only a sign, the Sabbath kept by God and man together, was not only at the doors but had actually dawned. If the good news of God was that the time was fulfilled, nothing less could have happened . . . This means (Eph. 1⁹ᶠ·) a complete re-appraisal of the human situation . . . The only real reason why men (before Christ) had time at all was that—although they did not realise it, apart from the prophets who prophesied " until John "—this day was to come. And the men after Christ have time only in order to orientate their lives in the light of this day which in the series of days has now appeared once and for all and is proclaimed with an explicit imperative. (III, 2, pp. 459–461. Man in His Time; cf. p. 622.)

Cf. also IV, 4, pp. 52–68 and p. 76.

2 TIMOTHY 1⁷⁻¹⁰ (VI)

Note that the relation between the two aeons is a relation of decision ("then "—" but now " v. 10; Col. 1²⁶; Rom. 16²⁶). The decision is made; that is the present; that is the proper content of the New Testament witness. (I, 2, p. 54. The Time of Revelation.)

It is not the New Testament understanding of time as such which makes man fearless, but He to whom the New Testament with its understanding of time bears witness. He has utterly destroyed death, i.e., not merely dying, but the nothingness which threatens and lurks behind it, and brought life and immortality to light (v. 10). He says: " Fear not! " He takes from the recognition and apprehension of our unique opportunity the atmosphere of anxiety, care and oppresion, and all the self-deception which derives from the fear of death and is really a fear of life. He removes the atmosphere in which our opportunity cannot be known or apprehended at all but can only be missed. He makes the recognition and apprehension of it the important, free, joyful, serious and responsible life work which it is as the required work of human obedience. He does this who by His dying and rising again is Himself our hope in face of our dying—God for us where we can no longer in any sense be for ourselves. (III, 4, p. 594. The Unique Opportunity.)

Cf. also II, 2, p. 597 f.

FIRST SUNDAY AFTER EPIPHANY

LUKE 2⁴¹⁻⁵² (I)

" They understood not the saying . . . " (v. 50) . . . How could the God worshipped in Jerusalem suddenly be His special Father and the temple His Father's house in particular? How could this Father suddenly intervene between their Son and themselves as His parents, and this Father's house between Him and the home in Nazareth? How could the first commandment fail to refer Him plainly and simply and directly to a keeping of the fifth in its obvious patriarchal sense? What was the new factor which suddenly seemed to alienate Him here from His parents and the obedience which He owed to them? The riddle is in fact insoluble for

any patriarchal or even matriarchal conception and interpretation of the
fifth commandment, and since such a conception and interpretation has to
a large extent been constantly accepted, or has been reaccepted, even in
the Christian Church, we need not be surprised that the important reserva-
tion expressed in the story of the twelve-year-old Jesus has not been
properly effectual in the sphere of the Christian Church, even though it
not only poses the riddle but also gives us the obvious answer in the conclusion (v. 51) . . . Jesus did not seek to evade the authority of His parents.
It is simply that He took it seriously—more seriously than they themselves
could realise and understand. He did not break with them, but was the
more genuinely bound. He showed this by returning with them as a
matter of course to Nazareth and remaining subject to them. The further
point . . . that " his mother kept all these sayings in her heart " . . . means
that she preserved them inextinguishably in the depths of memory. The
same phrase is used when it is said of Mary (Lk. 2^{19}) that she kept and
pondered in her heart the happenings in Bethlehem on the night of the
nativity. In both cases the meaning is that she took note of the
incident even though she did not penetrate its significance, or better
that even though she did not yet grasp its meaning, she took serious
note of it, regarding it as a problem but no longer as a tormenting problem,
accepting the unintelligible with the intelligible, i.e., the direct obedience
of the child to God together with the indirect in the form of the obedience
which He obviously did not fail to offer to His parents. (III, 4, p. 250.
Parents and Children.)

Cf. also III, 2, p. 57.

FIRST, SECOND AND THIRD SUNDAY AFTER EPIPHANY

ROMANS 12$^{1-6,\ 6-16b,\ 16c-21}$ (II)

Paul . . . summons his readers to present their bodies, their whole
existence (quite irrespective of its value before God and for others or
themselves), and to offer it up as a living sacrifice, holy and acceptable to
God. This is the " reasonable service " which they are both permitted
and commanded: the only true and reasonable and appropriate worship of
God . . . to be rendered with the decision and resolution of those who have
no option because they are disposed to make this sacrifice, because they
can dispose themselves only in accordance with this prior disposition,
because they are freed from the schematism of the world in which there
is no place for this presenting, because they are caught up in the renewing
of their mind and can will only this one thing. (IV, 2, p. 365. The
Direction of the Son.)

The community is betrayed into alienation when instead of or side by
side with the voice of the Good Shepherd to whom it belongs it hears the
voice of a stranger to whom it does not belong but to whom it comes to

belong as it hears his voice. This is something which does not have to happen, but which can happen in so far as it is in the world and forms a part of it. It does not have to happen, for it is not alienated by the mere fact that it belongs to the framework of the habits and customs and views of the men of this particular time and place and speaks their language and shares their general limitations and aspirations, rejoicing with them that do rejoice and weeping with them that weep (v. 15). Alienation takes place when it allows itself to be radically determined and established and engaged and committed and imprisoned in this respect ... It is always alienated when it allows its environment, or spontaneous reference to it, to prescribe and impose a law which is not identical with the Law of the Gospel ... As and so far as it hears this law as a law, it does not hear the voice of the Good Shepherd but that of a stranger. It hears the voice of the world in one of its phenomena, accommodating itself to it, being "conformed" (v. 2) to its pattern, and therefore belonging to it. (IV, 2, p. 667. The Upbuilding of the Community.)

In the " measure of his faith " (v. 3, 16) each has the honour due him and therefore the true honour of which he cannot boast because he has it either before God or before men or in his own heart, either in the world or in the Church, but which he can only have. (III, 4, p. 668. Honour.)

From what we have seen, Christian hope it too high a thing for the Christian not to have to seek afresh each new day and hour the freedom which he has and uses. Only the breath of the living God makes him a living man. That God should not take His Holy Spirit from him, but constantly grant him a new and right spirit (Ps. $51^{11\text{-}12}$), must be the continual if confident sigh and cry of the Christian. How else can he do that whereto he is called? " Not slothful in business; fervent in spirit; serving the Lord; rejoicing in hope; patient in tribulation " (v. 11 f.), the Christian will stride out of the present into the future if according to the last link in the chain he continues " instant in prayer. " (IV, 3, p. 942. Life in Hope.)

It is the will of God the Creator that man, as His creature, shall be responsible before Him. In particular, His command says that man is to keep His holy day as a day of worship, freedom and joy, that he is to confess Him in his heart and with his mouth, and that he is to come to Him with his requests ... The fact that we should " pray without ceasing " (v. 12; 1 Thess. 5^{17}) is not a suggestion to cease praying at definite times. (III, 4, p. 47 f. Freedom Before God.)

The " continuing instant in prayer " (v. 12, cf. Lk. 18^1 and Acts 1^{14}) must not be misunderstood at this point and made an excuse for abstaining from prayer altogether by appeal to the need for " constant adoration. " This is the inevitable result when prayer does not become an actual permission and necessity, a direct command, and when it is not observed as such. The parallel to the Sabbath commandment claims our attention. If prayer is to become and be the underlying note and basis of all human activity, it needs to be continually exercised in particular. Prayer as a particular act in some sense repeats and represents the holy day in the midst of the week. In these sayings, then, Paul was not merely pointing to a perennial attitude of prayer, but also to the fact that the concrete activity of the community and of each individual Christian in observance of the holy day may and must have its continuation and concrete correspondence on the work-day. (III, 4, p. 89. Prayer.)

The solidarity of the community with the world consists ... not in a cunning masquerade, but rather in an unmasking in which it makes itself known to others as akin to them, rejoicing with them that do rejoice and weeping with them that weep (v. 15), not confirming and strengthening them in evil nor betraying and surrendering them for its own good, but confessing for its own good and thereby contending against the evil of others, by accepting the fact that it must be honestly and unreservedly among them and with them, on the same level and footing, in the same boat and within the same limits as any or all of them. How can it boast of and rejoice in the Saviour of the world and all men, or how can it win them (1 Cor. 9[19f.]) to know him and to believe in Him, if it is not prepared first to be human and worldly like them and with them? (IV, 3, p. 774 f. The Community for the World.)

If the divine command summons the righteous: v. 18, this is not a charter of liberty to the unrighteous. God Himself resists them. Nor does He do so merely by calling them to order through His command. He does not oppose their transgression merely by citing them before His eternal judgment. Even in this life, in the course of human history, He does not do it merely by arranging that they keep one another in check, or by the establishments of the state and its laws, law-courts and other measures adopted and executed according to His will. On the contrary, it may well be that He commissions those who hear His command, who therefore accept the fact that it is He who resists and repays evil, and who are therefore not angry but give place to wrath in terms of v. 19, personally to withstand the disorderly, He Himself making them wise and strong and willing to oppose to them in word and deed, not their own human No, but His divine No. This can happen. God can will that a man should not allow his neighbour to be insulted, robbed, injured or even killed by a third party. He can command him, even at the cost of injuring the assailant, to rush to the assistance of the victim even before he is left lying by the wayside and needs a Good Samaritan to succour him ... Hence, even if from different angles, man may do this because God demands it, so that it is not merely legitimate but imperative that he should do so, and he may do it with pure hands and a clear conscience. (III, 4, p. 434 f. The Protection of Life.)

Cf. II, 2, pp. 713–732; IV, 3, pp. 856–859; IV, 1, p. 497.

FIRST SUNDAY AFTER EPIPHANY

MATTHEW 11²⁵⁻³⁰ (III)

It is in complete hiddenness that Jesus is who and what He is (v. 27) . . .
Who and what He is as the human bearer of that unlimited omnipotence,
and who and what is the One that has given it to Him, what there is of
divine majesty in the giving and receiving of it—this and the revelation of it
is not something which can be laid down and judged and evaluated from
without. It does not shine out clear and bright and sparkling in the world.
It does not appear to men as such. Its form does not correspond to it but
contradicts it, so that—although it is its form—it cannot be deduced from
it, it is more likely not to be recognised in this form, and in the ordinary
course of things it will not be recognised. This door to the majesty of
Jesus can open only from within. (IV, 1, p. 178. The Way of the Son
of God into the Far Country.)

The closed circle of the knowing of the Son by the Father and the Father
by the Son (v. 27) can be penetrated only from within as the Son causes a
man to participate in this knowledge by His revelation. (IV, 2, p. 344. The
Direction of the Son.)

A yoke which is not easy, a burden which is not light (v. 30), so that
those who bear it cannot draw their breath properly (v. 29), is certainly not
the yoke or burden of Christ which He lays on those who come unto Him.
And we have always to remind ourselves that so long and so far as we find
no relief in being Christians or even theologians, but do so only at bottom
with sighs and complaints, like the Saxons so harshly baptised by
Charlemagne or the Indians brought to baptism in no less cruel ways by
the 16th-century Spaniards, to this extent we should quietly admit that we
are not really Christians or theologians at all, and have every reason to
look about for the proper way in which we may finally become such. A
forced Christian is not a Christian . . . There can be no question of an act
of compulsion here. (IV, 3, p. 529. The Goal of Vocation.)

Cf. I, 1, p. 119 [134], (Luther); IV, 2, p. 170, 759.

1 JOHN 5⁹⁻¹³ (IV)
JOHN 1⁴³⁻⁵¹ (V)

Is this really an account of calling at all? In the intention of the Gospel,
it undoubtedly is, and exactly as it is narrated . . . Even if we prefer to
follow the Synoptists . . . we have to allow that from the purely material
standpoint the Johannine account constitutes a strangely original statement which is needed alongside that of the Synoptists to point to their
background. It tells us that it needed only the initial impulse of the saying
of the Baptist, and certain men had to follow Him, and did follow Him,
and were thus commissioned and sent by Him, without any verbal
summons on the part of Jesus and with supreme objective necessity.

According to the view of the Fourth Evangelist there existed between Him and them a kind of predestinarian, and as such highly efficacious, bond which was simply disclosed, confirmed and actualised in their encounter ... It is legitimate and indeed necessary to see in this Johannine account an indication and description of the basic process enacted between Jesus and the disciples when He came to them and they to Him, and to derive from the Synoptic accounts the explication of this basic process, in which the man Jesus did not in the first instance need to call men verbally because in His being as the One He was, as the completed work of God, He was also the Word of God which as such had both the content and the power of calling. (IV, 3, p. 585 f. The Vocation of Man.)

Heaven forms in many respects a kind of divine horizon of all life on the earthly cosmos ... Sent by Jesus, the Holy Spirit descended upon the Church from heaven (Acts 2[2]; 1 Pet. 1[12]). From this standpoint it can be said of heaven that it is open (v. 51; Acts 7[55]). By this is meant that it is opened from the inside outwards, so that between the upper and the nether world, and therefore between God and man—the initiative being wholly from above, from God—there is the possibility and actuality of a direct relationship. (III, 1, p. 141. Creation and Covenant.)

Cf. III, 3, p. 180 and 501.

GENESIS 28[10-22a]   (VI)

God's omnipresence is bound up with the special nature of His presence in His revealing and reconciling work ontologically (in its reality) and not merely noetically (as far as our knowledge of it goes). It is only the One who is present in this special manner and place who is also the God present in the world as a whole ... And so, when Jacob, waking from his dream (Gen. 28[16f.]), says: "... How dreadful is this place! this is none other than the house of God, and this is the gate of heaven, " this is not simply an expression of pious emotion. On the contrary, it describes the objective condition that lies at the basis of the whole covenant between God and man. Had the Lord not been at this particular place in a particular way, and had it not really been this particular Beth-El, then the dreams of this particular man, Jacob, which he had at this particular place and not at any other, would have been idle fancies. And then the whole covenant between God and man as a definite covenant with definite men would have been invalid both at that time and for all time. (II, 2, p. 478 f. The Unity and Omnipresence of God.)

Cf. on John 17[1-8] Palm Sunday.

SECOND SUNDAY AFTER EPIPHANY

JOHN 2[1-11]   (I)
ROMANS 12[6-16b]   (II)

Cf. on Romans 12 First – Third Sunday After Epiphany.

ISAIAH 61¹⁻³ (III)

This verse (v. 1 f.) speaks in one breath both of the Lord Yahweh and also of a bearer of the message of salvation who is anointed by this Lord and on whom the Spirit of this Lord rests. (I, 1, p. 313 [359]. The Root of the Doctrine of the Trinity.)

The author of Isaiah 61² saw already typified in the year of Jubilee the " acceptable year of the Lord, " i.e., the time of Messiah's redemption, and actually this utterly extraordinary year is according to Lk. 4¹²ᶠ. the time of Jesus Christ. (I, 2, p. 51. God's Time and Our Time.)

Old Testament scholars tell us that the provisions of Lev. 25 were never actually put into practice, at any rate literally. If that is so, it merely serves to underline the prophetic character of this part of the Old Testament Law. Israel may have failed on this as in other respects, but its failure made no difference to the promise which the Law contained. Its years, the years of its people, of rich and poor alike, were not to drag on indefinitely, but to issue in a year of welcome festivity, liberation and restitution. And this perhaps is the time-consciousness of Old Testament man, not the consciousness of indefinite time, but that of the time of an era destined to culminate in another, and therefore the explanation of a coming time, the end and new beginning by which the present time with its limitation is already illuminated and relativised, being drawn and controlled by it as though by a powerful magnet. (III, 2, p. 457. Jesus, Lord of Time.)

1 CORINTHIANS 2¹⁻¹² (IV)

The " demonstration of the Spirit and (therefore) of power " (v. 4) is shown unmistakably by the context not to be a demonstration which Paul thought he had given or could give in Corinth, but the demonstration which God had given and would continue to give there in Jesus Christ. (IV, 1, p. 650. The Work of the Holy Spirit.)

The personal liberation of the Christian consists further in the fact that, borne as with eagles' wings above the abyss, he is delivered from indecision and set in action . . . The confusion of his personal life may break over him again like a mountainous sea. But if he is engaged in the act of a called witness, he cannot and will not wholly succumb to it. He will emerge again—*non omnis moriar* (I shall not die totally, Horace). In spite of it, he will give what is perhaps a very small, yet also perhaps a greater, demonstration of the Spirit and of power, expressing in lively fashion, even though in narrow limits, that which he has to attest, namely, that God has had mercy on His world and man, and that man has found in Him his Lord. Each act of obedience by the Christian is a modest proof, unequivocal for all its imperfection, of the reality of what he attests. (IV, 3, p. 669 f. The Liberation of the Christian.)

To the image of God in man which was lost in Adam but restored in

Christ there also belongs the fact that man can hear God's Word (v. 9).

There are men—God has vouchsafed that there should be such—who know God's gracious acts (v. 12), who search out the " deep things of God " (v. 10), who can discern what is spiritual spiritually (v. 13), men to whom one can speak about their acquaintance with the Word of God (Jas. 1^{21}), who can " stand " in faith (1 Cor. 16^{13}). (I, 1, p. 241 [276]. The Knowability of the Word of God.)

Cf. I, 2, p. 515 f.; II, 1, pp. 324–327.

MARK 2$^{18-22}$ (V)

"No man also seweth a piece of new cloth on an old garment: else the new piece that filled it up taketh away from the old and the rent is made worse. And no man putteth new wine into old bottles: else the new wine doth burst the bottles, and the wine is spilled, and the bottles will be marred: but new wine must be put into new bottles. " For Jesus, and as seen in the light of Jesus, there can be no doubt that all human orders (sc. the Law, economic relations, the political order, the family and religious and cultic institutions as well as economic) are this old garment or old bottles, which are in the last resort quite incompatible with the new cloth and the new wine of the kingdom of God. The new cloth can only destroy the old garment, and the old bottles can only burst when the new wine of the kingdom of God is poured into them. All true and serious conservatism, and all true and serious belief in progress, presupposes that there is a certain compatibility between the new and the old, and that they can stand in a certain neutrality the one to the other. But the new thing of Jesus is the invading kingdom of God revealed in its alienating antithesis to the world and all its orders. And in this respect, too, the dictum is true: *neutralitas non valet in regno Dei* (Bengel). There is thus concealed and revealed, both in what we called the passive conservatism of Jesus and the individual signs and penetrations which question the world of human orders as such, the radical and indissoluble antithesis of the kingdom of God to all human kingdoms, the unanswerable question, the irremediable unsettlement introduced by the kingdom of God into all human kingdoms. (IV, 2, p. 177. The Royal Man.)

The wedding (v. 19) is in full swing, the Bridegroom is among His guests—this is the great change as compared with the sphere of the Baptist, and this change has come about with the intervening history of Jesus Christ. The dawn has given way to full morning, and the joy, the initial joy of the friend of the Bridegroom when he heard his voice, has now been fulfilled (Jn. 3^{29}). (IV, 4, p. 82. The Foundation of the Christian Life.)

HEBREWS 12^{18-25a} (VI)

THIRD SUNDAY AFTER EPIPHANY

MATTHEW 8[1-13] (I)

Those who believe in Jesus Christ have to do ... with the Lord of heaven and earth, i.e., with the One who can dispose in the whole realm of reality distinct from God, and who does actually dispose always and everywhere, whether secretly or (in signs) openly. The attitude and decision of those who believe in Jesus Christ is that they take into basic account this possible and actual power of disposal, and that they are ready to be summoned always and everywhere to take it into account. When they adopt this attitude and decision, the secret of creation cannot and will not be concealed from them. The faith which Jesus did not find in Israel, but in the Gentile centurion of Capernaum, is that confidence in Him in which the centurion begs Him to speak only a word ... But at this point we should really refer to all the accounts in the Gospels which show us that Jesus really possessed this power and freely exercised it; that He found faith, i.e., this trust in His power, in all kinds of hopeless sufferers, and that these people simply counted on the fact that He could help them if He were willing to do so. Again, we should quote all the occasions when He rebuked His disciples—it is noticeable that this time it is always the disciples—for their " little faith " because they failed in practice, in a given instance, basically to count on His power over nature and therefore to live always as those who expect His control over all things and situations. (III, 1, p. 35. Faith in God the Creator.)

ROMANS 12[16c-21] (II)

Cf. on Romans 12 First–Third Sunday After Epiphany.

JOHN 4[5-14] (III)

In the second creation story water is the element of life necessary to the earth and man and granted to them by God in His mercy. It is the sum of the blessing for which man hopes in the cosmos and which again by the gracious power of God is actually granted to them. Passages like Dt. 11[10f.]; Ps. 65[9f.]; Ex. 17[2f.]; Amos 5[24]; Is. 8[6f.]; 12[3]; 30[25]; 35[6]; 43[19]; 44[3]; 49[10]; 58[11]; Jer. 14[22]; 17[4f.]; Ps. 1[3]; 23[2] are taken up again in the New Testament, where Jesus is described as the One who gives living water to drink (v. 10 f.), who even promises to the man who believes on Him (7[38]) that from his body streams of living water will flow and who in heaven will not cease to lead His own to streams of living water (Rev. 7[17]) ... The passages at the end of the Bible (Rev. 21[6]; 22[1, 17]) and the passage at the beginning of the Bible (Gen. 2[8-17]) agree particularly in emphasising that the waters which bring life and blessing proceed from one definite place and thence spread out in all directions. (III, 1, p. 279 f. Creation and Covenant.)

Cf. on John 3[1-15] Trinity Sunday.

ISAIAH 49[1-6] (IV)

A (second) important qualification of the Old Testament concept of the covenant arises from the conception of the final mission of Israel to the nations (in Isaiah). Why did God separate and take to Himself and address this people? In the older tradition this question was left unanswered. But now in the light of the future an answer is given . . . in the form of a prophecy . . . In the last days it will be wonderfully shown that the covenant of Yahweh with Israel was not an end in itself, but that it had a provisional and a provisionally representative significance. Israel had and has a mission—that is the meaning of the covenant with it. In Israel—this is what will be revealed in the last days—there is to be set up a sign and a witness to all peoples. The redemptive will of God is to be declared to all humanity. That is what we are told in the particularly important word to the Ebed Yahweh (v. 6): " It is a light thing that thou shouldest be my servant to raise up the tribes of Jacob, and to restore the preserved of Israel: I will also give thee for a light to the Gentiles, that thou mayest be my salvation unto the end of the earth. " (IV, 1, p. 28. The Covenant as the Presupposition of Reconciliation.)

Cf. on Isaiah 42[1-8] Second Sunday in Lent (Reminiscere).

MATTHEW 4[12-17, 23-25] (V)

According to . . . the so-called harmony of the Gospels and Acts, the outline of the life of Jesus is consciously and expressly conceived and presented as a combination or fusion of word and deed, of acts of oral proclamation, of preaching and teaching and of mighty works which are objectively verifiable and effective . . . Against the powerful and too spiritualised conception of the picture of Jesus in the 18th and 19th centuries, it was and is necessary to draw attention to this, especially in relation to the bodily aspect and the whole range of the mighty works of the New Testament . . . The acts of Jesus do not merely accompany His spoken words. It is clear that in the view of the New Testament writers the reported bodily acts of Jesus are to be understood as the decisive indication, declaration and attestation of the speaking subject and therefore of His words, so that they cannot in any sense be regarded as mere incidentals and accessories. " Another teacher or prophet might also have spoken some or all the words; but here spoke One equipped with unique authority. " And it must be added at once: " Another miracle worker might have done some or all the acts; but here One operates who stood at the dawn of the kingdom of God actualised in Him and who in virtue of this forgave sins " (K. L. Schmidt, Art. " Jesus, " RGG[3], III, 118). But the first contrast is of equal weight with the second: Jesus not only announced the forgiveness of sins but really effected it; He met the physically sick not only with sympathy and words of comfort, not only as a skilful doctor, but as the One who makes whole. He is the man He is precisely in the unity of His work as it is apprehensible in this second moment. The " Christian Science "which isolates the Jesus of this second apprehensible moment, and in the Saviour sees only the Healer, evidently constructs an abstraction as remote from the text and as illegitimate as the Liberal theology which clings only to Jesus the Teacher and at most to His personal life . . . The kingly rule of God which is operative and evident in this man comprises these two moments. They are not parallels in Him, or two intersecting lines, or two agreeing or concurring functions. They permit no choice. They cannot be considered independently. In and with one another they are the oneness and wholeness of this life. (III, 2, p. 330 f. Jesus, Whole Man.)

Cf. on Mark 1$^{9-15}$ The Epiphany.

ROMANS 1$^{14-17}$ (VI)

Gospel and Law as the concrete content of God's Word imply always a seizure of man. No matter what God's Word says to man *in concretissimo*, it always tells him that he is not his own but God's. If in the light of its origin in revelation, in Jesus Christ, we understand the Word of God as the epitome of God's grace, grace means simply that man is no longer left to himself but is given into the hand of God . . . If a man knew nothing of this power that both sustains and stimulates, both protects and punishes, both pacifies and disturbs, if he merely heard about it without knowing it as a power, he would only give evidence that he knew nothing of the Word of God. We are acquainted with the Word of God to the degree that we are acquainted with this power. We speak of God's Word when we speak in recollection and expectation of this power, and when we do so in such a way that we realise that this power of the Word of God is not one power among others, not even among other divine powers, but the one unique divine power which comes home to us, to which we are referred, in face of which we stand in decision between the obedience we owe it and the unfathomable inconceivability of disobedience, and consequently in the decision between bliss and perdition . . . Where God has once spoken and is heard, i.e., in the Church, there is no escaping this power, no getting past it, no acknowledgment of divine powers that are not summed up in this power, that are not related to the manner of this power and active in its mode (Mt. 28^{18}; Col. 1^{17}). (I, 1, p. 150 [170 f.] The Speech of God as the Act of God.)

It is part of the commandment of God the Creator that man shall not be ashamed of the Gospel. If he were, he would be guilty of the folly of being ashamed of himself, of his existence as a creature. It is to the Word of God, and therefore to the Gospel, that he is indebted for his existence and nature. He himself exists as, consciously or unconsciously, gratefully or ungratefully, he is a kind of receipt for the creative Word of God. If he wants to be what he is, he must want this receipt to find expression, and therefore not to be silent or to contradict itself. If he is a man free before

God, he is free to want this and to act accordingly. And as the commandment of God the Creator demands of him in all circumstances that he be a
man free before Him—free in the execution of his responsibility before
Him!—it definitely claims his readiness to bear witness to Him; and not
His readiness only, but also the movement from this readiness to the
execution, the act of confession. Confession is the confirmation, declaration and impartion of what is known. (III, 1, p. 73. Confession.)

Cf. II, 1, pp. 605–607.

FOURTH SUNDAY AFTER EPIPHANY

MATTHEW 8²³⁻²⁷   (I)

Inevitably the New Testament community finds its own story in the
account of the crossing of the lake by Jesus and His disciples. But what
serious or final relationship is there between this and its high position in
relation to other wordly structures. For what does it imply? To be sure,
the ship is impressivly manned by the disciples whom Jesus has already
chosen and called to be His apostles. Carefully attired, according to
mediaeval fancy, in the correct episcopal vestments, they are the rowers . . .
They are not a motley group of inexperienced novices. Nor are they alone
with a mere tradition or recollection of the words and person of their Lord.
Jesus Himself is with them. But He . . . was asleep. And when the great
storm arose . . . these men who were elect and called, who had already
received so many promises and consolations in respect of their own existence
as His people, who had indeed the assurance of His own presence, seemed
to be cast back upon their own faith and in the last resort upon its bold
action in exercise of their seamanship. But lo! their apostolic office, their
episcopal habits, their experience, their tradition, even the living but sleeping Jesus among them, all appear to be useless . . . They are terrified that
the ship and they themselves and Jesus with them will all perish, that all
will be up with them, as the community has often since had cause to fear
and has actually feared. Basically, of course, it has never had any true
reason, but it has certainly had occasion enough . . . The story ends with
the noteworthy statement that . . . " they feared exceedingly " (Mark 4⁴¹)
. . . What was this fear? It was the great and necessary and legitimate fear
of the Lord which, as the beginning of wisdom, began with the end of the
little and unnecessary fear which could only lead the community to despair
of itself, its apostolate, its faith and indeed its Lord. "What manner of
man is this? " Could the community do any better, or show itself in any
better way to be the people placed at that high point, than by letting itself
be gripped and moved by this great and holy and joyous fear in face of His
self-declaration? It became and was indeed the light of the world, the
pillar and ground of truth, by letting itself be seized with this fear when it
saw Him as the One who showed Himself to be its Lord within world-

occurence. This was the decisive happening on the crossing. (IV, 3, p. 733 f. The People of God in World-Occurrence.)

ROMANS 13$^{8-10}$ (II)

The life-act of the Christian as such (v. 10b) finds its climax and visible expression in love . . . A love of God which does not involve also the required love of the neighbour is not the required love of God (v. 8b) . . . the Law requires a definite action. This action is love. This love is the fulfilment of the Law. The man who loves has done what the Law demands; he has fulfilled the Law. The same could not be said of faith (abstractly taken and considered), nor could it be said of hope and patience. Faith, too, is an act . . . But as faith it is the act of a pure and total reception. As this act it does not have to fulfil the Law . . . but it comes thankfully from the fulfilment which has already taken place for us in Jesus Christ. But Paul . . . knows nothing of a faith abstractly taken and considered, but only faith which has love as the complement (and also hope and patience and peace) within the one vital act of the Christian. And in love (not an abstract love, but the love by which faith works), and therefore in the self-giving which corresponds to this reception, the Christian fulfils the Law, doing that which God requires and which is right in His sight. (IV, 2, p. 732. The Problem of Christian Love.)

MATTHEW 14$^{22-34}$ (III)

The call to discipleship binds a man to the One who calls him. He is not called by an idea of Christ, or a Christology, or a christocentric system of thought, let alone the supposedly Christian conception of a Father-God. How could these call him to discipleship? They have neither words nor voice. They cannot bind anyone to themselves . . . Again, discipleship is not the recognition and adoption of a programme, ideal or law, or the attempt to fulfil it . . . In practice the command to follow Jesus is identical with the command to believe in Him . . . Discipleship consists in faith and it then at once consists in the act of obedience rendered to Jesus . . . Peter (v. 29) would not have believed if he had not obeyed Jesus' call to come, and left the boat and gone to him on the water. But Peter . . . did believe, and therefore he did at once and self-evidently that which was commanded. It is true . . . he looked at the raging wind instead of Jesus (v. 30), and was afraid, and doubted, and could go no further, but could only sink, and would have sunk if he had not been gripped by the hand of the One in whom he had so little faith. But this only shows that the disciple cannot obey without believing, or conversely that when he believes he must and can obey, and actually does so. (IV, 2, pp. 536–538. The Call to Discipleship.)

No matter how great the anxiety of the Christian may be or seem to be, he need not regard it as so great that the lordship of his Lord in face of it can consist only in a static superiority and not one which dynamically sallies out against it at the point where it contains it . . . Even though it does still totally embrace, darken and call in question his human and even his Christian being, it cannot prevent him from crying to Him like sinking Peter: " Lord, save me. "   It cannot prevent him from running to Him even in the midst of his anxiety like a child on the dark street running to meet its father as he returns home in the evening. He can and should pray to the God who encounters him in this Lord of his. His vocation is a vocation to prayer: not to particularly pious, fervent or beautiful prayer— the prayer of Peter could not be described as such—but simply to prayer. Nor can any anxiety, however great, impair, arrest or reverse this liberation for crying to God. (IV, 3, p. 672 f. The Liberation of the Christian.)

COLOSSIANS 2$^{8\text{-}15}$ (IV)

We recall once more Rom. 6^4 and Col. 2^{12} with their vivid description of baptism as a solemn burial of the old man. Burial is a renunciation of the deceased. To bury a man is to part from him for ever. Baptism is the burial of a dead man by the community and the candidate. It is their parting from him. They themselves were the dead man when he was alive: they themselves as men who sinned, and who above all sought to justify and cleanse themselves; they themselves as men who incurred guilt and came under condemnation by so doing . . . They themselves have not put to death this one who is now dead. He died when Jesus Christ died on the cross in place of the legalistic or libertine sinner. But he is now dead in both forms. He can only be buried. He can only be renounced. This is what has come about in baptism. Throughout the future they will have to remember that the old man is buried, that they have buried him, that they themselves, following the great decisive divine renunciation which took place and was revealed in Jesus Christ, have renounced him: " I renounce the devil and all his works, " as the candidate says to-day in the Roman office, though represented, of course, by his godparents. (IV, 4, p. 160. The Foundation of the Christian Life.)

Cf. on Colossians 2$^{3\text{-}10}$ Christmas Day and on Colossians 1$^{15\text{-}23}$ The Ascension Day; cf. also I, 2, p. 107, 731 f.; IV, 4, pp. 118–120.

EXODUS 14$^{8b\text{-}16b,\ 21\text{-}23,\ 26\text{-}31}$ (V)
III, 1, p. 146.

EPHESIANS 1$^{15\text{-}23}$ (VI)

" To know him " (v. 17) is the work of the Spirit of wisdom and reve- lation for whose gifts we pray . . . The terms faith and love and obedience are always near when reference is made to knowledge. Knowledge in the biblical sense directly includes, indeed, it is itself at root *metanoia*, conver- sion, the transformation of the *nous*, and therefore of the whole man, in accordance with the One known by him. Note should be taken of what is included in the knowledge of Jesus Christ according to v. 18 f.: " That the eyes of your understanding should be enlightened; that ye may know what is the hope of his calling, and what the riches of the glory of his inheritance in the saints, and what is the exceeding greatness of his power to us-ward who believe. " To know Him is to come into the sphere of this incomparable power of His. (IV, 3, p. 185. The Glory of the Mediator.)

Cf. on Luke 1[67-69] First Sunday in Advent.

When the New Testament speaks of Jesus Christ and His community it really speaks of the goal (and therefore of the origin and beginning) of all earthly things. Jesus Christ and His community is not an additional promise given to men ... It is not a further stage in actualisation of the divine will and plan and election which are the purpose of creation. It concludes this process. It is the complete fulfilment of the promise. It is the goal and end of all the ways of God. It is *the* eschatological reality. It cannot be surpassed, deepened or enriched by anything still to come ... For God has given Jesus Christ to be the " head over all things " to the community which is His body and in which He has His own divine fulness and His whole divine fulfilment (v. 22 f.). This completed fact is still to be shown to the cosmos. This completed fact must be revealed as the meaning of the whole cosmos. But it is already a completed fact. There is no salvation which has not already come to the world in the death and resurrection of Jesus Christ and the existence of the community which He has purchased by His blood and has gathered and still gathers by His Holy Spirit. (III, 2, p. 301. Man in His Determination as the Covenant-Partner of God.)

FIFTH SUNDAY AFTER EPIPHANY

MATTHEW 13[24-30]   (I)

At all times and in all situations holy members of the holy Church (Augsburg VII), and therefore true Christians, were and are the men assembled in it who are thereto elected by the Lord, called by His Word, and constituted by His Spirit: just so many, no more and no less, these men and no others. It is He who knew them and willed them and created them as such. It is He who knows and preserves them as His saints. But are there " others" in His community ... who take their confession on their lips and in some way participate in the life of the community—but only in appearance, who are not therefore saints, true Christians? It would be an obvious exaggeration to try to maintain that this is not possible. There is no doubt ... that the Church is also a human *civitas* or *societas*, a union of men. Hidden in this it lives as the body of Jesus Christ. But it does exist and recruit as this union on the basis of human insights and judgments and decisions. We cannot expect that these human insights and judgments and decisions (conditioned and limited as such) will be plainly and automatically and directly identical with those of its Lord, or that they can prejudice or even anticipate His, His knowledge of men and resolve concerning them, His activity by which He makes them members of His body. It may well be that they are blessed and ratified by Him, and to that extent made in His name . . . But the community constitutes and recruits itself knowing the fact, and knowing it as its limit, that in this, too, it is in His hand and is thrown back on the hope of His ratification and blessing, on the free grace of His Holy Spirit. It can constitute and recruit itself only in faith in Him. In this respect, too, it must acknowledge His sovereignty. But this involves an acknowledgment that it may make mistakes, that even amongst those who belong to it in the eyes of men there may be some who are not members of His body, who are not at all elected and called by Him, who are not awakened by His Holy Spirit to faith in Him . . . There may be tares among the wheat and bad fish (v. 47 f.) amongst those which came into the net. Who knows how many tares? Who knows how many bad fish? There was a Judas even among the twelve apostles. And so Augsburg VIII reckons with the fact that " in this life there remain many false Christians and hypocrites and even notorious sinners among the faithful." It may well be, therefore, that the fellowship of the Church as such can only be called a *societas mixta*, and in that case only *improprie*, improperly, the body of Christ. (IV, 1, p. 696 f. The Being of the Community.)

COLOSSIANS 3¹²⁻¹⁷ (II)

According to v. 12 f. love is the sum of all the mercy, goodness, humility, long-suffering and mutual forbearance and forgiveness that those who are chosen and sanctified and loved by God are to " put on " as a garment which is prepared for them and suits them. It is the " bond of perfectness," the bond which unites all the individual elements, which embraces their activity, and from which they move unitedly to their goal. Love is the fulfilling of the Law (Rom. 13¹⁰) . . . It is the form of life which characterises the existence of the community and its members, and which is indispensable if they are what they are. (IV, 2, p. 784. The Act of Love).

The ascribing of the name of Kyrios to Jesus is wrapped in all manner of obscurity. But in view of the close connexion between the early Church and the Palestinian and Hellenistic Synagogue it cannot possibly have happened unawares and unintentionally that this word was at any rate used as well to translate the Old Testament name of God Yahweh-Adonai, and was then applied to Jesus. We are pointed in the same direction by the practical meaning of the name Jesus as the name in which they prophesied, taught, preached, prayed and baptised, in which sins were forgiven, demons driven out, and other miracles were done, in which His followers were to gather, in which they were to receive one another, in which they were to believe, on which they were to call, in which they were to be upheld, for the sake of which they were to be hated and despised, to renounce all their earthly possessions and even perhaps to die, in which again they are washed, sanctified and justified (1 Cor. 6[11]), and which is, so to speak, the place, the sphere, in which all they speak and do is to take place (v. 17). (I, 1, p. 400 [458] God the Son.)

Cf. on Colossians 3[12-17] Fourth Sunday After Easter (Cantate).

LUKE 13[22-30]   (III)

Jesus Christ is the hope of all men, and therefore also of non-Christians, of the heathen, of the theoretically or practically ungodly ... He is the hope of these others too. And supposing more importance is attached to those who are not yet Christians? ... Supposing His light shines brighter here, and His Word is more living and active? Supposing the unconverted are sometimes dearer to Him than the converted? Supposing the knowledge of Jesus Christ which divides Christians from non-Christians, when imparted to the latter in fulfilment of the promise seriously given to the heathen too, brings forth among them more rich and varied and useful fruits than among those who already know Him, so that the last are first and the first last? Supposing the Christian is deceived when he adjudges his fellow a non-Christian, because the knowledge of Jesus Christ has already found a lodging in him in a form which the Christian and perhaps the man himself does not recognise? Supposing, finally, the Christian is deceived as to his own Christianity, being more of a non-Christian than a Christian, and basically perhaps not really being a Christian at all? In face of these by no means irrelevant questions the Christian should be glad that he lives under the lordship of Jesus Christ who is the hope even of those who are not for Him as He is for them, and under the promise, and in the power of the promise, which is also given to non-Christians of every kind. (IV, 3, p. 364 f. The Promise of the Spirit.)

Cf. also on Luke 19[1-10] Third Sunday after Trinity.

These are the decisive statements on the Church in the confession of the Protestant Batak-Church of Sumatra (which was drawn up without any Western participation at a synod held at Sipoholon in November 1951): "We believe and confess: The Church is the congregation of those who believe in Jesus Christ and are called, gathered, sanctified and maintained by God through the Holy Spirit ... (The Church comes ...) from all lands and peoples and races and tribes and tongues, although their customs and laws are different. The unity of the Church (based on Eph. 4[4] and 1 Cor. 12[20]) differs from what is usually meant by worldly unity. For it is a spiritual unity." (IV, 1, p. 707. The Being of the Community: *Credo catholicam ecclesiam.*)

1 PETER 3[15b-22]   (IV)

Biblical study ... is not merely the affair of a few specialists but fundamentally of all the members of the community. For none is infallible, and all need to be subject to the control of the rest. And again, it might some day be asked of any Christian to give an answer to those without concerning " the hope that is in you " (v. 15). For this no little knowledge of the Bible, and indeed some understanding and therefore study, are indispensable. The statement: " I am a mere layman and not a theologian " is evidence not of humility but of indolence ... The Christian must also be in a position to see his way clearly and not to be constantly bewildered in the dramas, tragedies and comedies of the past and present history of the community ... Hence there is need of the catechism and even of some memory work. (IV, 3, p. 870 f. The Ministry of the Community.)

The task of every Christian ... is his task as a bearer of the Gospel to the others who still stand without. To what end? To bring them into the Church, to make them Christians? In the event this too, but the real point is that to all those who by reason of their being outside demand an account of the living hope that is in him this account should be given by what he does and what he leaves undone, by his work and word. More restless than the most restless, more urgent than the most urgent revolutionaries in his immediate or more distant circle, he asks: " Where art thou, peace of all the world? "—and he asks it the more restlessly and the more urgently because he is sure of this future peace, because he consciously looks and moves forward to the future which is filled by it. To him who is thus endowed and blessed there applies the " go " of Mt. 28^{19}, not as a member of a Christian collective, but very personally. Here are the marching orders which are given directly and specifically to him. (IV, 4, p. 200 f. The Foundation of the Christian Life; cf. also p. 211 f. and p. 122.)

The place taken by Christ at the right side of God is definitely not that of a privileged spectator of the divine activity. On the ancient oriental view, the one who sits or stands or simply is at the right hand of a ruler (v. 22; Rom. 8^{34}) is the one who in his person represents that of the ruler, acting for him in his name and with his authority. In the first instance, therefore, the fact that Christ is at the right hand of God means metaphorically that in His relationship to God He is this agent or grand vizier of God, His first official act being to pour out upon the community the Holy Spirit whom He for His part has received from the Father (Acts 2^{33}). (III, 3, p. 439. The Kingdom of Heaven.)

Cf. also III, 2, p. 441.

MATTHEW 13^{47-52} (V)

ISAIAH 28^{23-29} (VI)

LAST SUNDAY IN EPIPHANY

MATTHEW 17[1-9] (I)

The transfiguration . . . is a good example of how the apostles regarded the pre-Easter life of Jesus from the present of their own time. It might almost be said to anticipate the Easter-history as the latter does the return of the Lord. At a first glance it looks like any other miracle story. But it is really unique, for this time the miracle happens to Jesus Himself, and is not something performed by Him. It comes wholly from outside. He does not say or do anything to bring it about. Perhaps it is to be taken as a preliminary key to all the other miracles . . . We are obviously in close material proximity to the resurrection story . . . The transfiguration is the supreme prefigurement of the resurrection, and its real meaning will not be perceived until the resurrection has taken place. It is surprising that 2 Pet. 1[16f.], speaking of the apostles as eye-witnesses and preachers of the " power and coming of our Lord Jesus Christ," says nothing about the resurrection itself, but seems to regard the preceding transfiguration as more important . . . In Jn. 2[11] the account of the miracle of Cana in Galilee closes with the words: " This beginning of miracles did Jesus . . . and manifested forth his glory." This would seem to imply that the miracles of Jesus are to be taken as " signs " in the sense that they point to what He already was, to the hidden presence of the kingdom of God which would later be unveiled during the forty days in an abiding manifestation, in a tabernacling of the Lord in the midst of His disciples—a disclosure which will become definitive and universal at the end of all time in His coming again. That there are such signs, and that in the transfiguration, as in no other miracle, this sign is performed on Himself, shows that the mystery of His being revealed at the resurrection has not been acquired in the meantime but had been present all along and was in fact *revealed* at this later point. (III, 2, p. 478 f. Jesus, Lord of Time.)

2 PETER 1[16-21] (II)

According to the Gospel record, Moses and Elijah had actually stood by the side of Jesus when He was transfigured before their eyes, and had spoken with Him. This prophetic word was not therefore outmoded, but acquired genuine relevance for those who had their origin in the appearance of Jesus. It was confirmed in its character as a prophetic word pointing to the future and became an indispensable light on their path. The disciples did not come down from the mount alone, or as eschatological innovators, but in company with the ancient witnesses, accredited by the fulfilment of the long-prepared history of the covenant and salvation. It was in this company that they moved afresh to meet the coming Lord. The visible and palpable unity of prophecy and fulfilment, of fulfilment and prophecy, is what factually distinguishes their proclamation of " the

power and coming of our Lord Jesus Christ" from all " cunningly devised
fables," v. 16. (III, 2, p. 494. Jesus, Lord of Time.)

Cf. I, 2, pp. 503–526.

Exodus 3¹⁻¹⁰   (III)

If God does not meet us in His jealous zeal and wrath—exactly as He
meets Israel according to the witness of the Old Testament, exactly as He
meets it later in the crucifixion of His own Son—then He does not meet
us at all, and in spite of all our asseverations about divine love, man is in
actual fact left to himself. That man is not abandoned in this way, that
God is really gracious to Him, is shown in the fact that God confronts him
in holiness. It is in this way that God is present without him, taking over
and conducting the cause which sinful man is impotent to conduct himself.
It is in this way that God reconciles man to Himself. The fact that God
does not permit Israel, the righteous, or the Church to perish means that
He cannot allow them to go their own way, unaccused, uncondemned and
unpunished, when they are and behave as if they were people who do not
participate in this salvation and protection. The burning bush of Exod. 3²
cannot be consumed. But the unconsumed bush must burn. This bush
is Israel. And the flame which burns it but does not consume it is the
God of Israel, the holy God. (II, 1, p. 366. The Grace and Holiness of
God.)

When the Old Testament speaks of the " land " promised and then given
to this people, the primary meaning, of course, simply is the land of Canaan
commended to the fathers by God. But again, whatever the qualities of
this geographical entity must have been at the time, as such they are
wholly unsuited to exhaust the full meaning that lies in the conception of
the promised land. When we look beyond the conception of a land
" flowing with milk and honey " and the promises associated with it
(particularly when things were really not going well in this land), our gaze
is necessarily directed to the paradise lost and restored which is to be the
dwelling-place of this people, to the miraculously renewed earth upon
which this people will some day live amid the other happily and peaceably
united peoples. Thus the " land " is certainly Palestine, but with equal
certainty, in and along with this land, there is meant the quite different
land which is not actually visible in the history of Israel, because it is its
goal, because it is therefore outside it. The one land is waiting for the
other. (I, 2, p. 96. The Time of Expectation.)

It is significant enough that this revelation of the name (Ex. 3¹³ᶠ·) is in fact,
in content, the refusal to give a name, for " I am that I am " can hardly
mean more than that " I am He whose true name no one can utter. " By
its very wording the revealed name is intended to recall the hiddenness even
of the revealed God. But under this name, which in itself and as such pro-
nounces His mystery, God does reveal Himself to His people, i.e., He

begins, as Ex. 3 instructively shows, to have dealings with Israel. (I, 1, p. 317 f., 322 [335, 339 f.] The Root of the Doctrine of the Trinity.)

Cf. II, 1, p. 60 f.; IV, 3, p. 577 f.

REVELATION 1[9-18] (IV)

The speaker in v. 4, 8, 17; 4[8]; 21[6]; 22[13] is not God *in abstracto*, but God *in concreto*, God in His identity with the man Jesus. It is equally clear that when the context speaks of His being in time it implies much more than that time has a beginning, duration and end . . . I am He who has life in Himself, v. 17. That is to say, I am sovereign over my own being. Even as present I am He who was and will be. All this is applied to the being of the man Jesus in time. The all-inclusive " I am " rules out any notion that the three dimensions, past, present and future, simply follow one another in succession. The very fact that 1[8] puts the " I am " and the " which is " first is a plain warning. It means: " I am all this simultaneously. " I, the same, am; I was as the same; and I will come again as the same. My time is always simultaneously past, present and future . . . How the author of the Apocalypse came to adopt this view of Jesus is indicated by v. 17 f., where the formula: " the first and the last, he that liveth, " is immediately followed by the reference: " I was dead, and, behold, I am alive for evermore. " There is no doubt that all this is meant to be taken in a concrete sense. It is because He rose from the dead that He liveth. As I am in my time, all time is my time, my before or after. (III, 2, p. 465 f. Jesus, Lord of Time.)

Jesus Christ does actually speak. He does so in the promise of the Spirit as the Crucified. And as such He does not merely murmur or whisper, but through the centuries, and therefore here and now among us, He speaks with a voice " as the sound of many waters " (Rev. 1[15]). He speaks so clearly and powerfully that when His Word goes forth all the non-Christian and Christian clamour of the world is reduced to a dying murmur. Even when they hear Him only from afar, others can only ask in astonishment whether it is possible that He should not be heard, and issue a summons to hear His voice. His Word is the sound which would fill heaven and earth even if there were no ear to hear Him. It did so even when specific individuals had not done so. It will do so even if they hear it no longer . . . He speaks where all others think they do, but in reality only lisp and stutter. He has something to say, and says it, where all others want to say something but have nothing worth saying compared with what He says. (IV, 3, p. 409. The True Witness.)

Cf. also III, 4, p. 50; IV, 3, p. 290.

JOHN 7[10-18] (V)

It is true that Jesus does not seek His own glory (v. 18). He does not seek it at all (8[50]). If He honoured Himself, His honour would be nothing

(8⁵⁴). Nor does He receive glory from men (5⁴¹). Those who receive glory from each other cannot even believe (5⁴⁴). How could He belong to them? In short, the glory which a man may ascribe to himself, or allow others to ascribe to him, has nothing whatever to do with the glory of Jesus. His glory is greater and comes to Him from a very different source. The One who honours and glorifies Him is His Father (8⁵⁴; 17²²ᶠ·). The text 17⁵ is particularly plain in this regard ... If He who would neither glorify Himself nor allow others to glorify Him seemed in a sense to disappear as the Subject, He obviously reappears as the object of the divine glorifying (*doxazein*). An object lacking in will and energy? One series of texts (7³⁹; 11⁴; 12¹⁶, ²³) speaks absolutely of His being glorified as if it were a transfiguration or investiture which simply came upon Him. But they are misunderstood if we take them in this sense. In no event which takes place between the Father and the Son is the Son merely an object. The texts about the glorification of the Son by the Father are counterbalanced by others in which the roles are clearly reversed (v. 18; 14¹³). To the prayer of 17⁵ should be added the prayer of 12²⁸ ... Here already is a hint that according to some most important passages of the Gospel the two aspects are to be brought into integral connexion with each other: " If God is glorified in him, God shall also glorify him in himself, and shall straightway glorify him " (13³²). And in the reverse order: " Father ... glorify thy son, that thy son also may glorify thee " (17¹). " Now is the son of man glorified, and God is glorified in him " (13³¹). It is clear that in this matter we have to do with a regular circle. It is the circle of the inner life of the Godhead. (III, 2, p. 65. Jesus, Man for God.)

2 CORINTHIANS 3¹²⁻¹⁸; 4⁶ (VI)

The Holy Spirit is not identical with Jesus Christ, with the Son or Word of God. Even in the saying in v. 17 we do not have an identification of Jesus Christ with the Spirit but rather a statement that to the Spirit belongs the *kyriotes*, the deity of the Lord, to whom there is reference in v. 16. The continuation is that where this Spirit is, who is the Lord, who is God, there is liberty, namely, liberty from the veiling of the heart which had continually made the reading of Moses unprofitable in the worship of the Jews, liberty to see and to hear. Then according to v. 18 there is reflected in us— our face is uncovered—the glory of the Lord, and so we are changed into His image, from His glory to a glory of our own, namely, through the Lord who is the Spirit. We are forbidden not merely by usage elsewhere but also by the meaning and context of the passage itself to identify the Spirit with Jesus Christ even here. (I, 1, p. 451 [516]. God the Holy Spirit.)

The Holy Spirit awakens a man to be a Christian, to be the kind of Christian who may hope in God, who in the service of God in and for the world, in the sphere of the penultimate, may hope for the ultimate. The Holy Spirit, however, is not a good daemon intervening between God and man like a *Deus ex machina* to make possible the impossible by a kind of magic. As there is no human skill, so there is no supernatural magic, to make possible the impossibility of a human life in hope. There is thus no daemon to grant this impossibility. Nor do we refer to a mere possibility, but to the actuality of such a life. The only One who can secure and introduce this reality of the Christian who hopes is God Himself in whom he may hope with reference both to the ultimate and the penultimate, and whom he may thus serve in his prophetic existence in the world. The reality of this prophetic existence of the Christian is not any kind of human or supernatural mystery. It is the mystery of God Himself ... Our reference is to the mighty activity of the Holy Spirit ... And God Himself is the Holy Spirit who awakens the Christian to life in hope. (IV, 3, p. 941. The Holy Spirit and Christian Hope.)

Cf. on 2 Corinthians 3^{3-9} Twelfth Sunday After Trinity; also IV, 1, p. 328.

PURIFICATION OF THE VIRGIN MARY
(Presentation of the Lord)
(February 2)

LUKE 2^{22-32} (I)

Cf. on Luke 2^{22-40} First Sunday After Christmas (December 29–31).

MALACHI 3^{1-4} (II)

Cf. on Malachi 3 Second Sunday in Advent.

SEPTUAGESIMA

MATTHEW 20^{1-16a} (I)

Klesis (*vocatio*) is the call of God. It comes from heaven and therefore from above. There can be no changing this. It is not to be co-ordinated with a human vocation and finally circuitously identified with the inner call. It is not the underlining or repeating of something old which men have already perceived and affirmed. It is always a new thing which God wants of man. But it is not a hermetically sealed ball suspended above him and neither touching nor touchable by him. It concerns him. It is for him. It simply cannot be strange to him. It falls from above into all his spheres and cuts diagonally across them ... We must not forget what K. L. Schmidt has correctly emphasised (in sharp opposition to Holl), namely, that *klesis* is the calling of God issued in Jesus Christ. But Jesus Christ as true Son of God is true man, who in all things human is certainly quite different from all other men, but to whom nothing really human can be alien. And the object of His work and recipient of His Word is man as he is and not as he is not. If Jesus Christ is the One who calls, and if His call goes forth to man as he is, then what the man called by Him is as such cannot be a matter of indifference or unconcern to the One who calls. Christ finds man precisely as the man he is; and He is found by the man who is obedient to His call. It is true enough that calling is revolutionary. It shakes what is wordly, or better what is human, not as a uniform and undifferentiated mass, but in its differentiation and multiplicity, just as calling itself is not uniform, but differentiated and multiple in correspondence with the differentiation of men. The servants in the parable in Mt. 25 receive from the one Lord their different talents, the one five, the other two and the third only one. The workers in the vineyard are called again by the one Lord, some early in the morning, others in the third hour, others in the sixth, others in the ninth and the last only at the eleventh hour. (III, 4, p. 603. Vocation; cf. pp. 600–607.)

1 CORINTHIANS $9^{24\text{-}27}$ (II)

This passage should be compared with Phil. $3^{12f.}$; together they bring out the fact that the Christian situation is a provisional one, in which we can only run but must run, and yet also—and this is what makes it a Christian situation—that there is a plain necessity to run to the very utmost of our resources. And this is the whole point of the instruction of the Holy Spirit. He does not put the Christian at a point or in a position. He sets him on the way, on the march. And it is a forced march which never ceases and in which there can be no halting. He does not put anything in his hands. He does not make him either a great or a little *beatus possidens*. He makes him a seeker: not, of course, an indecisive and planless seeker; one who knows what he is seeking; yet a real seeker whose hands are empty, who has not yet apprehended, but wants to apprehend because he is already apprehended. And He does not allow him to be merely an occasional and distracted seeker who divides his powers between this running and either resting or some other running; between this seeking and a possessing; or between the seeking of this one thing, his life in Christ, and that of other possibilities. The positive instruction of the Holy Spirit consists always in a gathering and mobilising and concentrating of the whole man who is instructed. (IV, 2, p. 376. The Direction of the Son.)

Cf. on Philippians $3^{12\text{-}17}$ Twenty-Fifth Sunday After Trinity.

LUKE $17^{7\text{-}10}$ (III)

To have our master in Jesus Christ means that we are subject to a command, in face of which there can be neither subterfuge nor excuse. We can find excuses and subterfuges for the commands of all other masters, even when we obey them in whole or in part. We can have doubts about their meaning. We can insist that we did not hear or understand. We can reply that we have already fulfilled them; or, *vice versa*, that we cannot

fulfil them, at any rate in the strict sense. But in face of this command these
devices are impossible . . . The relationship of lord and servant or of king
and subject seems to be the model for the relationship of Jesus to His
disciples. A single example (vv. 7–10) will illustrate the point. That is
how the children of God hear the Word of God. Their hearing is really
the hearing of an order and therefore obedience, a hearing which as such is
necessarily a doing of the Word (Jas. 1²²). When we remember this we
shall be on our guard against thinking that the commanding, ordering, or
lawgiving of the Old Testament belongs specifically to the Old Testament
. . . The purpose of the Law of God is not only to instruct and direct, to
judge and to terrify. It is also to comfort, to give us hope and joy and
help, to give us the very presence of God Himself in the act in which He
Himself is ours, in which He binds Himself to us to save us. In the 119th
Psalm we have an almost inexhaustible song of praise to the testimonies and
commandments and statutes and laws and precepts and words and ways of
God. But of the scriptural testimonies to revelation the 119th Psalm is one
which we must not despise, but carefully consider. It is, as it were, a con-
cretion of the saying about the omnipresence of God in Psalm 139: " Thy
Word encompasseth me on every side. " (I, 2, pp. 272–274. The
Freedom of Man for God.)

GALATIANS 2¹⁶⁻²⁰   (IV)
The fact that I live in the faith of the Son of God (v. 19 f.), in my faith
in Him, has its basis in the fact that He Himself, the Son of God, first
believed for me, and so believed that all that remains for me to do is to let
my eyes rest on Him, which really means to let my eyes follow Him. This
following is my faith. But the great work of faith has already been done by
the One whom I follow in my faith, even before I believe, even if I no
longer believe, in such a way that He is always, as Heb. 12² puts it, the
originator and completer of our faith, in such a way, therefore, that every
beginning and fresh beginning of our faith has its only starting-point in
Him, indeed, the only basis of its awakening. (II, 2, p. 559. The Basis of
the Divine Claim.)

When Paul says concerning himself in v. 20 that he no longer lives, but
Christ lives in him, this does not mean that he identified himself with
Christ, or gave himself out to be a second Christ. He at once interpreted
the statement by that which followed in v. 20b . . . Paul himself did not
take part—except in so far as he received it in faith as done for him—in this
self-offering of Christ, which took place for him as one who was loved by
Christ. He did not mean this in v. 19 or 6¹⁷ or 2 Cor. 4¹⁰, nor in 6¹⁴; 5²⁴;
Rom. 6⁶; Col. 3⁵. Both the text and the context of all these sayings completely exclude any idea of an interchangeability of Christ and the
Christian, the Head and the member, the One who leads and the one who
follows. They refer to a hard and painful and even mortal but redemptive

attack which must and is and will be made on the Christian in fellowship
with the suffering and crucified Christ, so that his whole life is determined
and marked and characterised by its influence and effects. (IV, 2, p. 600 f.
The Dignity of the Cross.)

Cf. IV, 2, p. 277 and p. 377; IV, 4, p. 9.

MALACHI 3$^{13-18}$, 4$^{1-2}$ (V)
Here the difference between the righteous and the wicked is equated
with the difference between those who serve and those who do not (v. 18).
We can then go on at once to Mt. 6^{24}. In both these sayings the word
" God " denotes the Lord of the covenant and the world acting in a definite
sequence of decisions, and therefore in both again the concept of " serving
God " obviously denotes an act of man in which a decision is executed on
his side, and the possibility of not serving God as Malachi puts it, or of
serving another lord or mammon according to the Sermon on the Mount,
is not chosen but rejected. To serve God is thus to choose God, to the
exclusion of neutrality or of another lord. And according to the saying in
Malachi, it is the act of this choice which makes us righteous. (III, 4, p.
475. The Active Life.)

Cf. on Malachi 3 Second Sunday in Advent.

ROMANS 9$^{14-24}$ (VI)
In his 1516–17 lectures on Romans Luther does great honour to Christian
repentance and humility in God's gracious judgment. But we should
seriously misunderstand him if we missed the constant emphasis and reminder that it is the work of God and not of man if we are led to Christian
repentance and humility . . . He (God) attests His power (*virtus*) to the
elect, by showing them their impotence, and hiding and destroying their
own power, so that they cannot boast of it any more (on v. 17). (I, 2,
p. 262 f. The Freedom of Man for God.)

We are not bowing (v. 20) before the caprice of a tyrant. Our submission cannot be such that it is accompanied by a still-remaining and
ever-increasing inward complaint and resistance. Rather, of ourselves, of
our own better knowledge, we will to be silent. It is not that our mouth is
stopped—for then our silence would not be a voluntary act of obedience,
but an act of disobedience which has been prevented and suppressed. It is
rather because our ears have heard the Therefore which is the truly
satisfying and convincing answer to every Wherefore. We are persuaded,
and have no more questions to put. God Himself . . . has given us Himself as the answer. What God does in freedom is in order . . . we can and
must perceive and recognise that it is in order without first measuring it by
our own conceptions of order and only then recognising it to be such. It
belongs to God to teach us what order is. It belongs to us to measure our
conceptions of order by His decision, and to learn from Him what order is.

(II, 2, p. 22. The Problem of a Correct Doctrine of the Election of Grace.)

If there is no neutrality towards God, we are already against God if we will to remain neutral ... Within the sphere described here (vv. 20–23) there is obviously no escape. We are obviously either lost and remain lost, or we pray the prayer which means either way that we leave the realm of neutrality and acknowledge God to be in the right instead of disputing with Him. When we do this we go over from disobedience to obedience, and therefore from God's left hand to His right, and we are therefore saved and not lost. According to Scripture the will of God is neither to be extolled nor feared as our fate. It is to be adored and done as the will of the Lord which is always justified and right (Ps. 135[5f.]; Job 23[13f.]; Ps. 33[8ff.]). We are not speaking of God's will at all if we do not grant it this range and worship it in it. (II, 1, p. 557 f. The Perfections of the Divine Freedom.)

Cf. II, 2, pp. 218–233; IV, 3, p. 393; II, 1, p. 538 f.

SEXAGESIMA

LUKE 8[4-15] (I)

The parable speaks (1) of the proclamation of the Word, (2) of the hearers of the Word and (3) of the differentiation between them ... We now come (3) to the point of the parable ... It is to be found in the fact that the normal case is confronted by so many unforeseen and startling abnormal cases in which, contrary to every rule, intention and hope, this knowledge (which is more than mere understanding: a reception, acceptance, appropriation and comprehension ... true inner apperception of the Word heard and understood) does not arise and the true and living and effective Word of the kingdom does not accomplish in the world that which it should accomplish in accordance with its nature and the world situation created by its proclamation. The differences between the wayside, the stony ground and the thorns certainly invite us to consider, as is done in the interpretation in vv. 18–23, the many different forms which the abnormal case usually assumes. On the one side, there is the man whose hardened self-will causes him to escape the Word immediately he has heard and understood it. Again there is the man of cheap enthusiasm who thinks that he has grasped what he has not really grasped at all, as is revealed by the first serious opposition which arises. Again, there is the man who is decisively claimed by very different forces, amongst which the interpretation (Mt. 13[22]) numbers not only carnal passions and ideological ties, but with great realism " the care of this world, and the deceitfulness of riches." We must all consider the ways in which we, too, might become abnormal cases ... There is no doubt that in all these cases there is depicted the great threat to which the work of the Sower is exposed. It might seem that the result of this work is inevitable. Is not the world in

which it takes place the world which is known by God? Has it any option
but to know the One by whom it is known? Yet the fact remains . . . that
in large measure it seems to have a very different option, namely, the
sinister possibility of the ignorance of God in whose actualisation the
exception threatens to become the rule, and the rule the exception. It
may well be " externally settled " that the Sower should now go forth to
sow in vain, that Jesus should be Victor. Yet in face of this threat to His
work, this is by no means self-evident. It has to take place that He
conquers. The enemy who aims at a different result, who is also intent
to triumph, is truly present in all the absurdity of his nature and existence.
It has to happen that he is driven from the field. (IV, 3, p. 189 f. Jesus
Is Victor.)

2 CORINTHIANS 12$^{1-10}$ (II)

Paul is speaking here . . . very personally of his own most intimate
religious experience. There are great things of which he might glory in
this sphere, of which, indeed, he could glory in truth, and without talking
nonsense . . . But who is it who can really glory in all these things (vv. 1–4)?
Three times (v. 2, 3, 5) Paul speaks of him impersonally: " I know a
man . . ." He calls him a " man in Christ." Undoubtedly he means himself. But—and this is the distinctive thing in the description of this
ecstasy—he puts a space between himself and this man. And it is only at
this remove that he will take part in the glory which this man—himself—
has by virtue of these high things. " To the honour of this man I will
boast; but to my own honour I will not boast, unless it be of weaknesses "
(v. 5 according to Schlatter). He is restrained from being lifted up by these
experiences (v. 7 f.), and is forced into this paradoxical glorying because of
weakness. For, like a thorn in the flesh, an angel of Satan stands at his
side to buffet him. Not even the most earnest prayer to Jesus Christ can
frighten away this enemy. Indeed, Paul obviously does not now want to
frighten him away. In his presence and activity he now sees the order in
the power of which he is held outside the circle of these experiences: at
the place where Christ dwells beside him, i.e., in his weakness. . . . But
what is his weakness? Well, it is what is left of his Christian experience,
i.e., humiliations, emergencies, persecutions, distresses for Christ's sake
(v. 10). In these he sees the power of Christ dwelling in him. In these
he knows that he is strong. In these he glories. (I, 2, p. 332. The Revelation of God as the Abolition of Religion.)

There is a form of human life and service in which man must be able to
do something different. At a first glance, this does not look like ability at
all, but its very opposite, since it has nothing whatever to do with the
attainment of aims, or the accomplishment of works. For when man stands
in the service of God, he must be able sometimes, and perhaps for long
periods, to be still, to wait, to keep silence, to suffer and therefore to be

without the other kind of capacity. This, too, is power; this is man's ability ... For the power of God Himself, reflected in the power which He gives to man, is the power of Jesus Christ, and therefore the power of the Lamb as well as the Lion, of the cross as well as the resurrection, of humiliation as well as exaltation, of death as well as life. To this there corresponds the way in which God gives power, ability, capacity to man. The power which comes from Him is the capacity to be high or low, rich or poor, wise or foolish. It is the capacity for success or failure, for moving with the current or against it, for standing in the ranks or for solitariness. For some it will almost always be only the one, for others only the other, but usually it will be both for all of us in rapid alternation. In each case, however, it will be true capacity, the good gift of God, ascribed to each as needed in His service. God demands one service to be rendered in the light, another which can be performed only in shadow. That is why He distributes this varied ability according to His good-pleasure. Either way, it is grace, being for each of us exactly that which God causes to be allotted to us. (III, 4, p. 396 f. Freedom for Life.)

For it is the strength of which Paul says in v. 9 f., and with more than a personal reference, that it is made strong and perfected in weakness. Even the strength of Jesus Christ neither was nor is strong except in supreme weakness. It is the glory of the community to follow Him in this too, and therefore to be totally strong only as it is totally weak, but to be really strong, of course, in this weakness. Weakness means inability. Of the Christian community in world-occurrence we have to say both that it can do nothing and that it can do all things. (IV, 3, p. 742. The People of God in World-Occurrence.)

MATTHEW 13[10-17] (III)

Jesus speaks to them in parables in fulfilment of the word of the prophet Isaiah about seeing and not perceiving, hearing and not understanding— the unalterable law that of himself man does not have the ability to turn to God, but that this is taken from him when God actually converts him to Himself. This law is the secret of the kingdom of heaven which they learn from Jesus as His disciples, and therefore actually know with Him. He has thus drawn them into His solitude before God and over against the whole world. (II, 2, p. 446. The Determination of the Elect.)

How can the mysteries of the kingdom of heaven be seen by men at all (v. 11)? The answer is that although they are divine and therefore heavenly orders, now that the kingdom of God as the kingdom of heaven is nigh they are reflected in the natural relationships and processes of earth. Hence the kingdom of God as the kingdom of heaven can be likened to or like good seed (v. 24), or a grain of mustard seed (v. 31), or leaven (v. 33), or the king (18[23]), or the more than dubious householder (20[1]), etc., and in this form it can be known by those to whom it is given and

missed by those to whom it is not, but either way it is in the circle of
human vision. (III, 3, p. 434. The Kingdom of Heaven.)

Cf. III, 2, p. 413; IV, 2, p. 204.

ISAIAH 55$^{6-11}$ (IV)

We are speaking of God's Word. Therefore we have to speak of its
power, its might, its effects, the changes it brings about. Because the
Word of God makes history, as Word it is also act (Jer. 23^{29}).

... The promise of the Word of God is not as such an empty pledge
which always stands, as it were, confronting man. It is the transposing
of man into the wholly new state of one who has accepted and appropriated
the promise, so that irrespective of his attitude to it he no longer lives
without this promise but with it. The claim of the Word of God is not as
such a wish or command which remains outside the hearer without im-
pinging on his existence. It is the claiming and commandeering of man.
Whatever may be his attitude to God's claim, man as a hearer of His Word
now finds himself in the sphere of the divine claim; he is claimed by God.
(I, 1, p. 152 [173]. The Speech of God as the Act of God.)

The Holy Spirit is simply but most distinctly the renewing power of
the breath of His mouth which as such is the breath of the sovereign God
and victorious truth. It is the power in which His Word, God's Word, the
Word of truth, is not only in Him, but where and when He wills goes out
also to us men, not returning to Him empty but with the booty or increase
of our faith and knowledge and obedience, and not remaining with Him
on its return, but constantly going out again to us to bring back new gain,
and thus establishing a communication between Him and us and initiating
a history of mutual giving and receiving. (IV, 3, p. 421. The True
Witness.)

Cf. II, 1, p. 417.

LUKE 10$^{38-42}$ (V)

The Christian community should never come together, except there
God's very Word be preached and prayer made.... Therefore where
God's Word is not preached, 'tis better people should neither sing nor
read, nor come together.... 'Tis better to leave out all, save the Word.
And nought is better pursued than the Word. For all Scripture showeth
that the same should be in full swing among Christians, and Christ also
saith Himself, Lk. 10^{42} " One thing is needful." For that Mary should sit
at Christ's feet and hear His Word daily is the best part to choose, and is
never taken away. It is an eternal saying that all else must pass away,
however much there is for Martha to do. (I, 1, p. 70 [78]. Luther: *Von
Ordnung Gottesdiensts*, 1523.)

It may well be that the older " friends of God " did sometimes slip into
the sphere of religious eroticism ... This cannot be condoned and must

not be imitated. But it does not mean that what they had in mind and tried to attest can be ignored or juggled away, namely, that which takes place at the centre where Christian love is originally direct love for God and for Jesus. Did Mary really choose the good part, or did she not? Here, then, we must think and speak with the measure of sober passion or passionate soberness which corresponds on the one hand to the fire which burns at this centre and on the other to its holiness and purity. In no case must we evade or suppress that which cannot be evaded or suppressed. If we do, we do not guard against the paganism of religious sentimentalism and religious *eros*. On the contrary, we open up the way for it. For this paganism finds its excuse in the vacuum created by such evasion and suppression. It flourishes all the more vehemently in this vacuum. We must not help it in this way. The only thing which has power against it is positive: that at this critical point we should think and say the right thing and not the wrong; and that we should think and say the right thing in all earnest. The Puritanism in relation to which this excursus is required was an unavoidable but dangerous contraction. The warning which it had to deliver is still valid. But as a contradiction it has played its part and is no longer necessary. (IV, 2, p. 798. The Act of Love.)

HEBREWS 3$^{1, \, 6b-14}$ (VI)

Why all the emphasis on " to-day " (v. 7, 13)? Because, as Heb. 4$^{1-8}$ explains, the Sabbath day has dawned . . . in the reality to which the sign had pointed so long. The day of rest has arrived for God and His people, and none must neglect to enter into it. The whole of the Old Testament is before them as an awful warning against neglect. This Sabbath has dawned " to-day " and must be kept, because " this day have I begotten thee " (1^5) . . . because " unto you is born this day . . . a Saviour " (Lk. 2^{11}); because " this day is salvation come to this house " (Lk. 19^9). All this happened yesterday for the sake of to-day—the birth of Jesus, His visit to the house of Zacchaeus, His death on the cross, His burial and resurrection. And as a consequence we to-day, in our time, have died and been buried and risen with Him in baptism. We can therefore walk in newness of life, as described in Rom. 6$^{1-11}$. (III, 2, p. 469. Jesus, Lord of Time.)

Taking the word in its most obvious sense a Christian means one who belongs in a special way to Jesus Christ, i.e., in a way different from that in which, since He died and rose again for all, and all are to bow the knee to Him and join in that confession, all men belong to Him and on the basis of His election and mission are His own, His possession and people according to John 1^{11}. The special way in which Christians belong to Him, however, is that their existence among all other men is determined, according to the commonest New Testament expression, by their faith in Him, by their liberating and yet also binding and active knowledge that all men and therefore they themselves belong to Him. In the active knowledge of this faith of theirs they anticipate the form of existence which one day is to be that of all men. In this special sense all men do not belong to Him here and now, but only Christians belong to Him and are His own, His possession and people. (IV, 3, p. 526. The Goal of Vocation.)

QUINQUAGESIMA (ESTOMIHI)

LUKE 18[31-43]   (I)

There is obviously a glaring contrast between the beginning and content and meaning of the existence of Jesus and its outcome and end. The Gospels see this and draw attention to it, and to the questions which it inevitably raises. They tell us how blind the disciples were when Jesus spoke of His approaching death (v. 34) . . . They also tell us of the impulsive reaction of Peter, who only a few moments before had made his inspired confession, and who was later to betray Jesus at the decisive moment, Matthew 16[22]. They tell us how at the last all the disciples forsook Him and fled, Mark 14[50f.]. They tell us with brutal frankness of the scornful taunts of His opponents when He was hanging on the cross, Mark 15[29f.]. And in Luke 24[20f.], even in the Easter story, we seem to catch an echo of this scorn on the lips of the troubled disciples . . . And Paul can still say (1 Cor. 1[23]) how self-evident it was that the crucified Jesus whom he proclaimed should be a stumbling-block to the Jews and foolishness to the Greeks. Even more important is the fact that the Gospels and the Epistle to the Hebrews (5[7f.]) are not afraid to represent Jesus Himself wrestling with the question—and they use the strongest possible terms, as in the Gethsemane passages—whether this end is really right or necessary, or whether there may not perhaps be some other possibility. Indeed, in Jn. 12[27] He could even pray: "Father, save me from this hour." And even more striking is the fact that in Mark (15[34]) and Matthew (27[46]) His only word on the cross, and therefore His final word, is a despairing question. The Gospels do not conceal the fact, but state it, that His death is a problem of the first magnitude. It is, in fact, the problem of all the problems of His existence and relationship to God and His life-work. The darkness of His end is a true and final darkness. It is a darkness which He Himself could not see through directly, but which had to be traversed like a tunnel. If this were not emphasised by the Gospels, it is hard to see how any real weight could be attached to the further and decisive thing which they have also to say about it. But there is one thing that the Gospels definitely do not do, and that is to invite their readers and hearers to prolong their consideration of this darkness and the problem it raises. As they represent it, even at the high points in the narrative, the passion of Jesus never assumes the character of a tragic entanglement which raises the possible and even necessary question of a partial error and therefore some possible guilt on the part of the hero. Nor does it have the character of a misfortune which breaks over Him either by chance or fate, so that the initiative is wrested from Him and He ceases to be the Lord. On the contrary, in His suffering and dying He is still the same as He always was, although in another form. (IV, 2, p. 250 f. The Royal Man.)

1 CORINTHIANS 13 (II)

He (man) must not imagine that he can be a Christian and therefore a witness on the authority of Paul or John, of Luther or Augustine, of pious elders or friends. If he hears them, if he goes to their school and remains in it, then he will be led by them to a personal part in the act and revelation of God. And it is in vain that he will shelter under the wings of their authority if he will not let them conduct him to their source and thus be instructed by them in his own responsibility in relation to this source. However else it may be with him, less than his own person is not enough if his true witness is to be declared as true by him, if it is not to be on his lips as sounding brass or a tinkling cymbal, and if therefore, in spite of its truth, it is not to be futile and even false witness with which he dishonours rather than honours his Lord, neither serving Him nor helping but only hindering the world and other men. He cannot be a herald to others and himself a castaway (9²⁷). (IV, 3, p. 657 f. The Liberation of the Christian.)

Since *agape* is from God . . . and *eros* from self-contradictory man, is it not one of the things which make comparison impossible that the former is absolutely superior to the latter, not only in dignity, but also in power? *Eros* can only flee and perish and cease, and with it the whole world which is dominated and impelled and built up and characterised by it. But love, *agape*, never fails (v. 8). With that which issues from it (as it does from God), it is imperishable even in the midst of a world which perishes. (IV, 2, p. 748. The Problem of Christian Love.)

For us, for our vision and understanding, the knowledge of Jesus Christ in His pure form is an indirect knowledge, i.e., knowledge in this other form, which certainly has its secret and force in the pure form, but which is not as such identical with it, which is rather alien and quite dissimilar to it. It is knowledge *in contrario*, *sub specie aliena* (v. 11 f.). Indirect knowledge is that which arises when the person or object to be known makes itself known. It can be known only in consequence of self-declaration. (IV, 3, p. 389. The True Witness.)

It is to be noted (v. 13) that faith also abides, even though in the coming great change it is taken up into sight. It is to be noted that hope abides, for how can it fail to do so when it is specifically the orientation of the life-act of the Christian on that which is perfect, whose coming will be its fulfilment? But faith and hope abide only as and because love abides. It is in love that faith and hope are active, and that there takes place that which is specifically Christian in the life-act of the Christian. Thus love is the " greatest of these. " It is the future eternal light shining in the present. It therefore needs no change of form. It is that which continues. For whatever else may be revealed in and with the coming of that which is perfect, in whatever new form Christian activity and the life of the community may attain its goal with everything that now is and happens, one thing is certain and that is that love will never cease, that even then the love which is self-giving to God and the brother, the same love for which the Christian is free already, will be the source of the future eternal life, its form unaltered. Already, then, love is the eternal activity of the Christian. This is the reason why love abides. This is the reason why to say this is to say the final and supreme thing about it. This is the reason why we had to say previously that it is love alone that counts (vv. 1–3) and love alone that conquers (vv. 4–7). This is the reason why it is *the* way (12³¹). (IV, 2, p. 840. The Manner of Love.)

EXODUS 33¹²⁻²³   (III)

It was for Luther no less than a principal rule of all knowledge of God . . . When we speak and hear about God we are not concerned with the *nuda essentia* or *natura* of God, but with the *velamen*, the *volucra*, the *certae species*, the *larvae* of His works. We must keep to them according to God's wise and unbreakable ordinance. We must be thankful for them. We must not disregard them, or prefer any direct, non-objective knowledge of God. If we do, we run the risk, not only of losing God, but of making Him hostile to us. We must seek Him where He Himself has sought us—in those veils and under those signs of His Godhead. Elsewhere He is not to be found . . . Exodus 33¹¹⁻²³ can hardly be understood except as a confirmation of Luther's general rule . . . It is precisely in the passing before of God that Moses is to hear His name . . . in God's passing before and going before, in God's work and action, in which he does not see God's face but in which he can only follow God with his eyes. In this case, more than that would not only be less, but even nothing at all—indeed, something negative. Man cannot see God's face, God's naked objectivity, without exposing himself to the annihilating wrath of God. It would indeed have to be a second God who could see God directly. (II, 1, p. 18 f. Man Before God.)

According to the dominant meaning of the terms *chen*, *chesed*, *charis* in the linguistic usage of the Bible, grace is an inner mode of being in God Himself. (II, 1, p. 353. The Grace and Holiness of God.)

HEBREWS 4⁹⁻¹³   (IV)

In v. 12 . . . it is said that the Word of God is sharper than a two-edged sword and pierces to the dividing asunder of soul and spirit, and that from this point of division, and obviously in such a way that the spirit comes to stand on God's side and the soul on man's, it becomes the discerner of the thoughts and intents of the heart. Scripture never says " soul " where only " spirit " can be meant. But it often says " spirit " where " soul " is meant; and there is inner reason for this in the fact that the constitution of man as soul and body cannot be fully and exactly described without thinking first and foremost of the spirit as its proper basis. We are nowhere invited to think of three entities. Even Augustine, when he once gave the almost intolerably harsh formulation: *Tria sunt, quibus homo constat: spiritus, anima et corpus,* immediately corrected himself: *quae rursus duo dicuntur, quia saepe anima cum spiritu nominatur* (*De fide et symb.* 10, 23). Trichotomism must necessarily issue in the view and concept of two different souls and therefore in a splitting of man's being. This makes understandable the force with which it was condemned at the Fourth Council of Constantinople in A.D. 869–70. (III, 2, p. 355. Man as Soul and Body.)

In different respects the Christian is a man who is notably helpless and vulnerable . . . He is in no position to make easy and cheap for men the hearing and receiving of what he has to attest. No self-evident friendliness, humanity and serenity with which he turns to them will deceive them. The glorious divine Yes which he may attest to them as the Gospel, and will perhaps do so in a way which is impossibly hard and cheerless and humourless, is necessarily enclosed in the No which they never like to hear because it not only gets on their nerves but touches them on the raw, radically challenging and overthrowing their existence. Not even in the name of love can he, to make it more acceptable, blunt either edge of the two-edged sword of the Word of God. He cannot make the free grace of God a comfortable grace, nor transform the good Lord into a good man. (IV, 3, p. 627. The Christian in Affliction.)

Cf. III, 2, p. 458; III, 1, p. 227; I, 2, p. 676.

LUKE 13[31-35] (V)

Cf. on Matthew 23[34-39] Saint Stephen's Day (December 26).

1 CORINTHIANS 1[18-25] (VI)

Truth (Jn. 18[38]) cannot be expected to encounter man as a phenomenon which is immediately and directly illuminating, pleasing, acceptable and welcome to him. He would not be who he is if the promise of the Spirit came to him easily and smoothly . . . That this is so in the case of the truth of God is grounded in the fact that this is identical with the true Witness Jesus Christ as the revelation of God's will and work for man enacted in Him. The glory of this Mediator, however, is a glory which is concealed in its opposite, in invisibility, in repellent shame. This Witness does not encounter man in a splendour which wins him easily and impresses him naturally. Raised from the dead by the power of God, He encounters him in the despicable and forbidding form of the Slain and Crucified of Golgotha. It is as the One whose way leads and ends there that He is the

Reconciler of the world to God, the justification and sanctification of man. It is with Him as this One that our life is hidden and secured in God. (IV, 3, p. 376 f. The True Witness. Cf. also pp. 389 ff.)

If we assume that it is given to us to be Christians, we can and must say that we know Him even in this concealment. He is our Lord and Hero, the Shepherd of the world and our Deliverer, even in this lowliness. He has acted as the true Son of God even in His suffering of death on the cross ... It was in His humiliation that there took place the fulfilment of the covenant, the reconciliation of the world with God ... Where the Holy Spirit intervenes and is at work between Him and us as the Spirit of Jesus Christ, we can believe and confess it in face of that hard antithesis. Christ the Crucified is a stumbling-block to the Jews and foolishness to the Greeks (v. 23 f.), but to those who are called He is the power of God and the wisdom of God. (IV, 2, p. 330. The Exaltation of the Son of Man.)

The whole truth is that in spite of all appearances to the contrary, Holy Scripture has more power than all the rest of the world together. The whole truth is that all other world-principles are already unmasked and delimited in Holy Scripture, that they are already overcome for all their supposedly final and absolute validity, that their power is already surpassed and their triumph outstripped. The whole truth—hidden but complete— is that of the story of the young David (1 Sam. 17$^{23f.}$). It was not in the helmet and armour of Saul, but with his shepherd's sling, that he overcame Goliath. Very rashly, from a human point of view, he confronted Goliath in the name of Yahweh Sabaoth. (I, 2, p. 678. The Freedom of the Word.)

Cf. II, 1, pp. 435–439, 605–607; IV, 3, pp. 389 ff.

FIRST SUNDAY IN LENT (INVOCAVIT)

MATTHEW 4$^{1-11}$ (I)

In none of the temptations is there brought before us a devil who is obviously godless, or dangerous or even stupid. And in none of them is the temptation a temptation to what we might call a breaking or failure to keep the Law on the moral or judicial plane. In all three we have to do " only " with the counsel, the suggestion, that He should not be true to the way on which He entered in Jordan, that of a great sinner repenting; that He should take from now on a direction which will not need to have the cross as its end and goal. But if Jesus had done this He would have done something far worse than any breaking or failure to keep the Law. He would have done that which is the essence of everything bad. For it would have meant that without His obedience the enmity of the world against God would have persisted, without His penitence the destruction of the cosmos could not have been arrested, and men would inevitably have perished . . . Jesus withstood this temptation (v. 3 f.). He persisted in obedience, in penitence, in fasting. He hungered in confidence in the manna with which the same God had once fed the fathers in the wilderness after He had allowed them to hunger. He willed to live only by that which the Word of God creates, and therefore as one of the sinners who have no hope apart from God, as the Head and King of this people. His decision was, therefore, a different one from that which all other men would have taken in His place, and in that way it was the righteousness which He achieved in their stead . . . Jesus did not do this (vv. 5–7). He rejected the supreme ecstasy and satisfaction of religion as the supreme form of sin. And in so doing He remained faithful to the baptism of John. He remained the One in whom God is well-pleased. He remained sinless. He remained in obedience. In our place He achieved the righteousness which had to be achieved in His person for the justification of us all and for the reconciliation of the world with God, the only righteousness that was necessary . . . Jesus resisted this temptation too (vv. 8–10). He refused to be won over to this attractive realism. As the one great sinner in the name and place of all others, without any prospect of this glory, quite unsuccessfully, indeed with the certainty of failure, He willed to continue worshipping and serving God alone. He willed to persist in repentance and obedience. This was the righteousness which He achieved for us. (IV, 1, pp. 262–264. The Obedience of the Son of God.)

Cf. III, 2, p. 67, 339; III, 3, p. 67; III, 4, p. 347.

2 CORINTHIANS 6$^{1-10}$ (II)

Before the end of all things there is no age whose work cannot be taken up again and continued and improved. Together with the whole ministry of the community, the critical scholarship of theology itself stands in constant need of criticism, correction and reform. For the same reason, it is inevitable that in constant self-testing it should be involved in continual warfare not so much with individual errorists as with the countless evil spirits of false or semi-false theology. To be sure, its weapons are those of " righteousness on the right hand and on the left " (v. 7), yet there can be no doubt as to the conflict. Always there must be serious questioning, analysis, argumentation, construction, discussion, and therefore directly or indirectly, and preferably only indirectly, polemics. From time to time, though not all the time, a little of the notorious *rabies theologorum* is thus in place. This does not alter the fact, however, that in itself and as such theology is supremely positive and peaceable, that it fosters peace, and that it is thus to be pursued soberly, good-humouredly, without any nervous excitement, and particularly without too much petty, self-opinionated bickering. It is to be noted further that it is a modest undertaking which like missionary work can aim only to serve rather than to dominate by rendering a certain limited and transitory assistance to the cause of the community and therefore of all Christians and the world as a whole. It is to be noted further that when it is conceived and executed correctly and resolutely, yet also freely and modestly, theology is a singularly beautiful and joyful science (cf. II, 1, p. 656 f.), so that it is only willingly and cheerfully or not at all that we can be theologians. (IV, 3, p. 881. The Ministry of the Community.)

Cf. IV, 3, p. 600 f.

MATTHEW 16²¹⁻²⁷   (III)

We have not concealed the fact that in the Jesus Christ who encounters us in His form of suffering we are concerned with a phenomenon which is strange, shocking and quite opposed to what we might for once call the natural feelings and desires and thoughts and beliefs and dreams of men. On the basis of what we regard as divine, who of us would look for the truth of God in this form? Who of us could or would acquiesce in the fact that we must find it in this form and in this form alone? This is what continually isolates Jesus Christ in every age and place, so that we would rather avoid Him, and prefer to have no dealings with Him. " This shall not be unto thee " (Mt. 16²²). And above all, we cannot have dealings with a Christ like this ... It is most unfortunate that the fact that we do not willingly look to him in this form is so obscured by the preoccupation of so much Christian art with this subject, and especially by the inane misuse of the symbol of the cross right into our own times. (IV, 3, p. 415. The True Witness.)

The man who is called to follow Jesus has simply to renounce and withdraw and annul an existing relationship of obedience and loyalty. This relationship is to himself. When he is called to discipleship, he abandons himself resolutely and totally. He can and must say of himself instead of Jesus: " I know not the man " (26⁷²). He cannot accept this man even as his most distant acquaintance. He once stood in a covenant with him which he loyally kept and tenderly nurtured. But he now renounces this covenant root and branch. He can confess only Jesus, and therefore he cannot confess himself. He can and will only deny himself. (IV, 2, p. 539. The Call to Discipleship.)

To follow Him involves for all those who are elected and called and willing and ready and really free to do this that they should deny themselves, i.e., that they should not try to save their life for themselves, but yield it freely to this total service. And this means concretely that each of them should take up his own " cross, " not fearing or hating or avoiding or evading or trying to escape by force or subtlety the affliction that falls on him, but freely accepting it and taking it up and carrying it. (IV, 2, p. 264. The Royal Man.)

Cf. IV, 1, p. 421 (Mark 8³⁵); IV, 2, p. 255 f.; IV, 4, p. 15 (Mark 8³⁵).
JAMES 4⁶ᵇ⁻¹⁰   (IV)

MARK 9[14-29] (V)

When a man begins to believe—even if only in a modest but unavoidable venture, even if only in the quantity, though also the quality, of a grain of mustard-seed, even if only, though seriously, with the petition: " Lord help thou mine unbelief "—he will not only not be unwilling, but will most earnestly desire, to overcome the ambiguity of a position in which apparently he might still be different or different again, to leave behind him the ostensible possibility of vacillating between Yes and No, between faith and unbelief. (IV, 4, p. 42 f. The Foundation of the Christian Life.)

What we are dealing with here . . . is the extremely fundamental fact that the disciples, while Jesus has called them, and they are His followers, belong to an " unbelieving generation " (v. 19). They are wholly and utterly outside even while they are wholly and utterly inside. So far as they stand on their own feet . . . they are wholly and utterly outside. It is clear that they have their religion, but it is equally clear that their religion is unbelief. (I, 2, p. 330. The Revelation of God as the Abolition of Religion.)

Cf. on Romans 8[24-30] Second Sunday After Christmas; also IV, 2, p. 234.

GENESIS 3[1-19] (VI)

It is not insignificant that the story of the creature in its relationship to God begins in Gen. 3 with a disastrous defeat, and that in the terrible form of human sin the chaos separated by God becomes a factor and secures and exercises a power which does not belong to it in relation to God but can obviously do so in relation to His creature. The creature had neither the capacity nor the power to effect that separation. It neither could nor should be God, judging between good and evil. It could and should live only by the grace of God and in virtue of the judgment already accomplished by Him. It could not and should not deal with nothingness as God did, nor master and overcome it like God. Only in covenant with God could it and should it confront nothingness in absolute freedom. And even in covenant with God, where God never fails, there can be and has been failure on the part of the creature . . . This is the disastrous defeat of the creature by nothingness as typically described in Gen. 3. (III, 3, p. 355 f. God and Nothingness.)

It should be noted that the *Eritis sicut Deus* (v. 5) is an element in the explanation of existence given by the serpent. We have to do here with a thought of chaos, the thought of chaos which can as such be very powerful but can never be other than false and destructive. Powerful, because it makes so plain the true and final purpose, almost the promise, of the aseity and independence indicated, and so very attractive the movement into the swamps of this aseity and independence. False, because it is contrary to the whole Old Testament concept of God, because the God that man resembles when he desires this independence can only be a false god. Destructive because the corresponding decision of man can, in fact, only lead him into a marsh in which he will sink hopelessly unless he is rescued from it. (IV, 1, p. 422 f., cf. also p. 420 f., 434 f., and 448. The Pride and Fall of Man.)

We are continually " permitting " ourselves all possible things, decisions and attitudes, thoughts and words and works, in which we regard ourselves as free, which we apparently do gladly, in which we think we are happy . . . It is apparently pure permission that rules (v. 6, 12 f.). Man permits himself to renounce the grace of God. He permits himself to be set up as one who knows good and evil and therefore as judge over both. He permits himself therefore to be established in the divine likeness. Man thinks that he is particularly free and happy even in his fall. (II, 2, p. 593 f. The Command as the Claim of God.)

There is no self-concealment from God. There is, of course, a desire for self-concealment which is the dire consequence of sin and the unwilling, compulsory, impotent admission of it. There is the flight to the denial of the undeniable God, dictated by anxiety, which is all that remains, when the desire to trespass has run its full course. There is the ostrich's strategy which confirms and seals the headlong fall into the realm of the non-existent and impossible before God, the overpowering by death and hell. But this policy can have no success. (II, 1, p. 553 f. The Constancy and Omnipotence of God.)

Therefore behold how boldly the Old Testament speaketh of matters. There it standeth that Adam was already a Christian so long before Christ was born, for he had precisely the faith in Christ which we have, for time maketh none difference to faith. Faith is the same from the beginning of the world to the end. Therefore he did receive by his faith that which I have received, Christ he saw not with his eyes any more than we did, but he had Him in the Word, so we also have Him in the Word. The sole difference is that then it should happen, now it has happened. The faith is all the same, so all the fathers just like ourselves were justified by the Word and faith and also died therein (Luther, Sermons on Genesis, 1527). (I, 2, p. 77. The Time of Expectation.)

Cf. II, 2, p. 670; IV, 1, p. 231 and 463.

SECOND SUNDAY IN LENT (REMINISCERE)

MATTHEW 15²¹⁻²³   (I)

I, 1, p. 177 f. [202]. Luther, Fastenpostille, 1525.

1 THESSALONIANS 4¹⁻⁷   (II)

It is integral to the event of sanctification—the *participatio Christi*, the call to discipleship, the awakening to conversion and the praise of good works—that as the life-movement of the Christian—as a human and earthly-historical life-movement—it is radically and relentlessly fixed and held and broken at a specific place. In the literal sense it is a movement which is crossed through, which is determined and characterised by a cross. The cross involves hardship, anguish, grief, pain and finally death. But those who are set in this movement willingly undertake to bear this because it is essential to this movement that it should finally . . . be crossed through in this way . . . It is quite in order that man . . . should try to ward off pain and death. Even the Christian does this. In themselves and as such, pain, suffering and death are a questioning, a destruction and finally a negation of human life. The Christian especially cannot try to transform and glorify them. He cannot find any pleasure in them. He cannot desire or seek them . . . He cannot be a lover of death as the natural man may easily become in a strange reversal and unmasking of his pretended affirmation of life and avid desire for it. His Yes to life is not one which can change surreptitiously into a No. He knows better than others what life is, and what he is doing when he secures himself against its negation. He affirms it just because it is for him more than a matter of life. What is at stake is that the will of God should be done, which is his sanctification. (IV, 2, p. 602. The Sanctification of Man.)

MATTHEW 21$^{28-32}$ (III)
HEBREWS 11$^{1f., 6, 8-10, 17-19}$ (IV)

Faith is not, therefore, a standing, but a being suspended and hanging without ground under our feet. Or conversely, in faith we abandon whatever we might otherwise regard as our standing, namely, our standing upon ourselves (including all moral and religious, even Christian standing), because in faith we see that it is a false and unreal standing, a hanging without support, a wavering and falling. We abandon it for the real standing in which we no longer stand on ourselves (on our moral and religious, or even our Christian state), and in which we obviously do not stand on our faith as such but—now at least firmly and securely—on the ground of the truth of God and therefore on the ground of the reconciliation which has taken place in Jesus Christ and is confirmed by Him to all eternity. It is a standing which seen from ourselves (but what we see from ourselves is a lie) may well appear to be an impossible and intolerable hanging and suspension. We will always be afraid of it as we see things from ourselves. We may well try to flee from it as if our lives were at stake (as indeed they are, though in the very opposite sense). We shall continually surprise ourselves on the flight from faith. (II, 1, p. 159. The Readiness of Man.)

Faith (v. 1) is " the conviction of things not seen," of things whose truth lies in God alone. Hence the believer who builds his life on such things has God alone and nothing else as his support and basis. (III, 2, p. 156. Man as the Creature of God.)

Calvin said concerning the relationship of *fides* and *spes* at the end of his great chapter *Inst*. III, 2 and with reference to Heb. 11 . . . Where there is a living faith in the Word of God, it cannot be otherwise than that faith should have hope as its inseparable companion, or rather, that it should beget and create it. If we have no hope, we can be sure that we have no faith. Those who believe, those who apprehend the truth of God with the certainty which corresponds to it, which is demanded and imparted by it, expect that God will fulfil the promises which He has spoken in truth . . . Waiting quietly for the Lord, hope restrains faith, preventing it from rushing forward in too great a hurry. It confirms it so that it does not waver in its trust in God's promises or begin to doubt. It revives it so that it does not grow weary. It keeps it fixed on its final goal so that it does not give up half-way or when it is in captivity. It continually renews and reestablishes it, thus seeing to it that it continually rises up in more vital forms and perseveres to the end. (IV, 1, p. 332. The Obedience of the Son of God.)

Cf. IV, 2, p. 597 f.; II, 1, p. 57.

ISAIAH 42$^{1-8}$ (V)

In the Ebed-Yahweh songs of Deutero-Isaiah the emphasis is unmistakably on the active co-operation of the human partner of Yahweh. The question whether this partner, the servant of the Lord, is meant as collective Israel or a single person—and if so, which? a historical? or an eschatological?—can never be settled, because probably it does not have to be answered either the one way or the other. The figure may well be both an individual and also the people, and both of them in a historical and also an eschatological form. What is certain is that in and with this servant of the Lord Israel as such is at any rate introduced also as the partner of Yahweh in an eschatological encounter with the nations, the powerful witness of Yahweh in the midst of the heathen. It is, therefore, in the light of a service which Israel has to perform that the actualisation of the prophecy of salvation is now understood . . . " I have formed thee . . . and will give thee for a mediator of the covenant on behalf of the race (Zürich Bible), for a light of the Gentiles " . . . It is the covenant people which lives and cries and suffers here, which is hemmed in and oppressed and threatened, which is more than threatened, actually overthrown and given up to destruction (and all according to the will and disposing of its God). The relatively short time of its modest existence in the sphere of world-history or of contemporary middle-eastern politics draws quickly to its close—in pain and grief and shame. What is it that the covenant-God is saying in all this? What is it that He wills by this work of His—He who has from the first and again and again shown and attested Himself as the One who is in covenant with His people? The prophets evidently associated the happenings primarily with the message that Israel had to see in it that judgment for its unfaithfulness to the Lord of the covenant which had been held before it from the very first . . . But they also spoke of the unchangeable faithfulness of the covenant-God, of the inflexibility of His purpose for His people, and therefore of the positive meaning of its history including its end. It is in this context that there arises the prophecy of the redemptive future of Israel in the last days. It presupposes the dark state of things at the present. It views it with pitiless clarity. And it does not overlay this view with the mere promise of better times to come . . . Its nerve and centre is the reference to an event which will terminate all history and all times, a history of the end . . . The last time, the day of Yahweh, will indeed be the day of final judgment . . . But as such it will also be the day of Israel's redemption—the day when the covenant which Yahweh has made will find its positive fulfilment. (IV, 1, p. 30 f. The Covenant as the Presupposition of Reconciliation.)

Cf. on Isaiah 49$^{1-6}$ Third Sunday After Epiphany.

HEBREWS 5$^{1-10}$ (VI)

But in individual figures whom we must not overlook the Gentiles also have a place in the redemptive history attested by the Bible . . . The most remarkable of them—they include Balaam, Rahab, Ruth, Hiram, Cyrus and the Syro-Phoenician woman—is Melchisedek (Genesis 14$^{18f.}$; Psalm 110^4), who appears again mysteriously as the representative of an otherwise unmentioned priestly order, by which even the Elect of Yahweh seems to be measured. According to 5$^{6,\,10}$; 6^{20}; 7$^{1f.}$, he is the type of Jesus Christ Himself and of His supreme and definitive high priesthood. It is therefore . . . obligatory to regard the figure of Melchisedek as the hermeneutic key to this whole succession. It is not on the basis of a natural knowledge of God and relationship with God that all these strangers play their striking role. What happens is rather that in them Jesus Christ proclaims Himself to be the great Samaritan: as it were, in a second and outer circle of His revelation, which by its very nature can only be hinted at. It must be noted that no independent significance can be ascribed to any of the revelations as we can call them in a wider sense. There is no Melchisedek apart from Abraham, just as there is no Abraham apart from Jesus Christ. They have no Word of God to preach. They are not witnesses of the resurrection. They have no full power to summon to the love of God. In this they differ permanently and fundamentally from the prophets and apostles, as does their function from that of the Church. Their witness is a confirmatory and not a basic witness . . . If we know the incarnation of the eternal Word and the glorification of humanity in Him, we cannot pass by any man, without being asked whether in his humanity he does not have this mission to us, he does not become to us this compassionate neighbour. (I, 2, p. 425 f. The Praise of God.)

The true God . . . is obedient (v. 8). We have to keep before us the difficulty of this equation if we are to be clear what we have to understand and to accept or reject as the content of the New Testament witness to Christ. Obedience—even obedience which serves—does not of itself exclude a way of outstanding human greatness and power and glory, a being as man which is fulfilled in the best sense, and effective and successful in the world, and in its own way satisfying and triumphant. But according to the New Testament it is not the being of the man Jesus which has this character. On the contrary, the New Testament describes the Son of God . . . not accidentally and incidentally, not merely to prove and show His mind and disposition . . . but necessarily and, as it were, essentially, and so far as can be seen without meaning or purpose . . . as a suffering servant who wills this profoundly unsatisfactory being, who cannot will anything other in the obedience in which He shows Himself the Son of God. (IV, 1, p. 164. The Way of the Son of God into the Far Country.)

Cf. I, 2, p. 157 f.

THIRD SUNDAY IN LENT (OCULI)

LUKE 11$^{14-28}$ (I)

In this matter we have to free ourselves . . . from the basically subjectivistic habit of thinking and speaking which would have it *either* that Jesus accommodated Himself in the interest of pedagogy to the current Judaistic idea (the suggestion of earlier Rationalists), *or* that He was Himself a prisoner of this view (the modern alternative). It is, of course, also a matter of " ideas, " but primarily and decisively it is a matter of objective facts, which cannot as such be jeopardised by a demonstration that the ideas in question are conditioned and limited. The truth was this. Jesus did in fact live in this Judaistic actuality with its presuppositions, which were not only subjective but also objective, not only anthropological but also theological and therefore cosmological. Like all other Jews therefore, but in a way incomparably more exact than all others, He saw and experienced what there was actually to be seen and experienced: an abyss of darkness which was not merely supposed or imagined or invented or projected into the sphere of being but was actual and concrete; the presence and action of nothingness, of the evil in the background and foreground of human existence. He saw and experienced man as he was, invisibly, but also visibly, and in any case really, claimed and imprisoned by this actuality, terrified of his human environment and therefore chained, constantly breaking his chains and really suffering in the freedom won in this way, " possessed " by nothingness in one or other of its different forms, inescapably delivered up to it, corrupted even in the forefront of his being by this corruptive background of the human situation. All this was at issue in the exorcisms of Jesus. And that is why they have a representative as well as an intrinsic importance, characterising the trend or direction of His whole activity. Like His raisings from the dead, they reveal the total and absolutely victorious clash of the kingdom of God with nothingness, with the whole world of the chaos negated by God, with the opposing realm of darkness . . . The activity of Jesus invaded at this point the sphere of that power which was introduced into the cosmos by the sin and guilt of man and works itself out in his need and tragedy, enslaving all creatures. It penetrated to the poisonous source whose effluents reach out to the whole cosmos and characterise its form as that of " this present evil aeon " (Gal. 1⁴). (IV, 1, p. 230. The Royal Man.)

EPHESIANS 5¹⁻⁹ (II)

What are we to do? We are to do what corresponds to the grace of God. We are to respond to the existence of Jesus Christ and His people. With our action we are to render an account to this grace. By it and by it alone we are challenged. To it and it alone we are responsible. Imitation (v. 1) is obviously related in the strictest possible sense to the gracious attitude of God to us men revealed and operative in Christ. This attitude is the Law which is given to us. It is to this attitude that we and all our activity are bound, and by it that we are measured, and must orientate ourselves. (II, 2, p. 576. The Command as the Claim of God.)

According to the speech and thought-forms of the Bible, concepts such as light, illumination, revelation and knowledge do not have . . . a more narrowly intellectual or noetic significance . . . The light or revelation of God is not just a declaration and interpretation of His being and action . . . In making Himself known, God acts on the whole man. Hence the knowledge of God given to man through his illumination is no mere apprehension and understanding of God's being and action, nor as such a kind of intuitive contemplation. It is the claiming not only of his thinking but also of his willing and work, of the whole man, for God. It is his refashioning to be a theatre, witness and instrument of His acts. Its subject and content, which is also its origin, makes it an active knowledge, in which there are affirmation and negation, volition and decision, action and inaction, and in which man leaves certain old courses and pursues new ones. As the work of God becomes clear to him, its reflection lights up his own heart and self and whole existence through the One whom he may know on the basis of His own self-declaration. Illumination and therefore vocation is the total alteration of the one whom it befalls. The light seen by seeing eyes becomes the light of the body, of the person of a man, in the shining of which it becomes wholly clear (Lk. 11³⁴ᶠ·) and is set wholly under the judgment and grace, the promise and command, of the One who calls him. The light thus bears " fruit " (v. 9). There is an " armour " of light which those whom it lightens must immediately put on (Rom. 13¹²). Far from being a mere spectator of the light, man becomes and the Christian is a

" child of light " (Jn. 12³⁶; 1 Thess. 5⁵; Lk. 16⁸), or " light in the Lord "
(v. 8). (IV, 3, p. 510. The Event of Vocation.)

GENESIS 22¹⁻¹⁴ᵃ   (III)

III, 3, pp. 3–57. The Doctrine of Providence, Its Basis and Form.
Cf. on Hebrews 11¹ᶠ·, ⁶, ⁸⁻¹⁰, ¹⁷⁻¹⁹ Second Sunday in Lent.

1 PETER 1¹³⁻²³   (IV)

The holiness required of Israel (Leviticus 11⁴⁴) has essentially the
character of cultic holiness. The holiness of man and of human actions,
of things and places, is constituted, so to speak, by their serviceableness in
the fellowship founded and initiated by God between Himself and man.
Unholiness is therefore unserviceableness to this end. The holiness of
God describes the form of His attitude in this fellowship. Sin is whatever
disturbs and makes this fellowship impossible. For this reason God's
attitude in this fellowship is characterised by holiness, exclusiveness, the
condemnation and annihilation of sin. The holiness of God thus involves
peril to the man with whom He has fellowship. Since his sin disturbs this
fellowship and makes it impossible, man himself becomes impossible. As
a sinful man he cannot stand before God. He must perish. That he
should himself be holy is not, therefore, a command by which God urges
him to secure for himself a status or merit in His presence. But as God's
command it is quite simply the command to cleave to His grace . . . Man
becomes holy in virtue of the holiness of the God who graciously takes
action on his behalf. (II, 2, p. 364. The Grace and Holiness of God.)
Cf. on Leviticus 19¹⁻³, ¹³⁻¹⁸ Eighteenth Sunday After Trinity.
Cf. also III, 2, p. 497.

MATTHEW 20²⁰⁻²⁸   (V)

The man Jesus is the " chiefest " (v. 27) . . . This is attested by what He
said at the institution of the Lord's Supper in the Synoptists and what He
did in the foot-washing in John. And He makes no demand upon His own
in this respect which He has not first inimitably demonstrated with the act
of His own life, thus giving it the character of a demand which can be
understood only as the proclamation and offer of the grace of God manifested in Him. (III, 2, p. 215 f. Jesus, Man for Other Men.)
Revealed as such by His resurrection and ruling as such by His Holy
Spirit, Jesus Christ is the King and Lord of the world and the community
as the One who on the cross was defeated and in that way victorious,
humbled and in that way exalted. He is the King and Lord as the One who
serves His Father, and therefore His own and all men. It is as this One
who serves that He rules and requires obedience. He is not, therefore, one
of the lords who do not serve but only rule and leave the serving to others.
He is the Lord as He is first the servant of God and all others . . . It is as

He serves that He rules ... The community attains its true order as His community when its action is service. And its members, Christians, attain their true order when they serve. In the Christian community, unlike all other human societies, there is no distinction between privileges and duties, claims and obligations, or dignities and burdens. There can be privileges and claims and dignities only in and with the duties and obligations and burdens of service (v. 27). (IV, 2, p. 690 f. The Order of the Community.)
Cf. IV, 4, p. 16.

REVELATION 5¹⁻¹⁴ (VI)

Something already before the seer, but not yet noted or named by him, now claims his attention (v. 1) ... That the roll of a book is sealed with seven seals characterises it as a will, or at least as a document which has to be executed as well as noted. Thus the opening of the book means that what is written in it takes place in history ... The book is in God's hand. It is obviously His will and counsel which will be executed when it is opened. And vv. 2–3 make it plain that it is in the hand of God alone. Who is worthy to open it? ... Even in heaven there is no answer. No one can or may or will execute what God has resolved. No one can even know it. No one can even look into the book in His hand. No creature can do this, not even the strong angel who addresses the question to his fellow-creatures. God is always sovereign. He alone decides and effects, and He alone knows the things which must be hereafter (4^1) ... The new and decisive vision and occurrence are to be found in v. 6 f. ... As yet there is no word of the opening of the book ... it is now in the hands of the Lamb. He will break its seven seals one after the other. The execution of all God's secret counsel will be His affair. Is God dead? Or has He gone into retirement? Far from it! The Lamb is not a second and different God. He is the one God. He will not change the counsel of the one God but execute it faithfully. What is revealed in His enthronement and seizure of power is that from all eternity the secret counsel of God, whatever may be its content in detail, has had the meaning which finds form and reality in the fact that this Lamb is the Lion, the all-powerful and all-wise Executor of His will and plan. The majesty of God as His mercy was the outline and shadow of the divine mystery as indicated already in c. 4. And now at the climax of c. 5 we are confronted by the form and reality of the same mystery. (III, 3, pp. 469–471, cf. 463–476. The Kingdom of Heaven.)
Cf. on Revelation 4¹⁻⁸ Sunday Next Before Advent.

FOURTH SUNDAY IN LENT (LAETARE)

JOHN 6¹⁻¹⁵ (I)
GALATIANS 4²²⁻³¹; 5^{1a} (II)

What Paul says in v. 25 f. with reference to the Synagogue may rightly be applied to every form of the people of God on earth—that " the Jerusalem which is above is free, which is the mother of us all. " Here again, however, the emphasis must fall on the other aspect. The Holy One does actually give it to His saints to be free: free to lift up themselves and look to Him; and therefore free from the compulsion to sin which results from their being as sinners . . . The apostolic admonition . . . is not given as a law or ideal proclaimed in the void. It is not given as though the question whether or not they can obey were still open and to be answered. It is obviously given on the assumption that they are free, and that they can make use of the freedom in which they have been made free in Christ (5^1). Without this assumption there would be no such thing as Christian ethics even for us. All the things that we have to develop in ethics in relation to the command of the God who reconciles the world with Himself can only be concretions of the lifting up of themselves, the looking to Jesus, of which Christians are capable because they have been given the freedom for them. It is true that in its original and proper form they have this freedom, not in themselves, but in the One who is above. But called by Him to fellowship with Himself, placed in it, united with Him by His Holy Spirit, they are free here and now in correspondence to His kingly rule . . . To their salvation they are free only for this. But they are genuinely free for this. They can look to Him and be His saints in everything that they do in this look. 2 Cor. 5^{17} is true of them . . .; and especially Heb. 12^{10} . . .; and above all Jn. 8^{36}. . . . It is all provisional, for the saints are still captives. But it is all very real, for they are already liberated. If it is true that they are still prisoners, it does not count. The captivity is behind them, freedom before them. And all this is in their fellowship with the Holy One. All this is in virtue of the fact that they are called by Him (Jn. 15^3). (IV, 2, p. 532 f. The Holy One and the Saints.)

The word " freedom " implies first and formally that when Scripture speaks of the Holy Spirit as an element in revelation we are dealing with an ability or capacity or capability which is given to man as the addressee of revelation and which makes him a real recipient of revelation. The problem by which we found ourselves confronted was: How can man believe? How does *homo peccator* become *capax verbi divini*? The New Testament answer is that it is the Holy Spirit who sets man free for this and for the ministry in which he is put therewith.

Christ has " set us free for freedom, " we read in v. 1. Here and everywhere the term is undoubtedly contrasted with the idea of the servitude overcome in Christ. Primarily—but only primarily—this servitude consists in bondage to a law of God which man has misunderstood and misused . . . But the nature and curse of this servitude lies deeper. Because man is bound in this way he is not able nor free to receive real revelation. The converse is also true: Because he is not free for real revelation, he is in bondage. At all events, although in appearance, but only in appearance, he believes in God and hearkens to Him and strives diligently to serve Him, he is in fact powerless in relation to the living God, i.e., powerless to know Him as He is and to obey Him as He desires. The freedom for which Christ sets us free cannot, then, consist merely in freedom from that servitude. It must also consist—and decisively so—in freedom from that powerlessness, in freedom for the real revelation of God. (cf. Jn. 8[30-59]). (I, 1, p. 456 [524]. God as Redeemer.)

Cf. II, 2, p. 215; pp. 589-593.

ROMANS 5[1-11] (IIb)

" We have peace with God . . . " (v. 1). Many serious and penetrating things result from this peace, as emerges in Rom. 5-8. But they result from the fact that we *have* this peace. Only half-serious and superficially penetrating things can result from a lack of peace with God, or from a supposed peace that we have or think we have in some other way than " through our Lord Jesus Christ. " The Christmas message is: " Peace on earth to men of (God's) goodwill. " And what is meant is the peace with God which is included for all the children of men in the child who was born there and then. (IV, 2, p. 273. The Direction of the Son.)

Jesus Christ fought His enemies, the enemies of God—as we all are (v. 10; Col. 1[21])—no, He loved His enemies, by identifying Himself with them. Compared with that, what is the bit of forebearance or patience or humour or readiness to help or even intercession that we are willing and ready to bring and offer by way of loving our enemies? But obviously when we look at what Jesus Christ became and was for us, we cannot leave out some little love for our enemies as a sign of our recognition and understanding that this is how He treated us His enemies. It is indeed a very clear commandment of God which points us in this direction from the cross of shame. (IV, 1, p. 244. The Judge Judged in Our Place.)

It is God first who is for man, and then and for that reason man is for God. God precedes therefore, and sets man in the movement in which he follows. He says Yes to him when man says No, and thus silences the No of man and lays a Yes in his heart and on his lips. He loves man even though he is an enemy (v. 10) and thus makes him the friend who loves Him in return. (IV, 2, p. 580. The Awakening to Conversion.)

Cf. II, 2, p. 600.

JOHN 6[22-29] (III)

In v. 29 we have the extremely succinct answer of Jesus . . .: " This is the work of God, that ye believe on him whom he hath sent." Is there not included in this all human work in its relationship to the work of God? . . . Man can only believe in the grace of God encountering and revealed to him . . . He can only pray that God will not hide His face or let him fall, as he must recognise each passing moment that he has deserved a hundred times . . . He will then act calmly and resolutely and vigorously, but always knowing that he must lay himself and what he wills and does and achieves wholly in the hand of the God who has so graciously chosen and called him to participate in His work. He will constantly commend it to Him, that He may forgive that in which it is sinful, that He may receive it like himself, that He may sanctify it, that He may use it and order it, that He may give it the character of a service rendered and acceptable to Himself—which is something that can never be given by the man who performs it. (IV, 2, p. 594 f. The Sanctification of Man.)

PHILIPPIANS 2^{12-18} (IV)

The Christian is summoned in v. 12 f. to work out (in " fear and trembling ") his salvation, or, as we may say, his life in hope, because it is God who works in him to will and to do of his good-pleasure. To be sure, his hope, like his faith and love, is a work which he himself has to perform either well or badly. It is a work which is required of him, so that he is responsible for its proper fulfilment. If a man looks for the day of the Lord, he must hasten unto it (2 Pet. 3^{12}). Of his own desire, according to his own judgment or whim, of his own ability or impulse? None has ever done this. On the contrary, he hastens or works or hopes with all his heart and soul and mind and strength, being concerned at all points, and with " fear and trembling " in view of the magnitude and importance of the task, for the genuineness of his hope, because the free God awakens him who in himself is unwilling and incapable to freedom, to freedom of thought and will and movement and action, and therefore to hope . . . In this freedom he will only desire and be able to live in this hope. What he has to keep in fear and trembling can only be this freedom, or, more exactly, his readiness continually to let himself b wakened by God to this freedom. (IV, 3, p. 940 f. Life in Hope.)

JOHN 6^{47-57} (V)

This is the verse (v. 56) to which Qu. 76 of the Heidelberg Catechism appealed in its explanation of the Lord's Supper: " What does it mean to eat the crucified body of Christ and to drink His own shed blood? It means not only to accept with a believing heart the whole death and passion of Christ, and thus to receive the remission of sins and eternal life, but also, by the Holy Ghost who dwells both in Christ and us, to be more and more united with His blessed body, so that, although He is in heaven and we on earth, we are bone of His bone and flesh of His flesh, and live and are ruled eternally by His Spirit (as the members of our body are by a soul)." Above all, we remember the all-embracing answer to Qu. 1: " What is thine only comfort in life and death? That with body and soul, both in life and death, I am not my own, but belong to my faithful

Saviour Jesus Christ." (IV, 2, p. 274. The Direction of the Son.) Cf. III, 2, p. 213 f.

EXODUS 16$^{2-7, 13b-15, 31, 35}$ (VI)

The knowability of God's Word in faith is not an extraordinary art. Or should one rather say conversely that is it a highly extraordinary art? Its practice does not presuppose any special endowment whether natural or supernatural. The believer is the same ungifted and idle or gifted and busy man he was as an unbeliever and may become again. He believes as the man he is, with the inventory corresponding to his condition . . . It is a possibility given for use, not for putting in an inventory or catalogue, not for storing on ice or placing in a museum.

Even in its details the story of the " manna " in Ex. 16 is an illustration of what has to be said about faith in this connexion.

The possibility, then, is not one we can exhibit but only one to which we can point, like faith, or the Word of God itself, or the child born of the Virgin Mary in the manger at Bethlehem. The force and seriousness of this pointer must be the force and seriousness of God if we are really to point. Thus the first thing that must be said about the knowability of the Word of God as the possibility given to us in faith is that it arises and consists absolutely in the object of real knowledge. (I, 1, p. 237 [272]. The Word of God and Faith.)

FIFTH SUNDAY IN LENT (JUDICA)

JOHN 8$^{46-59}$ (I)

One of the most outspoken representatives of recognition of the identity of the Old Testament and the New Testament, i.e., of the revelation of Jesus Christ in the Old Testament also, is Irenaeus, who especially in the fourth book of his chief work is never tired of speaking as follows . . . From the beginning there were those who recognised God and prophesied the coming of Christ, and if they did so, it was because they received revelation from the Son Himself (C.o.h. 7, 2) . . . Abraham's rejoicing (v. 56), so to speak, descended to his posterity, who really saw Christ and believed in Him—but again the rejoicing ascended to Abraham, who once desired to see the day of Christ (7, 1). (I, 2, p. 74 f. The Time of Revelation.)

God is pre-temporal . . . It may sound trivial to say that God was before we were, and before all the presuppositions and conditions of our existence. Yet in its unqualified, literal sense it is profound and decisive. God was in the beginning which precedes all other beginnings. He was in the beginning in which we and all things did not yet exist. He was in the beginning which does not look back on any other beginning presupposed by this beginning itself . . . We are not from eternity, and neither is our world. There was a time when we and the world did not exist. This was the " pre-time," the eternity of God ... In this time God wrote His decrees and books, in which everything is marked down that is to be and occur, including every name and the great and small events of the bearer of every name ... This pre-time is the pure time of the Father and the Son in the fellowship of the Holy Spirit ... If we understand eternity as pre-time—and we must understand it in this way too—we have to recognise that eternity itself bears the name of Jesus Christ (v. 58; Eph. 1[4f.]; 1 Pet. 1[18f.]). Note how in all these and similar passages the eternal presence of God over and in time is established by reference to a pre-time in which time, and with it the existence of man and its renewal, is foreseen and determined. What is to be said about time and its relation to eternity derives from the fact that eternity is also before time. (II, 1, pp. 621–623. The Eternity and Glory of God.)

Cf. on Galatians 4[22-31]; 5[1a] Fourth Sunday in Lent.

JOHN 17[9-19]   (Ib)

The hatred which will fall on the disciples is not an accidental nor exorbitant phenomenon; it corresponds to the general rule. The remarkable tense of v. 14 points in the same direction: "... and the world hated them." That is, in His giving them the Word of God, it was decided and took place already that the world hated them. It is to be noted that in the New Testament the word " hatred " nowhere seems to have, and does not have here, the sense of a personal emotion of personal aversion for the object of the hatred. The Christian is not hated as a human individual who is repulsive to the one who hates him on account of his personal being and action. He is hated as the bearer and representative of a specific claim and cause ... It is thus that the disciples are hated by all men and the world, being regarded and treated as outlaws—not because they are Peter, Paul or John, but because they represent to all men and to the world the alien and intolerable cause of the kingdom, the *coup d'état* of God. According to Mt. 10[22] this comes upon them, not because of what they are personally, but quite simply for the sake of the name which they preach, and of its import ... As those who are sent and commissioned by Him ... they can have no part in the self-understanding of the cosmos but can only contradict it. But since it is a matter of this basic and material thing, the New Testament *misein* (" to hate ") signifies a disproportionately sharper reaction than even the worst that might happen when one man cannot tolerate another for personal reasons. (IV, 3, p. 624 f. The Christian in Affliction.)

" All this I did for thee; What wilt thou do for me? " The New Testament does not speak in this way. It knows nothing of a Jesus who lived and died for the forgiveness of our sins, to free us as it were retrospectively, but who now waits as though with tied arms for us to act in accordance with the freedom achieved for us ... As we are not asked to justify ourselves, we are not asked to sanctify ourselves. Our sanctification consists in our participation in His sanctification as grounded in the efficacy and revelation of the grace of Jesus Christ. (IV, 2, p. 516 f. The Sanctification of Man.)

Cf. on John 17$^{1-8}$ Palm Sunday; on John 17$^{20-26}$ The Ascension Day Cf. also III, 2, p. 220 f.; II, 2, p. 459.

HEBREWS 9$^{11-15}$ (II)

Jesus Christ is the One who was accused, condemned and judged in the place of us sinners. But we can say the same thing in this way: He gave Himself to be offered up as a sacrifice to take away our sins . . . What does the term sacrifice mean? . . . Sacrifices (according to the Old Testament) are substitutes for what a member of the covenant people really ought to render to God, but never does so, and never will. They are gifts from the sphere of his most cherished possessions which represent or express his will to obey, which symbolise the life which has not in fact been offered to God. He can bring these gifts. He ought to do so. He acknowledges Yahweh and the fact that he belongs to Him by bringing them. He recognises his guilt and obligation . . . The real problem of sacrifice is not the imminent misuse to which like any cult it can be put, but the fact that in face of the sin of man . . . it does not in any way alter either sin itself or the situation of conflict and contradiction brought about by sin . . . It is only a " shadow of things to come " (v. 1). *Significat?* Yes. *Est?* No. That is the limitation and problem of sacrifice in the Old Testament . . . This is where the one sacrifice of Jesus Christ intervenes: the real sacrifice for sin, the sacrifice which sets it aside, which effects and proclaims its effective and complete forgiveness, which brings before God the just man which Israel could signify in its sacrifices . . . but could only signify, which it could introduce only in substitute, in a kind of *Quid pro quo*. The sacrifice of Jesus Christ, the offering of which is taken out of the hands of all priests, is entirely His own affair, and it is no longer a shadow or figure, but a fulfilment of the reconciliation of man with God . . . Our whole understanding depends upon our recognising that God's own activity and being, His presence and activity in the One who is His own Son, very and eternal God with the Father and the Holy Spirit, is the truth and power of that which takes place here as a history of human sacrificing and sacrifice. (IV, 1, pp. 277–280. The Judge Judged in Our Place.)

Cf. on Hebrews 7$^{24-23}$ Fifth Sunday in Lent (VI).

HEBREWS 4$^{14-16}$ (IIb)

Jesus was not a sinful man. But inwardly and outwardly His situation was that of a sinful man . . . Freely He entered into solidarity and necessary association with our lost existence. Only in this way " could " God's revelation to us, our reconciliation with Him, become an event in Him and by Him, 2^{18}; 4^{15}; $5^{2f.}$. Note: it is here that we find ourselves at the point where the biblical doctrine of the incarnation of the Word and familiar parallels in the history of religions part company. There are also incarnations of Isis and Osiris; there is an incarnation in Buddha and in Zoroaster. But it is only the New Testament that says " he hath made him to be sin " and " he became a curse for us." Only . . . it speaks of this divine solidarity and necessary association with us. To deviate from this, to try to make God's becoming flesh merely a becoming man or even a hero, is to descend to the level of the religions: they can all do this. (I, 2, p. 152 f. Very God and Very Man.)

" For we have not an high priest that cannot be touched with the feeling of our infirmities (" sympathise " with them is too weak a rendering and one that evokes false associations), but one that was in all points tempted like as we are, yet without sin." In His likeness He was also unlike in that He did not yield to temptation. That He learned obedience by the things which He suffered (5^8) means that He maintained it in freedom in a way which was not by any means self-evident. (IV, 1, p. 259 f. The Obedience of the Son of God.)

In practice, at least, it is to be noted that a living Christianity has always in its hymns and prayers, and above all in its administration of baptism and the Lord's Supper, experienced and seen and understood and expounded and proclaimed His presence within it and the world as the presence of the Crucified. Even in the most questionable feature of the Roman Mass, namely, its character as a representation of the sacrifice of Golgotha, we must acknowledge that it does at least make this clear. And Evangelical preaching must never lag behind it in this respect . . . It is not merely that He was once " touched with the feeling of our infirmities "; He is so still. It is not merely that He was once tempted as we are; He is with us and before us, tempted as we are (v. 15) . . . This is more than recollection, for it speaks of His presence here to-day among us in all our confusion, aberration and abandonment, before all our locked prison doors, at all our sick-beds and gravesides, and, of course, with questioning, warning, restraint and delimitation, in all our genuine or less genuine triumphs. He is still the Friend of publicans and sinners . . . All this is behind Him, yet it is also continually before Him. It is thus that He is among us and with us: " Slumbering and sleeping, We're safe in His keeping; On our awaking, The glory is breaking, Of His mercy so freely bestowed " (Paul Gerhardt). A man is merciful when he takes to heart the need of another. Jesus Christ has once and for all taken our need to heart. This was His passion. But although He did it once and for all, He did not do it once only. Risen from the dead, He lives and takes it to heart with undiminished severity. This is His passion to-day. (IV, 3, p. 395 f. The True Witness.)

Cf. on Hebrews 2^{10-18} Maundy Thursday.

JOHN 13²¹⁻³⁵ (III)

What makes the community a distinctive and serious partner in dis-cussion with the world is the fact that within it—but visible outwardly—it takes place that the men united in it do what is not done elsewhere: upholding one another instead of causing one another to fall (Eph. 4²); serving one another by love instead of ruling over one another (Gal. 5¹³); showing a brotherly love which is inward, unfeigned, sincere and constant (1 Pet. 1²²; 4⁸), not stagnating or declining but increasing in each individual member (2 Thess. 1³) and confirming itself even to the one who has fallen (2 Cor. 2⁸). . . . The similarity of the witness to God's love and to the freedom to love Him in return is to be found quite simply in the fact that the neighbour will love the neighbour, the brother the brother. He will do so in a human act of love. But within the limits and with all the frailty of human action he will do so in reality and truth. For he himself is loved by God and may love Him in return . . . On the level of what takes place between man and man he can proclaim it only in such a way that here too, in this encounter, there is love, the mutual love of these men. (IV, 2, p. 826 f. The Act of Love.)

1 CORINTHIANS 4⁹⁻²⁰ (IV)

It is obviously no mere figure of speech in biblical thinking that Paul in v. 15, 17 calls the Corinthian Christians his beloved children to whom he has given birth in Christ Jesus through the Gospel, and Timothy his beloved and faithful child in the Lord or his true child in the faith (1 Tim. 1², ¹⁸), as also Titus (Tit. 1⁴) and Onesimus (Philem. 10) whom he has begotten in his bonds. It is also clear that it is no mere symbolism, and even less an empty play on words, to talk of spiritual fathers, sons and brothers. Biological fatherhood has a weight and honour which physical sons must respect in the fact that it has as such a spiritual mission in execution of which it finds fulfilment. And we must add at once that at any rate in the New Testament, and already in the Old Testament Book of Proverbs, this mission of the older to the younger can seriously exist and be fulfilled, and is thus to be honoured, even apart from physical parenthood. (III, 4, p. 244. Parents and Children.)

EXODUS 32¹⁵⁻²⁰, ³⁰⁻³⁴ (V)

The " incident " (vv. 1–6) has already taken place, and has not passed without leaving a trace. What has happened has brought everything into question—the election, the grace, the covenant of God, the separation and divine mission and therefore the existence of Israel. It seems as though the dissolution of the covenant must at once follow its institution . . . v. 9 f. So greatly, so radically, so profoundly did that which Israel willed and did —its sin—run counter to that which God willed and did, that it seemed as though God could only renounce Israel in His anger and break off the connexion which He had made. But now Moses came forward and into the centre . . . in a different function from that so far allotted to him in this book. He is no longer merely the messenger of God and the prophetic and charismatic leader. Of course, he does still appear and act (vv. 15–29) in accordance with this mission. We might say that he is the one who fulfils the wrathful saying of God. He throws down and smashes the tables given to him for this people and written with the finger of God. He burns the image of the calf and grinds it to powder. He makes the people drink of it. He orders a partial mass-execution which brings out clearly the terrible nature of the presence of the One who had elected Himself the God of Israel. But surprisingly, the picture of Moses in accordance with his mission is itself only an " incident " in relation to the singular overall picture given in the book. It is framed by the accounts of the conversations which he had with God Himself (32^{7-14} and $32^{30}-34^{10}$), in which the same man plays quite a different part and one which is quite unique in the Old Testament. Anticipating the place of Israel among the nations . . . it is the role of a mediator between this people and its God . . . This man dares to remind God of His own promise, to appeal to His faithfulness, beseeching Him, but also very definitely remonstrating with Him, vv. 11–13. Is not this to flee from God to God, to appeal from God to God? And is it not the case that in this flight, this appeal of Moses, God finds Himself supremely and most profoundly understood and affirmed, that in a sense Moses has prayed, or rather demanded, from the very heart of God? He hears and answers this prayer which is so defiant and dogmatic. He does, of course, plague the people . . ., v. 35. But He repents of the evil . . ., v. 14. His destruction is well-merited and it seemed inevitable, but it does not take place. His covenant is not taken away . . . (IV, 1, p. 425f. The Pride and Fall of Man.)

Cf. I, 2, p. 328

Hebrews 7^{24-27} (VI)

It is the Crucified who was rasied again from the dead and ascended into heaven, where He sits at the right hand of God the Father Almighty. It is as this One, the Suffering and Afflicted, that " he continueth ever, and hath an unchangeable priesthood, and is thus able to save them to the uttermost that come unto God by him, seeing he ever liveth to make intercession for them " (v. 24 f.). The Lamb slain not only stood, but still stands, between the throne of God and the heavenly and earthly cosmos (Rev. 5^6), and according to the song in this chapter He not only was but is worthy to open the book and the seals, and to receive power and riches and wisdom and strength and honour and glory and blessing. (IV, 3, p. 397. The True Witness.)

Jesus Christ is a Priest after the order of Melchisedec. That is, He is an instance of priestly action for which there is no parallel, which cannot be deduced from anything else, which stands under no law but that established and revealed in the fact that there was this instance ... In His ministry, unlike other priests and high priests, He cannot and need not be replaced by any other priestly person. He does not have and exercise this office within the framework of an institution, as one of its many representatives, but on the basis of an oath which God swore by Himself, and therefore as a Priest for ever (vv. 20–24, not with daily or annual repetitions, but in a single action accomplished and effective once and for all (v. 27; $9^{12, 26}$; 10^{10}) ... In this way the work of Jesus Christ is at once the essence and fulfilment of all other priestly work but also that which replaces it and makes it superfluous ... The supreme and distinctive function of the priest is to offer sacrifice. But this Priest—and here the image breaks down completely and the parallel with Melchisedec is abandoned—is not only the One who offers sacrifice but also the sacrifice which is offered ... He does not offer anything else—not even the greatest thing—He simply offers Himself (v. 27; $9^{14, 23, 26}$; $10^{12, 14}$). (IV, 1, p. 276 f. The Judge Judged in Our Place.)

PALM SUNDAY

PHILIPPIANS 2^{1-11} (II)

This is also the practical significance of Phil. $2^{5f.}$. It serves, cf. verses 1–4, directly to emphasise the apostolic exhortation to humility, in which each member of the community is to subordinate himself to the other, not seeking his own but the things of others. In the community we are to be intent on the reality " in Jesus Christ. " And this is the divine condescension, the self-emptying and self-humbling. In it Christ is Christ and God is God. In it alone can Christians be Christians. Any " mind " which is not directed to it, however exalted or penetrating it may be, passes by Christ and therefore passes by God, and is therefore an un-christian " mind. " (II, 1, pp. 517 f. The Constancy and Omnipotence of God.)

In the New Testament this minister, servant or slave—the form of the Ebed Yahweh of Isaiah $52^{13f.}$ now revealed in its fulfilment—is ... Jesus Christ Himself. To be a man like all other men meant for Him, to whom it was proper to exist in the form and majesty of God, to exist rather, in a way which is exemplary for all men and especially for His own, in the form and lowliness of a *doulos* engaged only to obedience, in order that as such He might be distinguished by the name of *Kyrios* which is absolutely superior to all other names. (IV, 3, p. 601. The Christian as Witness.)

If this is so (v. 10, cf. Rev. 4^{12}; Col. 1^{15-19}), then there is no higher place at which our thinking and speaking of the works of God can begin than this name. We are not thinking or speaking rightly of God Himself if we do not take as our starting-point the fact which should be both " first and last ": that from all eternity God elected to bear this name. Over against all that is really outside God, Jesus Christ is the eternal Word of God (Jn. 1[1f.]), the eternal decree of God and the eternal beginning of God. (II, 2, p. 99. The Election of Jesus Christ.)

Cf. I, 1, p. 400 [458 f.]; IV, 1, p. 164, 635; IV, 2, p. 150 f.

JOHN 12[1-8] (III)

In the contrast here drawn between Judas and Mary, it is the latter's prodigality which Judas (v. 4) cannot and will not understand and accept. He is not opposed to the surrender of Mary's costly ointment. But he wants something for it—namely 300 denarii—not for himself, as he explains, but to give to the poor. He is not willing that the complete devotion, which by her deed Mary had in a sense given to the apostles as a pattern for their own life, should be an absolute offering to Jesus. For him it is too little a thing that the death of Jesus should be glorified by it. If there is to be an offering, he wants to exploit it. A good and profitable work is to be carried out in the strength and exercise of this devotion. It is to be for the benefit of the poor, of those who are injured or needy, to help improve their lot and that of others, and in that way it will be a meaningful devotion. This view, this attitude of Judas, is what makes him unclean. It finds relatively innocuous expression. It is not really evil. To correct it would be comparatively easy. But it was because of it that Judas " handed over " Jesus. If a man does not devote himself prodigally to Jesus, if he considers something too good to be offered to Him, if he thinks another purpose more important than the glorifying of His condescension, of His death, that man is as such unclean and opposes his election. He makes himself impossible as an apostle. He must and will hand Jesus over—hand Him over to men, to be crucified. (II, 2, p. 462. The Determination of the Rejected.)

It is practical love which is played off against an act which can be made explicable only as an act of love for Jesus. Ethico-religious (or " religio-social ") Puritanism protests against a very doubtful pietistic undertaking . . . What emerges clearly in all four accounts is that Jesus not only defends unconditionally the act of the woman but in all solemnity acknowledges that it is a good act which belongs necessarily to the history of salvation, even though it seems to be wholly superfluous, an act of sheer extravagance, which can serve " only " the purpose of representing direct and perfect self-giving to Him. (IV, 2, p. 797. The Act of Love.)

ZECHARIAH 9[8-12] (IV)

Cf. on 1 Timothy 3[16] Christmas Day (IV, 2).

JOHN 17[1-8] (V)

" If thou wilt fare securely and rightly teach or grasp God so that thou find grace and help with Him, then let not thyself be persuaded to seek Him elsewhere than in the Lord Christ, nor go round about and trouble thyself with other thoughts nor ask about any other work than how He hath sent Christ. Fix thine art and study on Christ, there let them also bide and hold. And where thine own thought and reason or anyone else leadeth or guideth thee otherwise, do but close thine eyes and say: I should and will know no other God save in my Lord Christ " (*Sermon on Jn.* 17³, 1528). What Luther wants is that deity in general and Christ's deity in particular should not be known along the path of autonomous speculation but along the path of knowledge of God's revelation. But Luther does want it to be known—and this must never be ignored or pushed into the background. More prudent than the Melanchthon of 1521, Luther does not fail to point out that in Jacob's dream we have angels both ascending and descending. The path is first from below upwards, from the *natura humana Christi* to *cognitio Dei*. But it does really lead upwards and therefore it leads downwards again too. (I, 1, p. 418 f. [479]. God the Son.)

Cf. on John 17⁹⁻¹⁹ Fifth Sunday in Lent (Ib); on John 17²⁰⁻²⁶ The Ascension Day (III).

Cf. also III, 2, p. 220 f.

HEBREWS 11², ³²ᵇ⁻⁴⁰; 12¹⁻³ (VI)

Perhaps the strongest New Testament account of this New Testament faith, which is not only bound up with hope but ultimately identical with it, is the eleventh chapter of the Epistle to the Hebrews . . . The statement is made in v. 2 that in the faith which they had in God as defined in v. 1 the elders obtained confirmatory witness. This is illustrated by the examples of Abel, Enoch, Noah, Abraham, Isaac, Jacob, Moses, and the harlot Rahab, with reference to the Judges Gideon, Barak, Samson and Jephthah, to David and Samuel, and to the prophets. Yet in their day they were not granted to see that which was promised . . . They will not therefore (v. 40) be made perfect without us, but with us, for whom God has laid up a new and better promise. And in the continuation in 12¹ᶠ. this is shown to mean that formally we have the same faith as this " cloud of witnesses. " On a better presupposition we, too, are in Advent. We look forward in hope. We are on the way to the fulfilment. (IV, 1, p. 331. The Obedience of the Son of God. Cf. on Hebrews 11¹ᶠᶠ. Second Sunday in Lent (Reminiscere) IV.

The beginning of the Christian life takes place in a direct self-attestation and self-impartation of the living Jesus Christ, in His active Word of power which goes forth *hic et nunc* to specific men in the work of the Holy Ghost. He, He alone, acts as the author of faith, just as He, He alone, is its finisher . . . The fact that a man becomes a Christian, and as such a member of the holy people of the covenant, is something which he owes . . . directly to the Lord of this people, to the Master, whom the community and all its members seek to serve, and can only serve, with their witness . . .

Hence, though the Word of Jesus Christ unquestionably calls a man to the Church, in the Church it immediately and directly calls him to Himself as the Lord of the Church, as the Head of this body of His, as the Good Shepherd. This Word of Jesus Christ which goes forth directly to a man and calls him directly to Jesus Christ Himself, and which all human words from Church dogma, indeed, even from the words of the apostles and evangelists down to the most modest *mutua consolatio fratrum* can only accompany, expound and illumine, is the divine change in a man's life, his baptism with the Holy Ghost, the beginning of the Christian life. (IV, 4, p. 31 f. The Foundation of the Christian Life.)

MAUNDY THURSDAY

JOHN 13$^{1-15}$ (I)

In the New Testament the concept of " serving " is given a new importance and urgency by the fact that the Lord Himself, who in the Old Testament is always the One whom men must serve in view of what He is and does for them, now appears as Himself the Servant . . . In the Fourth Gospel the story of the Last Supper is replaced by that of the foot-washing . . . How emphatically the latter emphasises the fact that the service of Christ is His true power and majesty and therefore the grace by which man receives His life!—the revealed grace of God which was already the secret of the Old Testament, though operative then only in a vertical movement from above. In the New, however, it has really come down into the depths and manifested itself there, becoming itself service in accordance with this end of its way. The action of God which absolutely precedes all human action and therefore human service is that He has placed Himself wholly and unreservedly in the service of man as revealed and effectual in the service of Jesus. This change is denoted linguistically by the fact that the terms *douleia*, *latreia* and *leitourgia* here recede into the background and the word *diakonia* is set more strongly and concretely in the foreground because on the self-evident presupposition of the service of God— the objective genitive now being taken as a subjective—it includes service among men and for them . . . According to the witness of the New Testament God Himself acts and is revealed as a Servant, and in this way as the Lord, in the person of Him who made Himself of no reputation and took upon Him the form of a servant (Phil. 2^7). To belong to Him, and to perform human action in this relationship, means *eo ipse* and *per se* to take His yoke upon oneself (Mt. 11^{29}), i.e., to serve and not to rule with Him, according to His example and in correspondence with His action, and to do so, not in a self-chosen way which might well be a secret path of domination, but in participation in His commission and therefore among men and in the service of men. This is the criterion and test whether it is really the service of God, whether man is really obedient in his active life, whether in his own choice he is really responding to the divine choice and not going his own way and living for himself under the pretext of a self-chosen service. (III, 4, p. 476 f. The Active Life.)

Cf. on John 13³¹⁻³⁵ Fifth Sunday in Lent (III); cf. also II, 2, p. 460 f.

1 CORINTHIANS 11²³⁻²⁹ (II)

And so they go and come to the gathering of the community to seat themselves, and to eat and drink, as brothers and sisters at the table where He Himself presides as Lord and Host, and they are invited and welcome guests. They go and come to the Lord's Supper. In so doing, they do the very thing which they also do for the strengthening and preservation of creaturely life; just as when they talk with and to one another they do something which is ordinarily done by men when they meet. They eat and drink. But as in their speaking in the community it is not a matter of the private and optional exchange of human convictions and opinions, so in the eating and drinking of the Lord's Supper it is not a question of the nourishment of one here and another there in company with neighbours, but of the eating of one bread and the drinking from one cup, of the common nourishment of them all, because it is He, Jesus Christ, who brings them to it, who invites them, who is the Lord and Host, who is Himself, indeed, their food and drink. It is thus a question of their nourishment by Him. It takes place in the fact that, as often as they here eat and drink together, He proffers and gives Himself to them as the One He is, as the One who is absolutely theirs; and conversely, that He continually makes them what they are, absolutely His. He strengthens and upholds them in their existence as those whom He, the Crucified and Risen, accompanies in the valley of the shadow. More strongly, He strengthens and upholds them in their existence as His body and its members, and therefore to eternal life in the concealment and glory of God . . . It is to be noted how the event of His own life is reflected and repeated in the event of the Supper (as in that of confession and baptism). In remembrance of Him there takes place here and now exactly the same as took place there and then between Himself and His first disciples, immediately prior to His death and resurrection. Provisionally in the place of all men, the community in its reaching out in all its members for eternal life necessarily lives by and in the fact that in its life here and now there may be this reflection and imitation. (IV, 2, p. 703 f. The Order of the Community.)

To examine ourselves (v. 28) means, therefore, to prepare ourselves for the encounter with our Judge. And it is not merely a warning against undisciplined and disorderly administration of the sacrament, but it has the deepest intrinsic significance, that we are invited to undertake this self-examination in relation to the Lord's Supper. What is involved in the readiness engendered by this *dokimazein*, emerges typically in our readiness for this action of actions, for our public and solemn participation in the communion of the body and blood of Christ. " Know ye not your own selves (the Pharisees of Lk. 12[56] certainly did not know, although as Israelites, instructed by the Law, they ought to have known) how that Jesus Christ is in you? " we read in 2 Cor. 13[5]. The goal of all *dokimazein* is finally and properly this self-knowledge correspondent to the action of the Lord's Supper, which is the good will of God to man, inviting him to partake in this sacrament and expecting him at the table of the Lord. To be prepared for our Judge is to be those who worthily partake in the communion of the body and blood of Christ, who expect their spiritual nourishment from this communion and find in it their life, who can say of Jesus Christ: " I am His, and He is mine." In this readiness, the Lord's Supper is rightly observed, and is the constant renewal of the community as the body of Christ, and of each of its members as such. In this readiness for the Lord's Supper all readiness for the Judge of our actions finds typical expression, and therefore all examination in this self-examination. If we examine ourselves at this point, we examine ourselves always and everywhere. If we fail to examine ourselves at this point, we do not examine ourselves at all. (II, 2, p. 640 f. The Command as the Decision of God.)

Cf. III, 2, p. 214.

JEREMIAH 31[31-34]   (III)

The covenant of Jer. 31[31f.] is based on the presupposition that Israel broke the first covenant whose commandments it was supposed to keep. As if this did not signify the end of any possible covenant, as if God were unfaithful to Himself, a new covenant is now proclaimed. In it, too, there is to be a Law, but it is not now revealed from afar amid thunder and lightning. This Law—but what does Law mean in this case?—is to be written in the hearts of the Israelites, so much so, so truly in their hearts, that all instruction in the knowledge of Yahweh from man to man will be superfluous. This new revelation of the Law, this completely new position of Israel close to Yahweh, this new covenant which is utterly inconceivable from the standpoint of the first, is to rest on the forgiveness of sins (v. 33). (I, 1, p. 180 [205]. The Speech of God as the Mystery of God.)

The time of salvation announced in v. 34 . . . has secretly dawned in the history of Israel and the history of Jesus Christ, but it has not yet come openly or in such a way that there is in fact no further need of a " Know the Lord." There is a real knowledge established in the power of the great acts of God and the prophecy of Jesus Christ. Yet . . . it is strangely but undeniably accompanied by an ignorance which is potent even within the community of the elect and called and therefore of those who are solidly enough instructed by the acts of God. Neither the apostles nor the prophets fear nor respect this fact. Yet they do not ignore it. They know how chronically and acutely dangerous it is. They know that it must be destroyed. They thus reveal it. They attack it. They treat it as a serious enemy. There are no writings in either the Old Testament or the New in which the authors do not reckon seriously with this opponent: not so seriously as with the reality whose truth they have to proclaim; yet with the seriousness appropriate to it. It is because of it, and to resist it, that they are empowered and commissioned by God to speak their word. (IV, 3, p. 194. Jesus is Victor.)

" I will put my law in their inward parts, and write it in their hearts." This and this alone is the basis of the love which is the fulfilment of the whole Law. And as God does this His Law, in virtue of which love is expected of man, is the Law of the Gospel. (IV, 2, p. 782 f. The Basis of Love.)

Cf. also IV, 1, pp. 32–34. The Covenant as the Presupposition of Reconciliation; II, 2, pp. 692 ff.

HEBREWS 2[10-18]   (IV)

According to 1 Cor. 1[30] Jesus Christ Himself is made unto us sanctification as well as justification. As E. Gaugler rightly observes . . . sanctification has to be thought of in terms of the history of salvation. Sanctification takes place as history because and as this man who is directly sanctified by God is its acting Subject . . . He is the One who sanctifies, by whose existence and action there are also saints. Everything that follows flows from this source and is nourished by this root. It is on this basis that the call goes out to others that they can and should and must " be holy in all manner of conversation " (1 Pet. 1[15]). (IV, 3, p. 515. The Holy One and the Saints.)

When He had Himself baptised with water by John, Jesus confessed both God and men . . . He became wholly and utterly one of them, not in an act of secret or even public condescension, like a king for a change donning a beggar's rags and mingling with the crowd, but by belonging to them in every way, by being no more and no less than one of them, by having no point of reference except to them. He became one of them, not in order to renounce full fellowship with them when the game was over, like the king exchanging again the beggar's rags for his kingly robes, not in order to leave again the table where he had seated himself with publicans and sinners, and to find a better place, but in order to be one of them definitively as well as originally, unashamed to call them brethren to all eternity because He was their Brother from all eternity (v. 11), a veritable King in this true form of His, and at His place of honour. (IV, 4, p. 58 f. The Foundation of the Christian Life.)

That Jesus could be tempted . . . is something upon which the Epistle to the Hebrews lays particular emphasis. Because " he that sanctifieth and they that are sanctified are all of one (Abraham? Adam?) he is not ashamed to call them brethren " (v. 11). " Forasmuch then as the children are partakers of flesh and blood, he also himself likewise took part of the same " (v. 14). " Wherefore it behoved him in all things to be made like unto his brethren, that he might be to them (in his likeness with them) a merciful and faithful high priest in things pertaining to God " (v. 17). Like them, therefore, in being able to be tempted and in the fight against temptation. How else could He represent them except in a serious entering into their whole situation? (IV, 1, p. 259. The Obedience of the Son of God.)

Cf. also IV, 4, p. 21.

MATTHEW 26$^{36-46}$ (V)

Jesus Christ was and is for us in that He took the place of us sinners . . . The divine subject of the judgment on man as which Jesus appears in the first part of the evangelical record becomes the object of this judgment from the time of the episode in Gethsemane onwards. If this judgment is fulfilled at all—and that is what the Evangelists seem to be saying in the second part of their account—then it is with this reversal. Jesus represents men at the place which is theirs according to the divine judgment, by putting Himself in the place which is theirs on the basis of and in accordance with their human unrighteousness. Jesus maintains the right by electing to let Himself be put in the wrong. He speaks for Himself by being silent. He conquers by suffering. Without ceasing to be action, as action in the strongest sense of the word, as the work of God on earth attaining its goal, His action becomes passion. The Gospel records betray something of the great and well-grounded astonishment at the unheard of nature of this happening, this transition, this reversing of roles. The shrinking of Jesus in the prayer in Gethsemane is a strong trace of it. According to this record it is not self-evident that He should be given this cup to drink and that He should take it upon Himself to drink it (v. 39). This prayer is, as it were, a remarkable historical complement to the eternal decision taken in God Himself, one which was not taken easily but with great difficulty, one to which He won through, which He won from Himself . . . In that strange and scandalous reversal we have a necessary fulfilment of the divine purpose which the Son accepts in fear and trembling as the will of the Father (Luke 24^{26}). (IV, 1, p. 235 and p. 238 f. The Judge Judged in Our Place.)

Jesus does not think about this God, but speaks to Him. And we have to seek the problem of Gethsemane (1) in the content of what He says, (2) in the fact that He is quite alone with what He says, without companion or helper, and (3) in the fact that the answer of God will be given only in the language of facts . . . The main question is that of the content and meaning of this address . . . Jesus prays that the good will and the sacred work and the true word of God should not coincide with the evil will and

the corrupt work and the deceitful word of the tempter and of the world
controlled by him . . . that for the sake of God's own cause and glory the
evil determination of world-occurrence should not finally rage against
Himself, the sent One of God and the divine Son . . . The riddle confronts
Him with all the horror that it evokes: that of the impending unity
between the will of God on the one hand, that will which He had hitherto
obeyed, and which He willed to obey in all circumstances, and whatever
it was, that will which He was quite ready should be done—and, on the
other hand, the power of evil which He had withstood, and which He
willed to withstand in all circumstances and in whatever form He might
encounter it, which He could not allow to be done. What shook Him was
the coming concealment of the lordship of God under the lordship of evil
and evil men. This was the terrible thing which He saw breaking on
Himself and His disciples and all men, on His work as the Reconciler
between God and man, and therefore on God's own work, destroying
everything, mortally imperilling the fulfilment of His just and redemptive
judgment. This was what He saw, and what His disciples, not to speak
of other men, did not see. It was to avoid this dreadful thing that He
prayed, He alone, while His disciples did not pray. It was to prevent this
event that He cried alone to God—that some other possibility should be
put into effect, that this future should not become the present. (IV, 1,
p. 267 and p. 269 f. The Obedience of the Son of God.)

Cf. III, 4, p. 92.

1 CORINTHIANS 10[16-21] (VI)

The eucharistic action as the crowning act of worship—*touto*, this, i.e.,
the common eating and drinking of the disciples according to His command
—is no more and no less than His body and blood, the communion of His
body and blood (v. 16) . . . In this provisional form as the action of the
community, it is His own action; the work of His real presence. Here and
now He Himself is for them—His offered body and His shed blood—the
communion of saints thanking and confessing Him in this action. (IV, 2,
p. 658. The Growth of the Community.)

The giving of His body and shedding of His blood for the many is the
true action, and He as the Doer of this work of atonement is the true
Actor, in the human event of the distribution and reception, of the common
eating and drinking of bread and wine in the Lord's Supper. It is He who
truly nourishes those who there receive and eat and drink bread and wine
together. The establishment and realisation of His fellowship with them,
the *koinonia* of His body and blood (v. 16), is the true reality of their
fellowship with Him and with one another as achieved in the Lord's
Supper. In this action they proclaim His death till He comes (11[26]) . . .
In the work of the Holy Spirit there takes place in the Lord's Supper, in
a way which typifies all that may happen in the life of this people, that

which is indicated by the great *touto estin* (" this is "), namely, that unity with its heavenly Lord, and the imparting and receiving of His body and blood, are enacted in and with their human fellowship as realised in the common distribution and reception of bread and wine. None of this can be taken for granted. It is all most strange and improbable. Indeed, from the human and even the Christian angle it is impossible. Yet on God's side it is not only possible but actual. If it may be perceived only in faith, which is itself the first of these counterparts or correspondents, in faith it may be perceived with clarity and certainty. (IV, 3, p. 758 and p. 761 f. The People of God in World-Occurrence.)

Cf. IV, 1, p. 665.

GOOD FRIDAY

JOHN 19[16-30]   (I)

Jesus Christ fulfilled the will of God . . . With His sacrifice He has left the sphere of that which is improper and provisional and done that which is proper and definitive. His offering was that which God affirmed, which was acceptable and pleasing to Him, which He accepted . . . The crucified Jesus knew (v. 28) " that all things were now accomplished." And His last word when He died was " It is finished " (v. 36). Jesus knew what God knew in the taking place of His sacrifice. And Jesus said what God said: that what took place was not something provisional, but that which suffices to fulfil the divine will, that which is entire and perfect, that which cannot and need not be continued or repeated or added to or superseded, the new thing which was the end of the old but which will itself never become old, which can only be there and continue and shine out and have force and power as that which is new and eternal. Notice the exposition of Ps. 40[7] in Heb. 10[8-10] . . . In this respect we can and must think of the positive intention and meaning of the Old Testament opposition to the sacrifices which Israel misused and therefore God rejected, and even to the institution of sacrifice itself. For now . . . the evil deeds of men are removed from the sight of God. The doing of evil ceases. It is now learned how to do good. Regard is had for right. The violent are now restrained, the orphans are helped to their right and the cause of the widow is taken up (Is. 1[16f.]). Thanks is brought to God, and in this way vows are paid to the Most High. In the day of need He is now called upon, that He may redeem man and that man may praise Him (Ps. 50[14f.]; 51[19]; 40[7f.]). All these things have now taken place: by the which will (the taking place of the sacrificial action of Jesus Christ) we are sanctified (Heb. 10[10]). There has been brought about that radically altered human situation to which all human priests and all the offerings brought by men could only look forward, the reconciliation which lit up their whole activity only as a promise on the horizon, warning and comforting, but only as an indication, not as presence and actuality. Now that Jesus Christ has done sacrifice as a priest and sacrificed Himself, all these things have come, for in Him that which God demanded has taken place; it has been given and accomplished by God Himself. (IV, 1, p. 281 f. The Judge Judged in Our Place.)

Cf. II, 2, pp. 357–389.

ISAIAH 52$^{12, 15b}$; 53$^{1-12}$ (II)

Cf. earlier on Isaiah 42$^{1-8}$ Second Sunday in Lent; on Isaiah 41$^{1-6}$ Third Sunday After Epiphany.

But above all there is in what is rightly the best known of all the Servant Songs—once again we have the eschatological event—it is now the nations themselves who acknowledge that they have at last understood the meaning of the existence of Israel among them—its historical role as a mediator and the message which it has addressed to them, 52$^{13-15}$. The historical background and outlook of the song is a time and situation of the last and deepest and most hopeless abasement of the people of the covenant, or of its (kingly? or prophetic?) representative. But according to this song, in the last days the nations will recognise and acknowledge that his mission, and the universally valid word and universally effective work of God, is present even in this utter hiddenness of the historical form of His witness, 53$^{1-3, 8f.}$. And then the great confession of the nations at the end of the age, which does not deny but confirms and even lights up this appearance, vv. 4–6. And all this means: " He shall see his seed, he shall prolong his days, and the cause of the Lord shall prosper in his hand " because he made himself " an offering for sin, " v. 10. Just as the passage begins with a soliloquy of Yahweh, so it also ends, accepting and confirming the confession of the Gentiles, v. 11 f. (IV, 1, p. 29 f. The Work of God and the Reconciler.)

Now suffering Israel, the suffering prophet, the suffering righteous man, is not Christ . . . But we obviously have to repeat our assertion, that Jacob, Jeremiah and Job, the whole obscure happening in and to Israel, points towards this real hiddennesss of God and so towards His real revelation, that the whole figure of " the servant " in Is. 53—and Is. 53 is only a recapitulation of what is to be found in almost every chapter of the Old Testament—typifies the suffering and crucified Christ. So far as the Old Testament is not only a problem but a solved problem, so far as Yahweh really acts mercifully, shows rivers of eternal gentleness to this nation, so far as these poor souls are nevertheless all comforted by the real and infinitely comforting nearness of God in spite of His hiddenness and in it, so far as God does not let them suffer in vain and they are not faithful to God in vain: to that extent Christ was indeed suffering Israel, the suffering prophet, the suffering righteous man. Not an idea of Christ, but the real, historical Christ *qui passus est sub Pontio Pilato*. As such, the Old Testament does not say that its problem is solved, or how. As such, the Old Testament does not know the God who is really hidden. It does not know, therefore, the God who is really manifest. But as such, and in and for itself, the Old Testament of which this must be said is not a reality at all, but a Jewish abstraction. (I, 2, p. 89. The Time of Expectation.)

In the words of v. 15: " He shall astonish many nations; kings shall shut their mouths at him ." This is said of the suffering righteous of the old covenant. But for this to happen he must open his own mouth and say something. How does he do this? How can he? How can Jesus Christ speak in this form? If His passion is the form of His action here and now, is He not by definition a mute and silent Witness? . . . " He shall not cry, nor lift up . . . " (43^2 and 53^7). But what will happen if this is so? What a contrast there is between the wordiness and noisiness of humanity and the Church of Jesus Christ in their tireless and inexhaustible attempts at self-communication and self-expression in their various more or less legitimate and urgent affairs, and Jesus Christ as the Proclaimer of the reconciliation accomplished in Him, and therefore as the Crucified! What a power of words on the one side, and what impotence on the other! For where all others, ourselves included, have the desire and the breath to speak with as much force, articulation and circumstantiality as possible, the only way in which He can and will present His cause is by means of the sigh on the cross which comes down through the centuries. What a Prophet this is, what a Witness, what a Word which is so very different from all human words whether temporal or spiritual, irreligious or religious, which is not in any sense one of the voices which may be heard in their common concert. (IV, 3, p. 408 f. The True Witness.)

Cf. II, 1, p. 665 f.; IV, 1, p. 172.

LUKE 23^{33-48} (III)

2 CORINTHIANS 5^{14-21} (IV)

To be a Christian is *per definitionem* to be in Christ. The place of the community as such, the theatre of their history, the ground on which they stand, the air that they breathe, and therefore the standard of what they do and do not do, is indicated by this expression. Being in Christ is the *a priori* of all the instruction that Paul gives his churches, all the comfort and exhortation he addresses to them. (IV, 2, p. 277. The Direction of the Son.)

As man's baptism with the Holy Spirit, the beginning of the new Christian life is and remains a real beginning. It is not perfect. It is not self-sufficient, definitive, or complete. It is a commencement which points forward to the future. It is a take-off for the leap towards what is not yet present. To be in Christ is to have become a new creature (v. 17) . . . Nevertheless, this carries with it a Forward. It intimates a work which goes further. In relation to this life, however, it has to be considered that the beginning in itself and as such does not necessarily imply the continuation. When the New Testament uses the concept of growth, this comprises the totality of the movement—not to be confused with Goethe's fine conception of an " impressed form which vitally develops itself. " It is not to be understood merely as the progress which corresponds to the beginning. In all its actions the work of the Holy Spirit is always and everywhere a wholly new thing. At each moment of its occurrence it is itself another change, a conversion, which calls for even more radical conversion. As the change to the Christian life was radical in its inception, so it must and will always be in its continuation.—As a " new creation " the Christian begins his life as one who is quite different, who starts again from the very first, who is in fact a little child in this sense. (IV, 4, p. 38 f. and p. 180. The Foundation of the Christian Life.)

It is true that God is with us in Christ and that we are His children, even if we ourselves do not perceive it. It is true from all eternity . . . And it is always true in time, even before we perceive it to be true. It is still true even if we never perceive it to be true, except that in this case it is true to our eternal destruction. " God was in Christ reconciling the world unto himself " (v. 19). " It is finished " (John 19³⁰). To this " perfect " of the truth of revelation nothing either need be added or can be added. It is not that there are, as it were, two different points: at the one the Son of God assumes humanity; and then, at quite a different point, the question of our destiny is necessarily raised and answered. In the one reality of revelation He is, in His assumed humanity, the Son of God from eternity, and we, for His sake, are by grace the children of God from eternity. Therefore the " perfect " of the truth of revelation already includes the conception of its existence in us. (I, 2, p. 238. The Freedom of Man for God.)

He is the assistance that comes to us . . . the exchange of status between Him and us: His righteousness and holiness are ours, our sin is His; He is lost for us, and we for His sake are saved. By this exchange (v. 19) revelation stands or falls. (I, 2, p. 308. The Revelation of God as the Abolition of Religion.)

Forgiveness obviously does not mean to make what has happened not to have happened. Nothing that has happened can ever not have happened. The man in whose life what had happened came not to have happened would not be the same man. He is this man in the totality of his history. He stands before God and is known to Him as this man. The man who receives forgiveness does not cease to be the man whose past (and his present as it derives from his past) bears the stain of his sins. The act of the divine forgiveness is that God sees and knows this stain infinitely better than the man himself, and abhors it infinitely more than he does even in his deepest penitence—yet He does not take it into consideration, He overlooks it, He covers it, He passes it by, He puts it behind Him, He does not charge it to man, He does not " impute " it (v. 19), He does not sustain the accusation to which man has exposed himself, He does not press the debt with which he has burdened himself, He does not allow to take place the destruction to which he has inevitably fallen victim. (IV, 1, p. 597. The Justification of Man: The Pardon of Man.)

The question indeed arises whether God and the world would not be far better served by a " word of reconciliation " (v. 19) spoken by Jesus Christ Himself and alone, without any co-operation on the part of Peter and Paul, let alone the rest of us. May it not be that Christians with their assistance actually do more to compromise, disrupt and hinder the prophetic action of Christ than to further it? If this co-operation of theirs is actually demanded by Christ in their unity with Him . . . and if it is not ordained in vain, this is to be established and explained only by the fact that the free action of Christ even in this prophetic form, being bound neither to anyone nor anything, is . . . the action of free divine grace, and as such it does not exclude but includes this human co-operation. It certainly does not need it. But it expresses its freedom in it. In a distinctive overflowing of divine grace it would have it so. He thus calls Christians to Himself, to His side, to His discipleship, to His service, and uses them as His heralds. (IV, 3, p. 607 f. The Christian as Witness.)

Cf. on 1 Timothy 1$^{12-17}$ Third Sunday After Trinity; cf. also IV, 1, p. 73–78 and p. 295.

Isaiah 50$^{4-11}$ (V)

Cf. on Isaiah 42$^{1-8}$ Second Sunday in Lent and on Isaiah 49$^{1-6}$ Third Sunday after Epiphany.

Hebrews 9$^{15,\ 24-28}$ (VI)

Cf. on Hebrews 9$^{11-15}$ Fifth Sunday in Lent; cf. also II, 1, p. 481 f. and III, 2, p. 637.

EASTER-DAY

Mark 16$^{1-8}$ (I)
Matthew 28$^{1-10}$ (III)
Luke 24$^{1-12}$ (V)

These stories (of the empty tomb and the ascension) are indispensable if we are to understand what the New Testament seeks to proclaim as the Easter message. Taken together, they mark the limits of the Easter period, at the one end the empty tomb and at the other the ascension. (It is worth noting that the limits are drawn not only backwards and forwards, but also downwards and upwards.) In the later apostolic preaching both events, like the Virgin Birth at the beginning of the Gospel narrative, seem to be presupposed, and are certainly never questioned, but they are only hinted at occasionally here and there, and never referred to explicitly. Even in the Easter narratives the empty tomb and the ascension are alike in the fact that they are both indicated rather than described; the one as an introduction, the other as a conclusion; the one a little more definitely, though still in very general terms, the other much more vaguely. Indeed, in the strict sense the ascension occurs only in Acts 1$^{9f.}$ . . . The content of the Easter witness, the Easter event, was not that the disciples found the tomb empty or that they saw Him go up to heaven, but that when they had lost Him through death they were sought and found by Him as the Resurrected. They empty tomb and the ascension are merely signs of the Easter event, just as the Virgin Birth is merely the sign of the nativity, namely, of the human generation and birth of the eternal Son of God. Yet both signs are so important that we can hardly say that they might equally well be omitted. The function of the empty tomb, with its backward, downward, earthward reference, is to show that the Jesus who died and was buried was delivered from death, and therefore from the grave, by the power of God; that He, the Living is not to be sought among the dead (Lk. 24^5; Mk. 16^6; Mt. 28^6). He is not here! . . . The empty tomb was obviously a very ambiguous and contestable fact (Mt. 27$^{62f.}$; 28$^{11f.}$). And what has happened around this sepulchre is a warning against making it a primary focus of attention. The empty tomb is not the same thing as the resurrection. It is not the appearance of the Living; it is only its presupposition. Hence it is only the sign, although an indispensable sign. Christians do not believe in the empty tomb, but in the living Christ. This does not mean, however, that we can believe in the living Christ without believing in the empty tomb. Is it just a " legend "? What matter? It is the sign which obviates all possible misunderstanding. It cannot, therefore, but demand our assent, even as a legend. Rejection of the legend of the empty tomb has always been accompanied by rejection of the saga of the living Jesus and necessarily so. Far better, then, to admit that the empty tomb belongs to the Easter event as its sign. (III, 2, p. 452 f. Jesus, Lord of Time.)

The whole historical difficulty occasioned by the Easter story itself has its foundation in the fact that in it the New Testament witness touches the point at which as witness, i.e., as human language about and concerning Christ, it comes up against its true object, against the point where everything else depends upon this object, which in itself contains the Word of revelation. Little wonder that human language begins to stammer at this point even in the New Testament. The Easter story is not for nothing the story whose most illuminating moment according to the account of Mark's Gospel consists in the inconceivable fact of an empty sepulchre, a fact which (in producing trembling and amazement) lays hold of the three women disciples and reduces them to complete silence (v. 8). Everything else related by this story can be heard and believed in the very literalness in which it stands, but can really only be believed, because it drops out of all categories and so out of all conceivability. It cannot be sufficiently observed that in the most artless possible way all the New Testament Easter narratives fail to supply the very thing most eagerly expected in the interests of clearness, namely, an account of the resurrection itself. How could it be otherwise? . . . In the slender series of New Testament accounts of the disciples' meetings with the risen Lord we are dealing with attestation of the pure presence of God . . . The Easter story actually speaks of a present without any future, of an eternal presence of God in time . . . Christ truly, corporeally risen, and as such appearing to His disciples, talking with them, acting in their midst—this is, of course, the recollection upon which all New Testament recollections hang, to which they are all related, for the sake of which there is a New Testament recollection at all . . . This fact, that the New Testament witnesses have this very recollection, and not just incidentally, but as the recollection which under-lies and holds together all others—this fact is the amazing circumstance which can never be overlooked or denied in these texts, nor directly or indirectly overlooked anywhere else in the New Testament. (I, 2, p. 114 f. The Time of Revelation.)

Cf. III, 2, p. 458; III, 3, p. 507 f.

1 CORINTHIANS 5[7f.]   (II)

1 CORINTHIANS 15[50-58]   (IIb)

The new Christian life . . . is only a beginning in the further sense that in its totality it hastens towards a goal which awaits it beyond its confines, or rather which comes to meet it . . . It is not yet the perfect life which it is properly and finally destined to be . . . It is only the first fruits and pledge of the perfection in which he will one day be manifested when Jesus Christ shall come, when He shall manifest Himself as the Pantocrator of all life, and hence of his mortal life, when He shall awaken him from his life in partial knowledge of God to life in the knowledge which is no longer in the riddle of a reflection, but " face to face." " We shall all be changed " (v. 51). This is the absolute future which the Christian is impelled and directed by the Holy Spirit to wait for and to hasten towards in this time of his which is one long Advent season. (IV, 4, p. 39 f. The Foundation of the Christian Life.)

There is no question of the continuation into an indefinite future of a somewhat altered life. The New Testament hope for the other side of death is the " eternalising " of this ending life. This corruptible and mortal life will be divested of its character as " flesh and blood," of the veil of transitoriness (v. 50). It will put on incorruption and immortality. This earthly tabernacle, which is doomed to destruction, will be " clothed upon " with the building prepared by God . . . the mortal will be swallowed up in life (2 Cor. 5[1f.]; Rom. 6[4]) . . . It can only be a matter, therefore, of this past life in its limited time undergoing a transition and transformation (v. 51) and participating in the eternal life of God. This transition and transformation is . . . the resurrection of the dead, which according to the indication given after the resurrection of Jesus is our participation in His future revelation. This is our hope in the time which we still have. (III, 2, p. 624. Ending Time.)

Why, apart from the fact that we see through that small chink, are we so fully dependent on faith? Why do we need to speak in terms of " only " and " still " and " not yet " (1 Jn. 3²)? Why is it, and to what end, that we must tarry in this tension between then and now and one day? Why is it that our freedom and joy can only be to accept this tension and thus to be continually on the march? What is the basis and meaning of the fact that Jesus Christ did not so come again that all further coming again is superfluous? Why is it that we and all creatures have still a long way to go to the home to which we belong, to the time when we shall enjoy our eternal life on the new earth and under the new heaven, to the investing of our corruptibility with incorruption (v. 53)? Why have we still to wait? These are not improper or unbiblical questions. Paul often put questions of this kind. The Apocalypse is plainly occupied with them. Indeed, they are found explicitly or implicitly in the whole of the New Testament testimony and characterise the assurance with which the New Testament bears witness to its subject . . . Would to God that with a more serious attitude to the Easter message there were in Christendom more of the unrest and impatience which—whatever else may have to be said—are necessarily expressed again and again in questions of this kind. (IV, 3, p. 319 f. The Promise of the Spirit.)

Cf. IV, 3, p. 646.

1 Corinthians 15¹⁹⁻²⁸ (IV)

By undergoing death in His person Jesus provided a total and conclusive revelation of its character. For He suffered death as the judgment of God. It would be out of place to say here that He did so as the sign of God's judgment. Here, in the person of the Messiah, it is God Himself, His embodied grace and help, who is genuinely and definitively present, both as Judge and Judged. He judges as He created between Himself and man the justice which had to fall on man, so that he had to suffer what he had deserved—death as a consuming force, eternal torment and utter darkness. But He is also judged as, knowing neither sin nor guilt, He caused this judgment to fall on Himself in place of the many guilty sinners, so that it availed for them all, and the judgment suffered by Him was fulfilled on them in Him, and their dying no longer has to be this dying, the suffering of punishment which they have deserved, but only its sign. What death is remorselessly as it encounters us is revealed in this act of judgment. At this point we cannot possibly fail to see that it hangs over us like a threat, and what it threatens us with. It is the enemy, the " last enemy " (v. 26), of man, whom God, in the death of Jesus, declares to be His enemy as well,

and treats as such by placing Himself at the side of man in the verdict there
pronounced, and snatching man from its jaws by the death of Jesus for
him. It remains for us as a sign of the divine judgment. We have no
longer to suffer the judgment itself. (III, 2, p. 600. Ending Time.)

Cf. on Romans 5^{12-21} Fourth Sunday in Advent.

What really oppresses the world and us in spite of the Easter event, or
rather in the light of a true appreciation of it, is not really a lack or failure
or absence of its efficacy but simply the fact that this is not evident to us,
and therefore its apparent absence . . . What confuses us, but ought not
to do so, is the fact that in the Easter event we have to do only with a
commencement of the revelation of reconciliation and its fruit in the
ensuing redemption and consummation, but not with this revelation in
its full development. In other words, we have to do with the return of
Jesus Christ in its first but not its final and conclusive form. The future
. . . has not ceased to be the future . . . From the first event we have still
to look to the second in which the light of life which has appeared in Him
will penetrate and fill even the remotest corner of the cosmos, in which
everything mortal and corruptible will put on and enjoy immortality and
incorruptibility (v. 53), and in which God will become and be all in all
(v. 28). We still cannot do more than wait for this event, for the future of
salvation in this conclusive and completed form. We can still see it as it
were only in a narrow chink in its first form. We have still to believe in
its second, coming, final and completed form. To this extent, even though
we are the children of God, we do not yet know what we shall be (1 John 3^2).
This tension exists, and cannot be relaxed. (IV, 3, pp. 317–319. The
Promise of the Spirit.)

1 Corinthians 15^{12-20} (VI)

The resurrection of Jesus Christ from the dead, with which His first
parousia begins, to be completed in the second, has in fact happened . . .
In the course of this particular history Jesus Christ appears to His disciples,
revealing Himself to them as the One who has risen again from the dead,
who is no longer under the threat of death, but under God (Rom. 6^{10}),
and therefore as the One who lives to-day as yesterday. That He has
appeared to them, with all that this implies, is the content of the apostolic
kerygma, the theme of the faith of the community which it awakened
(v. 14). The *kerygma* tells us, and faith lives by the fact, that God has
ratified and proclaimed that which took place for us, for redemption, for
our salvation, for the alteration of the whole human situation, as it will
finally be directly and everywhere revealed . . . That it has happened is
our justification . . . the verdict of God radically altering the human situation . . . In the light of it the community understands itself and its time in
the world, and looks forward to its end and goal in the second coming of
Jesus Christ. Because the resurrection of Jesus Christ has taken place

just as surely as the crucifixion, the cross of Jesus Christ is to us light and
not darkness, and it does not have to be changed from a " bare cross "
into something better by the fact that we take up our cross. We must not
miss the difference between the two events. They differ in substance as
God's right and God's justification, as end and new beginning, as work
and revelation. They also differ as the act of the obedient Son and the
act of the gracious Father. They also differ formally in the way in which
they take place in the human sphere and human time, and therefore in the
way in which they have to be understood as history. We cannot read the
Gospels without getting the strong impression that as we pass from the
story of the passion to the story of Easter we are led into a historical sphere
of a different kind . . . It is beyond question that the New Testament itself
did not know how to conceal, and obviously did not wish to conceal, the
peculiar character of this history, which bursts through all general ideas
of history as it takes place and as it may be said to take place in space and
time. There is no proof, and there obviously cannot and ought not to be
any proof (proof, that is, according to the terminology of modern historical
scholarship). (IV, 1, pp. 333–335. The Obedience of the Son of God.)

Cf. on 1 Corinthians 15$^{1-11}$ Eleventh Sunday after Trinity.

EASTER MONDAY

LUKE 24$^{13-35}$ (I)

This is the passage which shows most clearly what view of the earthly
life of Jesus was vanquished and removed by the resurrection and the gift
of the Holy Spirit in the second time, the time of the apostles and the
apostolic community; and also how this came about. As they were walking
on the road to Emmaus these two disciples were talking about . . . the
enacted life and death of Jesus (v. 14) . . . Hence it is not surprising that
when Jesus asked them what they were talking about, they stood still (v. 17),
gazing back like Lot's wife, and were gloomy and sullen and sad (cf.
Mt. 6^{16}; 9^{15}) . . . For them Jesus is now no more than a bit of past history
. . . " But we trusted that it had been he which should have redeemed
Israel . . ." (vv. 19–21). Even the beginning of the Easter story had found
its way into this sad history, and they tell how the women had found the
tomb empty . . . but . . . this news had merely plunged them into further
despondency (vv. 22–24), while v. 11 goes even so far as to say that " their
words seemed to them in their sight as idle tales; and they believed them
not." Even the Easter message . . . is still the object of mere recollection,
and of very dubious recollection at that. Nor was their gloom dispelled
when Jesus reproached them (vv. 25–27) for their stubborn incomprehen-
sion and refusal to believe . . . Not until He performed a certain action was
this state of affairs changed (v. 31). That action was not something new
and special, but the very action He had performed on the night of His

passion when He re-interpreted the Passover as a prefigurement of His own passion ... This was what dispelled their gloom: " He was known to them in the breaking of bread." That was the momentous news they brought back to the eleven and their companions when they returned to Jerusalem. Clearly the meaning is that the full power of the earthly life of Jesus, hitherto veiled from their eyes, was now made manifest ... The historical Jesus as such had removed the veil of the merely " historical " from their eyes and came to them as the Lord, the same yesterday and to-day. This was the burden of the apostolic account of the resurrection, of their Easter history. The limitation of the past had been burst. The past of Jesus had become a present reality. (III, 2, p. 471 f. Jesus, Lord of Time.)

Thus Scripture is a book, to which there belongeth not only reading but also the right Expositor and Revealer, to wit, the Holy Spirit. Where He openeth not Scripture, it is not understood ... But whoso knoweth not Christ, may hear the Gospel or hold the book in his hands, but its import he doth not have, for to have the Gospel without understanding is to have no Gospel. And to have the Scripture without knowledge of Christ is to have no Scripture. (I, 2, p. 508—Luther.)

Cf. IV, 2, p. 259.

ACTS 10³⁴ᵃ, ³⁶⁻⁴³ (II)

The Word or Son of God became a Man and was called Jesus of Nazareth; therefore this Man Jesus of Nazareth was God's Word or God's Son ... In regard to the exegetical question, it must be said that this twofold statement, whether as such or in its two constituent parts, is not very often found in so many words in the New Testament. As a rule, only one of its two parts appears at certain solemn climaxes in the New Testament witness, where it is manifestly the writer's business to gather up what has been said before coming to the ultimate fact, i.e., before coming to the name Jesus Christ itself. But this confession does not seem to come easily from their lips. Nor is it frequent. On the whole they prefer other ways of laying bare its truth to explicit formulation. There is, moreover, no single passage in which this confession is formulated with the dogmatic exactitude which we might like, or in which it is actually formulated at a later period. The christological dogma, like that of the Trinity, is obviously not the text but the commentary on the text. Nowhere in the Bible is it to be found word for word ... In the passages in Acts, which reproduce the apostolic *kerygma*, the confession occurs only once in so many words, namely, at Ac. 10³⁶ᶠ·, though there it is set most impressively at the very beginning. It is lacking in 2²²ᶠ·; 3¹³ᶠ·; 13²³ᶠ·. It appears indeed at the climax of the Johannine Easter narrative (Jn. 20²⁸), but not in the Synoptic parallels. As a rule it is to be found between the lines and inferred by the reader or hearer from what is otherwise said directly or indirectly about the name Jesus Christ. It waits, as it were, the reader's or hearer's own confession ... The New Testament is the instrument of proclamation and witness; it is neither a historical exposition nor a systematic treatise. The modest task of dogmatics it has left to the Church, to us. (I, 2, p. 13 f. Jesus Christ the Objective Reality of Revelation.)

According to the New Testament (Phil. 2[6f.]; 2 Cor. 8[9]; Heb. 2[14, 17f.]; 4[15]), this sympathy, help, deliverance and mercy, this active solidarity with the state and fate of man, is the concrete correlative of His divinity, of His anointing with the Spirit and power, of His equality with God, of His wealth. It is genuinely the correlative of His divinity, so that the latter cannot have any place in the picture of His humanity, as, for example, in the form of His " religious life," but, on the presupposition of His divinity, His humanity consists wholly and exhaustively in the fact that He is for man, in the fulfilment of His saving work. (III, 2, p. 210. Jesus, Man for Other Men.)

Cf. IV, 2, p. 196 f.

LUKE 24[36-49]   (III)

The proof of the reality of the resurrection (v. 41 f., cf. v. 31, 35) is also the proof of its tremendous import and far-reaching consequence. No longer, as at the Last Supper, will they sit at meat with Him in anticipation of His sacrifice, but in retrospect of its completion; not in a representation and repetition, as in the Romanist doctrine of the Mass, but in a simple and full enjoyment of its benefits, of the eternal life won for us in Him, within the revelation of the completion and benefits of this sacrifice, and therefore with open eyes and ears, and even open mouths, within the kingdom of God. For this reason the " Lord's Supper " of the primitive Church, formally celebrated in repetition of the pre-Easter passover " in rememberance " of the Lord (1 Cor. 11[20]), is materially a continuation of these festive meals in the personal presence of the Resurrected. While in the Lord's Supper the Church looks back upon " the night in which he was betrayed, " it cannot confine the memory to this night. On the contrary, " the death of the Lord " is " proclaimed " (1 Cor. 11[26]) through the action of the community. It is continually made known to the community and the world, on the basis of His self-revelation at Easter as a saving event. (III, 2, p. 502. Jesus, Lord of Time.)

How striking it is that in the Easter story in v. 41 this joy is not merely that of faith, or connected with faith, but precedes faith and can even be a hindrance to it ... (IV, 2, p.182.)

Repentance for the remission of sins ... cannot be separated from the proclamation of His name. It is only in His name, in the revelation and reality of His person, that it becomes ... meaningful proclamation. The world, then, is to be summoned to faith in Him, to the recognition and acknowledgment of the repentance in which the bearing away of sin which He has accomplished becomes recognisable and real for the world. (II, 2, p. 434. The Election of the Individual.)

1 CORINTHIANS 15^{35-44a} (IV)

Concerning heaven itself and its nature a first cautious statement which we can make is that, as earth exists as the sphere of man, heaven also exists, thus constituting the inalienable counterpart of earth. What exists and takes place in our sphere exists and takes place in the presence and with the participation of this other sphere, this counterpart, heaven. It belongs to earth as our sphere to be open to the other. And it belongs to happenings in our sphere to be set against that other sphere and thus to take place in relationship from and to it. To the outlook of man in the Old and New Testament there belongs the consciousness of existing as an earthly creature in the presence and with the participation of this other sphere. Even apart from his relationship to God this man is not alone. With his cosmos which he can see and in which he is at home he is not alone even apart from God. Another cosmic sphere has also been created by God and is also present in addition to his own. There are celestial as well as terrestrial bodies . . . (v. 40). There are knees which can bow in heaven as well as on earth (Phil. 2^{10}) . . . There is here a connexion, a relationship, a common tie (Lk. 15^{18}; 2 Chron. 28^9; Jer. 4^{28}; Ps. 96^{11}; Is. 49^{13}; Rev. 12^{12}). Together heaven and earth grow old and are renewed. And if in Eph. 1^{10} the end of the ways of God is described as the process in which heavenly and earthly reality come to have their Head in Christ, this is to be understood as a confirmation of their mutual relationship and confrontation as grounded in their creation (Col. 1^{16}). (III, 3, p.423f. The Kingdom of Heaven.)

JOHN 20$^{1-18}$ (V)

The New Testament is speaking of an event in time and space. It must not be overlooked that in this event we have to do on the one hand with the *telos*, the culminating point of the previously recorded concrete history of the life and suffering and death of Jesus Christ which attained its end with His resurrection, and on the other with the beginning of the equally concrete history of faith in Him . . . Since the presupposition and the consequence of the Easter message of the New Testament are of this nature, it would be senseless to deny that this message (between the two) does at least treat of an event in time and space. It would be senseless to suppose that it is really trying to speak of the non-spatial and timeless being of certain general truths, orders, and relationships, clothing what it really wanted to say in the poetical form of a narrative . . . We therefore presuppose agreements that a sound exegesis cannot idealise, symbolise or allegorise, but has to reckon with the fact that the New Testament was here speaking of an event which really happened, as it did when it spoke earlier of the life and death of Jesus Christ which preceded it and later of the formation of the community which followed it . . . In what did this history consist? What was it that God did in this happening? . . . The result of it was the awakening and establishing of the faith of the disciples in the living presence and action of Jesus Christ, and by the creation of this Easter faith the laying of the foundation of the community . . . But we have to distinguish between the act of laying a foundation, the creation of a presupposition, and the result of this act or action. In the strict sense the Easter narratives do not speak so much of the result as of the act as such . . . In this respect ought we not to take warning from the lexico-graphical observation that the word *pistis* does not occur at all in the Easter narratives and the word *pisteuein* only in John 20? What interests these narratives is who and what brought and impelled and drove the disciples to this faith, but not, or not primarily, the fact and the manner of their coming to it, of its development in them. (IV, 1, p. 336–339. The Verdict of the Father.)

Cf. on 1 Corinthians 15$^{1-11}$ Eleventh Sunday after Trinity; on 1 Corinthians 15$^{12-20}$ Easter Day.

Cf. also III, 3, p. 507 f.

EZEKIEL 37$^{1-14}$ (VI)

Ezek. 37 is the most powerful commentary on Gen. 2^7. In this passage Israel has reached the climax of its history, and this climax is the end which always threatened and has now come. It shows us a valley full of dry bones (v. 1 f.), and the Israelites can only complain: v. 11. To the question whether these bones can live, the prophet can only answer: " O Lord God, thou knowest " (v. 3). But the prophet is commanded to pro-phesy over these bones: vv. 4–6. And so it came to pass: vv. 7–10. One thing obviously was not killed and did not die when Israel became a valley of dry bones, and this was the prophetic Spirit by whom this people had become a nation. He might have shunned it, or withdrawn Himself, or scattered Himself to the four winds, thus giving up the body and soul of this people to vanity, as He had the right and freedom to do and as this people had deserved a hundredfold. But He for His part could not be destroyed. Thus the same Spirit who had once quickened it and kept it alive was now to quicken it afresh after its necessary and merited disappear-ance. It was of this return of the breath of life to an Israel already dead that Ezekiel spoke. If he really spoke of the fulfilment of its history as this took place in Jesus Christ on the far side of Israel's destruction, he did not prophesy in vain but in the name of God. For what took place in Jesus Christ is precisely the resurrection of Israel from the dead by the power of the prophetic breath of life which for the sake of the nations had created it as a nation, and which was not killed and did not die with Israel.

That this God-given breath as the vital principle of the soul and body of man can and will be withdrawn; that in respect of both soul and body man is subject to death and has no immortality; but that even when this breath is taken from him it does not vanish, or cease to be the living and quickening Spirit; that by God's free disposal He can and will return and genuinely requicken man from the death to which he has fallen victim and in which he has actually perished—these are the lessons which we have to learn from Ezek. 37, as a commentary from salvation history, in our understanding of the anthropology of Gen. 2. (III, 1, p. 248 f. Creation and Covenant.)

FIRST SUNDAY AFTER EASTER (QUASIMODOGENITI)

JOHN 20[19-31]   (I)

According to Jn. 3[8]; Ac. 2[2] *pneuma* means wind, which comes from one place and moves mysteriously to another. More precisely it is in 2 Thess. 2[8]; Jn. 20[22] breath, which comes out of the mouth of a living creature and can reach another living creature, invisibly, without removing the spatial distance between them. This little and removable paradox becomes in the New Testament and already in the Old Testament a metaphor for the great and irremovable paradox of divine revelation. The fact that God gives His *pneuma* to man or that man receives this *pneuma* implies that God comes to man, that He discloses Himself to man and man to Himself, that He gives Himself to be experienced by man, that He awakens man to faith, that He enlightens him and equips him to be a prophet or apostle, that He creates for Himself a community of faith and proclamation to which He imparts salvation with His promise, in which He binds men to Himself and claims them for Himself, in short, in which He becomes theirs and makes them His. (I, 1, p. 450 [515]. God the Holy Spirit.)

The particular content of the particular recollection of the apostolic community at this particular time (the forty days) consisted in the fact that in this time the *man* Jesus was manifested among them in the mode of *God*. It is essential to a true understanding that both His humanity and His deity should be kept in view. The Resurrected is the man Jesus who ... was before them as true man, *vere homo* ... Relevant here is the story of " doubting " Thomas (vv. 24–29). Much injustice has been done to the latter through wrong exegesis. The fact that he wanted to touch Jesus before he came to believe shows only that he had no more doubts than the other disciples had according to the accounts. It is the fact that the risen Christ can be touched which puts it beyond all doubt that He is the man Jesus and no one else. He is not soul or spirit in the abstract, but soul of His body, and therefore body as well. To be an apostle of Jesus Christ means not only to have seen Him with one's eyes and heard Him with one's ears, but to have touched Him physically. This is what is meant by Ac.

1^{22}, where we are told that what makes an apostle is the fact that he is a " witness of the resurrection. " By beholding His glory, by seeing, hearing and touching in the flesh in which this glory is made manifest, those who consorted with Jesus during this time were brought to believe in Him, and thus authorised and consecrated to proclaim the Gospel ... It is impossible to erase the bodily character of the resurrection of Jesus and His existence as the Resurrected. Nor may we gloss over this element in the New Testament record of the forty days, as a false dualism between spirit and body has repeatedly tried to do. For unless Christ's resurrection was a resurrection of the body, we have no guarantee that it was the decisively acting Subject Jesus Himself, the *man* Jesus, who rose from the dead. But it is equally important to note that the man Jesus appeared to them during these days in the mode of God ... For the disciples this was not a self-evident truth, nor a discovery of their own, but a conviction which went utterly against the grain. This is made abundantly clear in the resurrection narratives, where the disciples begin by doubting and even disbelieving. But their doubts and disbelief are soon dispelled, never to return. They are definitively overcome and removed in the forty days. " Be not faithless, but believing " (v. 27 f.), says Jesus to Thomas. This is not just pious exhortation, but a word of power. And to this Thomas gives the appropriate answer: " My Lord and my God. " In and with the presence of the man Jesus during this time, in the unique circumstances of the forty days, a decision is taken between the belief and unbelief of His disciples. There takes place for them the total, final, irrevocable and eternal manifestation of God Himself. God Himself, the object and ground of their faith, was present as the man Jesus was present in this way. That this really took place is the specific content of the apostolic recollection of these days. (III, 2, p. 448 f. Jesus, Lord of Time.)

Cf. on Matthew 18$^{15-20}$ Fourth Sunday after Trinity; also III, 2, p. 330; IV, 2, p. 238; IV, 4, p. 25.

1 JOHN 5$^{1-5}$ (II)

The attitude of the men of the Bible and the recipients of revelation will again help us to see our way clearly at this point. It is marked by the fact that the strictness with which they are claimed for the things of God is directly paralleled by a particular attraction to the things of God. In the Old Testament prophets and especially in Paul in the New Testament, particularly in the latter case, we do not see anything of the rigidity or Zelotism or anxious zeal, in short, the spiritual cramp which always results when men think and act as if the *causa Dei* were really their own anxiety and concern. They do not really aim to do what God does. They aim only to participate. They do not do the work; they assist. It is in this way that they are the recipients and witnesses of revelation. The commandments which they keep in love to God are God's commandments, and therefore not grievous (v. 3). His yoke is easy and His burden is light (Mt. 11^{30}). They need not be ashamed of the Gospel, because it does not need their own dynamic . And it does not need it, because it is itself the " power of God, " and indeed " to salvation " (Rom. 1^{16}). (I, 2, p. 276. The Freedom of Man for God.)

Cf. IV, 4, pp. 123–127.

JOHN 21^{1-14} (III)

We may also ask how it came about, as the text so clearly implies, that in the scene by the lake the disciples were able and even compelled to leave off questioning: " Who art thou? " because they knew " that it was the Lord " (v. 12). The common meal in which Jesus took the place of host plays again a very important, if subordinate, part in this incident. But surely the simplest explanation of their recognition is that the whole incident is an unmistakable reflection, for all the variations in detail, of Peter's great draught of fishes as recorded in Luke 5^{4-11}. It is true, of course, that the first to recognise Jesus as He stood on the shore waiting for the ship with its rich haul is " the disciple whom Jesus loved " (v. 7). But it is Peter who plunges out of the ship to reach Him in the quickest possible way—the same Peter who had once done something like this before (Mt. 14^{29}), but who above all had been told in Lk. 5^{10}: " Fear not; from hence-forth thou shalt catch men." The closing section of John's Gospel, which comes immediately after, has as its theme the sending and future of Peter (21^{15-23}). Is Lk. 5^{4-11} one of the many anticipations of the event of Easter? Or is it not perhaps more natural to understand that part of the Easter occurrence described in Jn. 21^{1-14} as the actualisation of this important element in the pre-Easter history?

The event consisted in a series of concrete encounters and short con-versations between the risen Jesus and His disciples. In the tradition these encounters are always described as self-manifestations of Jesus in the strictest sense of the term. In this context self-manifestation means (1) that the execution and termination as well as the initiative lie entirely in His own hands and not in theirs. Their reaction is a normal one, but it is to an action in whose origination and accomplishment they have no part at all. They have really encountered their Lord. He controls them, but they do not control Him. Self-manifestation means (2) that the meaning and purpose of these encounters consists simply and exhaustively in the fact that the risen Christ declares Himself to them in His identity with the One whom they had previously followed and who had died on the cross and been buried. (IV, 2, p. 143–145. The Exaltation of the Son of Man.)

ACTS 3^{1-21} (IV)

There is no hearing or receiving of Christ which does not have the form of a hearing and receiving of His disciples (Lk. 10^{16}; Mt. 10^{40}) . . . " Look on us " is what Peter can and must now say to the lame man before the Beautiful Gate of the temple, although he has nothing to give him other than the Word in the name of Jesus Christ of Nazareth (vv. 4–6). It is the fact that they have to speak this Word, that is, therefore, that they have to speak in fulfilment of the revelation accomplished in Jesus Christ of Nazareth, in such a way that He Himself is always with them (Mt. 28[20]); it is this which marks them out, so that now we have to look at them . . . " As men Paul and Peter do not deserve our confidence at all " (J. Wichelhaus). The decisive confidence, i.e., confidence in what they say, is something which they certainly cannot create by the incidental glimpses of their humanity. On the contrary, it is only what they say that by its own credibility can create confidence in their humanity. But necessarily this means —and it applies to all of them—a judgment on their humanity. To look on them, as we are requested to do in v. 4, always means to look on Him who has sent them. (I, 2, p. 487 f and p. 491 f. Scripture as the Word of God.)

The future which even in all the misery of his past and present, of his ignorance, awaits the one addressed in the task given to the community is a future of joy . . . It is the refreshment promised to the weary and heavy-laden whom Jesus calls to Himself (Mt. 11[28]). It is the time of the restitution of all things (Acts 3[21]). According to the content of the Word of God, what is allotted to and appointed for the man whom God addresses in it is not only the removing of his ignorance, the acknowledging of His Word, his awakening to faith and obedience, his conversion from a potential Christian to an actual, but the meeting of the need in which he engulfs himself with his self-contradiction, with his denial of his new reality already created in Jesus Christ, and the dispelling of the anxiety which as the fear of even greater need both agitates and oppresses him in this need and causes movements of anxiety which in fact produce this greater need. Man's persistence in ignorance and therefore his continuance in misery is indeed the danger under threat of which he stands of himself and to which he would be a hopeless prey if he were only what he is of himself. In virtue of the work and Word of God, however, he has not only fallen victim to this persistence and continuance, to this fatal progress of his ignorance; he has actually been rescued from it. (IV, 3, p. 810 f. The Holy Spirit and the Sending of the Christian Community.)

Cf. III, 2, p. 495.

LUKE 20[27-40] (V)

It does not actually say that man and woman will be angels but " like the angels " (v. 36), i.e., those who according to 1 Cor. 13[12] no longer see God, themselves and all things in a glass darkly but face to face, and are thus liberated from the problematical, burdensome and complicated nature of their existence in the form which they now know (through a glass darkly). To this form there belongs marrying and giving in marriage with such implicated questions as that raised by the Sadducees on the basis of Deut. 25[5f.], and the overriding concern for children. It is not from the insights of the world of the Song of Songs that the Sadducees ask concerning the solution of such complicated matters in the future aeon, and the stern rebuke which Jesus gives them is fully justified ... This whole concern for marrying and giving in marriage and the raising up of children, says Jesus, can no longer occupy men in the resurrection when according to v. 36 they cannot " die any more. " God is (v. 38) ... the God for whom, and before whose eyes which span the centuries, all men are alive in their time. As such they will be revealed in the resurrection, and with their death the necessary cares which now lie like a cover over their lives will be lifted and left behind. Thus the fact that that woman had belonged to seven successive husbands, and must still belong to them according to the law of marriage, could cast no shadow on her temporal life as disclosed in the resurrection, nor on the life of the seven men. For the fact that she married and was married will then be a past event with many other happenings and finally with the death of those concerned. The only thing that will count is that like Abraham, Isaac and Jacob they have lived in their time for God, the God of the living, and therefore live eternally. To that extent they will be as the angels of heaven (Mk. 12[25]), not in heaven, but on the new earth under the new heaven—new because the cosmos will then be revealed in which there will be no more possibility or place for tears and death and sorrow and crying and pain (Rev. 21[4]). They will thus be as angels of heaven because this is how it is already with the angels. But there is no reference here, and cannot be, to an abolition of the sexes or cessation of the being of man as male and female. (III, 2, p. 295 f. Humanity as Likeness and Hope.)

1 PETER 1[3-9]   (VI)

The right of divine sonship ascribed to man is really his future, the given promise, to the fulfilment of which he can only look and move in every present. Who amongst us looking back to his past has ever found that he is a child of God and therefore in a kinship of being with Him, just as indispensable to God as God is to him, in possession of this whole and truly princely right in relation to Him? We know this, if at all, only as that which God promises and ascribes, and as we trust and receive and accept God's promise. We are " begotten again unto a lively hope " (v. 3) in this being. (IV, 1, p. 600. The Pardon of Man.)

The Christian with his witness anticipates the penetration of the light of the fulfilled covenant of grace into the darkness which still surrounds it ... Deriving from the death and passion of Jesus Christ, he finds that even in the storm into which he is plunged as a witness of this Word he is engaged in a movement and transition towards the future of that revelation and therefore that penetration. He is still in the night, but he moves towards the day when " God shall wipe away all tears ... " (Rev. 21⁴). He is necessarily carried as on a powerful wave, through and beyond all that the world can do, by the hope which he may proclaim to a world which does not yet see and grasp it, himself begotten unto this lively hope (v. 3). (IV, 3, p. 643. The Christian in Affliction; cf. also p. 929.)

Christians—men who come from baptism—are those (v. 3) who through the overflowing mercy of God, who is the Father of their Lord Jesus Christ, are in His resurrection from the dead begotten anew to a living hope. Not through their baptism, but in the power of the resurrection of their Lord! When they asked for baptism in His name, when they confessed Him in the community and were baptised in His name, they took the first step of the Christian life as those who were begotten anew to a living hope. Since this first step is always a model for those which follow, their Christian life, as the life of those who are begotten anew, can only become and be a life in this hope. Their future—that which comes to them—can consist only in a living hope which is continually confirmed and exercised. (IV, 4, p. 197. The Foundation of the Christian Life.)

SECOND SUNDAY AFTER EASTER (MISERCORDIAS DOMINI)

John 10¹¹⁻¹⁶ (I)

Extra ecclesiam nulla salus? The Church proclaims the redemptive act of God as it took place in Jesus Christ. Yet it is not outside adherence to the Church, but outside the adherence of all men to Him as known and confessed and proclaimed by the Church, that there is no salvation, no participation in the reconciling act of divine redemption: *extra Christum nulla salus* ... We have to reckon with the hidden ways of God in which He may put into effect the power of the atonement made in Jesus Christ (v. 16) even *extra ecclesiam*, i.e., other than through its ministry in the world. He may have provided and may still provide in some other way for those who are never reached, let alone called to Him, by the Church. It does not detract from the glory of the community or weaken its commission if we keep at least an open mind in this respect. What we can say of the community is only this, though we can say it in all seriousness: *extra ecclesiam nulla revelatio, nulla fides, nulla cognitio salutis.* (IV, 1, p. 688 f. The Being of the Community.)

1 Peter 2²¹ᵇ⁻²⁵ (II)

The connexion between the cross of Jesus Christ and that of the Christian ... is only an indirect connexion. Those who have to take up their cross only follow Him in this ... they follow in His steps (v. 21). They do not accompany Him in an equality of their cross with His. And they certainly do not precede Him in the sense that His cross acquires reality and significance only as they take up their cross. Behind this view there stands the ancient mystical notion that it is Christ's own cross that Christians have to take up and carry. This notion is quite false. The cross of Jesus is His own cross, carried and suffered *for* many, but *by* Him alone and not by many, let alone by all and sundry. He suffers this rejection not merely as a rejection by men but, fulfilled by men, as a rejection by God—the rejection which all others deserved and ought to have suffered, but which He bore in order that it should no more fall on them. Their cross does not mean that they have still to suffer God's rejection. This has been suffered already by Him (as their rejection). It can no longer be borne by them. (IV, 2, p. 600. The Dignity of the Cross.)

Discipleship very properly describes the relationship between Him and His followers as a history which in this way is proper to Him and to Him alone. Jesus goes, and the disciple accompanies Him on the same way. It is Jesus who chooses the common way, and treads it first. The Christian follows Him on the way which He has chosen, treading in His steps (v. 21). He believes in Jesus, not in a theoretical and general way, as in a good leader alongside whom there might be others, but in such a way that He is the inescapable Leader who leaves him no option but to go after Him in the way which He has chosen. And believing in Him, he obeys Him . . . in such a way that his own sovereignty is completely forfeit . . . And obeying Him, he confesses Him . . . by publicly entering the way which is chosen by Him, by irrevocably and bindingly accepting his own relationship to Him, by thus compromising himself with Him, by making himself a fool for His sake, as we must add for the sake of clarity . . . His discipleship, which is the history of the relation of the Christian to Him, embraces the whole life of the Christian. The fact that His call is the call to this discipleship, and therefore to fellowship with Him, thus shows us particularly clearly that vocation is not merely *vocatio unica* but *vocatio continua*. (IV, 3, p. 535 f. The Goal of Vocation.)

JOHN 21[15-19]   (III)

The existence of the man Jesus and the event of the direction of the Holy Spirit as issued by Him involve the shaming of all other men . . . Man is shamed . . . because he finds that he is compared with God. With God? Yes, if he is radically and totally shamed it is because he is compared with God, and measured by His holiness he necessarily sees his own unholiness revealed. When we compare man with man there can and will be occasional and partial and superficial shamings . . . The basic and total shaming which we cannot avoid is either from God or it does not take place at all . . . It is striking, and worth considering, that in the Gospels the shaming of man is expressly revealed in a figure which is given great prominence—that of Peter. Peter is obviously shamed already (although the word itself is not used) . . . when . . . he has to be told quite plainly (Mk. 8[33]) that he must remove himself from the sight of Jesus (" behind him "). He is shamed already when . . . (Lk. 22^{32}; Mk. 14$^{30f.,\ 37}$; Mt. 26^{52}; Jn. 18^{11}). Again, his particular distinction and commission (v. 15 f.) are preceded by the shaming question whether he really loves Jesus: whether he loves him more than the other disciples as he had previously boasted; whether he really loves Him at all . . . . (Mt. 14^{31}; Gal. 2$^{11f.}$; Lk. 5^{8}; 22$^{61f.}$ and finally Jn. 21^{17}). This was the appearance, in relation to Jesus, of the rock on which He willed to build His community, and did in fact do so. Again, it is obviously the intention of the tradition to characterise in the person of this first disciple *mutatis mutandis* the situation and shame of all others in their relation to their Lord; the Christian situation in its typical significance for the human situation as such. As it sees it, neither in the community nor the world is there anyone who is not shamed by Him as Peter is when measured by Jesus. (IV, 2, pp. 384–388. The Man of Sin in the Light of the Lordship of the Son of Man.)

EZEKIEL 34$^{1-16,\ 31}$ (IV)

This (vv. 2–6, cf. Mt. 9^{36}) is how Jesus saw the multitudes around Him. He had compassion on them when He saw them because they had shepherds who were no shepherds . . . According to Ezekiel, the true Shepherd who was lacking was One who would know that He was responsible for them and would therefore act solely on their behalf. He would hear the general and foolish crying and bleating as each tried to assert his own individuality, and He would understand the basic reason for it better than the people themselves. He would not, therefore, reject or despise them. He would know what they need and how they can be genuinely helped . . . They would not be merely a nameless and inhuman mass for Him, but a company of men. He would know and call them each one by name, and feed them individually, each one having his or her place . . . Without encroaching on their freedom, He would be their Head. Without having anything to forgive Himself, He would be their servant . . . There was no lack of other, so-called, but only ostensible shepherds . . . Someone had always to think and speak for the people. They had always to group themselves round an individual whom they could follow. A general assertion of individuality could only lead them to tread one another down, and bring them to an isolation in which they had to begin again in a state of bewilderment and confusion. In these circumstances ostensible shepherds continually offered themselves. It was always a fine and honourable and lucrative occupation to be a shepherd and head of the people, to fill this gap, to be the man who could instruct and lead the people. Thus there have never been lacking those who seemed to have the desire and even for a time the equipment for it . . . But the ostensible shepherds were not real shepherds, and the hopes put in them never materialised. They all had good heads, but there was no head. Their real concern was not for the people, but for themselves. They simply fed themselves. They

acted as all the rest did. How, then, could they really help them? . . .
" And they were scattered, because there is no shepherd." They were
scattered the more terribly each time they thought that they had a shepherd
and were again disappointed and " became meat to all the beasts of the
field " (v. 5) . . . In exact fulfilment of Ps. 23 . . . the man Jesus came among
and for all other men as the Good Shepherd, Jn. 10[11]. (IV, 2, p. 186 f.
The Royal Man.)

JOHN 10[1-5, 27-30]   (V)

The offence in this parable, particularly in the contrasting of the one
Shepherd with strangers who are described as " thieves and robbers " or
" hirelings," is not concealed: " They understood not what things they
were which he spake unto them " (v. 6). Nor is it removed but aggravated
by the claim in v. 11: " I am the good shepherd." This, and everything
which underlies the " I," seems to raise up a division (schisma) among the
Jews (v. 19). Can Jesus say this? " He hath a devil, and is mad." Or must
He say it? " These are not the words of him which hath a devil." The
healing of the man born blind had preceded. Has this not validated the
claim of Jesus to be the Shepherd whose voice must be heard in contrast
to all others (Deuteronomy 18[15]; Mark 9[7])? " Can a devil open the eyes
of the blind? " The drift of the story is plain. Jesus has the authority to
make this claim to an exclusive hearing. In and with His existence He
rightly advances and emphatically exercises and successfully presses this
claim. Hence Acts 4[12] and 1 Cor. 2[2] . . . It is thus incumbent, not that
we should merely repeat these or similar biblical texts, but that we
should so enter into the biblical mode of thought which underlies and is
expressed in them that the thesis of the uniqueness of the prophecy of
Jesus Christ impresses itself upon us as no less self-evident than it is
presupposed and sometimes stated to be in Holy Scripture. But if we do
this, this means that we shall be guided by the direction of Holy Scripture,
that we shall not have to champion the thesis in our own strength or on
our own responsibility, and that we may thus champion it without anxiety
because it is not really exposed to the charge of arbitrariness. There can
be no question, however, of merely learning clever tricks of thought. The
distinctive thought-form of the Bible is not something which is discovered
in that way; it is demanded, enforced, and indeed created by that which
is attested, namely, by the lordship of Jesus Christ Himself. Hence we
have first and foremost to allow ourselves to be confronted by Him
through the biblical witnesses in order that we may learn from the latter,
as from older and more experienced fellow-students, how we shall think
and speak as those who are confronted by Him. (IV, 3, p. 95 f. The Glory
of the Mediator.)

In John (10[30]; 17[11]) believing is equally both coming from the known
Father to the unknown Son and also coming from the known Son to the

unknown Father. There can hardly be anything contrary to the sense of John if in this context we substitute for Father and Son the concepts of form and content in their distinction and unity. (I, 1, p. 176 [201]. The Nature of the Word of God.)

Cf. also II, 1, pp. 172–178.

1 PETER 5$^{1-5}$ (VI)

The authority of parents proclaimed in the fifth commandment (Ex. 20^{12}) is not that of a power posited and exercised as a right, but that of a spiritual power. And the honouring of parents required of children does not mean the outward and formal subjection of the will of the younger to that of the older generation, but the respecting of the latter as the bearer and mediator of the promise given to the people with regard to its existence. That children should honour their parents means that they should receive from them this promise and themselves live under this promise in Canaan until the meaning of the existence of Israel in this God-given land is revealed and the Son towards whom the whole succession of generations is tending has come. Without the honouring of parents there is no life under this promise. There is also a law of subordination to the power of authority claimed and exercised as a right. But this belongs to other connexions, and the present requirement ought not to be mentioned in the same breath with it. It is all very well to speak of territorial fathers and mothers, but there is no basis for this concept in either Testament. The one analogy to what is meant in the fifth commandment . . . is the relationship of the elder to the younger (v. 5) in the Christian fellowship. In general terms, this is the human, relative and limited authority, yet serious because spiritual, of predecessors and leaders in the community of the saints, the importance and dignity of their witness, confession, teaching and other traditions for all who succeed them. Here we can and may recall the fifth commandment and so speak of the " fathers " who as bearers and mediators of the promise are to be honoured—not as God but as God's representatives. (III, 4, p. 242 f. Parents and Children.)

THIRD SUNDAY AFTER EASTER (JUBILATE)

JOHN 16^{16-23a} (I)

(In the message of Jesus) men were not only told not to fear but to find comfort. They were also told—much more strongly—that they should rejoice . . . The whole purpose and meaning of the mission of Jesus is to bring joy (Jn. 15^{11}; 17^{13}). According to Jn. 16$^{20f.}$ this was also the purpose of the sorrow which would come with His death . . . As we are told in Jn. 8^{56}, Abraham had already rejoiced to see the day of Jesus and he saw it and was glad . . . In the first instance, however, both in the Johannine passages and in Lk. 10^{21}, this joy is the joy of Jesus Himself, His rejoicing

in the Holy Ghost. Men neither appropriated it to themselves nor produced it of themselves, but it came to them in and with the man Jesus.
It was given them in Him and by Him. In the first instance it was present
for them objectively—and obviously identical with the kingdom of God,
which is joy as well as righteousness and peace (Rom. 14^{17}). It was this
objective joy which could and should be reproduced in the joy which they
too were permitted and commanded. In the presence of the man Jesus it
was already actual for them and could not be resisted or destroyed by
anything or anyone, v. 22. (IV, 2, p. 182. The Royal Man.)

I PETER 2^{11-20} (II)

It is characteristic that in the New Testament, so far as I can see, there
is no summons to the direct defence of one's honour, but only the admonition to remember and actively to respect the honour of others, often quite
obviously in view of some special position of service which they occupy,
e.g., the honour of fathers and mothers especially, or of officers of the state
(v. 17; Rom. 13^7), or of the elders (1 Tim. 5^{17}), or of women as they are
to be respected by men (1 Pet. 3^7). Cf. Rom. 12^{10}; Phil. 2^3. And in v. 17
we have the all-embracing words: " Honour all men." It is obvious that
in the question of the direct representation of his honour the command
as such first points man away from himself and refers him to the honour of
others, demanding that he should champion this and obviously implying
that it is only by this circuitous route that a legitimate answer can be given
to the question. (III, 4, p. 684 f. Honour.)

" The world cannot hate you; but me it hateth " (Jn. 7^7). The meaning
obviously is that the world would not hate you, would have no cause to
do so, would not even be allowed by God to do so, were it not that I am
the true object of its hatred. In the light of this we can understand in what
sense v. 19 f. regards it as a danger threatening Christians that as the doers
of good deeds they should be affected by this hatred and should thus have
to suffer. You are called to do so—this is the only passage in which the
line from the concept of *klesis* is expressly drawn in this direction—because
Christ has suffered for you and has left a *hypogrammos* (literally, a model
for a writer or artist to copy), that you should follow in His steps, v. 21.
That He has died for them implies their suffering with Him. . . . It is not,
therefore, the disposing of the world, nor that of the Christian, but
primarilly and finally Jesus Christ Himself who is the true reason for the
necessity of the Christian's affliction. (IV, 3, p. 638. The Christian in
Affliction.)

Cf. IV, 3, p. 188.

ISAIAH 40^{26-31} (III)

In the context (v. 18, 25, 27) the drift of the complaint seems to be that
Yahweh is only one of many gods, and a small one among many greater,

so that it is not surprising that His people is in this sorry predicament among the great nations. What is the reply of the prophet of the Exile? Simply to put to those who sigh in this way the counter-question whether, in face of who and what Yahweh is and has done and still does, in face of His self-evident majesty which reduces to the dust all the majesties of the world in their apparent triumph, there can be even the remotest possibility of the comparison of Yahweh with the gods of the nations—a comparison fatal for Israel and therefore for Himself . . . The arguments in vv. 21, 28, 12–14, 21, 26 and 19 f. then lead to the positive conclusion of vv. 22–24 and 15–17. What does this mean for poor little Israel, so impotent by human reckoning? It means that its complaint and accusation are quite pointless, vv. 28–31. The train of thought is remarkable. What is at issue—the incomparable uniqueness and therefore the absolute sovereignty of Yahweh, and with this the absolute security of Israel—is not just quietly but with supreme and joyous assurance represented as something which is quite self-evident and speaks for itself. This is how the biblical mode of thought pursues the matter. And it is obvious that the comprehensive answer to the question of the uniqueness of the revelation of God in Jesus Christ can basically be no more than that which is so forcefully anticipated in Isaiah 40. (IV, 3, p. 104 f. The Glory of the Mediator.)

Cf. II, 1, p. 431 f. The Patience and Wisdom of God.

The will for power also belongs to the actuality of life. And as God calls man to life, and so long as he addresses him as a living person, He wills that man should not neglect this capacity, the power, strength and force which he has been given, but affirm, will and accept it. (III, 4, p. 390. Freedom for Life.)

Acts 17¹⁶⁻³⁴   (IV)

Is it really possible to maintain that, in distinction to what Paul had to say elsewhere to Jews and heathen, the Areopagus address consisted for the greater and decisive part in a declaration that without and before God's revelation in Jesus Christ men already stood in a relationship to God, and that in the proclamation of the Gospel they were to be addressed on this basis as a possession in which they had at least the possibility of becoming, independently and of themselves, witnesses to the truth of the Gospel? If the author of Acts understood the sermon in this sense, it is obviously very strange that, at the end of the story, the stoic and epicurean philosophers addressed on this possibility are not seen in the kind of light the sermon itself would lead us to expect according to this understanding. Paul has addressed them on a possibility which on this occasion, at any rate, does not become an actuality. The story should not have ended in this way if this was the meaning of the sermon; for this story, at any rate, does not bear witness to a natural addressability of man for the Gospel. Surely Luke ought to have seen this? Surely he ought to have seen it on this second occasion? For a similar question arises in relation to the short speech at Lystra (c. 14[15-17]). And there, too, the supposed attempt at contact ends in an open failure. Perhaps we can explain it as a literary blemish which Luke has repeated. But if not, neither speech can have had this superficial meaning as Luke himself saw them. On the contrary, what appears a failure of the Pauline missionary preaching is for him the crisis upon man brought about by the Word, 1 Cor. 1[23] . . . Paul proclaims on the Areopagus the crucified Christ in what is basically the same manner as he proclaimed Him always and everywhere. One thing at least is clear: the sermon on Mars Hill contradicts the opinion that in the apostolic Gospel we are perhaps concerned with one of the many spiritual novelties which capture the world's interest just because they are novelties. The Gospel does not belong to this category. It is the utterly and really strange and new thing because it does not belong to this category. From it we can see, and see through, this category—the category of the spiritual novelties of man mutually concurring and surpassing one another—as something which has been wholly and utterly surpassed, as the category of one long and guilty and as such empty misunderstanding. This is what the sermon says. It is not an attempt to understand the world of the Athenian philosophers from their own viewpoint and to overcome it from within. It is the announcement of the judgment which comes upon this world from without. (II, 1, p. 121 f. The Knowability of God.)

Paul is not deluded when (presumably accepting and adopting as his own a saying and certainly a sentiment of pagan wisdom) he confesses that in God we live and move and have our being (v. 28). For God attests Himself to him on the Areopagus and wherever he may be, as the One who has possessed and occupied this one unique place on earth (Jesus) in virtue of His good-pleasure and omnipotence. There is, therefore, no reason to doubt that for the sake of this one place, in view of it and by the proclamation and power of it, He can and will also be present also here and now in other earthly places relatively to this one place, but really. It is to be noted that the reality of God's special presence in other places rests on this relationship, but so too does the distinction between them and His presence in this one place. They would not have existed as places of His presence without this proper place, just as the circumference of a circle cannot exist without its centre. God is really present in these other places too. Indeed, He is really present everywhere. But He is present in them and everywhere because and as He is present here. He is first present here, and then (either before or after Jesus Christ's epiphany) there and everywhere. He is present here primarily, there and everywhere secondarily. (II, 1, p. 484 f. The Unity and Omnipresence of God.)

Cf. on Rev. 14[8-18] (Harvest) Thanksgiving; also IV, 3, p. 808.

LUKE 10$^{17-20}$ (V)

II, 1, pp. 172–178 (*Declaration of Barmen*); III, 4, p. 677; IV, 2, p. 228.

REVELATION 21$^{1-7}$ (VI)

It is of the very essence of the cross carried by Christians that it has a goal, and therefore an end, and therefore its time (v. 4). It signifies the setting of a term. That is why it is so bitter. But this limitation is not itself unlimited. Borne in participation in the suffering of Jesus, it will cease at the very point to which the suffering of Jesus points in the power of His resurrection and therefore to which our suffering also points in company with His. It is not our cross which is eternal, but, when we have borne it, the future life revealed by the crucifixion of Jesus. V. 4 will then be a present reality. P. Gerhardt is thus right when he says: " Our Christian cross is brief and bounded, One day 'twill have an ending. When hushed is snowy winter's voice, Beauteous summer comes again; Thus 'twill be with human pain. Let those who have this hope rejoice." There cannot lack a foretaste of joy even in the intermediate time of waiting, in the time of sanctification, and therefore in the time of the cross. (IV, 2, p. 613. The Dignity of the Cross.)

Cf. III, 2, pp. 462–511.

FOURTH SUNDAY AFTER EASTER (CANTATE)

JOHN 16$^{5-15}$ (I)

Thus we find the Holy Spirit only after the death and resurrection of Jesus Christ or in the form of knowledge of the crucified and risen Lord, i.e., on the assumption that objective revelation has been concluded and completed. We have seen already that Christ is the revelation of the Father in His passage through death to life. Those who believe in Him and confess Him believe in Him and confess Him as the exalted Lord. Thus the Spirit in whom they believe and confess and He who is the object of this faith and confession stand as it were on two different levels. What comes over or down to us from above, from the exalted Lord, is, therefore, the Spirit.

In spite of all this, it can hardly be the idea of the New Testament that chronologically it was only after Good Friday and Easter that there were men who received the Holy Ghost. If so, what could it mean that faith is in all seriousness ascribed to many disciples and non-disciples even before Good Friday and Easter? What would Jesus' reply to Peter's confession mean (Mt. 16^{17})? And one might well ask whether the miracles of Jesus are not all to be regarded as, so to speak, backward-striking rays of the glory of the risen Lord, whether ultimately the entire life of Jesus is not meant to be considered in this retrospective light. Even in John, where the chronological schematism seems to be more consciously and strictly applied, the temporal relationship between Him who lived as a man among the disciples and the exalted Christ, and hence also between the promised Spirit and the given Spirit, is undoubtedly more complicated than might appear at a first glance.

We must now add at once that while the Spirit is the element of revelation which is different from Christ as the exalted Lord, while He is revelation to the extent that it becomes an event on us and in us, nevertheless He is still to be regarded wholly and entirely as the Spirit of Christ, of the Son, of the Word of God. He is not to be regarded, then, as a revelation of independent content, as a new instruction, illumination and stimulation of man that goes beyond Christ, beyond the Word, but in every sense as the instruction, illumination and stimulation of man through the Word and for the Word. (I, 1, p. 451 ff. [517 f.]. God the Holy Spirit.)

Cf. I, 2, p. 310 (Luther).

MATTHEW 5¹⁻¹⁰ (Ib)

It is evident that what is determined as the situation of these men (vv. 3–6) is not a happy or desirable one in itself. Nor is there even the slightest hint of any secret or immanent value of any kind to which these beatitudes refer. The New Testament, like the Old, does not regard or magnify the happy and positive and vital as a secret quality of that which is unhappy and negative and dead. It does not call black white, or interpret the evil case of these men as their true well-being. It is not to men who are miserable only in appearance that the beatitudes refer, but to men who are genuinely miserable. Yet their misery is not seen abstractly and independently any more than their action. It is not seen in a vacuum. It is seen in a definite relationship. Not now in their action, but in their suffering, they are seen in confrontation with the kingdom of God. From this kingdom, or, as we must say, from Jesus, there falls a definite light on the situation which they have neither brought about nor desired and willed, on themselves in this unhappy situation which is already redolent of death. In their misery they find themselves on the outer edge of the cosmos as it is confronted with the kingdom of God and to be renewed by the man Jesus. Its vulnerability is revealed and can be seen in their misery. In the glory of the man who is wealthy and laughing and mighty and righteous and lucky as the world sees it, its mortal wound is concealed. But it is brought to light in the misery of those who suffer. It is not for nothing that the man Jesus comes and acts and is revealed as Himself a sufferer, the supreme sufferer and the partisan of all others. For it is in the existence, the situation, of the poor and sad and meek that the new thing of the kingdom of God shines in all the different spheres of the life of the old man ... The beatitude of Jesus ... is not merely a promise and proclamation, but the present (if hidden) impartation of full salvation, total life and perfect joy.

We cannot rate it lower than this when it is a matter of the salvation and life and joy of the kingdom of God, the salvation and life and joy which have appeared and are resolved in Jesus. This man does not only speak. He accomplishes what He says. He makes actual what He declares to be true. He tells us in and with the beatitudes that to-day, here and now, He is for those whom He addresses in this way; that He is their *soter*, the One who shows them His powerful mercy, the One who gives them all that is His by giving them Himself. (IV, 2, pp. 190–192. The Royal Man.)

Cf. also on Matthew 5[1-10] Reformation Day.

JAMES 1[17-21] (II)

Again, the judgment of the Word of God is not a mere aspect under which man himself remains untouched, just as the same man may seem to be a giant from the standpoint of the ant or a dwarf from the standpoint of the elephant without in fact being any different either way. The judgment of God as such creates not only a new light and therewith a new situation, but also with the new situation a new man who did not exist before but who exists now, being identical with the man who has heard the Word.

. . . We find all this expressed in the strongest imaginable way in Jas. 1[18], where (cf. also 1 Pet. 1[23]) there is reference to the fact that the Christian is begotten of the word of truth. Then v. 21 goes on logically to speak of an implanted word, i.e., a word which, so to speak, belongs to man himself, without which man, would no longer be himself. And because the word at issue is the Word of God, we must add explicitly that its efficacy, its power to change, is not just relative as in the case of other powers. It is not uncertain. It is not conditioned or restricted by the behaviour of other factors, e.g., man. All this may be true of what it effects in man, of what may be seen of its operation in the life of man. But it is not true of its operation in itself and as such. The power of the Word of God in itself and as such is absolute power. (I, 1, p. 152 f. [174]. The Speech of God as the Act of God; cf. also on Isa. 55[6-11] Sexagesima.)

The Modernist view from which we must demarcate ourselves here goes back to the Renaissance and especially to the Renaissance philosopher Descartes with his proof of God from human self-certainty . . .

Karl Holl once formulated as follows the fundamental principle that is " common to all men " and that constitutes " the plumb-line of their religion." " Nothing, " he said, " is to be recognised as religiously valid but what can be found in the reality present to us and produced again out of our direct experience. " This principle is in fact the principle of Cartesian thinking, which is quite impossible in theology. On the basis of this principle there is no knowledge of the Word of God. For we do not find the Word of God in the reality present to us. Rather—and this is something quite different—the Word of God finds us in the reality present to us. Again it cannot be produced again out of our direct experience. Whenever we know it, we are rather begotten by it according to Jas. 1[18]. (I, 1, p. 195 f. [223]. The Word of God and Man.)

Cf. IV, 3, p. 675.

JOHN 6[64b-69]   (III)

The whole difficulty would be removed if we could be content with the mere assertion that Jesus Christ is one light of life, one word of God: the clearest perhaps; a particularly important one, and of great urgency for us; but only one of the many testimonies to the truth which have been given by others and which have also to be studied and assessed together with His ... This could be received ... It need not be disputed by the modern Synagogue. It is actually stated in the *Koran*. It can be accepted by Western Idealism. With this message we need not expose or compromise ourselves, or provoke suspicion or unpopularity, or give offence to anyone, least of all to ourselves. Noble rivalry or peaceful co-existence is possible with those who prefer other lights of life or words of God ... But supposing that we cannot be content with this? Supposing the ... meaning of the confession of Jesus Christ is that *Thou* hast the words of eternal life, Thou alone and no other (for there are no others to whom we may go), Thou alone not merely for me but for all others and all men, yet Thou particularly for me, so that I have no option but to hear these words from Thee? Supposing that the confession excludes as quite illegitimate and prohibited the free and friendly acceptance of many lights of life and words of God among which that spoken by Thee is only one? Supposing that the freedom of the confession consists in thinking and speaking in this way? What will happen when a Christian or the community or theology makes use of this freedom? (IV, 3, p. 87 f. The Light of Life.)

Cf. II, 2, pp. 459–461; I, 2, pp. 350–352.

ACTS 16[16-40]   (IV)

We certainly do not have in the Bible stories of conversion such as that which Augustine recorded in his autobiography, or the numerous legends of the saints stimulated by Augustine in the Middle Ages, or the Christian portraits of which the first half of the 19th century was so particularly fond, or the testimonies given in gatherings of the Salvation Army and Moral Rearmament by those who at first were not interested in personal salvation, then sought it in the wrong place and finally sought and found it in the right place. There can be no contesting the significance of an experience like that of Luther in the cloister. But where do we find even the remotest likeness to it in the Bible? Certainly there was no question of Paul finding a gracious God in his conversion. To be sure, there are places in the Bible, especially in Luke and Acts but also in the typical stories of calling, where we can glimpse something of the fact that such a personal experience was directly or indirectly linked with the decisive thing, i.e., with what came upon the called from the hand of God, so that in and with the true thing which re-determined their lives on the basis of their vocation there took place an illuminating and salutary alteration in their own being and status. Yet we can hardly speak of more than glimpses. The personal history of the called and its happy outcome never became a real theme, not even in the stories of the publican Zacchaeus and the Philippian gaoler. The killing and eating of the fatted calf is as little the burden of the parable of the Prodigal Son as is David's dancing before the Lord when the ark was brought up to Jerusalem the burden of his vocation (2 Sam. 6^{14}). (IV, 3, p. 571 f. The Vocation of Man.)

Cf. on 2 Peter 2^{11-20} Third Sunday After Easter (Jubilate)

MATTHEW 21^{14-17} (V)

" Hearest thou what these say? " They are not asking the children, for what do they know what they are saying? They are asking Jesus, who tacitly approves what they are saying. These ecclesiastics and theologians think that He is to blame. They are accusing Him. But He is pleased with what the children say. He gives His approval even though those who cry thus are not independent or responsible, even though at best this is only their childlike or childish reaction to the healings, even though it is possibly their childish imitation of what they had heard the people cry out in His entry into the city. Though neither independent nor responsible, though childlike and childish, it was an echo of the truth which was spoken for them and to them. Jesus confessed Himself in confessing the children who cry thus . . . The complainants should have read the saying in Ps. 8^2 and should realise that it is now being fulfilled . . . There is also—as an event *sui generis*—this reaction to the work and word of Jesus which is not independent or responsible, but which is supremely real and significant. The Evangelist certainly cannot have imagined, however, that it should be understood as faith, obedience, confession and discipleship, or that babes and sucklings ought to be baptised because they can be deemed worthy to participate in the praise of God. (IV, 4, p. 183. Baptism with Water.)

COLOSSIANS 3^{12-17} (VI)

The existence of the community as such and of all Christians has to serve the praise of God . . . In v. 16 f., it is not merely insisted that the community should allow the Word of God to dwell in it richly, nor that Christians should sing to God in their hearts, nor that they should do everything in word and deed in His name and therefore with thanksgiving to God the Father, but also quite expressly that in wisdom they should teach and admonish one another " in psalms and hymns and spiritual songs. " And is it not worth noting that in Mk. 14^{26} we are told that the disciples sang a hymn immediately after the last highly significant meal with Jesus and just before the commencement of His passion? The praise of God which constitutes the community and its assemblies seeks to bind and commit and therefore to be expressed, to well up and be sung in concert. The Christian community sings. It is not a choral society. Its singing is not a concert. But from inner, material necessity it sings. Singing is the highest form of human expression. It is to such supreme expression that the *vox humana* is devoted in the ministry of the Christian community. It is for this that it is liberated in this ministry. It is hard to see any compelling reason why it should have to be accompanied in this by an organ or harmonium. It might be argued that in this way the community's praise of God is embedded by anticipation in that of the whole cosmos, to which the cosmos is undoubtedly called and which we shall unquestionably hear in the consummation. The trouble is that in practice the main purpose of instruments seems to be to conceal the feebleness with which the community discharges the ministry of the *vox humana* committed to it. There is also the difficulty that we cannot be sure whether the spirits invoked with the far too familiar sounds of instruments are clean or unclean spirits. In any case, there should be no place for organ solos in the Church's liturgy, even in the form of the introductory and closing voluntaries which are so popular. What we can and must say quite confidently is that the community which does not sing is not the community. And where it cannot sing in living speech, or only archaically in repetition of the modes and texts of the past; where it does not really sing but sighs and mumbles spasmodically, shamefacedly and with an ill grace, it can be at best only a troubled community which is not sure of its cause and of whose ministry and witness there can be no great expectation. In these circumstances it has every reason to pray that this gift which is obviously lacking or enjoyed only in sparing measure will be granted afresh and more generously lest all the other members suffer. (IV, 3, pp. 865–867. The Ministry of the Community.)

Cf. also on Colossians 3$^{12-16}$ Fifth Sunday After Epiphany.

Cf. I, 2, pp. 252–257.

FOURTH SUNDAY AFTER EASTER (ROGATE)

JOHN 16^{23b-27} (I)

True prayer is prayer which is sure of a hearing. By " hearing " is to be understood the reception and adoption of the human request into God's plan and will, and therefore the divine speech and action which correspond to the human request. And the assurance of prayer is the confident anticipation of this hearing which accompanies the human request—the assurance that when we address a petition to God it is not only received by Him but infallibly passes over into His plan and will and cannot lack the corresponding divine speaking and doing . . . But what is its basis and origin? How can we so boldly and unquestioningly take the content of our human asking into our hope in God, into the very will of God Himself? What does faith mean here? There cannot, of course, be any question of trying to build a bridge into the darkness and emptiness, of a titanic movement of defiance. This could only issue in an impotent challenging of God, and would quickly enough break up. Here, too, faith must have its basis. And indeed, it does . . . The man who really prays, and therefore prays with this assurance of being heard, belongs to the " we, " to the body whose Head is Jesus Christ. But " in Christ, " in the fellowship of the Holy Spirit and therefore in fellowship with Him, the praying man is not separated from God nor God from him. Rather, in Jesus Christ man is from eternity bound up with God, and God from eternity with man. And now " we " may pray with and after Him, making the great request which He as man has uttered and still utters at God's right hand in this union, establishing, confirming, renewing and assuring it in His obedience, in His whole existence, in the work of His life and death, and summarising it in the Lord's Prayer as the request for God's cause and man's. We ask *comme par sa bouche* (Calvin). In this respect we move within the specifically Johannine thought of prayer " in the name of Jesus. " In His name means under His leadership and responsibility, in the unity of our asking with His, in obedience to the summons of this One, but also with the support of His power as that of the Son, of His unity with the Father (v. 23 f.; 15^{16}; $14^{13f.}$.) (III, 4, pp. 106–108. Prayer.)

JAMES 1^{22-27} (II)

To want to be hearers only would mean to want to isolate the Word from our existence, to make ourselves onlookers at heart, and independent judges in our own consciences, to debate with the Word. In short, it would mean that we maintain our autonomy over against it as those who know the Word and are interested in it and reverence and adore it. But although we can do this with the word of man, we cannot do it with the Word of God. Because it is the Word of the Lord, to hear the Word of God is to obey the Word of God. Not to obey the Word of God is therefore to deceive oneself. The deception is twofold: first by dealing with the engrafted Word (v. 21), as though it were not the Word of the Lord; and then by imagining that to ignore the engrafting is to rob it of its power, as though resisted grace does not become judgment by the very same power with which it may be blessing. (I, 2, p. 365. Man as a Doer of the Word.)

The Christian must indicate and attest this word in the act of his whole existence . . . That he should do this is the concrete goal of his vocation, the *ratio* of his Christian existence. He may be a hearer of the Word to become a doer. But his doing of the Word can consist decisively only in the fact

that, commissioned and sent by Christ and himself existing in the world as
man, he may turn to the world and other men who have not yet heard this
Word, and make known to them what he was enabled to hear. (IV, 3, p.
609. The Christian as Witness.)

No less plainly the " law of liberty " referred to in v. 25; 2^{12} is the order
which is directly contrasted, but positively so, with the law of the Jews, an
order under which a man stands who is not just a hearer but also a doer—
and in James this means, not a forgetful nor a merely reputed hearer, but a
real hearer of the Word of God who is claimed in his life-act, in his existence. The man who is capable of being a doer of the Word of this kind, i.e.,
a real hearer, is free in the New Testament sense of the term. The reference
is not to any kind of freedom or any kind of ability. In accordance with the
freedom of God Himself, His freedom to be Himself, what is at issue here
is a man's freedom for God, for the " glorious liberty " of the children of
God (Rom. 8^{21}), the *analogia fidei* of the divine freedom which alone really
deserves to be called freedom. (I, 1, p. 457 [523]. God the Redeemer;
cf. on Gal. $4^{22\text{-}25}\text{-}5^1$ Fourth Sunday in Lent (Laetare).)

Cf. I, 2, p. 719 and II, 2, p. 588 and p. 593.

1 TIMOTHY $2^{1\text{-}8}$ (IIb)

His then living and speaking and acting, His being on the way from
Jordan to Golgotha, His being as the One who suffered and died, became
and is as such His eternal being and therefore His present-day being every
day of our time . . . In virtue of His resurrection from the dead Jesus
Christ—" the man Christ Jesus who gave Himself a ransom for all "—is
(in the same way as the One God) the one Mediator between God and man
(v. 5). He was this in the event of Good Friday to be it for ever—this is
what the event of Easter Day revealed and confirmed and brought into
effect. He not only did represent us, He does represent us. He not only
did bear the sin of the world, He does bear it. He not only has reconciled
the world with God, but as the One who has done this, He is its eternal
Reconciler, active and at work once and for all . . . His history did not
become dead history . . . He is the living Saviour. This would be a fantastic
and not very helpful statement if it simply meant that He is something like
this for certain men of His own age, and that He can be something of the
same for certain men of other ages by their recollection of Him, by the
tradition and proclamation concerning Him, by a sympathetic experience
of His person, or by some form of imitation of His work. He would then
be alive only in virtue of the life breathed into Him as a historical and
therefore a dead figure by the men of other ages. But the fact that He is
the living Saviour is true and helpful because He is risen from the dead
and therefore—the Father of whom the same can be said has given it to
Him—He has life in Himself (Jn.5^{26}) and in His own omnipotence, on
His own initiative, and by His own act, He is the same here and now as He

was there and then: the Mediator between God and us men. (IV, 1, p. 313 f. The Verdict of the Father.)

Cf. II, 2, p. 421 and IV, 4, p. 29.

LUKE 11$^{5\text{-}13}$ (III)

True prayer is prayer which is sure of a hearing. By " hearing " is to be understood the reception and adoption of the human request into God's plan and will, and therefore the divine speech and action which correspond to the human request. And the assurance of prayer is the confident anticipation of this hearing which accompanies the human request—the confidence that when we address a petition to God it is not only received by Him but passes infallibly over and into His plan and will and cannot lack the corresponding divine speaking and doing. It goes without saying that this assurance, since its object is the attitude of the sovereign God, has the character of hope. But as such it cannot merely precede or only follow the human request. On the contrary, the human request is made wholly and utterly under the determination of this hope. And this hope, as and because it is directed to God, has on its side the character of unreserved and unquestioning certainty, and therefore not in any sense that of a problem or an open question. Asking is an action which does not query the divine hearing; otherwise it cannot be the asking of true prayer. (III, 4, p. 106. Prayer.)

We need not hesitate to say that on the basis of the freedom of God Himself God is conditioned by the prayer of faith. The basis is His freedom. It is thus a form of His sovereignty, and therefore of His immutable vitality, that He not only permits to faith the prayer which expects an answer but has positively commanded it. The Bible is completely unambiguous about this: Prv. 15^{29}, Ps. 50^{15}, Jas. 5$^{16\text{-}18}$. (II, 1, p. 510 f. The Constancy and Omnipotence of God.)

COLOSSIANS 4$^{2\text{-}6}$ (IV)

Cf. on 1 Corinthians 1$^{26\text{-}31}$ Eleventh Sunday After Trinity.

MATTHEW 6$^{5\text{-}13}$ (V)

Prayer is not confession, not the outward witness to the knowledge of God before one's generation (v. 5 f.) . . . Fundamentally, prayer is not proclamation. Prayer takes place fundamentally " in thy closet, and when thou hast shut thy door," i.e., in secret. Prayer is the aspect of the praise of God which is directed only towards God, and to this extent it is strictly its inward aspect. This is true of both personal and common prayer. Prayer as a demonstration of faith, as disguised preaching, as an instrument of edification, is obviously not prayer at all. Prayer is not prayer if it is addressed to anyone else but God . . . Where man is concerned only with God . . . the only thing that counts is that he shall really be concerned with

God and with a request addressed to Him. It may well be that he can only sigh, stammer and mutter. But so long as it is a request brought before God, God will hear it and understand it, and He will accept it as right, as the prayer demanded by Him, as an act of obedience, infinitely preferring it to the sublimest liturgy which does not fulfil this condition . . . True prayer may and must probably be short rather than long (v. 7 f.). It is based on assurance of being heard . . . It is not a confession of God before men, but an address to Him personally, an urgent flight to Him in supreme objectivity. It has thus no reason to spin itself out in the form of meditations or theological or rhetorical formalities. Strict discipline is perhaps required in this respect, especially in public worship . . . Luther kept to this in the formularies of the *Smaller Catechism*. The extemporary prayers with which Calvin concluded his sermons are also short and good; and this is also a laudable feature in the extant prayer of Christopher Blumhardt. But we can only say with shame that from the 17th century a terrible verbosity and volubility began to distinguish Protestant liturgies from the conciseness of the Roman Mass. It is to the credit of the modern liturgical movement that it is apparently trying to return to prayer which is taut and compressed. But unfortunately this does not mean that we do not have to suffer dreadful things in this respect even to-day and from the lips of good people in the form of so-called " extemporary " prayer. (III, 4, p. 88 and p. 112 f. Prayer.)

Where two or three are gathered together in the name of Jesus, they are called by Him to pray with one another . . . They also pray, of course, individually and in small groups. But this is not enough . . . The prayer of Christians demands that it should find its true and proper form in the prayer of the assembled community; in the united calling upon God: " Our Father, which art in heaven . . ." The reason why it must be united is not merely that it is easier and finer and more consoling to pray in company than individually—for this is an open question. It is because those gathered to the community may pray with the One by whom they are united and who is Himself present in the midst—their predecessor in prayer. The distinctive value and importance of the " Our Father " as the Lord's Prayer consist in the fact that in it Jesus ranges Himself alongside His disciples, or His disciples alongside Himself, taking them up with Him into His own prayer. The " we " of this prayer is the " We " to which the Lord attaches Himself with His people. The We in which He does this is the We of the community. (IV, 2, p. 704 f. The Holy Spirit and the Upbuilding of the Christian Community.)

When we speak of God's glory we do emphatically mean God's " power." Yet the idea of " glory " contains something which is not covered by that of " power." For the idea of " kingdom " which precedes the other two concepts in the doxology of the Lord's Prayer seems to say something of wider range than can be described by power alone. Light, too, has power and is power, but it is not this that makes it light. Has not and is not God more than is covered by the idea of power when He has and is light and is glorious? (II, 1, p. 650. The Eternity and Glory of God.)

JEREMIAH 29$^{1, \; 4\text{-}14a}$ (VI)

He is the God who lets man come to Him with his requests, and hears and answers them. He is God in the fact that He lets man apply to Him in this way, and wills that this should be the case. Here, then, we stand before the innermost centre of the covenant between God and man which is the meaning and inner basis of creation, God's gracious will. It is so superior, so majestic, so clear that it makes man's prayer immediately necessary. It is the basis, permission and necessity of prayer, the basis which the man who is free before Him cannot escape. It is here an imperative command and a strict order. As prayer is uttered, it is not only said but it avails: Ps. 50^{15}. Or, as the prophet heard: Jer. 33^{3}; 29^{12}; Is. 55^{6}. And in the decisive dominical saying: Mt. 7^{7}. (III, 4, p. 93. Prayer.)

THE ASCENSION-DAY

MARK 16$^{14\text{-}20}$ (I)

As this washing with water, Christian baptism is, so far as we can tell, a custom which was self-evident in the New Testament Church in all places and from the very outset ... Why did the primitive community have to be a community of the baptised and a baptising community? Was this necessary? Could it not be content with the baptism of the Holy Ghost which it had received or was expecting, with its faith in Jesus Christ and all that this included by way of gifts and obligations? ... How many exegetes have wished they could cut these verses (v. 16; Jn. 3^{5}; Acts 2^{38}) out of the New Testament, since then everything would be, or would appear to be, much simpler! But there they are, and in their own place they have to be taken into account and honoured. One can expound them, one can explain the surprisingly self-evident attitude of the primitive community and its members which finds expression in them, only if one accepts the fact that the community and its members were under the pressure of an imperious—because authoritative—injunction in this matter —so imperious that in the main they could recognise it only by actually taking the step of human decision which was demanded and by practically regarding it as self-evident in the way they did as men who had received such an order, and could only follow it, even if they would rather things had been different and baptism dispensable. (IV, 4, p. 46 f. Baptism with Water; cf. also p. 122.)

" Healing," which constitutes an essential part of the apostolic task (Lk. 9^{1}), does not reappear in the missionary command of Mt. 28, just as

Jesus does not perform any miracles after His resurrection. The fact that mention is again made of the healing work of the apostles in the presentation of the missionary command given in Mark 16[17f.] is a significant internal sign that the whole passage vv. 9–20 does not belong to the original content of the Gospel, but to a period when this difference was no longer understood. The fact that after Jesus' resurrection healing no longer formed part of the Church's task does not mean—as is shown in the Acts of the Apostles—that all such healings were in future excluded. Even less does it mean that the power over demons and death, given to the apostles, was withdrawn from them and from the Church. But it does mean that once the resurrection of Jesus has happened it no longer requires to be particularly indicated. All healing, all cleansing, all victory over death and the devil, are now to be regarded and believed and proclaimed as accomplished in Him. With reference to Mt. 28[18f.] we have probably to say that the healing commanded of the apostles in the first stage of the account found its legitimate and complete continuation and fulfilment later in the baptism which they were commissioned to give in the name of the triune God. (II, 2, p. 448. The Election of the Individual.)

ACTS 1[1-11]   (II)

The resurrection and ascension of Jesus Christ are two distinct but inseparable moments in one and the same event. The resurrection is to be understood as its *terminus a quo*, its beginning, and the ascension as its *terminus ad quem*, its end ... The resurrection of Jesus Christ is the " whence ": " Jesus came "—but where did He come from? ... His ascension is the " whither ": " Jesus went "—but where did He go to? We can and must give a twofold answer. It must first be to the effect that He went to the absolutely inaccessible place, to the cosmic reality by which man is always surrounded (for even on earth he exists under heaven) and from which to that extent he derives, but which he cannot attain or enter. The spheres which are accessible to him are earthly spheres, and only earthly spheres ... That He went there is only stated and not described in the New Testament. . . . It was only Christian art which unfortunately was not afraid to try to depict it ... But there is another and decisive aspect ... When He went into this hidden sphere He went to God. In His identity with the Son of God, when He was lifted up into heaven, He was not deified, or assumed into the Godhead (for this was unnecessary for Him as the Son of God and impossible for Him as the Son of Man), but placed as man at the side of God, in direct fellowship with Him, in full participation in His glory. (IV, 2, pp. 151–153. The Homecoming of the Son of Man.)

" Heaven " in biblical language is the sum of the inaccessible and incomprehensible side of the created world, so that, although it is not God Himself, it is the throne of God, the creaturely correspondence to His glory, which is veiled from man, and cannot be disclosed except on His initiative.   There is no sense in trying to visualise the ascension as a literal event, like going up in a balloon.   The achievements of Christian art in this field are amongst its worst perpetrations.   But of course this is no reason why they should be used to make the whole thing ridiculous.   The point of the story is . . . that He entered the side of the creaturely world which was provisionally inaccessible and incomprehensible, that " before their eyes " (v. 9) He ceased to be before their eyes . . . The most important verse is the one which runs: " A cloud received him out of their sight " (v. 9).   In biblical language, the cloud does not merely signify the hiddenness of God, but His hidden presence, and the coming revelation which penetrates this hiddenness . . . the heaven which is closed for us, but which from within, on God's side, will not always be closed . . . The conclusion to the Easter history gives to the whole retrospective memory of the Resurrected a joyous character.   It shows that Jesus did not enter and is not to be sought after the Easter history and the Easter time in any kind of hiddenness, but in the hiddenness of God.   And it describes the hiddenness of God in such a way as to suggest that it burgeons with the conclusive revelation still awaited in the future (v. 11).   As this sign, the ascension is indispensable, and it would be injudicious as well as ungrateful on any grounds to ignore or reject this upward and forward-looking sign.   (III, 2, p. 453 f.   Jesus, Lord Time.)

Cf. also on Mark 16[1-8] Easter Day.

" Ye shall be witnesses unto me " (v. 8)—this is enough for the one to whom Christ speaks and who has heard Him.   Whether strong or weak, willing or unwilling, successful or unsuccessful, the Christian is a witness . . . In all circumstances and with his whole existence he is a responsible witness of the Word of God.   He is called to be this.   As such he is set at the side of God in the world, and therefore set over against the world. As such he is bound both to God and men.   He exists in this engagement, but he is also invested with the honour which it implies to be bound in this function.   It is in this way that he and his service, his very existence, are the appointed sign of the living Word of God and therefore of its substance, of the kingdom of God drawn near in all its concealment in the person and act of the One who alone can and does reveal it.   (IV, 3, p. 609 f. The Christian as Witness.)

JOHN 17[20-26]   (III)

It is an impossible situation that whole groups of Christian communities should exhibit a certain external and internal unity among themselves and yet stand in relation to other groups of equally Christian communities in an attitude more or less of exclusion.   It is an impossible situation that such groups should confront each other in such a way that their confession and preaching and theology are mutually contradictory, that what is revelation here is called error there, that what is heresy here is taught and reverenced as dogma there, that the order and cultus and perhaps the ethics of the one should be found and called strange and alien and unacceptable and perhaps even reprehensible by the other, that the adherents of the one should be able to work together with those of the other in every possible secular cause, but not to pray together, not to preach and hear the Word of God together, not to keep the Lord's Supper together.   It is an impossible situation that either tacitly or expressly, with an open severity or a gentler friendliness, the one should say to the other, or, in fact, give it to be understood, or at any rate think of the other: You have another spirit; You are not within but without; You are not what you presumptuously call yourselves, the community of Jesus Christ.   We have to recall the effects of this disunity on the mission fields of Asia and Africa, in the face of Islam and Buddhism. But we have also to recall its effects on the so-called home fields of the Christian Church . . . where with the dispelling of the mediaeval illusion of a Christian West the Church is mercilessly confronted . . . with the tremendous alienation of the baptised masses from the Gospel . . . The matter itself (we should read vv. 21–23 word by word) demands always, and in all circumstances, *unam ecclesiam*.   And if history contradicts this, then it speaks only of the actuality and not the truth.   Even under the fatherly and effective providence of God which can cause it to work for good, a scandal is still a scandal.   The disunity of the Church is a scandal. And there are some cases where the scandal is not even serious, but has only the character of a foolish embroilment. (IV, 1, p. 676 f. The Being of the Community.)

Cf. also IV, 3, pp. 35–38.

COLOSSIANS 1¹⁵⁻²³   (IV)

In Jesus Christ we are not merely dealing with one of the many beings in the sphere of the created world and the world of men.   He is this too. Because He is this, because He is a being like us and with us, He enables us actually to hear the Word of God . . . As such He is born in time, at His own time.   But in Jesus Christ we are not merely dealing with the author of our justification and sanctification as the sinners that we are.   We are not merely dealing with the One who has saved us from death, with the Lord and Head of His Church . . . But at the same time and beyond all that—and the power of His saving work is rooted and grounded in this— He is " the first-born of all creation " (v. 16)—the first and eternal Word of God delivered and fulfilled in time. (IV, 1, p. 47 f. The Work of God the Reconciler.)

Both sentences (v. 19; 2⁹) undoubtedly speak of a bodily and proper dwelling of God in His fulness or completeness.   They therefore speak unreservedly of a divine position above or behind it which cannot partake in this indwelling.   And they say of this . . . dwelling . . . that it is His dwelling even in creation. In Jesus Christ there does exist the distinction between Creator and creature, between God and the created world of heaven and earth, and therefore between divine and created space. Yet there is no diversity or separation, but rather the unity of the two. For here the Creator is at the same time creature, which means in this connexion that the Creator has given the creature not only space but his own most proper space. God has raised man to His throne. God's most proper space is itself the space which this man occupies in the cradle and on the cross, and which He cannot therefore leave or lose again, for, as His resurrection and ascension reveal, it is now His permanent space. How can the dwelling of the fulness of God in Him be cancelled? (II, 2, p. 486. The Unity and Omnipresence of God.)

Through the blood of His cross He has created a cosmic peace which embraces all things both in earth and heaven. (IV, 2, p. 257. The Royal Man.)

Cf. II, 2, p. 99.

JOHN 14¹⁻¹² (V)

Notable figures may be recalled even from the Old Testament in this connexion: the Moabite prophet Balaam and his fellow-countrywoman Ruth; the Canaanite harlot Rahab; Hiram, king of Tyre, and the queen of Sheba; the Syrian Naaman, and Cyrus with his outstanding role in Deutero-Isaiah and the Book of Ezra. In the New Testament we can think of the wise men from the East, and rather strangely of a whole series of Gentile soldiers—the centurion of Capernaum, the centurion at the cross and the centurion Cornelius of Caesarea. Above all, and typical in his significance, there is king Melchizedek of Gen. 14, who in Hebrews is set even against Abraham as a type of Jesus Christ. And it is not for nothing that in the parable of Lk. 10 it was a Samaritan who . . . provided the classic instance and definition of a neighbour in answer to the question of the scribe. If it is the case that God can and actually does raise up children to Abraham from " these stones " (Mt 3⁹), in what relationship do these stand to the children of the household, and the latter to them? They bring both comfort and warning, reminding them that they are not in their own house but in that of the Father of Jesus Christ, and that in this house there are many mansions, including some which they themselves do not yet know. (IV, 2, p. 808. The Act of Love.)

If the freedom of divine immanence is sought and supposedly found apart from Jesus Christ, it can signify in practice only our enslavement to a false god. For this reason Jesus Christ alone must be preached to the heathen as the immanent God, and the Church must be severely vigilant to see that it expects everything from *Jesus Christ*, and from Jesus Christ *everything*; that He is unceasingly recognised as the way, the truth, and the life (v. 6). This attitude does not imply Christian absolution or ecclesi-

astical narrowmindedness, because it is precisely in Jesus Christ, but also
exclusively in Him, that the abundance and plenitude of divine immanence
is included and revealed. If we do not have Christ, we do not have at all,
but utterly lack, the fulness of God's presence. If we separate ourselves
from Him, we are not even on the way to this richness, but are slipping
back into an impoverishment in which the omnipresent God is not known.
The freedom of God must be recognised as His own freedom and this
means—as it consists in God and as God has exercised it. But in God it
consists in His Son Jesus Christ, and it is in Him that God has exercised it.
In all its possibilities and shapes it remains the freedom which consists and
is exercised in Jesus Christ. If we recognise and magnify it, we cannot
come from any other starting-point but Him or move to any other goal.
(II, 2, p. 320. The Being of God in Freedom; cf. also pp. 172–178 in
exposition of the *Declaration of Barmen*.)

COLOSSIANS 3¹⁻¹¹   (VI)

For there, above, hidden with Christ in God, is their true life, v. 1 f.
There God acts for them, there, consequently, is the norm and principle
of their own action, in the sense that what is done there is to be seen, discovered, considered, observed and valued by us, and then confirmed con-
tentedly, joyfully and willingly in and by what we do. All other things
which might try to claim us elsewhere . . . are an earthly authority which
does not deserve to be considered and valued and confirmed by us and
therefore cannot really become normative, because it can never be divinely
normative, because God does not stand behind these claims. The claim
behind which God stands, and which is therefore binding, is " above. "
But it is not a heavenly power or spiritual force which is " above. "
It is Christ as the outstretched and active right arm of God Himself, as
God's gracious dealing and gracious work in person. " To seek " and " to
set the affection on " what is " above " is, therefore, to seek and set the
affection on Christ, and then to live as one who does this, who from his
heart accepts as right the gracious dealing and gracious work of God which
he has experienced and is experiencing, who takes pleasure in these ways
of God. (II, 2, p. 580. The Content of the Divine Claim.)

What this nekrosate " mortify " (v. 5; cf. Gal. 5²⁴; Rom. 8¹³; 13¹⁴; 1
Pet. 2¹¹) does not mean is plainly enough said in the warning given a few
verses before against the Colossian errors (2²³) . . . A powerful ascetic can
be a vessel of much greater wickedness than even the most indulgent. We
cannot forget so easily that one may be a non-smoker, abstainer and veg-
etarian, and yet be called Adolf Hitler. (III, 4, p. 347 f. Freedom for Life.)

Anthropological and ecclesiological assertions arise only as they are
borrowed from Christology. That is to say, no anthropological or ecclesiological assertion is true in itself and as such. Its truth subsists in the
assertions of Christology, or rather in the reality of Jesus Christ alone. We

can certainly say to man that he can and should believe. But if we want to understand and say truly what this means, we must understand and say it of the One in whom he believes . . . In Christian doctrine, and therefore in the doctrine of the knowledge and knowability of God, we have always to take in blind seriousness the basic Pauline perception of v. 3 which is that of all Scripture—that our life is hid with Christ in God. With Christ: never at all apart from Him, never at all independently of Him, never at all in and for itself. Man never at all exists in himself. And the Christian man is the very last to try to cling to existing in himself. Man exists in Jesus Christ and in Him alone; as he also finds God in Jesus Christ and in Him alone. (II, 1, p. 148 f. The Knowability of God.)

We believe that we are redeemed, set free, children of God, i.e., we accept as such the promise given us in the Word of God in Jesus Christ even as and although we do not understand it in the very least, or see it fulfilled and consummated in the very least, in relation to our present (v. 3 f.). We accept it because it speaks to us of an act of God on us even as and although we see only our own empty hands which we stretch out to God in the process. We believe our future being. We believe in an eternal life even in the midst of the valley of death. In this way, in this futurity, we have it. The assurance with which we know this having is the assurance of faith, and the assurance of faith means concretely the assurance of hope. (I, 1, p. 463 [530]. God the Holy Spirit.)

Cf. also I, 1, p. 219 [251] (Luther); II, 1, p. 483; III, 3, p. 438, 441; IV, 1, p. 729.

SUNDAY AFTER ASCENSION-DAY (EXAUDI)

JOHN 15^{26}–16^4 (I)

We have to note that He is Himself the free active Subject in this event of the sending, imparting and outpouring of the Holy Spirit. But we have also to note that . . . without Him, without His free and sovereign address to specific men, there is no Holy Spirit as a factor in the existence of other men. Nor is there any Holy Spirit except as the One whom He sends to them as the Crucified and Risen, who cannot deny that as a factor in their existence He comes from Him as the Crucified and Risen . . . Both these points are brought out very clearly in the New Testament. To quote the Baptist again (Jn. 1^{30}), the One who comes after him is the One who baptises in the Holy Spirit, in the power of the Holy Spirit and with the Holy Spirit, as the giver of the Holy Spirit. Or as He Himself puts it . . . He will send the Spirit from the Father (15^{26}; 16^7). Or as He tells the disciples: " I send the promise of my Father upon you " (Lk. 24^{19}). Or as we are told in Peter's sermon at Pentecost (Acts 2^{33}), it is He who, exalted at the right hand of God, and as such the recipient and bearer of the promise, of the Holy Ghost, " hath shed forth this, which ye now see and hear. '' Or according to the abbreviated account in Jn. 20²² He breathes on His disciples as the Resurrected and says: '' Receive ye the Holy Ghost. '' It is He Himself who does this, but He Himself on the far side and not on this side of that frontier; He Himself as the One who has crossed it, who in His death has fulfilled both His humiliation and His exaltation, and in His resurrection proved Himself to be the '' holy servant '' (Acts 4²⁷ᶠ·) and therefore the Lord. It is He, the One who is crowned in His death and revealed as the King in His resurrection, who achieves His presence and action in the existence of other men. If they have the Spirit, they have the Spirit from Him, from this One, and therefore as the Holy Spirit. Prior to this fulfilment, and otherwise than from it, there is no Holy Spirit, no empowered witnesses, no apostles, no Christians, no community. As we are told in Jn. 7³⁹, ''the Holy Ghost was not yet (for others); because that Jesus was not yet glorified.'' '' If I go not away, the *parakletos* will not come unto you '' (Jn. 16⁷). The power of the reconciliation of the world with God as already accomplished and revealed, and therefore the power of the occurrence of Good Friday and Easter Day, is the presupposition which is made in the New Testament with reference to these other men. That this occurrence is reflected in their existence is the event of their reception and possession of the Holy Spirit, of their life by and with Him, of their government by Him. That they partake of the Spirit means that in distinction from all other men they are made witnesses to all other men. By Him they are to believe His being and action, His completed being and action. To live in the Holy Spirit is to live with and in and by and for this message. (IV, 2, p. 325 f. The Exaltation of the Son of Man.)

1 Peter 4⁷⁻¹¹   (II)

What does it mean that the end of all things has already begun, and that time and human existence are to be seen and fulfilled only from this standpoint? That it is not worth while to take them seriously? Quite the contrary! Just because this is true, there is a demand for prudence, soberness in prayer, persevering love, generosity, the service of each according to the gift which he is given, speech and action in responsibility before God and in the strength to be expected and received from Him (v. 7 f.). Just because the night is vanishing and the day dawning, there must be no more sleeping as though we had not yet realised it and were still living in the night in the illusion that we might still live on in peace and safety (1 Thess. 5³). No, we must awake and '' walk honestly as in the day '' (Rom. 13¹¹ᶠ·). We must put on '' the whole armour of God. '' We must admonish one another and edify one another (1 Thess. 5⁴ᶠ·). For what purpose do we have this time of ours? It is for us a kind of market or exchange that we might make the most of it in careful transactions, '' not as fools, but as wise '' (Eph. 5¹⁵ᶠ·; Col. 4⁵) . . . New Testament ethics is one powerful summons to take frankly and seriously the existence of man in his limited time as such and therefore to grasp it to-day, at once, this very moment, as his opportunity. But the power of this summons lies in the fact that it understands the time of man— obviously the time of every man—as a moment within the interval of time which begins and ends with Jesus Christ, which belongs to Him, in which man also belongs to Him, which is short, and in which the only thing known to man is that time, already bearing its end in itself, can suddenly come to an actual end. The summons of New Testament ethics is urgent. Every- where it emphasises that the limited time loaned to man is important be- cause everywhere it sees concretely, not merely that this time has a limit, but that God is its limit. Thus in its preaching of Jesus Christ it does not proclaim the man who is in some way halted by his limitation, and it certainly does not proclaim the faith of this man, but it proclaims the Lord who is superior to the man existing in this limitation, yet who has turned to him in His superiority. (III, 4, p. 583 f. Freedom in Limitation; cf. also on Romans 13$^{11-14}$ First Sunday in Advent.)

Praedicatio verbi Dei est verbum Dei (*Conf. Helv. post.*, 1562, *Art* I, 2). According to the translation: " Therefore when even to-day the Word of God is proclaimed in the churches by duly called preachers, we believe that the Word of God is proclaimed and accepted by the faithful. "

Proclamation is human speech in and by which God Himself speaks like a king through the mouth of his herald, and which is meant to be heard and accepted as speech in and by which God Himself speaks, and therefore in faith, as divine decision concerning life and death, as divine judgment and pardon, eternal Law and eternal Gospel both together. (I, 1, p. 52 [56]. Talk about God and Church Proclamation.)

Cf. on Luke 7$^{36-50}$ Eleventh Sunday After Trinity and on Romans 13$^{8-10}$ Fourth Sunday after Epiphany.

JOHN 7$^{37-39}$ (III)

According to the unanimous view of modern commentators the body from which these rivers flow is not that of the believer but the body of Him in whom he believes, the body of Jesus Christ. Thus one reads also in 4^{14} ... But what is this water which flows forth from Jesus, which is to be received from Him, which is, when received, to be drunk? The Evangelist himself comments in v. 39 ... According to the Johannine view, the exalting and glorifying of Jesus took place in His crucifixion and death. Without this, before it, the water could not yet flow forth, the outpouring of the Spirit could not yet take place, 16^7. This happens. When there is no doubt as to His death, immediately the water begins to flow out, the Spirit comes forth from Him and begins His work. 19^{34} tells of the fulfilment of the promise given in 7$^{37f.}$ and 16^7. (IV, 4, p. 126. Baptism with Water.)

Cf. also III, 2, p. 363; IV, 2, p. 326; IV, 4, p. 77.

ACTS 1¹⁰⁻²⁶   (IV)

In the New Testament Judas is always described as " one of the twelve," and the concept of election is expressly applied to him. The power of the apostolic cause which can be seen in him to the ultimate degree that he must serve it in his sin and guilt, is the power of the divine election which has fallen on him too. His election excels and outshines and controls and directs his rejection; not just partly, but wholly; not just relatively, but absolutely . . . It is of decisive importance for the New Testament teaching on predestination that the man rejected by God, the counterpart of the elect, should not be shown at a distance but in the most intimate and direct proximity to Jesus Himself. This helps to bring out the sinister threat which results for the elect from the fact that the rejected is among them . . . (II, 2, pp. 458–506, quoting here from p. 504). This description (v. 18) obviously suggests that Judas perished from within himself. It was because of an inward impossibility—in the New Testament the *splanchna* mean the inward part of a man as this is revealed—that he came to destruction. His creaturely being could no longer endure the monstrousness of the contradiction in which he had enmeshed himself, and so it had to explode like a released hand-grenade. He could only die therefore—Ac. 1 does not say by his own hand, but of himself . . . Whoever does what Judas did, does more than the deed itself. He does that which makes him insupportable to himself. He passes judgment upon himself. His inmost being moves irresistibly to this explosion of his whole existence. The man who kills Jesus also kills himself, even though he may not technically be a suicide. (II, 2, p. 470 f. The Determination of the Rejected.)

Cf. also on Acts 1¹⁻¹¹ The Ascension-Day and III, 3, pp. 509–511.

GENESIS 11¹⁻⁹   (V)

It is worth noting that the divine reaction to the building of the Tower of Babel (v. 8) does not consist in His destroying it by an earthquake or some other miracle. This confirms the fact that it is not the building, the technical invention, the attempt at civilisation facilitated by it, or the underlying intention, which constitutes the evil against which God takes these measures. What is brought under this judgment is the care and therefore the arrogance with which humanity tried to help and assert and maintain itself, to make itself a name, to play the part of providence in respect of the blessing of unity entrusted to it. An end was put to this procedure by depriving it of an object, i.e., by taking away this unity. The building thus ceased of itself. That it could cease shows that it was not harmless in intention but directed against God and therefore evil. This being the case, it had to cease: Ps. 127¹. The later destruction of these buildings, the ruins of which may still be seen, was a self-evident and factual commentary on this " in vain." Everything is in vain, and moves self-evidently to destruction sooner or later, that is enterprised by man with the same intention as this building. (III, 4, p. 316, cf. pp. 313–316. Near and Distant Neighbours; cf. also pp. 320–323.)

2 CORINTHIANS 4[7-18] (VI)

It is provided that they always have this treasure in very earthen vessels (v. 7), that their thanks are always very equivocal, that their faith is smaller than a grain of mustard seed, that their knowledge is wrapped in obscurity, that their confession is an impotent stammering. It is provided that their praise of God will always be that " poor praise on earth " in which ultimately they can only pray that it will be received in grace, in the hope that "it will be better in heaven when I am in the choirs of the blessed." There is no perfection in it, only the deep and radical imperfection of the cry, " Abba, Father." Even the voice of this minority is only the voice of the sinful humanity justified only in Jesus Christ, which can only believe in its right as established by Him. It certainly cannot escape a wonderful similarity with its Lord who became a servant. (IV, 1, p. 738 f. The Time of the Community.)

The life of Christians as a life in this hope begins with the decision made in their baptism. The whole of the further progress on this way which they plainly enter here can consist only in further responses to the Word of God which they accepted here, and hence in mere repetitions and variations of the grasping and exercising of this hope. Any step taken in thought, word or deed without this hope, they can only recognise and confess as quickly and radically as possible as sin, seeking the divine forgiveness, repenting, trying to make amends as they proceed on the appointed way ... On the basis of their baptism they have freedom only to stride forward in the direction of the Lord who comes in His new, final and comprehensive revelation, of the Lord and His dominion. This freedom, however, they do have. Its exercise is decisively that which is described in v. 16 as the daily renewal of the inward man, which corresponds—it is the inner man who is renewed from baptism, not the outer man—to the daily perishing and corruption of the outward man. (IV, 4, p. 198 f. Baptism with Water.)

Cf. II, 2, p. 499; III, 2, pp. 621–623; IV, 1, p. 329.

WHIT-SUNDAY

JOHN 14[23-27] (I)

" And mark well this text, how here Christ bindeth the Holy Ghost to His mouth and setteth Him His goal and measure that He go not beyond His own word ... Therewith He sheweth that henceforth in Christianity naught else must be taught by the Holy Ghost than what they, the

apostles, heard from Christ (but did not yet understand) and were taught
and reminded of by the Holy Ghost, that therefore it always pass out of
Christ's mouth from one mouth to the other yet remain Christ's mouth,
and the Holy Ghost is the schoolmaster, to teach and recall such."
(Luther, *Cruz. Somm. Post.*) (I, 2, p. 251. The Holy Spirit the Subjective Possibility of Revelation.)

The Spirit shows Himself to be holy, i.e., the Spirit of Jesus Christ
Himself, by the fact that He testifies of Him. The men to whom He is
given by Him are called to Him, reminded of Him, set in His presence
and kept close to Him. They are brought to the place to which they
belong according to the will of God revealed in Him. The Spirit reveals
to them, not only Jesus Christ, but also their own being as it is included
in Him and belongs to Him. He does this by causing them to see and
hear Jesus Christ Himself, as the One who has power over them, as the
One to whom they are engaged and bound, as the One whom they have
to thank for everything, as the Lord and salvation of the whole world
whom they are called to proclaim. The Gospel of John is particularly
explicit and impressive on this point. The Spirit is " the Spirit of truth "
(14^{17}), the power which does not work arbitrarily or independently, but
simply declares Jesus, accomplishing again and again the disclosure and
revelation of His reality. He will lead them to the fulness of the revelation
of this reality, and finally to its last and perfect form ($16^{13f.}$; 14^{26}; 15^{26}).
(IV, 2, p. 326. The Exaltation of the Son of Man.)

ACTS 2^{1-14a}, $^{22f.}$, $^{32f.}$, ^{36} (II)

The statements about the significance and work of the Holy Spirit in
the event which is called revelation in the New Testament can be arranged
in three groups. 1. The Spirit guarantees man what he cannot guarantee
himself, his personal participation in revelation (Rom. 8^{16}) ... 2. The
Spirit gives man instruction and guidance he cannot give himself ...
3. Exegetically most obscure but materially of crucial importance is the
fact that the Spirit is the great and only possibility in virtue of which men
can speak of Christ in such a way that what they say is witness and that
God's revelation in Christ thus achieves new actuality through it.

A Whitsun sermon cannot be an exposition of Ac. 2^{1-14} if it does not
see and show that the outpouring of the Holy Spirit to which this passage
refers consists very concretely in the fact that cloven tongues are seen and
that the disciples on whom these alight begin to speak in other tongues:
καθὼς τὸ πνεῦμα ἐδίδου ἀποφθέγγεσθαι αὐτοῖς. (Repetitions of this event
are reported in Ac. 10^{46} and 19^{6}). The second effect of this Whitsun
miracle then consists in the fact that the members present from every
possible nation both near and far hear the disciples declare the " wonderful
works of God " in their own tongues (Ac. $2^{7f.}$). A Whitsun sermon which
aims to be an exposition of Ac. $2^{1f.}$ will have to talk about this speaking of

the disciples and this hearing by Parthians, Medes and Elamites, etc. The impact of the address of Peter which follows in vv. 14–36, in so far as this is not a presentation of the *kerygma* itself, also consists purely and simply in the fact that what has happened is declared to be a fulfilment of the prophecy of Joel about the outpouring of the Spirit on all flesh, which will mean that men—both men and women is the surprisingly strong emphasis—will " prophesy." This is what is fulfilled at Pentecost. Over against the Lord Jesus, absolutely subordinate to Him but distinct from Him, there is another element in the reality of revelation, an apostolate, men commissioned, authorised and empowered by Him to witness, men whose human word can be accepted by all kinds of people as proclamation of the " wonderful works of God." This is the doing of the Holy Ghost. The difficult exegetical question here is how this gift of " tongues " at Pentecost is related to the special gift of individual members of the Christian community to which Paul gives the same name in 1 Cor. 12 and 14, and which he takes very seriously and values highly, but in respect of which he has many reservations and even criticisms . . . But there is no doubt that what Paul knew by this name did not have either for himself or, on his view, for the community, the same central significance as that which is recorded in Ac. 2. There is also no doubt that what gives the thing recorded there its central significance, the commissioning, authorising and equipping of the apostolate, is for him too—and for him too as the work of the Holy Ghost—the presupposition of his own activity and message. I, 1, pp. 453 ff. [518 ff.], God the Holy Spirit.

Cf. also III, 4, pp. 321–323.

JOEL 2²⁸⁻³² (III)

After the occurrence, completion and manifestation of the history of Jesus Christ, after the Day of Pentecost, Christian baptism, in distinction from that of John, derives from the outpouring and impartation of the Holy Spirit which took place for the first time at Pentecost, but which has taken place repeatedly since . . . The relation of Christian baptism to the baptism of the Spirit is no different from its relation to the imminent kingdom of God. Precisely because it derives from the event of a baptism with the Holy Spirit, as baptism with water it cries more urgently, earnestly and intensively for this event than does John's baptism. What were the three thousand who (Acts 2⁴¹) had themselves baptised on the Day of Pentecost when they had been added by the Holy Spirit, and what were all the thousands who followed them, when measured by the promise of Joel 2²⁸: " I will pour out my spirit upon all flesh," with which Peter (Acts 2¹⁷) began his Pentecost sermon? And what was the instalment (2 Cor. 1²²; 5⁵; Eph. 1¹³ᶠ·), the first-fruits (Rom 8²³), of the Spirit, when measured by the fulness promised to Christians in and with this beginning? *Venit Creator Spiritus*—but *Veni Creator Spiritus* is the cry of need uttered by the very ones who know and have the Spirit of Christ in this beginning of His work. (IV, 4, p. 76 f. Baptism with Water.)

ROMANS 8¹⁻¹¹ (IV)

Only God, our Lord and Creator, could stand surety for us, could take our place, could suffer eternal death in our stead as the consequence of our sin in such a way that it was finally suffered and overcome and therefore did not need to be suffered any more by us. No creature, no other man could do that. But God's own Son could do it. He could do it physically (p. 399 f.) and He could do it lawfully (p. 400). We must now add specifically that He could also do it effectually, i.e., in such a way that His suffering is in fact reckoned to us, that it need not be suffered any more by us, that we can be free from fear, that in view of the righteousness of God in necessary condemnation and punishment we may cling to Him as to the One in whom satisfaction is done to this necessity . . . If we hear Him as the Word made flesh, we hear what God also hears as the blood of His own Son cries to heaven to Him. But in His own Word made flesh, God hears that satisfaction has been done to His righteousness, that the consequences of human sin have been borne and expiated, and therefore they have been taken away from man—the man for whose sake Jesus Christ intervened. In the Word spoken by the blood of His Son God hears that for those whose flesh this His Son has made His own, for those who are in Him, in Jesus Christ, there is now no more condemnation (v. 1). (II, 1, p. 403. The Mercy and Righteousness of God.)

The man who can know this (v. 1 f.) without presumption or self-deception, and who can and must say it with such definiteness, is the same man who has before him and knows and says that which precedes it, the man who comes from the one to go forward to the other. Obviously he is the only one who can do this. But he can. The justified man speaks of his sin as in Rom. 7. No one else could do this so mercilessly. (IV, 1, p. 582. The Justification of Man.)

Have I the Holy Spirit (v. 9)? . . . Just because He is the Spirit of Christ, this question of " having " is not decided by what we can never do more than think we " have," but only by Christ. For it is only from Christ that we can have it, and therefore we can have it for ourselves only by continually turning to Him. And He says always: " Him that cometh to me I will in no wise cast out " (Jn. 6³⁷). The Church and Holy Scripture and preaching and the sacrament are therefore again the only possible criteria in any practical investigation. And true and proper proclamation of the subjective possibility of revelation, true preaching about the Holy Spirit of Pentecost, will not consist in pointing to our own or other men's seizure, but in pointing to the divine seizing, and therefore once again to Christ Himself. Consciously or unconsciously, every hearer is necessarily faced with the question whether and how he can be a real hearer and doer of the Word. And true preaching will direct him rather " rigidly " to something written, or to his baptism or to the Lord's Supper, instead of pointing him in the very slightest to his own or the preacher's or other people's experience. It will confront him with no other faith than faith in Christ, who died for him and rose again. But if we claim even for a moment that experiences are valid and can be passed on, we find that they are marshy ground upon which neither the preacher nor the hearer can stand or walk. Therefore they are not the object of Christian proclamation. If it is really applied to man in a thoroughly practical way, Christian proclamation does not lead the listener to experiences. All the experiences to which it might lead are at best ambiguous. It leads them right back through all experiences to the source of all true and proper experience, i.e., to Jesus Christ. (I, 2, p. 249. The Holy Spirit the Subjective Possibility of Revelation.)

Cf. IV, 3, pp. 545–547.

MATTHEW 16$^{13-20}$ (V)

To the picture of Jesus Christ presented in the New Testament tradition there belong various accounts which show that He was regarded by those around as a Prophet after the manner of the Old Testament, v. 14; Mt. 21$^{11,\ 46}$; Lk. 7^{16}; 9^{19}; 24^{19}; Jn. 4^{19}; 9^{17}. Nowhere do the Evangelists reject the possibility of numbering Jesus Christ with the prophets, nor the right to do so. But we detect a certain reserve in their accounts of these opinions and statements. For is He really just one prophet after and alongside so many others? He is a Prophet indeed, but in the Messianic confession of Peter in face of these opinions concerning Him it is maintained that as such He is more than all those who bear this title, and therefore that in relation to them He is a Prophet in a qualified sense. (IV, 3, p. 49. The Glory of the Mediator.)

Peter, proved to be a disciple by his confession, serves as the rock on which a wise man (7^{25}) will build. But it is Jesus Himself who builds His Church. And it is because He builds that it is invincible. To the best of my knowledge, this is the only passage in the New Testament—Vielhauer calls it " an erratic block "—in which Jesus is explicitly described as the One who builds up the community. But how can He be anything else . . . in relation to it than its Builder? Who else can be that? As He is a man among men, He builds up His community, integrating—not all men—but those who are called by Him into a common knowledge and faith and life and ministry. (IV, 2, p. 633. The Holy Spirit and the Upbuilding of the Christian Community.)

Can it really be characteristic of the communion of saints to increase in consequence and prestige and influence and outward pomp in the world around; to command increasing authority and esteem for itself as a recognised force, both from the state and from all other human societies; to win an assured place in the structure and activity of worldly politics and scholarship and literature and art? We need hardly demonstrate or bemoan the fact that the Church has often acted as if a positive answer had to be given to this question. But the very opposite is the case. The Church has the promise that " the gates of hell shall not prevail against it " (v. 18), but it has no promise to this effect. Its glory will be manifest when that of its Lord is manifest to the world. In the time between it is thankful for all the necessary space that it is granted in the world to fulfil its task. But the enlargement (or diminution) of this space has nothing whatever to do with its nature or commission. Its enlargement is not promised, nor its diminution demanded. It has its hands full with the task of filling it in the service of its cause according to the measure in which it is given (whether great or small). It will not be surprised or annoyed if it is pushed into the corner; or if sometimes it is forcefully deprived of its outward majesty and pushed even more into the corner. It is always seriously mistaken if it tries to grow in this dimension. The Church of Jesus Christ can never—in any respect—be a pompous Church. (IV, 2, p. 648. The Growth of the Community.)

Cf. I, 1, pp. 402–404 [460–463]; II, 2, pp. 435 ff.; IV, 2, pp. 673–675; IV, 3, p. 840; cf. also on Matthew 16[13-19] June 29.

ACTS 2[36-41]   (VI)

In the light of the miracle of Pentecost, Acts is bold to end the address of Peter with the proclamation (v. 36): " Therefore let all the house of Israel know assuredly . . . " This assurance is *in nuce* the alteration of their existence as it is effected by the Holy Spirit. " All the house of Israel " is assembled in this sure knowledge of Jesus as it is to be received and fulfilled by the Holy Spirit. By this knowledge it is marked off from the nations and enters on its mission to them. By this knowledge men are divided, not into the good and bad, the elect and reprobate, the saved and lost, but into Christians and non-Christians. They are divided, we may add, in the relative and provisional way in which they can be divided in the relative and provisional state of human history, where sin and death are still powerful, this side of this aeon. They are divided, we may add further, subject to the judgment of Jesus Christ on those who are divided in this way, on the relative and provisional genuineness of their division, and therefore on whether or not they are really Christians or non-Christians. And we must also add that this division has to be made continually. Each new day we are all asked whether we are Christians or non-Christians. Each new day we must cease to be non-Christians and begin to be Christians. Each new day we need the Holy Spirit for this purpose. Yet it is still the case that there is a division at this point, 1 Cor. 12[3]; 1 Jn. 4[2f.], [6]. (IV, 2, p. 327 f. The Direction of the Son.)

The witness of the community must be evangelical address, i.e., address in which men are claimed in advance for what is to be made known to them as the content of the Gospel. This content must form not only the declaration and explanation but the appeal with which the community turns to the world . . . To address men evangelically is decisively to present to them the great likeness of the declaration and explanation of the Gospel in such a way that they come to see its crucial application to them, that so far as any human word can do so it pricks their heart (v. 37), that it brings them to realise that the reference is to them, or to a supremely general truth which as such demands their personal cognisance and knowledge. (IV, 3, pp. 851 and 852 f. The Holy Spirit and the Sending of the Christian Community.)

With some variations in detail, but general agreement in substance, the process as described in vv. 37–41; $8^{12, 38}$; $10^{44f.}$; $16^{14f.}$; 22^{16}, is as follows. Individuals or groups have been reached by the Word of God, i.e., the apostolic preaching. Having heard it, they face the question: What shall we do? They want to obey the demand for confession of sins, for faith, for conversion. They do obey it. In keeping with this, in visible execution of the act of obedience, they ask for baptism and have themselves baptised. In all these accounts baptism has the character of an action in which there is a common affirmation by the candidates of the Gospel preached and received, which involves their conscious and voluntary participation, and which rests upon and takes place in an act of free decision. In these accounts it is not even conceivable that infants might be the recipients of baptism. This is certainly possible in other passages to which appeal is often made, $16^{15, 33}$; 18^8 and 1 Cor. 1^{16}. These verses speak of the baptism of whole houses or households, in which there might have been infants. This is, however, a slender rope, for it should be noted that even in these verses we have the sequence preaching—faith—baptism. (IV, 4, p. 179 f. Baptism with Water.)

Cf. IV, 4, p. 46, 78, 184.

MONDAY IN WHITSUN-WEEK

JOHN 3^{16-21} (I)

Now the object of the divine loving was the cosmos, which means (for what follows cf. R. Bultmann, *Das Evangelium Johannes*, 1950) the human world as a single object in hostile antithesis to God. Not from the very first. Not because it is bad in itself. For the world was made by God, 1^{10}. Not because it is posited against God in itself. Not because it is authorised or empowered to stand in this position of hostility to God. It is His possession, 1^{11}. Not because God has left it to itself. Not because He has given it cause for this hostility. The true light, the light of the covenant promising life, was and is present: and bright enough for every

man, 1^9. But the world knew it not, 1^{10}. In contrast to it the world is darkness, 1^5 It does not understand God—either in itself as His creature or as illuminated by that light. But with all these characteristics it is the object of the divine loving. For with all these characteristics it is the cosmos. Created by God and illuminated by Him from the beginning, not recognising Him and therefore dark, it is still the object of His loving. This event takes place absolutely. It has this in common with the creation of the world ... that God does not owe it to the world to love it. The world is not, as Philo and others imagined, the son of God. It is not begotten by Him. It does not share His nature so that He is bound to it by nature, essentially. It is the free will and the free act of God that He willed to be the basis of its existence and its light. The meaning of this event is from the very first a free loving ... There can be no question of any claim of the cosmos to be loved, or consequently of any mitigation of its character as darkness, which is only revealed in all its impossibility in this event, and for which it will now be plainly accused and judged and sentenced. But this does not take place because God rejects it, but because He loves it. And His love is not merely a disposition but an act, an active measure in relation to it. V. 16 describes the fulfilment and scope of this measure. (IV, 1, p. 70 f. The Fulfilment of the Broken Covenant.)
Cf. IV, 3, pp. 487–490.

ACTS $10^{34-36,\ 42-48a}$ (II)
IV, 3, pp. 487–490; IV, 4, p. 85.

JOHN $4^{19-30,\ 39-42}$ (III)
This does not mean that the freedom of the divine dwelling had suddenly ceased to be the freedom of an actual dwelling of God, and that its relativity would now rule out its reality. It does not mean that the divine presence in the world had suddenly become that of a mere undifferentiated ubiquity, and not of definite and distinct places. The opposite of Jerusalem and Gerizim and all temples made with hands—and we can apply it and say the opposite of Rome, Wittenberg, Geneva and Canterbury—is not the universe at large, which is the superficial interpretation of Liberalism, but Jesus. And the worship of the Father in spirit and in truth is not the undifferentiated worship of a God undifferentiatedly omnipresent. On the contrary, we have only to glance at the way in which the terms " spirit " and " truth " are used elsewhere in St. John's Gospel and we shall see at once that it is worship of God mediated through Jesus as the One who makes everything known to us. According to the testimony of the New Testament, God does not cease to dwell in the world in definite and distinct ways, i.e., even as omnipresent, and without detriment to His omnipresence. (I, 2, p. 481. The Unity and Omnipresence of God.)
After this manner and reality which are spiritual both ontically and

noetically, the vocation of man consists decisively in the fact that the living Jesus Christ encounters definite men at definite times in their lives as their Contemporary, makes Himself known to them as the One He is for the world, for all men, and therefore for them too, and addresses and claims them as partners in His covenant and sinners justified and sanctified in Him. He does this in the witness of the prophets and apostles. But in this witness it is He, Jesus Christ, who does it, so that these men may say with the Samaritans: v. 42. The historical process of vocation is thus highly extraordinary and yet also supremely simple. It is a temporal and historical event among others, and yet it is distinguished by this manner and content. (IV, 3, p. 502. The Event of Vocation.)

Cf. on v. 22 II, 2, p. 204; on v. 24 I, 1, p. 459 f. [526]; on v. 42 IV, 2, p. 183.

EPHESIANS 4$^{11-16}$ (IV)

The Holy Spirit is the quickening power with which Jesus the Lord builds up Christianity in the world as His body, i.e., as the earthly-historical form of His existence, causing it to grow, sustaining and ordering it as the communion of His saints, and thus fitting it to give a provisional representation of the sanctification of all humanity and human life as it has taken place in Him. (IV, 2, p. 614. The Holy Spirit and the Up-building of the Christian Community.) Cf. also pp. 623–626.

Christ is primarily (1^{20-23}) the Head of all things ... It is as such that God has given Him to be the Head of the community, and to Him as such that He has given the community as the body. He cannot and must not be without it as the *totus Christus* ... It believes in him as its Head. It looks and moves up towards Him from the depths and distance as to the One who exists in this heavenly form. And believing in Him it believes in itself as His *soma* and therefore His *pleroma*. But it does not see this. It is still on the way to this future when it will be revealed that He is the *pleroma* of all things and that it is His *pleroma*; that He is the One who rules the world and it is ruled by Him; that He and itself with Him, as the *totus Christus*, is the perfect man, v. 13 (cf. p. 623). Of course, all this—the *totus Christus*—has not still to evolve or to be made. In accordance with the predetermination of God ($1^{10f.}$), He has been instituted as such once and for all: not only in His relationship to the community but also in His relationship to the cosmos; and both not merely in heaven but also on earth; yet not visibly on earth even to Christians, and to that extent only in the sphere of the future. Thus the community *is* His body, the *pleroma* without which He would not be that which He has been appointed by God. (IV, 2, p. 659. The Growth of the Community.)

JOHN 15$^{9-17}$ (V)

The relation between the name of Jesus Christ and the Christian religion cannot be reversed: Ps. 100³; Jn. 15¹⁶. Both these "sayings" are particularly directed to the religious community of the religion of revelation as such. For the Church and for the children of God there is a recurrent temptation to regard themselves as those who elect in this matter. It is their faith and their love, their confession, tradition and hope which is its proper substance. Its grounding in the name of Jesus Christ can then appear as a free concession. We may perhaps decide upon it very seriously, but by thinking that it is something which we ourselves can and should decide, we show that we no longer realise with what name we have to do . . . There is no doubt (as Mt. 16¹³ᶠ·; Jn. 6⁶⁷ᶠ·; Josh. 24¹⁵ᶠ· show) that an election does take place: but it is an election upon which, just because it is our own election, we can only look back as upon something which has taken place already. In the act of electing we are not confronted by two or three possibilities, between which we can choose. We choose the only possibility which is given to us . . . Those who choose the name of Jesus Christ choose the only possibility which is given to them . . . They elect, but they elect their own election . . . Their election is election of the name of Jesus Christ . . . The Reformers and the older Protestantism knew well enough what they were doing when with one breath they challenged man to this decision and to that extent undoubtedly appealed to his freedom, and then (with greater or lesser emphasis) described predestination, i.e., the choice in the eternal decree of God, the election effected and perceived in Christ, as the proper object and content of the decision of faith. It is only in the decision of faith as ordered and understood in this way that we really have to do with the name of Jesus Christ . . . The power of affirming the name of Jesus Christ is either its own power or it is impotence. And it is only in the decision of faith as ordered and understood in this way that the truth can emerge and become certainty. The truth illumines and convinces and asserts itself in the fulfilment of the choice whose freedom and power is only that of the name of Jesus Christ Himself. As such it becomes, it makes itself, the truth of the Christian religion, whereas in the alleged possession of an abstract Christianity we always look in vain for the truth of the name of Jesus Christ and therefore strive in vain for certainty of the truth of the Christian religion. (I, 2, pp. 350–352. The Revelation of God as the Abolition of Religion.)

Cf. on John 16¹⁶⁻²³ᵃ Third Sunday After Easter (Jubilate) and on Joshua 24 Fourth Sunday After Trinity; cf. also III, 4, p. 402; IV, 2, p. 605.

ISAIAH 44¹⁻⁸　　　　　　　　　　　　　　　　　　　　　　　　　　　　　(VI)

TRINITY-SUNDAY

JOHN 3¹⁻¹⁵　　　　　　　　　　　　　　　　　　　　　　　　　　　　　　　(I)

"Born of water and the Spirit" in v. 5 expounds the "born from above" in the first saying of Jesus in v. 3. The reference is to the unique event in a man's life which can be expected and effected only from above, from God, the event of his total transposition into one who may see (v. 3) the kingdom of God and who may thus enter into it, receiving an active part in its establishment. How does this come about? We note that the man described as born from above is later described in v. 6 and v. 8 as " born of the Spirit " (with no " of water "). The natural conjecture that " of water " in v. 5 was added in an ecclesiastical redaction of the Gospel and should thus be excised has been advocated by several modern commentators, including R. Bultmann. This removes the difficulty, but it perhaps sets aside as well the true point of the verse. It has no textual support . . . What is meant by " of water and of the Spirit "? Since the two terms could later be reduced to one, we do not seem to have here two different events . . . It is natural to assume that we have in this formula one of the many pairs-in-tension which are characteristic of the thought and utterance of the Fourth Gospel: 1^{17}; 4^{23}; 5^{24}; $6^{30, 45, 69}$; 11^{25}; 17^3; 19^{34} . . . It is surely strange if the pair " water and Spirit " does not belong to this series of dynamically critical syntheses. What the " water " is by which a man is born from above is explained wholly and exclusively by " Spirit." In the function ascribed to it there is no water at all outside or alongside the Spirit: not the water of Jacob's well ($4^{6f.}$), nor that of the pool of Bethesda ($5^{2f.}$), nor the water of Christian baptism which many were perhaps extolling in circles around the Evangelist; not this water even as a representative, means or witness of the Spirit. Water is to be defined in this function solely by Spirit. He who begets a man from above is He who moves where He wills, whose voice may be heard but not localised (v. 8). He, the Spirit alone, is the " living water " ($4^{10f.}$; 7^{38}). His baptism, the baptism of the Spirit, is the true and proper baptism, namely, that which begets a man from above, that which gives him the ability and power to see and enter the kingdom of God. (IV, 4, p. 120 f. The Foundation of the Christian Life.)

Cf. I, 1, p. 221 [253] (Luther); IV, 2, p. 320 and p. 562 f.

ROMANS 11^{33-36} (II)

Whatever may be the literary and religious derivation of the well-known formula in v. 36 with which Paul concludes his great discussion of Christ, Israel and the Church . . . there can be no doubt that it does actually describe most exactly the presence and action of God in history . . . *Ex autou* has obvious reference to a beginning which produces and controls and determines and already anticipates everything that follows. *Di autou* has reference to a power and its operation which strive from this beginning to the corresponding goal and mediate the transition from the one to the other. *Eis auton* has reference to a goal which shows itself to be the genuine goal, i.e., anticipated by this beginning and attained by this power and its operation, by the fact that from it it is possible only to look back to this beginning and to return to it—the looking back, the return, the *eis auton*, obviously taking place in the same power, the same *di autou*, by which it is attained as a goal. And then *ta panta*: the whole occurrence stands under the threefold sign that it is all of Him and through Him and to Him. And therefore He, *autos* . . . is the one Lord in this history in a threefold manner and form, as its origin and means and goal. Thus . . . the liturgical conclusion . . . must be understood as the worship in which the Christian thought of God can alone be thought . . . (IV, 2, p. 388. The Exaltation of the Son of Man.)

Even the world without, which seems to be and is so very different . . . is wholly and utterly from Him and by Him and to Him, v. 36 . . . What takes place without in the cosmos in distinction from the history of the community of Jesus Christ is not occurrence which is alien to this one God, which evades or escapes the will of His love, the omnipotence of His mercy and forbearance, or His gracious overruling, which is finally and properly directed by man or by itself or by some other lord. . . . The community of Jesus Christ has a very inadequate view of its Lord, the King of Israel who is also the King of the world, if it is not prepared to recognise that even world-occurrence outside takes place in His sphere and under His govern-ance, or if it tries to imagine that in this occurrence we are concerned either with no God at all, or with another God, or with another will of the one God different from His gracious will demonstrated in Jesus Christ, and therefore with another kingdom of God on the left hand directed by God to another end and in another spirit. That which really takes place on the left hand of God, not outside but in hostility and opposition to His will, can only be nothingness and the devil. (IV, 3, p. 685 f. The People of God in World-Occurrence.)

Cf. IV, 1, p. 519.

MATTHEW 28[16-20] (III)

On the assumption of v. 18 and v. 19 f., one thing is required of the disciples, namely, that they are to help all nations to become what they themselves are, i.e., disciples of Jesus. They are to conduct them to membership of the one people of God . . . What is added in the participle clauses is not a second or third alongside the first, but its elaboration. They are to make disciples by calling them, in the name of the Father, the Son and the Holy Spirit, and therefore in appeal to the authority of God to which they know that they themselves are subject, to conversion, to the forsaking and forgetting of their former way, to a new beginning, to the state of hope, to prayer for the Holy Spirit, in short to the baptism which is then to be administered. And they are to make disciples by teaching them what they themselves have been taught by Jesus, by causing them to participate in the knowledge granted by the self-declaration of Jesus . . . but this one and indivisible whole in the light of and in reliance on the fact that as they do this He, Jesus, is not far from them but present among them to the end of this age as the One who primarily and properly speaks and acts. (IV, 3, p. 860 f. The Holy Spirit and the Sending of the Christian Community.)

In mission the Church sets off and goes (v. 19), taking the essentially and most profoundly necessary step beyond itself, and beyond the dubiously Christian world in which it is more immediately set, to the world of men to which, entangled as it is in so many false and arbitrary and impotent beliefs in so many false gods of ancient or most recent invention and authority and reflecting its own glory and misery, the Word which God has pronounced in Jesus Christ concerning the covenant of grace which He has concluded with it is still alien and must therefore be taken as a new message. The vocation which constitutes the community is directly the command to take this message to this world, to the nations or the "heathen." As it is obedient to this command, it engages in foreign missions ... As the community goes to the nations, to all nations (v. 19), calling them to discipleship, it certainly does not remove the frontiers and differences between them. On the other hand, it does not sanction them. Rather it constitutes right across them a new people in which the members of all peoples do not merely meet but are united. Gathered to it, men are first members of this new people, i.e., Christians, and only then, without disloyalty to their derivation but above all without compromising their unity, are they members of the different nations. A Church whose members sought to regard and conduct themselves first and decisively as members of their own nation and only then as Christians, i.e., a national Church in the strict and serious sense, would necessarily be a sick Church, since it would resist the witness to the fellowship of all nations, not helping to achieve this but making it if anything more difficult. The community which is true to its witness, while it does not question its particular membership of and responsibility to this or that nation, recognises the primacy of its own citizenship over all others, and *eo ipso* is not merely one of the uniting factors in the common life of humanity, but *the* such factor. (IV, 3, p. 874 and p. 899. The Ministry of the Community.)

Cf. IV, 4, pp. 95–100 and 155; I, 2, p. 165, 544, 671; III, 2, p. 453 f.; IV, 1, p. 735; IV, 2, p. 107, 658; IV, 3, p. 121, 288, 350.

Isaiah 6$^{1\text{-}13}$ (IV)

We misread the situation as Isaiah himself saw it (vv. 1–4) if we expect that a word along these lines, the proclamation of the universal rule of Yahweh as such, will be his task and the purpose of his mission. So far there has been no mention of any commission. What shatters and seizes Isaiah in face of the exalted King and as a hearer of the hymn or ascription of the seraphim is a recognition, which pierces asunder to the very joints and marrow, of the total disparity and discrepancy between the being and rule of Yahweh, as disclosed to him by the declaration articulated in the saying of the seraphim, and himself as a member of the temple community and the people of Jerusalem and Judah. The contrast is a mortal blow, v. 5. It is to be noted that he does not speak of the unclean heart, but of the unclean lips of himself and his people. It is thus clear to him from the very first that what he has seen and heard demands to be expressed and proclaimed. It must go out as a human word on human lips, to be sounded forth and heard in its immeasurably positive and negative significance among all men throughout the earth. But he knows of no human mouth which is able and worthy to form and express that which corresponds to the matter. He must confess that he is a member of the community and people in which there are only unclean lips which contradict rather than correspond to the matter. He thus knows that what he has seen and heard must be expressed and yet cannot be expressed by a human mouth. It is in view of this dilemma that he cries: " Woe is me! for I am undone. " And the distinctiveness of his calling is to be found in the fact that his own commissioning is thus delayed and he himself must first be made able and worthy . . . v. 6 f. There must be no mistaking the fact that the remission and purging which he is granted—whatever personal or private significance they might have—relates strictly to his enabling, to his being made worthy, for a service of his lips which is not yet but obviously will be required. Its purpose is strictly to make him free to render this service in distinction from the other members of his community and people. (IV, 3, p. 579 f. The Vocation of Man.)

Cf. III, 3, pp. 465–467.

LUKE 10²¹⁻²⁴ (V)

Within the structure of the thought and language of the Synoptists (v. 22 and Mt. 11²⁷) this element of pre-Johannine tradition is rather like a foreign body. But whatever may be its origin and age, according to this saying, revelation imparted to the *nepioi* (v. 21; Mt. 11²⁵) is grounded in the preceding movement in God Himself between the Father and the Son; in the fact that the Father has already delivered all things to the Son. The saying tells us with what authority and power the Son calls the *nepioi* and enables them to know Him, and (within the appointed limits) to know the Father as the Son knows Him. The very least that we can say is that this saying is a close, exact and illuminating parallel to the Johannine statement about the love of the Father and the Son and those called by the Son. The New Testament as a whole forces us even more than the Old to the question whether it is only casually and externally that the One whom it calls God fulfils the fellowship with man foreshadowed in the Old Testament covenant by humbling Himself so deeply, and exalting man so highly, that He was ready to take the being and nature of man to Himself and to be concealed and revealed as the Lord in the man Jesus of Nazareth. If this act was not casual, if in it He did not estrange Himself from His divine essence, if on the contrary He was supremely true and just towards it, in this act and in His essence He was again the God who cannot in any sense be equated with the unmoved deity of Plato and Aristotle and therefore with a God who is to be loved erotically. In His very essence He was the Father who loves the Son and the Son who loves the Father, and as such, in the communion and reciprocity of this love, as God the Father, Son and Holy Ghost, the God who is self-moved, the living God, the One who loves eternally and as such moves to love. (IV, 2, p. 759. The Holy Spirit and Christian Love.)

Cf. on Matthew 11²⁵⁻³⁰ First Sunday After Epiphany.

EPHESIANS 1³⁻¹⁴ (VI)

It is of God alone, but of God truly and effectively, that the community of the Old and New Testaments is His people. This is how it understands itself. It is thus that it recognises and confesses its invisible being in and with the visible. (IV, 3, p. 731. The People of God in World-Occurrence.)

It is at this height (v. 4) that the decision concerning our sanctification was resolved—and since the resolve is God's already taken. It is at this depth that Jesus Christ is and acts for us as our Lord and Head even as concerns our own conversion to God. In so far as this is its meaning and content, the history of the royal man Jesus crowned in His death at Calvary had this dimension from the eternity of the will of God fulfilled by Him on earth and in time. That is why Paul can hazard a statement like that of 1 Cor. 3¹⁷. That is why those gathered into the community can and must be called "saints." They are sanctified and therefore " saints in Christ Jesus " (1 Cor. 1²; Phil. 1¹); in and with the One who originally and properly is alone the Holy One. For He is their Head and Lord and King. They do not belong to themselves, but to Him. They are saints, not *propria*, but *aliena sanctitate*; *sanctitate Jesu Christi*. They are holy in the truth and power of His holiness ... That it is given to men to be saints (only, but with supreme reality) in their participation in the sanctity of the One who alone is holy means that there is created in the world a fact by which the world cannot be unaffected but is at once—wittingly or unwittingly—determined and altered. It is now the world to which there belongs also the existence of these men, this people, and it has to contend with this fact. (IV, 2, pp. 517 f. The Holy One and the Saints.)

Cf. II, 2, pp. 60–76.

FIRST SUNDAY AFTER TRINITY

LUKE 16¹⁹⁻³¹ (I)
1 JOHN 4¹⁶ᵇ⁻²¹ (II)

It is a frightful thing to say, but ... there is indeed a love which is mere philanthropy, a sympathetic and benevolent concern and assistance which we can exercise with zeal and devotion without taking even a single step away from the safe stronghold of being without our fellow-man, but in a deeper withdrawal into our shell. There is a form of love—mere charity— in which we do not love at all; in which we do not see or have in mind the other man to whom it is directed; in which we do not and will not notice his weal or woe; in which we merely imagine him as the object of the love which we have to exercise, and in this way master and use him. Our only desire is to practise and unfold our own love, to demonstrate it to him and to others and to God and above all to ourselves, to find ourselves self-expression in this sublime form. There is thus a form of love in which, however sacrificially it is practised, the other is not seized by a human hand but by a cold instrument, or even by a paw with sheathed talons, and therefore genuinely isolated and frozen and estranged and oppressed and humiliated, so that he feels that he is trampled under the feet of the one who is supposed to love him, and cannot react with gratitude. The great tragedy is that it is perhaps in the sphere of the neighbourly love established and shaped by Christianity, in Christian families and houses and societies and institutions, that we seem to have more frequent and shattering examples of this than in that of the worldly love, courtesy, affability and fellowship which are so much more shallow and discriminating, and therefore so much the less exacting. (IV, 2, p. 440. The Sloth and Misery of Man.)

" He that loveth not his brother whom he hath seen, cannot love God whom he hath not seen " (v. 20). He cannot, he cuts the root of his whole Christian existence. Positively v. 21: it is to be noted that here we do not really have an imperative but an indicative: " he that loveth " (on the vertical plane, in direct answer to God's own love) " loveth " (on the horizontal plane, in indirect but necessary repetition of this answer). There is thus a general inter-connexion, the one thing entailing the other. God's love evokes the love of the Christian for Him, and the two together the mutual love of Christians. (IV, 2, p. 817. The Act of Love.)

Cf. on 1 John 4$^{1-8}$ Twentieth Sunday After Trinity; also II, 1, pp. 32 ff.

MATTHEW 10$^{16-20}$ (III)

The individual Christian . . . is himself outside as well as inside. He is very much a man as well as a Christian. He is not only in the congregation but totally in the world as well, and therefore in the dark and alien and opposing sphere to which the community is sent as " sheep in the midst of wolves " (v. 16). In this true service he can co-operate only in faith. He cannot face the world from a safe harbour, but only as he faces himself, and the wolf in himself. (III, 4, p. 502. The Active Life.)

" As sheep "—it may be noted in passing that they are not sent out as shepherds who have to feed the sheep, though this is indeed their function (Jn. 21$^{15f.}$), but as themselves sheep in the midst of wolves. Nor are they sent out as wolfhounds who can bite no less powerfully than the wolves themselves, and are a good match for them, but as creatures who have no power to fight them and by human reckoning can only be chased and devoured by them. This is not a very heroic or comforting aspect of Christian existence. There is nothing here for Nietzsche . . . The addition (which is lacking in Luke): " Be ye therefore wise as serpents, and harmless as doves, " is hardly to be understood as a direction as to the way in which they might perhaps help themselves in this terrible situation by superior skill. (IV, 3, p. 630, cf. pp. 630–633. The Christian in Affliction.)

In the New Testament, and during the centuries which followed, the Christian existence and confession and life was always latently at least (if not uninterruptedly) an enterprise which stood under the threat of repression even to the point of physical violence. Later, and in our own time, the cross indicated in the New Testament has become rare, and for the most part exceptional, in this unequivocal form. Yet . . . even to-day the Christian is a *rara avis*, under constant threat, even in an environment which is ostensibly, and perhaps consciously and zealously, Christian. (IV, 2, pp. 609 f. The Dignity of the Cross.)

Cf. IV, 3, p. 633; III, 4, p. 79; IV, 2, p. 264.

EPHESIANS 2$^{17-22}$ (IV)

After Pentecost Christian baptism, in distinction from John's, is baptism in the name of Him who is the Messiah of Israel and the *Soter* of the world. It is thus baptism in one body, which is the Church of both Jews and Gentiles. The world, the Gentiles, may be seen from afar, but only from afar, in John's baptism . . . In the meantime, however, this slightly opened barrier had been pushed wide open. Strangely enough, even as the expected Messiah of Israel appeared and was delivered up by Israel itself to the Gentiles to be put to death, and even as the Gentiles, dramatically enough as executors of the sentence of rejection passed by the spiritual leaders and the people of Jerusalem, incurred the guilt of practical murder in respect of Him, " strangers and foreigners " became " fellow-citizens . . . " (v. 19), " fellow-heirs, and of the same body, and partakers " of the promise (3^6)—the promise which according to the counsel of God was fulfilled in that very crime. (IV, 4, p. 84. The Foundation of the Christian Life.)

Building up means integration (v. 20). This is what is done by God, by Jesus Christ, by the apostles and charismatics too, and finally, if it is a true Church, by the whole community in all its members . . . When they are gathered into the community, they are dedicated to the goal of all goals, and therefore their union must be total and complete and unconditional. It must be a union in brotherhood. Not in a collective in whose existence and activity the individual is not required as such and his particularity is a *pudendum*. Union in brotherhood is a solid union, but it is a union in freedom, in which the individual does not cease to be this particular individual, united in his particularity with every other man in his. In this context, therefore, upbuilding and therefore integration does not mean the erection of a smooth structure with no distinctive features, but of one in which the corners and edges of the individual elements used all fit together in such a way that they are not merely aesthetically harmonious but also exercise their technical function of mutual dependence and support ... The true form of this *synharmologein*/integration in the New Testament seems to consist always in an action as between man and man which necessarily has the character of love. And the simplest form of this action consists in a reciprocal relationship in which the one man is a neighbour and brother to the other, and *vice versa*, and they meet and act accordingly ... At this " joint " it takes place that " each one receives the consolation of the Gospel and passes it on to others " (Michel). (IV, 2, p. 635 f. The True Church.)

On Acts 15^{1-12} cf. June 24.

EZEKIEL 2^{3-8a}; 3^{17-19} (V)

In the Old Testament it is especially in Ezekiel (e.g., $3^{16f.}$; $18^{4f.}$, $^{20f.}$) that we find an " existential " application of the promise and call to the individual—that he should turn from his former way and live. Self-evidently, that which becomes explicit in Ezekiel is the meaning of both Testaments. The proclaimed conversion to God is an action and being ascribed and promised personally to each individual. It is a happening which applies particularly to him; which reaches to the heart and reins, the bones and marrow, of this or that particular man. And there is biblical precedent in the Book of Proverbs for what becomes so important in the later Church as the individual cure of souls. In general, however, we cannot overlook the fact that in the Bible the call for conversion is usually addressed—even when it is in the singular—to a plurality of men, to the people Israel, to Jacob-Israel in its totality, to Jerusalem or Ephraim ... We cannot make the conversion of man into a purely private matter, as though it were only a concern of the individual, the ordering of his own relationship to God and his neighbour, of his inward and outward life, of his own achievement of pure and essential being. It is right to emphasise its personal character, its singularity, and the isolation in which the individual must perish as the man he was, and can and may become new. But we must remember at this point the basis on which alone, if it takes place, it is an affair of the individual. The biblical individual is not selfishly wrapped up in his own concerns. It is a matter of God—that God is for him and he for God ... His conversion and renewal is not, therefore, an end in itself, as it has often been interpreted and represented in a far too egocentric Christianity. The man who wants to be converted for his own sake and for himself rather than to God and to entry into the service of His cause on earth and His witness in the cosmos, is not the whole man. When we convert and are renewed in the totality of our being, we cross the threshold of our private existence and move out into the open. The inner problems may be most urgent and burning and exciting, but we are not engaged in conversation if we confine ourselves to them. We simply run (in a far more subtle way) on our own path heading to destruction. When we convert and are renewed in the totality of our being, in and with our private responsibility we also accept a public responsibility. For it is the great God of heaven and earth who is for us, and we are for this God. (IV, 2, p. 565 f. The Awakening to Conversion.) Cf. IV, 3, p. 582 f.

2 TIMOTHY 3¹³⁻¹⁷ (VI)

Paul orders Timothy—it is noted that we are almost on the edge of the Canon—to " continue " in the things which he has learned, and received in faith ... All that he has said so far he has said in clear and express remembrance of the fact that the Scriptures have already played a definite, decisive role in the life of his reader, that they have already ... proved themselves. But then Paul goes on to give the assurance that these same Scriptures will also be profitable to thee " for doctrine, for reproof, for correction, for instruction in righteousness " (all obviously as much for himself as through him for others), " that the man of God may be perfect, thoroughly furnished unto all good works." The same Scriptures have now become the object of expectation. The content of the expectation does not differ from that of the recollection of which he spoke earlier, but all that was previously represented as a gift now acquires the character of a task which has still to be taken up and executed ... Scripture was able and it will be able for what is said about its meaning for the life and activity of the reader both before and after. In the middle of these two statements, throwing light both backwards and forwards, there stands the sentence: all, that is the whole Scripture is—literally: " of the Spirit of God," i.e., given and filled and ruled by the Spirit of God, and actively outbreathing and spreading abroad and making known the Spirit of God. It is clear that this statement is decisive for the whole. It is because of this, i.e., in the power of the truth of the fact that the Spirit of God is before and above and in Scripture, that it was able and will be able for what is said of it both before and after. But it is equally clear that at the centre of the passage a statement is made about the relationship between God and Scripture, which can be understood only as a disposing act and decision of God Himself, which cannot therefore be expanded but to which only a —necessarily brief—reference can be made. At the decisive point all that we have to say about it can consist only in an understanding and delimiting of the inaccessible mystery of the free grace in which the Spirit of God is present and active before and above and in the Bible. (I, 2, p. 504. Scripture as the Word of God.)

SECOND SUNDAY AFTER TRINITY

LUKE 14[15-24] (I)

IV, 3, p. 550; cf. on Matthew 11[25-30] First Sunday After Epiphany and on Matthew 22[1-14] Twentieth Sunday After Trinity.

1 JOHN 3[13-18] (II)

The second form of the witness consists in the fact that I give assistance to my neighbour as a sign of the promised help of God ... Supposing we take the most obvious and illuminating case of possible assistance which one man can give another in this sphere. By sacrificing himself he can save the physical life of another. (This is the case which is, of course, emphasised in v. 16, cf. Jn. 15[13], as a confirmation of love for the brother.) Can he really help him by doing this? No, he has not saved him from death; sooner or later death will overtake the one who is saved. Can he give his act the character of a sign of real help in face of death? No, for even the purest intention which he may have in this expressive act cannot create for it this character if it does not have it already, whatever may be his intention. Can he give to this expressive act the effect that the one who is saved does, in fact, recognise the sign of real help in face of death, the witness to Jesus Christ which is given him by it? Again: No, he cannot do that. Many a person has been saved from death by another without receiving and accepting in that event the witness of the one who saves him. He cannot really make the one who is saved see what there is to see in the act. Even, then, in this simplest and clearest instance of one man assisting or acting for another there has to be at least a threefold divine miracle if witness is to be borne by the service of the one to the other and if that witness is to be real assistance ... But how can it be disputed that the saving of physical life, which the one can do for the other, can actually mean for this other a knowledge of the limit of his need, a redemption in the light of which he learns to believe in *the* redemption, a comfort which will not fail, when the death which has for the moment been averted comes? ... We shall have to be clear that our action does not give us control of the decisive miracle. But we act rightly, and therefore with the promise that it will be a brotherly action, only when we count on the decisive miracle as a miracle of God. (I, 2, pp. 444–447. The Life of the Children of God.)

Cf. IV, 2, p. 810 f.

MATTHEW 9[9-13] (III)

The righteous are those who in their own judgment and that of other righteous people, who are never lacking in the world even without the intervention of Jesus, are standing in the right place as distinct from others, namely, at the side of God. Apart from their reconciliation to God effected in Jesus, and therefore apart from His prophecy, there is a relatively large minority of men who see in themselves and one another those who are already placed at the side of God, who are already called, who seem in some sense to form God's party in the world, and who can advance many good reasons for claiming to do so, in contrast to the majority of the godless with whom as such they are already in conflict . . . The publicans as sinners obviously do not belong to this party, but belong to the part of the godless assailed by them. And now Jesus comes to the scene of battle and finds the righteous on the one side and the ungodly on the other. To whom does he belong? . . . There now comes (for the righteous) the great disappointment and alienation. It is astonishing enough that Jesus calls a notorious publican to be His disciple. But this may be condoned on the natural assumption that He is calling him out of the great company of worldlings and ungodly and leading him into their camp. To make proselytes has always been a fine occupation for the righteous. Yet this is not what happens. What happens is that Jesus seems to follow the one who is called by Him rather than *vice versa*. He accepts his invitation, goes to his house, sits down at table not only with him and the existing disciples but with a highly dubious company of worldlings, eats and drinks with them, and in this way openly and publicly dissociates Himself from the righteous and associates with the ungodly . . . Who, then, is Jesus if this is His company? He has not come to strengthen the righteous in their righteousness, nor to give validity and new thrust to their party politics. Nor can He use them in His discipleship for what He has in mind for those who are called by Him. They are the very last who can become and be His witnesses. As those who are already righteous, they can never be His. As His disciples, as Christians, they could only cause confusion and offence by understanding and representing His Gospel as a new and higher kind of Pharisaism. He, Jesus, is not against publicans and sinners at the side of God. He is for them. He is for the worldlings and ungodly. (IV, 3, p. 586 f. The Vocation of Man.)

1 Peter 2¹⁻¹⁰ (IV)

What is it that makes individuals elect men (in Jesus Christ, and by means of His community)? We begin with a general answer. They are made this by a distinction of God's relationship to them and their relationship to God which is in fact peculiar to themselves (though independent of their personal peculiarities and independent of their conduct and actions). It is on the basis and assumption of this distinction that the guidance granted them, and their own conduct and actions and ultimately their role and task in the world about them, find their appointed, decisive character in relation to those of others . . . Just as Christians have their being as a whole elected race of priests and kings, a holy and peculiar people (v. 9), similarly every one of them has his being on the basis of his personal election. Each individual Christian is what he is no less definitely than Abel, Abraham, Moses, David and all the prophets, i.e., he lives and manifests the very presupposition and distinction peculiar to his being; he fulfils his personal predestination. The fact that in the Church all are elect, elect individuals, constitutes its difference from Israel. But the fact that they are elect is something which the Church has in common with Israel. And in this it shows itself to be a fulfilment of that of which Israel has been a prophecy. (II, 2, p. 340, 342. The Election of the Individual.)

Cf. on Revelation 3^{1-6} Second Sunday in Advent; on Hebrews 10^{32-39} December 26.

MATTHEW 10^{7-15} (V)

It is the *keryssein* of Jesus Himself, His self-proclamation, that is to form the content of their *keryssein*. How, then, can it turn in upon itself? How can it be grounded in itself? How can it crowd out the *kerygma* of Jesus? How can it make it superfluous? It is a call to hearing, faith and confession, news of an accomplished salvation, to the extent that it derives from His sending, consists in the execution of His commission, and therefore, dependent absolutely on His sending and commission, takes up and reproduces the *kerygma* of Jesus. The power of their action lies in this relationship. It is because of this relationship that there can be said of them and their work: " He that heareth you heareth me " (Lk. 10^{16}). As they speak in this relationship, they are authorised, and, as is so emphasised in the commissioning speech in v. 26 f., they do not need to fear anyone or anything. (IV, 2, p. 208. The Royal Man.)

Cf. II, 1, p. 355.

ISAIAH 55^{1-5} (VI)

THIRD SUNDAY AFTER TRINITY

LUKE 15^{1-10} (I)

God's loving is concerned with a seeking and creation of fellowship without any reference to an existing aptitude or worthiness on the part of the loved. God's love is not merely not conditioned by any reciprocity of love. It is also not conditioned by any worthiness to be loved on the part of the loved, by any existing capacity for union or fellowship on his side . . . The love of God always throws a bridge over a crevasse. It is always the light shining out of darkness. In His revelation it seeks and creates fellowship where there is no fellowship and no capacity for it, where the situation concerns a being which is quite different from God, a creature and therefore alien, a sinful creature and therefore hostile. It is this alien and hostile other that God loves . . . This does not mean that we can call the love of God a blind love. But what He sees when He loves is that which is altogether distinct from Himself, and as such lost in itself, and without Him abandoned to death. That He throws a bridge out from Himself to this abandoned one, that He is light in the darkness, is the miracle of the almighty love of God (Mt. 15^{24}; Lk. 5$^{31f.}$; 19^{10}). According to Luke 15 it is the lost sheep, the lost coin and the lost son that are the object of the Messiah's work; while to the Pharisees Jn. 9^{41} must be quoted . . . (II, 1, p. 278. The Being of God as the One who Loves.)

1 PETER 5^{5b-11} (II)

The anxiety and fear which are so strongly forbidden (in many New Testament passages) obviously meet in the fact that when man is anxious and afraid, instead of going his way in confidence and hope, he lets himself be burdened and arrested (or burdens and arrests himself) by looking at a threat which confronts him, and by the consideration which he lets this threat obtrude on him—as if he knew that it might, or necessarily would, involve a catastrophe. The way in which the two conceptions are related is that anxiety is in a sense the term for a little fear, and fear the term for a great anxiety. Anxiety has to do expressly with penultimate things which we can more or less envisage. It has to do with questions of the future external form of life. The anxious man wants security in face of the uncertainty of the future before he goes further and decides to live for that for which he should properly live . . . He, too, is really afraid . . . He has postponed that which really ought to happen. He is not genuinely and seriously moved and claimed by it. He is moved and claimed by the non-essentials of which he believes and maintains that they must first be thoroughly regulated before that which is properly essential can come into its own. But he will never admit that he is afraid. He will " only " postpone the real essential . . . When he is anxious, he creates a small fear, and conceals from himself the fact that he is no less afraid because his fear takes this shape . . . In what they have in common, anxiety and fear, both in their difference and in their inner connexion, are obviously the direct opposite of what the New Testament describes as freedom and of what we have described as the permission given to man by the command of God. (II, 2, p. 597 f. The Command as the Claim of God.)

Cf. on 1 Peter 5$^{1-15}$ Second Sunday After Easter (Misericordias Domini) and on Matthew 6$^{24-34}$ Fifteenth Sunday After Trinity; cf. also III, 3, p. 43.

LUKE 15$^{11-32}$ (III)

It would be a strained interpretation to try to give this parable a direct christological reference . . . In what it says directly . . . it speaks of the sin of man and the mortal threat which comes to him in consequence, of his repentance and return to God, and of the overwhelming grace with which this one who turned away and then turned back to God is received by Him. According to v. 1 f. this is all with a view to the " publicans and sinners " who come to Jesus and hear Him, whom He receives, and with whom He eats—in contrast to the scribes and Pharisees, who seem to shun Him for this reason. In the parable the latter correspond to the elder son (v. 28 f.) . . . the—indispensable—contrast, just as the scribe or Pharisee, the righteous who needs no repentance, has only the significance of contrast in relation to the main statement of the passage. The real message . . . in this story tells of the turning away and turning back of man in his relationship to God, in which there is not only no diminution but a supreme heightening and deepening of the fatherly mind and attitude of God towards him . . . I will not press the point, but will only say that in v. 28 f. we are invited by the text itself to indirect, not allegorical, but typological, or *in concreto* christological exposition. So much we may say, and it will have to be taken into account in even the most cautious exegesis of the parable. (IV, 2, pp. 21–25. The Homecoming of the Son of Man.) The insight that " I have sinned . . . and am no more worthy to be called thy son " (Lk. 15[18f.]) is not an insight of abstract anthropology. Only the son who is already recalling his father's house knows that he is a lost son. (I, 1, p. 407 [466], God as Reconciler.) Ezekiel 18[1-4], 21–24, 30–32.

Cf. on Ezekiel 2[3-82]; 3[17-19] First Sunday After Trinity and also II, 1, p. 414.

LUKE 19[1-10]   (V)

Jesus Christ is the hope of all men, and therefore also of non-Christians, of the heathen, of the theoretically or practically ungodly. How could we limit the positive sign of life in the midst of the times to Christians? The main concern of the ongoing of the history of the prophecy of Jesus Christ which fills our time is with non-Christians. Their existence is a reminder of the darkness which resists it. It is for their sake that it must go forward, that Jesus Christ as the living Word of God is still on the way to-day. Their conversion from ignorance to knowledge, from unbelief to faith, from bondage to freedom, from night to day, is the goal of His prophetic work so far as it has a temporal goal. He wills to seek and to save those who are lost, who without Him, without the light of life, without the Word of the covenant, will necessarily perish, v. 10. He is for them specifically this light, this Word. He is their hope . . . Christians have many reasons to see this. In days past were they not themselves non-Christians, or sleeping and even dead Christians, and therefore in fact and at bottom non-Christians? Is it not the case that they were not for Him as He was for them? Have they not every cause to be grateful that in spite of this, without their response of love, even when they were enemies (Rom 5[10]), He was for them, their hope, and the Holy Spirit was obviously promised to them in this way? (IV, 3, p. 364 f. The Promise of the Spirit.)

Cf. on Luke 13[22-30] Fifth Sunday After Epiphany.

1 TIMOTHY 1[12-17] (VI)

What did Saul not know? . . . What it all amounts to is that he did not know Jesus. Looking back later (2 Cor. 5[16]), he said that he then knew Christ " after the flesh," i.e., as the author of a sect which despised all that was most holy, which destroyed the Israelitish economy of reconciliation and revelation, and which was thus guilty of serious apostasy from God. This was how he saw and understood Him from the standpoint of an unrepentant Israel ignorant of its own peace. And seeing and understanding Him in this way which made him a persecutor of the community, he did not know Him at all. To know Christ in this or some other carnal way is not to know Him at all and thus necessarily to hate the witness concerning Him, and those who bear it. Saul of Tarsus did not know Him and therefore he did not know the divine election resolved for the deliverance of Israel in the existence of this Israelite rejected by Israel. He could interpret His existence only to the detriment of Israel and therefore as hostile to God. This was the ignorance of his unbelief, v. 13. It was in this darkness of ignorance that in his zeal for God he finally went rushing to Damascus. (IV, 3, p. 200. Jesus is Victor.)

Cf. III, 2, p. 443.

FOURTH SUNDAY AFTER TRINITY

LUKE 6[36-42] (I)

That He is the Judge, and that He makes judgment impossible for us . . . is the indicative which stands behind the evangelical command not to take the top seats but the lower (Lk. 14[8]), not to exalt but to abase ourselves (Mt. 23[12]), and especially the prohibition in v. 37 (Mt. 7[1f.]). The One who forbids men to judge, who restrains and dispenses them from it, is the One who has come as the real Judge. He makes clear what is true and actual in His existence among men as such: that the one who exalts himself as judge will be abased, that he can only fall into the judgment which will come upon himself. The evangelical prohibition frees us from the necessity of this movement in a vicious circle. Freed in this sense, Paul writes in triumph: 1 Cor. 4[3f.]; Rom. 8[34]. (IV, 1, p. 235. The Judge Judged in Our Place.)

The evangelical warning (v. 37; Mt. 7[1]) not to judge is not intended or to be kept only occasionally; it goes right home to the kingdom of demons which is opposed to the kingdom of God and devastates the earth. (IV, 1, p. 452. The Pride and Fall of man.)

ROMANS 8[18-23] (II)

It is to be noted that in vv. 19–23 the *ktisis*, creation, which also includes humanity, is set over against the children of God. Both are waiting and sighing for a future revelation. But it will be the revelation of what the children of God are *hic et nunc*, of the freedom which, even though its glory is hidden from them too, is already granted and proper to them *hic et nunc*, 9^{26}; Gal. 3^{26}; 1 Jn. $3^{1f.}$. (IV, 3, p. 532. The Goal of Vocation.)

A passage like v. 19 f., is shot through by the conception that the cross of Christians also consists in their particular share in the tension, transience, suffering and obscurity by which every man is in some form constricted and disturbed and finally condemned to death, and in which man also seems to find himself in painful connexion with creation as such and as a whole. The older Evangelical hymn depicted the cross of the Christian primarily in this light. In so doing, it departed to some extent from the New Testament. But it did it very impressively. If it is in its own way right, then in relation to the cross laid on the Christian we have also to think of the afflictions of creaturely life and being which come on him either suddenly or gradually, momentarily or continually, but in the long run with overwhelming force: misfortunes, accidents, sickness and age; parting from those most dearly loved; disruption and even hostility in respect of the most important human relations and communications; anxiety concerning one's daily bread, or what is regarded as such; intentional or unintentional humiliations and slights which have to be accepted from those immediately around; the sense of a lack of worthwhileness in respect of particular tasks; participation in the general adversities of the age which none can escape; and finally the dying which awaits us all at the end. (IV, 2, p. 611. The Dignity of the Cross.)

Cf. I, 1, p. 457 [523 f.]; III, 4, p. 355; IV, 3, p. 310 and p. 915.

GENESIS 50^{15-22a} (III)

1 CORINTHIANS 12^{12-27} (IV)

In New Testament passages like Rom. $12^{4f.}$; 1 Cor. $10^{16f.}$; $12^{12f.}$; Col. $1^{18, 24}$; Eph. $1^{22f.}$; 4^{12}; $5^{23, 29f.}$ etc., the Church is undoubtedly described as the body of Christ. One meaning of this description is undoubtedly this: that the existence of the Church involves a repetition of the incarnation of the Word of God in the person of Jesus Christ in that area of the rest of humanity which is distinct from the person of Jesus Christ. The repetition is quite heterogeneous. Yet for all its heterogeneity it is homogeneous too (although the uniqueness of the objective revelation forbids us to call it a continuation, prolongation, extension or the like) . . . The Church has its origin in Christ, i.e., it derives from the Word that became flesh. (I, 2, p. 214 f. The Freedom of Man for God.)

There were two insights which constantly forced themselves on Paul . . . in the question of the plurality and unity of the community . . . and which he constantly tried to make clear and explicit to the readers of his letters by means of the image of the body and its members, cf. also Rom. 12^{4-8}; Eph. 4^{1-16}. They are both stated alongside one another in v. 12 . . . The two basic principles, and their complementary relationship to one another, can only be fully clear and necessarily illuminating when it is understood that for Paul . . . there is in this image not merely an image but something real, indeed, primarily and ultimately the only real thing in the world. He has the community before his mind as the body and members of the Head Jesus Christ, v. 27 . . . It is as he looks up to this Head that he understands as he does the community, the unity and plurality of its ministry and witness, and the relation of the fellowship to the fellowships, and that he is so certain of the one Spirit and yet also of the multiplicity of His gifts. The " communion of the Holy Ghost " (2 Cor. 13¹³) is for him neither a prison nor a maze of human caprice, invention, freedom of opinion and thirst for adventure, but the " bond of perfectness " (Col. 3¹⁴) which neither represses nor withholds the perfect bond uniting the community (and called the bond of peace in Eph. 4³), since it is for him the same thing as the " fellowship of his Son Jesus Christ our Lord " (1 Cor. 1⁹) . . . The total meaning of the v. is thus as follows: " As the body is one, and hath many members, and all the members of that one body, being many, are one body: so also is Christ. " (IV, 3, pp. 857–859. The Ministry of the Community.)

Matthew 18¹⁵⁻²⁰ (V)

If this reflects the language of the synagogue, binding and loosing means forbidding and permitting. In Jn. 20²³, however, the two concepts are linked with the forgiving and non-forgiving of sins. Since this agrees more closely with the image of the keys which open or shut the kingdom of heaven in Mt. 16¹⁹, it would probably be more accurate to use the terms " retain " and " release " in the verses in Matthew, since these would also include forbid and permit. The saying has obviously played a more decisive role in the theory of later penitential or Church descipline, as unfortunately explained and applied e.g., in the *Heidelberg Catechism, Qu.* 83–85. Indeed, Mt. 18¹⁸ seems in the context to point in this direction. Nor can it be contested that it has an inward significance for the Church, if hardly perhaps in the technical sense later acquired. The solemn connexion with the founding of the community in which it occurs in Mt. 16¹⁹ and Jn. 20²³, however, makes it probable that primarily and properly it is to be referred to the function of the community in and in relation to the world. If so, it speaks of that which, as the community is at work, either takes place or does not take place in the world and among men, including the members of the community itself. If everything is in order, and its work is well done, there must be a great opening, permitting and releasing i.e., the promise and reception of the forgiveness of sins. If its work is not done or done badly, then contrary to its task the community closes the kingdom of heaven and excludes men from it instead of pointing them to the door which is open to all. It holds where it should release. The remission which is the content of its witness is kept from men . . . Heaven is at stake in what it does or fails to do on earth. By its work God Himself is either glorified or compromised and shamed in His work. God Himself rejoices or weeps over what it does or fails to do, over its lawful opening or unlawful closing. (IV, 3, p. 861 f. The Holy Spirit and the Sending of the Christian Community.)

First, where two or three are gathered in His name (i.e., have been brought together by the revelation of His name), they speak with and to one another in human words; . . . Secondly, they will mutually recognise and acknowledge that they are those who have been gathered by Him as their one Lord, and regard and receive one another as brothers because they are all brothers of this First-begotten; . . . thirdly, it is in order that they may be unitedly strengthened and preserved to eternal life; . . . fourthly, they are called by Him to pray with one another . . . Its public worship . . . is the place where this takes place, in its concrete life as a fellowship, not only of confession and baptism and the Lord's Supper, but also of prayer. (IV, 2, pp. 699–706. The Holy Spirit and the Upbuilding of the Christian Community.)

Cf. on 1 Corinthians 10$^{16-21}$ and cf. 11$^{23-29}$ Maundy Thurdsay; cf. also IV, 2, p. 658; IV, 3, p. 757 f.

ROMANS 14$^{7-19}$ (VI)

The Christian cannot be a lover of death . . . he knows better than others —than those who for different reasons have lost their zest for life and long for its end and dissolution—what he is doing when he says Yes to the negation of his life, to pain and suffering and death. He says Yes to these because his sanctification in fellowship with Jesus Christ, in His discipleship, in the conversion initiated by Him, in the doing of good works, ultimately includes the fact that he is to see and feel and experience the limit of his existence—even of his Christian existence engaged in sanctification—as the limit of his human and creaturely life, which necessarily leads to pain and suffering and death, leading to death, and proclaiming it, and finally involving it. To save his life he must surrender and lose it. He will not seek or induce this loss. It will come to him. But as a Christian, and because it is a matter of life, he will not negate or affirm it, just as elsewhere and right up to this frontier he will not negate but affirm life. He will not affirm either for its own sake. But he will definitely affirm both, even death, for Jesus' sake (Mk. 8^{35}). He will accept the fact that this limit or frontier is set, and that he has to note it. He will take up his cross. (IV, 2, p. 602 f. The Dignity of the Cross.)

FIFTH SUNDAY AFTER TRINITY

LUKE 5$^{1-11}$ (I)

There can be no real faith in God which in the presence of the marvellous work of divine election and favour does not feel compelled to utter the cry of Peter in v. 8 ... Rightly understood, it is the believer and the believer alone who speaks in this way. For from grace and only from grace does the judgment proceed which compels men to speak in this way. The man without grace and faith will not speak in this way. Rather he will attempt to evade the judgment and hide it from himself. In fact, he will not be able to appreciate it. He will merely be judged in fact, and fall an eternal victim to judgment without realising it. He will suffer without surrendering himself to that which encounters him, without repentance and without knowledge, and therefore without help and without hope. It is a well-known fact that Luther referred to the consciousness of sin, the fear of God's wrath and penitence, to a special revelation of divine law, holiness and wrath, separate from the revelation of divine grace; to a special aspect of God's being, its majesty and hiddenness. In this respect we do not follow Luther because this scheme cannot honestly be maintained in face of the apparently more complicated but in truth far simpler testimony of Scripture. In Scripture we do not find the Law alongside the Gospel but in the Gospel, and therefore the holiness of God is not side by side with but in His grace, and His wrath is not separate from but in His love. But Luther seems fortunately to have contradicted himself many times. That the Holy Spirit, the One who convicts the world in respect of righteousness (i.e., in the resurrection of Jesus Christ) and of judgment (upon the prince of this world), also convicts the world in respect of sin (Jn. 16$^{8f.}$), was after all written effectively in his Bible too ... The holiness of God consists in the unity of His judgment with His grace. God is holy because His grace judges and His judgment is gracious. (II, 1, p. 362 f. The Grace and Holiness of God.)

Cf. also IV, 3, pp. 588 ff.; IV, 1, p. 82, 290.

1 PETER 3$^{8-17}$ (II)

Cf. on 1 Peter 3^{15b-22} Fifth Sunday After Epiphany; also II, 2, p. 577 f.

LUKE 9^{57b-62} (III)

The call to discipleship is the particular form of the summons by which Jesus discloses and reveals Himself to a man in order to claim and sanctify him as His own, as His witness in the world. It has the form of a command of Jesus directed to him ... Because the command of Jesus is the form of grace which concretely comes to man, it is issued with all the freedom and sovereignty of grace against which there can be no legitimate objections, of which no one is worthy, for which there can be no preparation, which none can elect, and in face of which there can be no qualifications ... The man mentioned in v. 61 f. lacked true discipleship, not merely because he offered it to Jesus as a matter for his own choice, but because he also made a condition ... Those who offer themselves to be disciples are obviously of the opinion that they can lay down the conditions on which they will do this. But a limited readiness is no readiness at all in our dealings with Jesus. It is clear that this man does not really know what he thinks he has chosen. It is certainly not the following of Jesus. This is commanded unconditionally, and therefore it cannot be entered upon except unconditionally. (IV, 2, p. 535 f. The Call to Discipleship.)

The concept of discipleship points in quite a different direction from *imitatio*. In the first place it is descriptive of someone who accompanies another, who takes the same road as he does. But more pregnantly, it indicates the follower who respectfully walks behind his master or prince, the scholar who strides along at a distance behind his teacher. And in cases like this imitation is not only unnecessary, but impossible. Further, we have to note that this following is distinguished from an arbitrary action, like imitation, by the fact that it is conditioned by the call of Jesus. It is therefore a Messianic gift. The individual who decides (v. 61 f.) to tread this way on his own initiative, at once proves that he is not suited for the kingdom of God. (I, 2, p. 277. The Freedom of Man for God.)

Cf. also under 3 (a–e) in I, 2, pp. 265–278.

Acts 9^{1-20} (IV)

The essential feature in this event is . . . that Jesus Himself makes Saul acquainted with Himself, enlightening him concerning Himself, namely, that He is the One for whom Paul is elected from his very birth, that He is the *telos* of the Law and covenant so vehemently asserted by Saul, that Saul has to do with Him in the witness of the Christians whom he persecutes . . . He gives Himself to be perceived by him . . . as acting Subject . . . as his Lord . . . But this necessarily means that Saul must give place to this Other as his Lord, that he must accept His lordship, that he must end his headlong rush as a persecutor of this Subject, or more positively that he must bend to His rule, subject himself to His will and work, and thus in a right-about turn become His disciple, a witness and an apostle instead of an enemy of this Jesus. The call which overtakes him when this Jesus makes Himself known and he is brought from ignorance to knowledge is a summons to leave his former path and to enter and tread the new and opposite path which is indicated to him as one who now knows Jesus and which he cannot hesitate to take as such. Saul of Tarsus does not live any more. Christ lives in him. To the extent that he still lives, it is in faith in the Son of God (Gal. 2^{20}). He is now free to obey this superior Other. He is the prisoner, the slave, the apostle of Jesus Christ. (IV, 3, p. 202 f., cf. pp. 199–211. Jesus is Victor.)

Are there not indeed Christians whom like the Pietists we can describe as " chosen vessels " (v. 15) in relative distinction from others, and whose existence is absolutely necessary to the life and witness of the community? If this brings us inevitably into close proximity to Roman Catholic doctrine and practice, we should not let this prevent us from perceiving a serious problem and tackling it as such. It is naturally intolerable that ... we should describe these models of Christian existence as " saints " in distinction from others, that we should call upon these sometimes very singular saints as guardians and helpers, that by curious processes we should ascribe to them the honour of altars and that we should direct upon them a whole mass of popular superstition. Yet we should still recognise the genuine concern concealed behind these confused developments ... To the active witness of the community there belong the production and existence of definite personal examples of Christian life and action ... It makes no odds what higher or lower function or office these men have. It makes no odds whether they have any official function at all. It is not a matter of the form or quality of their character, culture, morality, or human appearance and achievement. In this field the last may by first and the first last. (IV, 3, p. 887 f. The Holy Spirit and the Sending of the Christian Community.)

Cf. on Acts 16$^{16-40}$ Third Sunday After Easter (Cantate).

LUKE 14$^{25-33}$ (V)

Hate (v. 26)! It is not the persons that are to be hated, for why should they be excluded from the command to love our neighbours? It is the hold which these persons have and by which they themselves are also gripped. It is the concentration of neighbourly love on these persons, which really means its denial. It is the indolent peace of a clannish warmth in relation to these persons, with its necessary implication of cold war against all others. The coming of the kingdom of God means an end of the absolute of family no less than of possession and fame. Again, there is no general rule. No new law ... has been set up. But there is proclaimed the freedom of the disciple from the general law as it is given to him, and has to be exercised by him, in a particular situation ... There can be no doubt that in its fear of the bogy of monasticism Protestantism has very radically ignored this proclamation of Jesus Christ, as also that of other freedoms. To a very large extent it has acted as though Jesus had done the very opposite and proclaimed this attachment—the absolute of family. Can we really imagine a single one of the prophets or apostles in the role of the happy father, or grandfather, or even uncle, as it has found self-evident sanctification in the famous Evangelical parsonage or manse? They may well have occupied this role. But in the function in which they are seen by us they stand outside these connexions. In this respect, too, no one who really regards himself as called by Jesus to discipleship can evade the question whether he might not be asked for inner and outer obedience along these lines. The life of the new creature is something rather different from a healthy and worthy continuation of the old. When the order is given to express this, we must not refuse it an obedience which

is no less concrete than the command. (IV, 2, p. 551. The Call to
Discipleship.)

Cf. on John 17$^{9-19}$ Fifth Sunday in Lent (Judica) and on Matthew 10$^{34-39}$
Twenty-First Sunday After Trinity.

1 KINGS 19$^{1-8}$ (VI)

JUNE 24. SAINT JOHN BAPTIST'S DAY

LUKE 1$^{57-80}$ (I)

According to the Synoptists, at any rate, the function of John the Baptist
is almost wholly Old Testament. He arraigns, he preaches repentance,
he proclaims the nearness of judgment . . . Also Old Testament is the last
thing we hear in the Synoptics about his attitude to Jesus, the question of
Mt. 11^3. Moreover he also dies the typical death of a prophet . . . But this
line of exposition is strangely intersected by another . . . It is especially
the Fourth Gospel which has so very emphatically stressed this line (from
Mt. 3$^{13f.}$; 11^9), cf. 1$^{15f., 29, 36}$; 3$^{27f.}$; 5^{36} . . . And finally, does not this
extremely Old Testament John administer the same sacrament of water
baptism that is also the permanent sacrament of the Church? True, he
cannot baptise with the Holy Ghost; but neither can the apostles. Only
One can do that . . . " Hence John is also put midway between Old Testament and New Testament to bring the people to heaven and take away hell.
For his voice made the letter live, and brought the Spirit to Scripture, and
led Law and Gospel together. For the two preachings of John are these;
the first that depresseth, the second that exalteth; the one that leadeth to
hell, the one that leadeth to heaven; the one that killeth, the other that
maketh alive; the one that woundeth, the other that maketh whole. For
he preacheth both, Law and Gospel, death and bliss, letter and Spirit, sin
and righteousness " (Luther). (I, 2, p. 120 f. The Time of Revelation.)

Cf. on Luke 1$^{67-79}$ First Sunday in Advent.

ISAIAH 40$^{1-8}$ (II)

Cf. on Isaiah 40$^{1-11}$ Third Sunday in Advent.

JOHN 3$^{22-30}$ (III)

In the Gospel of John . . . the Baptist is a kind of prototype of . . . the
witness of Jesus . . . Taken strictly, this would mean that with his water-
baptism he would have at least one foot in the Christian community, as a
kind of apostle before the apostles. It can hardly be denied that in John's
Gospel he is taken to be on this threshold. But how about the rest of the
tradition? . . . As viewed by the Synoptic tradition (Lk. 1; Mt. 11$^{2-15}$),
the Baptist belongs to the history of the fulfilment of the Old Testament
promise even in his Old Testament character, even as the last and greatest

bearer of pure promise. Even as he promised, he was himself promised—not the promised One, but promised: Mt. 11[13f.]. Thus, while he is still outside, he is already inside . . . It cannot be contested that the Johannine presentation of the relationship between the witness of the Baptist and Jesus Himself involves a certain smoothing out or foreshortening of the problem. But it is certainly not avoided or obscured. On the contrary, the same differentiation and conjunction which were obviously the concern of the Synoptic presentation with its more complicated strands are both clear and illuminating in this Gospel. (IV, 2, pp. 205–207. The Royal Man.)

The Christian can confront the world only as a witness. His action is wholly dependent on the truth and reality of what he attests. He can only point men to the speaking of Jesus Christ, drawing attention to the fact that He speaks . . . He cannot (v. 28 f.) come and speak among them as a second Christ, as if Christ spoke through him. He can encounter them only as the friend of the Bridegroom. If Christ speaks through him, giving to his witness the power of His own self-witness, as He can and will, this is not in the Christian's hands and he cannot boast of it to the world. He has no power to baptise with the Holy Ghost, for, even though he may receive and have Him, he does not control Him. Hence it does not stand in his own power to cause the Gospel so to shine that it must enlighten the world, to create and give men the freedom to grasp and appropriate the kingdom of God and therefore their reconciliation, to recognise and confess Jesus Christ as Lord. He cannot convert anyone. (IV, 3, p. 629. The Christian in Affliction.)

Cf. IV, 3, pp. 611–613.

Acts 19[1-7] (IV)

A saying which v. 4 attributes to Paul when he was talking to the disciples of John found at Ephesus is perhaps typical of the view of John's baptism which perhaps came to be held quite generally—and it is interesting that the saying is traced back or attributed to Paul. It runs as follows: " John verily baptised with the baptism of repentance, saying unto the people that they should believe on him which should come after him, that is, on Christ Jesus. When they (not John's disciples, but the people at the Jordan) heard this, they were baptised in the name of the Lord Jesus." What needs to be said authoritatively to these disciples of John (v. 6 f.) by the laying on of Paul's hands is simply that in being baptised by John they did in fact accomplish the conversion to Jesus which was the point of his baptism, and therefore, baptised in His name, they already belong to His people and are Christians. That this is so is confirmed at once by the fact that their earlier disturbed confession to Paul: " We have not so much as heard whether there be any Holy Ghost " (v. 2), is rendered pointless, since there at once comes on them that which on the Day of

Pentecost had come on the disciples, who had probably been baptised by John too: " The Holy Ghost came on them; and they spake with tongues, and prophesied." Those baptised by John in the Jordan were as such truly called, invited and summoned to faith in Jesus Christ. Accepting John's baptism, they made in fact a genuine confession of Jesus Christ. (IV, 4, p. 62. Baptism with Water.)

MARK 6$^{14-29}$ (V)
ISAIAH 49$^{1-6}$ (VI)
    Cf. on Isaiah 49$^{1-6}$ Third Sunday After Trinity.

JUNE 25. ANNIVERSARY OF THE AUGSBURG CONFESSION

MATTHEW 10$^{26-33}$ (I)

    Christian faith is a confession . . . In general terms, confessing is the act of faith in which the believer stands to his faith, or, rather, to the One in whom he believes, the One whom he acknowledges and recognises, the living Jesus Christ; and does so outwardly, again in general terms, in face of men. Confessing as the act of faith in Jesus Christ means " to confess him before men " (v. 10), not to conceal the fact that we belong to Him, and the involved alteration of our attitude, which would be to deny Him, but . . . to be that alerted man who belongs to Him in our whole being and therefore outwardly as well. To that extent confessing is not a special action of the Christian . . . It is striking and extraordinary and surprising and spectacular and aggressive . . . only in the eyes and ears of those who lack categories to understand what he is and does on this basis . . . If his action acquires the character of a venture, if he does something which is perhaps annoying to others and dangerous to himself, if he accepts the risk of a collision with their action, if he provokes unfriendly or even hostile reactions on their part, if, as a confessor, he has to suffer in some way, it is not because he intends all this. It proceeds from his action, but he himself does not impart to it the quality to provoke it. It has this from the object and origin of his faith. It has it from the mystery of his existence which he himself cannot control. Because he is a little light reflecting the great light, he becomes a witness of the great light, without especially willing to do so, and without in any way helping to do so. His task is that he should not cease to be that little light reflecting the great light. His task is that he should not place that little light under a bushel. If he sees to this, he does the act of confessing which is required of him, the confession of faith. (IV, 1, pp. 776–778. The Act of Faith.)

    Cf. on Matthew 10$^{24-33}$ October 31.

I TIMOTHY 6^{11b-16} (II)

    The being of the Christian in the sovereignty imparted to him is demonstrated in his exercise of it. He is hidden in God as he does what he who is hidden in God has to do, and does not do what such an one cannot do ... There is no alternative; what is unconditionally and unassailably given has to become a task. In accordance with the nature of the gift, it necessarily becomes a task. The good fight in which the Christian finds himself must be accepted and fought. He must really lay hold on the eternal life to which he is called, v. 12. What is meant by the terms " fight " and " lay hold "? He is to be what he is, namely, a disciple, a witness, a Christian. He is to remain, and continually to become again, what he is. In affliction, in face of it and through it, he is set in the ministry laid upon him, and summoned, engaged and challenged to discharge it, in order that in so doing he may be and become that man who is absolutely secure. (IV, 3, p. 646. The Christian in Affliction.)

Cf. on 1 Timothy 6[11b-16] Second Sunday in Advent.

JUNE 29. SAINT PETER'S (AND SAINT PAUL'S) DAY

Matthew 16[13-19]   (I)

As a man, of this human essence, Jesus Christ can be known even by those who do not know Him as the Son of God. They can see and know and in some way interpret Him like all other men. He stands before Caiaphas and Pilate, and can be judged and condemned and put to death by them. At a distance He appears before Josephus, and at an even greater distance before Suetonius and Tacitus ... As Jesus of Nazareth He is a figure of world-history and of different views of the world. But even for Caiaphas and Pilate, for Josephus, Suetonius and Tacitus, for so-called historical scholarship and the authors of different views, He does not exist apart from the grace of His origin, and therefore in virtue of the fact that He is the Son of God. They know Him and His existence, but they do not really know them. They do not know with whom they have to do. They call Him by His true name—Jesus of Nazareth. But they do not know to whom they give this name, or how it is that they come to see and know and in different ways interpret Him. They do not know what they are really doing, as their action itself shows. Conversely, where He is known as the Son of God who became man and exists in human essence, this does not mean that something is conferred on Him, or that His appearance as such is penetrated and interpreted. The question whom men (the people) or the disciples say that He the Son of Man is, is critical and divisive, v. 13, 15. To recognise Him is to see and know Him— without any penetration or interpretation—as the One who He, Jesus of Nazareth, really is. It is not a matter of interpreting and appearance but Himself, His existence, beside which He has no other. And it is a matter of interpreting it in the light of the origin from which He comes, without which He would not be, without which there would not be any appearance.

It is a matter of interpreting Him as the One He is.   It is to recognise Him
as the Son of God, as identical with this Son—" Thou art . . .," in the
traditional words of Peter in v. 16. (IV, 2, p. 91. The Exaltation of the
Son of Man.)

The reply of Peter (v. 15 f.) is the expression of a central Christian
insight, but it is not confession in the strict sense, although it is always
called this.   What he should have said in the courtyard of the high-priest,
but thrice failed to say and actually denied while the cock crowed twice,
would have been confession (26[59ff.]). And what after Easter and Pentecost
he actually did say before the high-priests and elders and scribes (Ac. 4[8f.]
and 5[29f.]) was undoubtedly confession.   It is in confessions of this kind,
in such words of direct aggression, that the Christian community always
was and is built up. (III, 4, p. 85. Confession.)

Cf. II, 2, pp. 435–442; IV, 2, p. 633 f.; cf. on Matthew 16[13-20] Whit-
Sunday and on Matthew 18[15-20] Fourth Sunday After Trinity.

EPHESIANS 2[19-22]   (II)
Cf. on Ephesians 2[17-22] First Sunday After Trinity.

JOHN 21[18-22]   (III)
The drama of age . . . is that the pure future obtrudes with increasing
concreteness, thus making the view of life *sub specie aeternitatis* more and
more unavoidable.   From the time of Cicero much has been said *de
senectute* that is true, wise, melancholy or even consoling.   From the
Christian standpoint there can be added only the supremely positive fact
that the old man has the extraordinary chance to live, indeed, to have the
privilege of living, in terms of a verse which he has often sung with gusto:
" With force of arms we nothing can . . ."   The divine promise and
command sought to call him to this from his youth.   All genuine obedience
begins with it . . . When he was younger he could imagine that it was a
matter of his own going to meet his Sovereign on his own initiative.   When
he grows old it can be his special opportunity to discover that the Sovereign
comes to meet him and to take him to Himself.   Obedience to Him can
now be more natural.   It should be the wisdom of age to accept this . . .
In the light of this, we are not to understand the saying of Jesus to Peter
(v. 18) as an exhortation to resignation . . . The continuation (v. 19)
harmonises with Deut. 33[25]: " As thy days, so shall thy strength be," or,
according to Luther's translation: " May thine age be as thy youth."
(III, 4, p. 617 f. Vocation.)

ACTS 15[1-12]   (IV)
The mystery of Jesus Christ (of His delivering up by the Jews and
crucifixion by the Gentiles, Eph. 3[4]) was not disclosed at once even to the
apostles and the first communities.   Were they really to go forth?   Could

they be the Lord's witnesses, not only in Jerusalem and Judaea, but also in Samaria and to the ends of the earth (Ac. 1⁸)? Could they make disciples of all nations (Mt. 28¹⁹)? At first there is obvious hesitation in this matter. But this is how it had to be. What God had called clean—and in the death of Jesus Christ He had called the Gentiles clean—even Christians from Israel could not regard as unclean (Ac. 10¹⁵; 11⁹). In the long run they neither could nor would do so. It is interesting that according to the presentation in Acts, the second half of which is devoted exclusively to the story of the apostle Paul, who took the lead in this matter, the modest figure of Philip the deacon is mentioned as the first to preach in Samaria (Ac. 8⁴ᶠ·) and then to baptise a Gentile, the Ethiopian eunuch (8²⁶ᶠ·). It is even more interesting that Peter (10¹ᶠ·) is named as the one who, resistant at first, but then willing and resolute, went to the Roman Cornelius, proclaimed to him and his house the word of Jesus Christ, witnessed the descent of the Spirit on these pagan listeners, baptised them forthwith, and then (11²ᶠ·) interpreted what had happened to the brethren in Judaea: " Then hath God also to the Gentiles granted repentance unto life " (11¹⁸) —a conclusion which was solemnly confirmed when Paul and Barnabas conferred with the leaders in Jerusalem (15¹ᶠ·), Peter again playing a normative role. Luke was obviously concerned to show that this great step into open country was no mere fad of Paul's but an act which was taken by the whole of the Christian community, not self-evidently or without anxiety, yet in the long run resolutely, and from the theological standpoint rightly, no matter how things might have turned out historically. The great debates in Galatians and Romans, and in its own way Ephesians, and even Acts, bear witness to the problems and difficulties by which the process was attended and beset on both sides. But it could no longer be arrested. A restraining of the Gentiles from baptism (8³⁶; 10⁴⁷) was quite impossible. The Church could now be only the Church of both Jews and Gentiles, bound together by one Lord, by one faith, and therefore also by one baptism (Eph. 4⁵). (IV, 4, p. 85. Baptism with Water; cf. also on Ephesians 2¹⁷⁻²² First Sunday After Trinity.)

LUKE 22²⁴⁻³² (V)
Cf. on Ezekiel 2³⁻⁸ᵃ; 3¹⁷⁻¹⁹ First Sunday After Trinity.

1 CORINTHIANS 12²⁷⁻³¹ᵃ (VI)
Cf. on 1 Corinthians 12¹²⁻²⁷ Fourth Sunday After Trinity.

SIXTH SUNDAY AFTER TRINITY

MATTHEW 5¹⁷⁻²² (I)
Whether we like it or not, the Christ of the New Testament is the Christ of the Old Testament, the Christ of Israel. The man who will not accept

this merely shows that in fact he has substituted another Christ for the Christ of the New Testament, v. 17; cf. Jn. 10[35]. Let us remember what is said on this score by that Gospel of Luke, which Marcion preferred, but also assiduously corrected: 4[21]; 18[31]; 24[13f.]. (I, 2, p. 488 f. Scripture as the Word of God.)

Jesus has not, of course, come to deny or destroy or dissolve the Israelite religion of revelation (v. 17 f.). He Himself accepts it, and He does not require His disciples to abandon or replace it. But He does demand that they should go a new way in its exercise; that they should show a " better righteousness," i.e., not better than that of the people, the common herd, but better than that of its best and strictest and most zealous representatives, the scribes and Pharisees (v. 20); better than the official form which it had assumed at the hands of its most competent human champions. The better righteousness is not more refined or profound or strict. It is simply the piety which the disciple can alone exercise in face of the imminent kingdom of God. It has nothing whatever to do with religious aristocracy. On the contrary, the kingdom knocks at the door of the sanctuary of supreme human worship. The disciple must act accordingly. According to two groups of sayings ... Jesus summoned to this advance on two fronts. It is a matter of morality on the one side (vv. 21–48) and religion on the other (6[1-18]). (IV, 2, p. 551. The Sanctification of Man.)

ROMANS 6[3-11]   (II)

V. 3 f. is in the first instance a dramatic underlining of the statement which dominates the narrower context of vv. 2–10, namely, that Christians are men who as concerns the " old man," the " body of sin," are crucified with Christ. They are dead to sin in Him. They have no future as sinners, because they have no possibility of existence as such. Thus reduced to nullity, dead with Christ, they may also live with Him, live to God. Also underlined hereby is the point which Paul is making in the larger context of vv. 1–11. Not even with the pious ulterior motive of v. 1: " That grace may abound," can Christians try to continue in sin. There can be no such continuance because they are no longer in sin. Since they are dead with Christ, their existence as sinners is irrevocably behind them. What is before them in and with Him can only be a new and different life. This is the real thesis of the passage. It is thus over-hasty exegesis to derive from vv. 3–4 the secondary statement that in baptism Christians have died with Christ and, if possible, been raised up with Him also to a new life; that in practice this radical change has taken place in and through baptism; that in baptism the old things have passed away and all things are made new (2 Cor. 5[17]) ... The reference to baptism in v. 3 f. underscores the thesis of the whole context. As Christians are baptised ... they register the fact, and it is registered of them, that there is no going back on their way, but that there is for them a promised, permitted and commanded Forward beyond the point behind which they can never go back again . . . This is the great change in their situation which is graphically indicated, but not brought about, by their burial with Christ, and hence by their baptism. A subsidiary and incidental appeal can thus be made to this too. Subsidiary and incidental—for the burial of Christians with Christ to which v. 3 f. alludes is one thing, their actual death and future resurrection with Christ is quite another. Baptism cannot be—as though this were necessary—a repetition, extension, re-presentation or actualisation of the saving event which is the true theme of the argument in vv. 2–10. It is a basic human Yes to God's grace and revelation, but not a " sacrament," not a means of grace and revelation. (IV, 4, p. 117 f. Baptism with Water; cf. also p. 79. 91, 196 f.)

Cf. III, 2, p. 441, 470; IV, 1, 295.

MARK 10$^{13-16}$ (III)

The children (infants according to Lk. 18^{15}) who were brought to Jesus were not figurative children but real children of flesh and blood. It may be assumed that their mothers brought them, though we are not actually told this. What did they want from Him? According to Mark and Luke they wanted Him to touch the children, and according to Matthew they wanted Him openly to pray for them—probably the original signification of the laying on of hands. They wanted Him to make it manifest that He was for them too, that He represented them too before His Father. They wanted Him to show that as He came to all adults, good or bad, healthy or sick, satisfied or needy, so He came to these non-adults. Those who came with this request, the disciples wanted to " drive away." Why? Bengel can hardly be right when he suggests that they were mostly young men who had no time for children or infants. It is more likely that they regarded the request as the product of non-existential thinking, and the object of the request—the confirmation of the grace of Jesus Christ as a grace which applied to infants as a *gratia praeveniens*—as a mythological affair which was quite unworthy of their Master. Jesus, however, was displeased . . . and did what He was asked to do, acknowledging that it was right, v. 16. He is already the Saviour of these children who are not yet called to decision for Him or capable of it. He already prays for them, takes them in His arms and blesses them. He has already laid His hands on them. The text is a very intimate but for that reason all the more powerful witness to the universal scope of the work and word of Jesus. (IV, 4, p. 181 f. Baptism with Water.)

A credible doctrine of infant baptism . . . should prove what it has to prove as such. It should not prove something else which, though true and theologically demonstrable, does not prove in the very least the legitimacy of infant baptism . . . It has not to prove that in the children of v. 13 f. Jesus promised in advance to all children access to Himself, and that as the Saviour of all He blessed and embraced all children . . . It has not to prove that it is the destiny of every man, and therefore of every child, to come to faith, to belong to God's special people in the world, and as a member of this people to lead the life of a witness of Jesus Christ. (IV, 4, p. 175 f. Baptism with Water.)

ACTS 8²⁶⁻⁴⁰   (IV)

In order to be proclaimed and heard again and again in the Church and the world, Holy Scripture requires to be explained, v. 31. As the Word of God it needs no explanation, of course, since as such it is clear in itself. The Holy Ghost knows well enough what He has said to the prophets and apostles and what through them He wills also to say to us . . . But this Word in Scripture assumes the form of a human word. Human words need interpretation because as such they are ambiguous, not usually, of course, in the intention of those who speak, but always for those who hear. Among the various possibilities, the sense intended by the speaker has to be conveyed, and as the sense which they have for the speaker, it has to be communicated to the thinking of the hearer, so that the words have now a meaning for him, and indeed the meaning intended by the speaker. Perhaps this twofold interpretation, which can be distinguished as exegesis and application, can be made at once by the hearer; perhaps the speaker himself is in a position to offer this twofold interpretation of his words, or, if not their application, at least their exegesis; perhaps a third party must intervene and perform this service of interpretation for speaker and hearer. All human words without exception need one of these interpretations. Now, since God's Word in Scripture has taken the form of a human word, it has itself incurred the need of such interpretation. (I, 2, p. 712 f. Freedom under the Word.)

Christian faith is a free human act . . . It is an acknowledgment, a recognition and a confession . . . We are not dealing with an automatic reflection, with a stone lit up by the sun, or wood kindled by a fire, or a leaf blown by the wind. We are dealing with man. It is, therefore, a spontaneous, a free, an active event. (IV, 1, p. 757 f. The Act of Faith.)

ISAIAH 43¹⁻⁷   (V)

It is with this freely electing love that according to the witness of the Old Testament Yahweh concluded His covenant with Israel . . . It is as He decides that Israel is separated from other peoples. It is as He elects Himself to be its God that it becomes His elected people. Yahweh has created and formed Israel—and we have to give to this statement the strict sense that He has caused it to be made new. It is for this reason, in the free grace in which He is its Creator, that He addresses it: vv. 1–3. This " I " must be taken in all its sovereignty. It is He, Yahweh, who guarantees this promise, and the fact that Israel is the people which may receive it and live with it comes from Him, from above, and not from below, from Israel, which is only the creation and construct of His free good will, Dt. 7[6f.]; 10[14f.]; 14[2]. (IV, 2, p. 768. The Basis of Love.)

This self-sacrifice of God in His Son (Jn. 3[16]) is in fact the love of God to us. " He gave Him," which means that He gave Him into our existence. Having been given into our existence He is present with us. Present with us, He falls heir to the shame and the curse which lie upon us. As the bearer of our shame and curse, He bears them away from us. Taking them away, He presents us as pure and spotless children in the presence of His Father. This is how God reconciles the world to Himself (2 Cor. 5[19]). We can, indeed, speak of the love of God to us only by pointing to this fact. It is the work and gift of the Holy Spirit that the fact itself speaks to us, that in the language of this fact God says: " I have loved thee ... fear not, then; for I am with thee " (v. 4 f.). No other saying is needed, for this one says all there is to say. (I, 2, p. 378. The Love of God.)

EPHESIANS 5[9-14]   (VI)

We should set alongside the concept of illumination that of awakening, not putting it either above or below the other but side by side with it in order to gain a deeper view. Under the influence of Pietism and Methodism this has become an important word in the Christian vocabulary. Yet it is not so compelling a New Testament word as illumination. To be precise there are only two passages which are expressly dominated by it (Rom. 13[11] and Eph. 5[14]), and even in these it appears only in the closest connexion with illumination, from which we cannot separate it materially if we are really to describe the vocation of man ... Awakening is instructive, thirdly, because the reference in both the New Testament passages which mention it is not to Jews or Gentiles or children of the world but quite unmistakably to Christians and therefore to those who are already called but who obviously ... both need and are granted a new and further calling; just as elsewhere in the New Testament Christians are continually addressed as people who are indeed awakened, roused and awake, but in such a way that they, too, are not prevented from falling asleep again, like even the wise as well as the foolish virgins who slept according to Mt. 25[5], and thus stand in constant need of, and are constantly granted, a new call to awaken. This is the extent to which the vocation of man is concerned with the establishment of the totality and not merely of a part or beginning of Christian existence. What makes a man a Christian is that the One who has wakened him once is not content with this, but as the faithful One He is (1 Thess. 5[24]) wakens him again and again, and always with the same power and severity and goodness as the first time. What makes him a Christian is that he has a Lord who to his salvation will not leave him in peace but constantly summons him to wake up again. (IV, 3, p. 512 f. The Event of Vocation.)

Cf. on Hebrews 10³³⁻³⁹ December 26 and on Ephesians 5¹⁻⁹ Third Sunday in Lent (Oculi).

SEVENTH SUNDAY AFTER TRINITY

MARK 8¹⁻⁹   (I)
MATTHEW 6¹⁶⁻¹⁸   (Ib)
 II, 2, p. 693; III, 4, p. 667.

ROMANS 6¹⁹⁻²³   (II)
 In itself and as such man's death is the wages which sin pays him, v. 23. Death came into the world, and passed upon all men, through sin (5¹², ¹⁷). Death is the sting of sin (1 Cor. 15⁵⁶). Sin reigns in death (Rom. 5²¹) so long as it can and may. Man dies through sin (Rom. 7¹⁰). Christian mysticism in every age, which has often, in pagan fashion, led to death mysticism, ought to have taken warning from these passages. It leads into a blind alley. In itself and as such man's death is in no sense a transition to life. Death is destruction into which all the *phronema* of the flesh plunges as into a cataract. It is the evil fruit which man, having sown to the flesh, must reap (Gal. 6⁸; Rom. 8⁶). (IV, 4, p. 16. The Foundation of the Christian Life.)

LUKE 11³⁴⁻³⁶   (III)
 Bureaucracy is the form in which man participates with his fellows when this first step into mutual openness is not taken, and not taken because duality is evaded for the sake of the simplicity of a general consideration and a general programme. Bureaucracy is the encounter of the blind with those whom they treat as blind. A bureau is a place where men are grouped in certain classes and treated, dismissed or doctored according to specified plans, principles and regulations. This may very well have the result that the men themselves, both those who act and those who are acted upon, are invisible to one another. A bureau does not have to be an office. Many a man unwittingly sits and acts all his life in a private bureau from which he considers how to treat and dismiss men according to his private plans, and in the process he may never see the real men and always be invisible to them. Certainly, there can and must be the bureau, both public and private. Bureaucracy does not hold sway in every bureau. But every bureau is situated hard by the frontier beyond which bureaucracy raises its head, and with it inhumanity, even on the presupposition of the most altruistic intentions. It is not the man who works in a bureau, for to some extent we all have to do this, but the bureaucrat who is always inhuman. In this whole matter we may perhaps refer to the parable of the eye (v. 34⁻Mt. 6²²ᶠ·). With this human picture of the good or bad eye the parable refers to the open or closed relationship of man to the

imminent kingdom of God. (III, 2, p. 252. The Basic Form of Humanity.)

1 CORINTHIANS 6⁹⁻²⁰ (IV)

How will Paul continue after this solemn statement (v. 9 f.)? With the demand that there should be no backsliding in this direction? That there should be a destruction of every remnant of this type of conduct? That there should be a concern for restitution and a corresponding new beginning in the opposite direction? Is there not every occasion for this? Is it not the natural drift of what he says? Yet he himself develops his " be not deceived " and his charge very differently: " But ye are washed . . . " (v. 11 f.). To oppose to the raging flood of human vice a barrier by which it is set effectively in the past all that is needed is the " But " of recollection of what has taken place in Jesus Christ, and in Him for them and to them (Col. 1²¹ᶠ·; Eph. 5²⁷; Heb. 13¹²). (IV, 2, p. 517. The Holy One and the Saints.)

At this critical point Paul set the anthropological question as that of man's humanity in the light of Christology, and answered it accordingly . . .

There is possible for man only the becoming " one body " in which there is clearly and unequivocally reflected the full and serious and genuine fellowship of Jesus Christ with His community and each of its individual members. There is possible only the becoming " one body " of which he does not need to be ashamed in face of the fact that he is " one spirit " with Jesus Christ, and in respect of which the man and woman have no cause for mutual shame but for rejoicing as in a reflection of light from above . . . Paul brings the concrete form of the fellow-humanity of man and woman, and sexual intercourse as its most concrete form, into connexion with the relationship between Jesus Christ and His community, and derives his normative concept of the human—not without express reference to Gen. 2—from this basic norm. The necessary stringency is not lacking. But there is none of the papistical severity which is so often encountered in this sphere. Paul knew how to give a categorical and effective warning on the basis of the whole Gospel, and his warning is far more categorical and effective than that of many who before and after him have tackled the problem purely from the standpoint of the Law. (III, 2, p. 308. Man in his Determination as the Covenant-partner of God.)

Cf. III, 4, p. 135 f.

MARK 9⁴³⁻⁴⁸ (V)

GENESIS 1²⁶⁻²³ (VI)

From the Christian point of view, is the exercise of birth control permissible, and if so may it sometimes be obligatory?—We may observe first that in this matter there are no longer any fundamental differences between Christians. Increasingly an essentially affirmative answer is being given, not only by Christian doctors ... not only by Evangelical moralists ... but also partially, yet with a fundamentally decisive break from the former consistent negative, by the supreme teaching office of the Roman Catholic Church (Enc. *Casti connubii*, 1930). In every case it has not been a surrender to contemporary influences which has caused this change of attitude, but a deeper examination of the question which has been long overdue, and which necessarily includes a positive but critical appraisal of these influences ... *Post Christum natum* the propagation of the race (v. 28) has ceased to be an unconditional command. It happens under God's long-suffering and mercy, and is due to His mercy, that in these last days it may still take place. And it does actually do so with or without gratitude to the One who permits it. There may even be times and situations in which it will be the duty of the Christian community to awaken either a people or section of a people which has grown tired of life, and despairs of the future, to the conscientious realisation that to avoid arbitrary decay they should make use of this merciful divine permission and seriously try to maintain the race. But a general necessity in this regard cannot be maintained on a Christian basis. (III, 4, p. 268 f. Parents and Children.)

The blessing and hallowing of the seventh day (v. 2) means that, *mutatis mutandis*, every seventh day shall have for the creature the same content and meaning as the seventh day of creation has for God Himself ... It is to be for the creature a day free from work. On this day the creature, too, is to have a " breathing space " in consequence of and in accordance with the fact that God the Creator also rested on the seventh day, celebrating, rejoicing, and in freedom establishing His special lordship over the finished creation ... Man may and shall " rest " with God, imitating His action, doing no work, celebrating in joy and freedom ... This is just what he is commanded to do. Hence his history under the command of God really begins with the Gospel and not with the Law, with an accorded celebration and not a required task, with a freedom given to him and not an imposed obligation, with a rest and not with an activity, in brief, with a Sunday and not with a working day which could lead to Sunday only after a succession of gloomy working days. (III, 4, p. 52. The Holy Day.)

Cf. III, 1, pp. 176–228; III, 2, p. 457; III, 4, pp. 349–353 and p. 472.

EIGHTH SUNDAY AFTER TRINITY

MATTHEW 7[15-23]   (I)
I, 2, p. 461.

ROMANS 8[12-17]   (II)
Paul hazarded the strongest expressions about the unity with Christ into which Christians enter with their acceptance as evoked by the Holy Spirit: 1 Cor. 2[16]; 6[17]. The whole context of vv. 14–17 refers to the relationship

of the Christian to Christ as created by the Holy Ghost (cf. Gal. 4⁶⁻⁷), and here the Spirit is described as the Spirit of adoption, and therefore as the power in which the Christian is granted a part in the filial being and authority of Christ. In virtue of this *pneuma* they can be sons of God here and now, and therefore free from the servile fear for which they would have good reason of themselves. Here and now *de profundis*, but in the depths in which they still dwell, they can cry with the one Son of God: " Abba, Father. " Here and now they can already say of themselves: " We are the children of God, " and, because sons, heirs of the inheritance which this Father alone, God Himself, controls—joint-heirs with Christ. They can bear their suffering as a subsequent suffering with Him, following the One who has gone before them, and with Him they can move toward the glory, their own glorification in the light of God. (IV, 2, p. 328 f. The Direction of the Son.)

Obviously the New Testament concept of divine sonship cannot compete in any sense with that of the divine sonship of Jesus Christ. On the contrary, it is absolutely dependent on this. The fathers made the distinction that Jesus Christ is *Filius Dei natura* while believers are *filii Dei adoptione*. They can be this *adoptione* because Jesus Christ is so *natura*. The constant indicatives underline what the New Testament says of believers, that they are (Rom. 8¹⁴), we are (Rom. 8¹⁶), we are called and are (1 Jn. 3¹), we are now (1 Jn. 3²), you are (Gal. 4⁶), and even you all are (Gal. 3²⁶) sons or children of God.

In a decisive passage Paul mentions only one thing in which everything is obviously included for him, v. 15, Gal. 4⁶. Remarkably, and certainly not by accident, this is the same cry as the Gospel narrative (Mk. 14³⁶) puts on the lips of Jesus when He is at prayer in Gethsemane. So then, in this form, the Son of God is the prototype of the sonship of believers. (I, 1, pp. 457 f., 460 [524–526, 529 f.]. God the Holy Spirit.)

Cf. IV, 1, p. 600 and p. 604; IV, 2, p. 570.

JOHN 15¹⁻⁸ (III)

If God's claim on man is to be comprehended in a word, on the one side (predominantly in the Johannine writings) it is that we should abide, and on the other (predominantly in Paul) that we should stand. In the most concentrated expression (6⁵⁶; 15⁴) we read of an abiding " in me, " or, according to 1 Jn. 2⁶, ¹⁰, ¹⁷, " in him, " " in the light, " " in eternity, " even " in God " Himself (1 Jn. 4¹⁵ᶠ·). This abiding is concretely fulfilled, however, as an abiding " in the grace of God " (Ac. 13⁴³), " in his goodness " (Rom. 11²²), in faith, in the doctrine of Christ, in the doctrine of the apostles, in the special calling to which each is called, in brotherly love. In the same way, we also read of a standing ... The essential unity of the two conceptions is clear ... The place of their abiding and the ground of their standing are identical. In both cases the reference is to the Lord, grace, faith, the apostolic proclamation. The concern, and the only concern, is that they should abide at this place and not leave it, that they should stand on this ground and not stumble or stoop or fall or be brought down because they exchange it for another. (II, 2, p. 600. The Form of the Divine Claim.)

While the authors of the New Testament presuppose the being of Christ in the Christian ... they look more in the opposite direction, namely, to the being of the Christian in Christ. The whole emphasis of the speech concerning the vine is obviously laid on the fact that, as the branches can bear fruit only as they abide in the vine, so the disciples, if they are to be what they are fruitfully, must abide in the One who speaks to them. This ... is impressively repeated in the First Epistle of John ($3^{6,\ 9}$; 4^{16}). For "without me ye can do nothing" (v. 5). That they are called to abide in Him presupposes that the free and responsible participation of Christians in their status is envisaged in the description of the fellowship between Christ and them. It presupposes that they are already in Him, and obviously because first and supremely He is in them and has made their being a being in Him. "I in you" (14^{30}) comes first, but secondly and on this basis it must also be said: "Ye in me." (IV, 3, p. 545 f. The Vocation of Man.)

PHILIPPIANS $4^{10\text{-}20}$ (IV)

The New Testament often speaks of the power and force to which man may and should say Yes. But it leaves us in no doubt that it understands by it exclusively the strength that God has lent to man. The young men of 1 Jn. 2^{13} are "strong" because and as the Word of God remains in them and they have overcome the wicked one. Abraham "was strong in faith giving glory to God" (Rom. 4^{20}). Hence the prayer that the Father grant Christians "to be strengthened with might by his Spirit in the inner man" (Eph. 3^{16}). Hence the admonitions: 1 Cor. 16^{13}; Eph. 6^{10}, cf. 2 Tim. 2^1. Hence the claim of Paul: Phil. 4^{13}, cf. 1 Tim. 1^{12}. Because these texts view human power only in its relation to its origin in God, in Christ and in the Spirit, they can speak of it quite freely and raise the will for human power almost to a command. (III, 4, p. 393. Freedom for Life.)

JEREMIAH $23^{16\text{-}29}$ (V)

We are reminded here of Heb. $4^{12f.}$ .... The opposite of this Word is obviously an imagined Word of God, but, however well and truly imagined, as a mere dream it remains outside the real world and existence of man, leaving the other subjects in the sphere of our world and existence unmolested, but also unilluminated and unconsoled in the depths of their creaturely existence. But now God has become man, and therefore Himself a creaturely being, in His Son, and in this human world of ours His Son lives on in the form of His instruments and their witness. So His power in this testimony is also a concrete power at the heart of this sphere, consoling and healing, but also judging and assailing. Therefore no matter how vivid and lifelike it may be, that imagined word which remains aloof is not as such the true word of God . . . The Word of God (or rather what is in this case called the " Word of God ") can be understood in a quietistic sense only if it derives from an absolute which is not identical with Jesus Christ, which is not therefore realised in and by Him alone, but surreptitiously introduced along mystical lines. It is only in this way that there can be relapse into the view that the Word of God is a transcendent authority above and beyond the dialectic of actual reality and therefore not a fire and a hammer, as in the saying of the prophet (v. 29), but the telling of a dream. (I, 2, p. 676 f. The Freedom of the Word.)

JAMES 2[14-24] (VI)

The knowing of faith and its recognition can never be an abstract knowing. It is to be feared that when our older dogmaticians found the beginning of faith in *notitia* they were thinking of an abstract knowledge of all kinds of truths of faith as formulated in the Bible or dogmatics, the sort of knowledge which a man may amass and enjoy without its having any further relevance to him. They then thought it necessary to proceed to the *assensus* in which a man decides to accept these truths for himself, to make them his own, until finally he attains to *fiducia* in them and penetrates to their true meaning and flavour . . . In all the so-called truths of faith we have to do with the being and activity of the living God towards us, with Jesus Christ Himself, whom faith cannot encounter with a basic neutrality, but only in the decision of obedience. The idea of an abstract knowledge of this object—we might almost say the idea of a theologian abstracted from the fact that he is a Christian—is one which has no substance. But positively the knowing of faith cannot be an abstract knowledge because it is only one element in the active recognition of faith. It is an indispensable element. It is an integral element. It decides its meaning and direction. It shows us what must be the object and origin of the recognition of faith. But it is only one element. Taken alone, as an abstract knowledge of God and the world and even of Jesus Christ, it can only be described as unimportant and even, as v. 29 tells us, negative, a possibility or impossibility of demonic being. (IV, 1, p. 765. The Act of Faith.)

Cf. IV, 2, p. 731.

NINTH SUNDAY AFTER TRINITY

LUKE 16[1-9] (I)

The wisdom of the world or of men is not, therefore, something which we must rate too low. It many cases it may have a very high value . It is never simply and unequivocally devilish. Within its limits, it is often

worthy of the most serious respect. In its own way it may even have
exemplary significance for those who are truly wise, for Christians . . . In
v. 8 we read that the Lord Himself praised the " unjust " steward, or his
worldly skill, concluding that the children of this aeon are in their generation (on their own level or in their own sphere) wiser than the children of
light are in theirs. (IV, 2, p. 417. The Sloth of Man.)

I once had two experiences closely related in time. The first was on a
Saturday evening when I attended a variety show which was perfect in all
its items and therefore, so far as I could see, executed with a real righteousness of works. The second was on the following Sunday morning when
I listened to an extremely poor sermon, a real piece of theological bungling.
Could I resist the impression that, formally at least, the right thing had
been done at the place of very secular amusement and not at the place
where the Gospel is preached and worship offered? Vengeance is swift if
we think that the service of the Christian community is not also a human
activity, that it does not fall under the concept of work and the question of
right work, and that theological and ecclesiastical work does not also
possess its own distinctive orientation to an end and the resultant objectivity. Vengeance is swift if in virtue of the Holy Spirit we think that we
need not do our best in the same modest but definite sense in which this is
almost taken for granted by the children of the world and thus constitutes
a promising aspect of so much secular activity. What is it that we are told
in v. 8? " And the lord commended the unjust steward, because he had
done wisely." (III, 4, p. 529. The Active Life.)

1 Corinthians 10$^{1-13}$ (II)

So in confirmation of this statement that revelation, i.e., genuine
expectation of revelation, is to be found in the Old Testament, we cannot
ultimately and in principle point to any other authority than to revelation
itself, i.e., to Jesus Christ Himself . . . The fact which is confirmed in itself
because it confirms itself, namely, that Jesus Christ is also manifest in the
Old Testament as the expected One, we cannot bring forward as being
ourselves witnesses; but, with reference to this ultimately sole witness and
so to the axiomatic character of the statement, we can bring up the counter-
proof, by addressing the question about Jesus Christ in the Old Testament
to the New Testament, in which we have before us the witness to recollection of Christ . . . The fact that, according to Paul, His promise in the Old
Testament already signifies His real presence in the pre-time is shown by
vv. 1–4, which speak about baptism and the Father's gift of spiritual meat
and drink in the desert, and which say expressly of the rock from which
they drank: That rock was Christ. Luther's comment on this passage is
exegetically sound, that " no allegory or spiritual interpretation " must be
admitted: " for 'twas not a figure but a plain seriousness, God's Word that
maketh alive and the right faith was there, thus it befell them in no

appearance, but 'tis the fact itself was there." (I, 2, pp. 72–74. The Time of Expectation.)

Cf. IV, 4, p. 90.

MATTHEW 7²⁴⁻²⁹   (III)

It is not possible to be with Jesus without being called and drawn into the occurrence indicated by these demands (of discipleship). What Jesus says cannot be heard, and what He does cannot be seen, without coming under His lordship ... He has authority, He does not speak "as the scribes," His doctrine is not a way of life or programme of world-betterment, nor is His life a pattern for its execution, but wholly and utterly the event of God's dealing with man. We cannot, then, be with Him merely to learn and accept this or that and leave on one side what we find inconvenient. Being with Him means at once the separation of those who do not desire and are not able really to be with Him, and the acceptance of those who desire it and can do it because they belong to Him. But the claim which His existence implies—just because it is God's own claim—is still addressed to the former and valid for them. Perhaps to-morrow they will have the desire and the capacity that they do not have to-day. And perhaps those who have it to-day will no longer have it to-morrow. (II, 2, p. 570. The Content of the Divine Claim.)

Those who heard Jesus, whether they believed or not, were confronted with the same new thing, the same alien will and unknown power, at the heart of man's known and customary possibilities and fulfilments. With the same actuality as those who were eye-witnesses of these particular acts of Jesus they stumbled against the kingdom of God drawn near. The Sermon on the Mount ... was no less a miraculous Word, the irruption and occurrence of something incomprehensible to man, than the raising of the young man at Nain. (IV, 2, p. 211. The Royal Man.)

JAMES 1²⁻¹²   (IV)

It needs faith to participate in temptation. Temptation is a divine work, like the comfort from which it is not to be separated. If we do not believe, then we may indeed doubt, and doubting fall on the right hand and on the left, seeking refuge now in this and now in that unreal contention. But faith ... does not doubt; it cannot doubt, because the divine work of temptation comes upon it by which it is deprived of the time and desire for doubting. Faith falls into temptation and "counts it all joy" when this happens, v. 2. It confesses: v. 12. For temptation is God's question as to its existence. Nothing can be dearer to faith than to accept this question. By temptation faith is completely destroyed, and in that way completely established. In temptation faith is taken from man in order that it may be restored to him by its object. In temptation faith is killed in order that it may be quickened again by Him in whom it believes. This is the blessedness of temptation. We still do not know anything about faith, and therefore about God . . . if we do not know about the blessedness of temptation, which is as distinct from doubt as heaven is from earth. (II, 1, p. 247 f. The Limits of the Knowledge of God.)

Cf. IV, 3, pp. 641–649.

MATTHEW 13[44-46] (V)

But if there is a human action which, as an obedient step into freedom in answer to the call of God, fulfils the essence of human action and the active life, it is the simple but very strange action, which is not at all cheap but which risks and ventures everything as in the purchase of the pearl of great price (v. 45 f.), of associating oneself with the community of the coming kingdom and of thus confirming in oneself the necessity of the reality of this community on earth in order that testimony may be borne to Jesus Christ. In other words, the obedient action of man consists basically in joining the community. We have only to grasp the range of this step to see that the life of man cannot be more active than in this simplest basic form. Again, joining and belonging to the community is itself this obedient action which can be performed only in the obedience of faith—no more, no less, no other. All else is already included in this. The fact that men have belonged to the community in this action is the thing which from the human standpoint has always made it the community of God and qualified and equipped it for service. By this fact alone, from the human standpoint, has it continued to exist as that which it essentially is—the *ecclesia semper mansura*. (III, 4, p. 493. The Active Life.)

JOSHUA 24[1, 2a, 13-25] (VI)

The Old Testament covenant is a covenant of grace. It is instituted by God Himself in the fulness of sovereignty and in the freest determination and decree. And then for that reason it is a matter of free choice and decision on the part of " Israel." God chooses for Himself this His people: this people, the community of tribes, chooses for itself this their God. This mutual choice, which takes place in this order and sequence, we have described as the basic fact and presupposition of Old Testament religion, the standing of man before God which is always found in it . . . The covenant remains . . . the event of a divine and human choice . . . for this reason there is no single and definitive narration of the original conclusion of this covenant. According to the opinion advanced by many to-day, it is in the account in Joshua 24 . . . that we have a representation which approximates most closely to an event of this kind. The conclusion of the covenant is portrayed in a very striking and solemn manner in this passage, so that if we did not know to the contrary, we might conclude that it was necessarily the only occurrence of this nature. But according to Deut. 26–30, already at the end of Moses' life and under his leadership...

it had been preceded by a conclusion of the covenant which is described as equally unique and definitive. And both these accounts stand under the shadow of the account in Ex. 24 of a covenant mediated by the same Moses at Sinai, which became so important in tradition right up to the time of the Christian Church. And even the priority of this covenant is apparently shaken by the covenant between God and Abraham which is narrated in two versions in Gen. 15 and 17, and later recalled with particular emphasis. But according to 2 K. 13^{23} this could be understood as a covenant " with Abraham, Isaac and Jacob," and in any case it was preceded by the covenant with Noah in Gen. 8 and 9 . . . It is enough that all the accounts are at one in this, and that even in their puzzling variety they make it clear, that the presupposition of all the Old Testament happenings has itself always to be understood as an event, the event of the mutual electing of the God of Israel and His people. (IV, 1, p. 23 f. The Covenant as the Presupposition of Revelation.)

Cf. on John 15$^{9-17}$ Monday in Whitsun-Week; also IV, 2, p. 781.

TENTH SUNDAY AFTER TRINITY

LUKE 19$^{41-48}$ (I)
1 CORINTHIANS 12$^{4-11}$ (II)

If the gifts of the grace granted to this community are many and varied (vv. 4–11), they all have one thing in common which guarantees their co-operation and the unity of the Church. It is not that they are co-ordinated by a constitution or a confessional position or the existence of an office. Only from the 2nd century onwards, when there was no longer the same certainty of the Spirit, was it thought necessary to find this kind of assistance. The real point is that they are all gifts of the same Spirit, who divides to every man severally as He will—for He is not a spirit of the community who exercises a neutral rule, but One who has as such His particular will for each Christian. All differences in the community rest on the variety of His distribution. According to Eph. 4$^{3f.}$ " one body " is identical with " one Spirit." (IV, 2, p. 321. The Direction of the Son.)

We know as little concerning the substance of the *charismata iamaton* mentioned in v. 9 as concerning most of the " gifts of grace " of the Holy Spirit mentioned in this and other passages. But there can be no doubt at least that we are to think of a power against sickness which is effective and known in the congregation as a transitory or lasting characteristic of some of its members, not as something belonging to these people, but as a free gift of God, and yet exercised by these people. Perhaps we do well not to bring this power into too close relation with the cures of Jesus as the unique " signs and wonders " of the kingdom come on earth in Him and Him alone, but rather to understand it as a possibility of a secondary type. Yet there can be no doubt that the apostolic proclamation of the kingdom and of the name of its Bearer did also include this possibility, and that we see the community, in the possession and exercise of these gifts and in the following of Jesus Christ, engaged in conflict against sickness and not at peace with it. It is not a wilful fight, but one which is laid upon it and for which it is empowered by the grace of God. It is necessary to recall at this point . . . J. C. Blumhardt. In word and deed Blumhardt made it plain that from one standpoint sickness is the exponent of an ungodly and inhuman reality in relation to which the Christian attitude can only be one of indignation and conflict in co-operation with God and faith in Him and prayer to Him. " The stories of Blumhardt are an abomination to me " (R. Bultmann, *Kerygma und Mythus*, 1948, p. 150) . . . Ernst Gaugler (*J. C. Blumhardt*, 1945, p. 36) has rightly stressed that Blumhardt . . . has no interest in producing anything new . . .: " He only read afresh what was already known to him from the old book of biblical truth. He did what every preacher must always adequately or inadequately attempt, namely, to make present the Word of God." This (Ps. 77^{10}) is what we have to learn regarding sickness as a mortal power consequent upon sin. And we must learn it, not from Mrs. Eddy, but from Blumhardt, or, better, from the place where Blumhardt himself learned it. (III, 4, p. 370 f. Respect for Life.)

Cf. on 1 Corinthians 12^{12-27} Fourth Sunday After Trinity; cf. also IV, 3, p. 895.

ROMANS 9^{1-5}; 10^{1-4} (IIb)

The existence of the Synagogue side by side with the Church is an ontological impossibility, a wound, a gaping hole in the body of Christ, something which is quite intolerable. For what does the Church have which the Synagogue does not also have, and long before it (v. 4 f.)— especially Jesus Christ Himself, who is of the Jews, who is the Jewish Messiah, and only as such the Lord of the Church? The decisive question is not what the Jewish Synagogue can be without Him, but what the Church is as long as it confronts an alien and hostile Israel. " Jewish missions " is not the right word for the call to remove this breach, a call which must go out unceasingly from the Church to these brethren who do not yet know their unity with it—a unity which does not have to be established but is already there ontologically—who will not accept what they already are, and what they were long before us poor Gentiles. And what a dreadful thing when the Church has so little understood its own nature that it has not only withheld this knowledge from its brethren but made it difficult if not impossible for them! *Credo unam ecclesiam?* This confession gives rise to other and very difficult questions. But here in the so-called Jewish question we face the deepest obscurity which surrounds it.

The Jewish question? If Paul is right, then in the light and context of that confession it is really the Christian question. (IV, 1, p. 671. The Being of the Community.)

Cf. II, 2, pp. 202–205, 240–259; IV, 3, p. 68, 877 f.

JEREMIAH 7$^{1-7}$ $^{(8-15)}$ (III)

The Old Testament testimony does not, of course, say (as do those who according to v. 3 f. trust in " lying words ") that the place is holy in itself, trying to have the Lord Himself, possessively, with the holy place. Those who think in this way must be told without any ceremony: " Amend your ways and your doings." They must be reminded by the prophetic preaching of repentance and judgment that it is God who dwells here and who will be recognised and honoured as God. But Jeremiah, too, did not doubt for one moment that God does actually dwell here. God is not imprisoned in this place. What the prayer of Solomon says in this connexion may be regarded as characteristic of the tenor of the whole Old Testament. According to v. 14 f. He can destroy and forsake this house as He forsook that of Shiloh. But He always was and always will be the One who dwells in the midst of Israel and possesses a definite place. (II, 1, p. 480. The Unity and Omnipresence of God.)

ROMANS 11$^{25-32}$ (IV)

There is an obvious continuity between the witness of the New Testament to the love of God and that of the Old Testament. In the New Testament this love has not ceased to be the love which elects Israel . . . How can Samaritans and Gentiles possibly have any claim to be the fellow-elect of the children of Abraham (Mt. 10^5)? How can God owe it to them to make them such? If they are this, it is in a new and no less inconceivable revelation of His free good-will than that in which the children of Abraham are first elected. It is simply a fulfilment of Hos. 2^{23} and 1^{10} as quoted in Rom. 9$^{25f.}$. The Gentiles will then be " cut out of the olive tree which is wild by nature, and grafted contrary to nature (against every rule of horticulture!) into a good olive tree " (v. 24). The one—and only—thing which helps the Gentiles is that there has now actually taken place a new and inconceivable revelation of the free good-will of God. The crumbs do fall from the table of the Lord, and the request of the Syro-phenician woman is fulfilled (Mt. 15^{28}). There has actually taken place an engrafting of the branches of the wild olive into the fruitful branches of the good (v. 17). Gentiles who followed not after righteousness have attained to righteousness (Rom. 9^{30}). The dividing wall between Jews and Gentiles is broken down (Eph. 2$^{14, 19}$). (IV, 2, p. 769. The Basis of Love.)

V. 32 is to be understood in the light of 9$^{16-18}$, God's mercy is God's freedom. Hence it is impossible to understand this " all " mathematically and mechanically, as the sum of all mankind, to whom God owes His grace as such. On the contrary, according to the passages in Rom. 9 they are undoubtedly the elect people which was once no people, but has now become His people, the people of those who were once without grace but have now found grace (1 Pet. 2[10]) ... In passages like Ps. 78[37f.] and Is. 54[7-10] we must understand the predicates in the light of the subject and then interpret the subject in its predicates. That God who is provoked to anger is not only angry, but for the sake of that which provokes Him sets bounds to His anger and is compassionate, and that His compassion is His and is therefore active, where His wrath slays, to make alive and renew and enlighten—that is the secret and at the same time the simple and manifest reality of His mercy. (II, 1, p. 372 f. The Mercy and Righteousness of God.)

Cf. I, 2, p. 110; II, 2, pp. 298–305; IV, 1, p. 501 and pp. 503–505; IV, 3, pp. 876–878.

MATTHEW 21[33-46]   (V)

The old aeon which passes away in revelation and yet in passing away is still present, stands to the new one that comes in revelation by no means in the neutral relation of any time to any other time following upon it. The old aeon is rather God's time confronting men who boast of their own power and in that very fact are sinful and fallen; and in these men we recognise ourselves, if we really recognise God's revelation—ourselves as God's enemies ... It was when the lord of the vineyard sent his beloved son that the vine-dressers' rebellion first became fundamental and final, v. 38; Heb. 12[3]; Jn. 1[5]. In respect of the irruption of the new aeon, over against Jesus Christ, the old aeon, Adam's sin, comes to its true proportions. Revelation and only revelation brings it to its true proportions, draws it into the light in its totality, in which it now confronts and resists revelation, so that now nothing can be more hidden than revelation. It is just this revelation that the whole man resists. It is against the new fulfilled time that every time necessarily fights, and indeed " our " time also, because even we ourselves fight against it. It is primarily only at revelation that one can—and inevitably must—be offended. " God in time, " " God in history "—that is the offending thing in revelation. God in Himself is not offending. Time in itself is not offending. But God in time is offending ... because we are thereby gripped by God, as it were, in our very own sphere, namely in the delusion that we possessed time. Fulfilled time in our midst is the enemy who has forced himself in, the centre of confusion which, driven by necessity, we want to destroy or at least render innocuous or conceal from our sight. What becomes of our time if it is really limited and determined by a " fulfilled time, " described as an aeon already·past, thrown as it were wholesale upon the scrap heap? What a menace! And— for us as members and citizens of our own time—what a challenge! (I, 2, p. 62 f. The Time of Revelation.)

ACTS 13⁴²⁻⁵²   (VI)

It may sound like a general truth of reason when Paul says in Rom. 3^{29}: Is he the God of the Jews only? is he not also of the Gentiles? Yes, of the Gentiles also: seeing it is one God. In fact, however, this is a description of the altered situation, the history and the way which are the theme of the second part of Luke's historical record, and above all the decisive content of the apostolic action of Paul himself, v. 46. But this action of Paul is only a reflection of the way which the man Jesus went and was led in obedience to the will of His heavenly Father. And the decisive turning-point in this way was His delivering up (Mk 15^1) to Pilate and the Gentiles by the representatives of Israel itself—the event which necessarily transformed the mission to Israel (Mt. 10$^{1f.}$) into a world-wide mission: " Go ye therefore, and make disciples of all nations " (Mt. 28^{19}). But again, this way of the man Jesus is a reflection of the way which God Himself went from those who have all things to those who have nothing. The saying of Mary in the *Magnificat* (Lk. 1$^{51f.}$) might well be set over the whole of this inversion. (IV, 2, p. 171. The Royal Man.)

Cf. II, 2, p. 279.

ELEVENTH SUNDAY AFTER TRINITY

LUKE 18$^{9-14}$ (I)

God so gives Himself to us in His revelation that we are and remain and indeed only truly become rich in Him and poor in ourselves. And yet again only the man who seeks nothing in himself seeks everything in God.

What we have to offer, to sacrifice to God in order to pray aright, is ourselves in this total lack of any claim.

Whether prayer is made aright and answered depends on this total lack of any claim (Ps. 51^{17}). (I, 1, pp. 464 ff. [531 f.]. God the Holy Spirit.)

This man (v. 11) is not quite so easy to see through as his colleagues in Mt. 6 and 23. He does not want honour before men; he wants it before God. He thus stands and repeats a kind of psalm. He does not praise himself, but God, that he is not like other men (v. 11 f.). Of the three marks of modesty which we have suggested, thankfulness certainly seems to be present in this case. The only trouble is that humility and humour seem to be all the more lacking. The theme of the psalm of thanksgiving is unfortunately the psalmist himself in his abstention and action, even though under the sign of the grace of God. The point of it is obviously to bring to God's attention his wonderfully successful efforts. He might have magnified the grace of God even more strongly. Like the Roman Church in its songs of praise, he might have commemorated the Holy Ghost as the self-evident presupposition of his distinguished honour. His attempt is impossible from the very outset. The more honourable than he (Lk. 14$^{7f.}$) has already been invited and is already present. Even though he does not hear it, there is already said to him: " Give this man place. " Even though he does not notice it, he has already had to take the lowest seat. (III, 4, p. 667. Honour.)

Cf. IV, 2, p. 385.

1 CORINTHIANS 15$^{1-11}$ (II)

Whether we take the accounts of the resurrection appearances in detail or put them together, they do not give us a concrete and coherent picture, a history of the forty days. Rather we are confronted by obscurities and irreconcilable contradictions, so that we are surprised that in the formation of the canon no one seems to have taken offence at them or tried to assimilate the various accounts of this happening which is so basically important for the New Testament message. There is the further difficulty that Paul not only presupposes and gives (vv. 4–7) another account of what happened which is different again from the Gospels, but that in v. 8 (cf. Gal. 1^{16}) he connects the appearance to himself (obviously the Damascus experience as presented several times in Acts) with the events of those days, although it took place long after the forty days, and the *schema* of the forty days is thus strangely broken . . . Vv. 4–8 cannot be claimed as an attempt at proof, and therefore as an attempt at the external objective assurance that the history did, in fact, take place. For the witnesses to whom Paul appeals with such solemnity are not the outside impartial witnesses which such an attempt would demand. They are the tradition which underlies the community, which calls for a decision of faith, not for the acceptance of a well-attested historical report. They are those who have themselves made this decision of faith, Cephas, the Twelve, five hundred brethren, James, then all the apostles, then finally, and in the same breath, Paul himself. In these well-known verses there is an appeal to faith, not on the basis of Paul's knowledge, but in recollection of the faith which constitutes the community. (IV, 1, p. 335. The Obedience of the Son of God; cf. on 1 Corinthians 15$^{12-20}$ Easter Sunday.)

Cf. III, 2, p. 638; IV, 4, p. 48.

1 CORINTHIANS 1$^{26-31}$ (IIb)

It is not a bad sign for the Church, but an indication of the genuineness of its calling, that not many wise after the flesh, not many mighty, not many noble are in it. In keeping with the presumed folly of this Gospel (v. 18: that of the death of Jesus Christ with or without His resurrection), God has chosen the so-called foolish ones of the world to confound the wisdom of the wise, the weak to confound the strong, the trivial and contemptible, the things that are not to bring to nothing those that are, in order that it may be manifest that no flesh can glory in His presence (vv. 26–29). From this God, in whose presence no flesh can glory, Christians have their life in Jesus Christ. They have it by the power of His resurrection from the dead. Therefore, on the one hand they clearly participate in the folly, weakness and contemptibility of the divine action which has taken place in Jesus Christ ... But they participate, on the other hand, in the triumph of real divine wisdom over the false human wisdom from which this judgment stems—a judgment which can only reveal the folly of this human wisdom. For them, Jesus Christ ... has been made by God Himself by His resurrection, not only justification, sanctification and redemption, but also and above all wisdom (v. 30), in order that in them may be fulfilled the words of Jer. 9$^{23ff.}$ ... If a man boasts in the Lord, there are three reasons why he cannot at the same time boast also in his own wisdom, the human wisdom of the world. 1. Since he boasts in this other, the real wisdom of God, he has no more room for his own, human wisdom. 2. By this wisdom in which he may now glory human wisdom is for him unmasked as unwisdom, as utter and contemptible folly in his eyes. 3. He cannot wish to withdraw from his solidarity with divine wisdom even in regard to its supposed folly and the judgment to which it must be content to submit in this world. (II, 1, p. 435 f. The Patience and Wisdom of God.)

LUKE 7$^{36-50}$ (III)

That love covers a multitude of sins (1 Pet. 4^8) is said in the first instance of sins committed by the neighbour who is to be loved, but it applies also to the sins of those who exercise love towards him. As he does this—and the Christian does—he acts as one who is justified before God, and, in and with what he himself does, he passes into a place which is sheltered from storm and sin. He is empowered and free to do this, and passes into this place, as one who receives purely and totally in faith. *Ama et fac quod vis.* If you love as a Christian, you cannot and will not sin. You can and will sin only if you do not love as a Christian. The man who loves as a Christian cannot blame the Law or be backward in respect of its demands. He fulfils it. For the pure and total reception of justification by faith alone cannot be separated from his pure and total self-giving in love. The two are one and the same. And conversely, the fact that against all his deserts but in genuine earnest God shows benevolence and beneficence to him as a sinner, and that he may know this, is confirmed by the Christian in the act of his surrender: " Her sins, which are many, are forgiven; for she loved much " (v. 47). When a man performs this act, the will of God does not remain undone in his life, nor the Law of God unfulfilled. But the will of God is done, and His Law fulfilled. (IV, 2, p. 732 f. The Problem of Christian Love.)

2 SAMUEL 12$^{1-10,\ 13f.}$ (IV)

The Old Testament version of the election of a man is that it is the distinction of one who is a sinner with all others ... who shows himself to be a sinner and is punished as such ... It stands or falls with that which God purposes and will effect and accomplish with him, and on this very account it can only stand and not fall ... It does not stand because of his virtues, nor does it fall because of his failures. It does not stand because he commits only refined sins (Saul), nor does it fall because he sins grossly (David). It does not in any state stand because he conforms to the testimony laid upon him, nor does it fall because he contradicts it. Who or what he may be, for good or evil, is God's concern, and only to that extent his own concern. If we understand this, we can also understand that the story of David's sin ... far from being in contradiction to the presentation of him as a figure of light in contrast with Saul, is absolutely indispensable to this presentation. The king by God's grace has the bull-king within him, not merely a minute trace, not merely in harmless intimations, but as completely and devastatingly as is described in 2 Sam. 11. And yet it is as this man that he is the king by God's grace—as the man who in this sinfulness is utterly dependent upon the mercy and forgiveness of God, who is enabled to stand only because God stands and supports him, who has nothing to offer God except his need. (II, 2, p. 383, cf. pp. 381–384. The Elect and the Rejected.)

Cf. IV, 2, pp. 464–467.

MATTHEW 23$^{1\text{-}12}$ (V)

To have our master unavoidably in Jesus Christ (v. 8) means always (a) to have found someone over against us, from whom we can no longer withdraw ... (b) to have discovered His supreme authority, to which in all our obedience or disobedience we are always responsible and subject ... (c) to be subject to a command, in face of which there can be neither subterfuge nor excuse ... (d) to exist in an ultimate and most profound irresponsibility ... (e) to be subject to a definite formation and direction ... and finally and comprehensively (f) to have no concern of our own but to have Christ's concern as ours ... Where the Word of God is master by the outpouring of the Holy Spirit, there enters in an interest or concern which does not allow any rivals. (I, 2, pp. 270–278. The Freedom of Man for God.)

" All ye are brethren " (v. 8). This does not mean, as it has often been understood and depicted in recent years, that a social impulse derived from their common situation, faith and community sense brings Christians together and makes them brothers. Other religious unions and fellowships of all kinds may arise in this way. And the strength of the social impulse which constitutes them is the more or less sure guarantee of their continuation. But Christianity, the community of Jesus Christ, neither arises nor continues in this way. It does not rest on the natural need of union and co-operation felt by those who share a common aim ... It is Jesus Christ Himself ... who calls these individuals in their plurality and unites them with one another ... There is no *vocatio*, and therefore no *unio cum Christo*, which does not as such lead directly into the communion of saints, i.e., the *communio vocatorum*. (I, 3, p. 682. The People of God in World-Occurrence.)

Cf. on Matthew 6$^{1-4}$ Thirteenth Sunday After Trinity; also IV, 2, p. 261 and IV, 3, p. 888.

ROMANS 9^{30b-33} (VI)
II, 2, pp. 240–242.

TWELFTH SUNDAY AFTER TRINITY

MARK 7$^{31-37}$ (I)
" But He keepeth specially before Him two members, ears and tongue; for the kingdom of God is founded upon the Word which one cannot grasp or conceive without these two members, ears and tongue, and ruleth alone through the Word and faith in the hearts of men. The ears grasp the Word and the heart believeth it: but the tongue uttereth or confesseth it as the heart believeth. So if we do away with the tongue and ears, there remaineth no marked difference betwixt the kingdom of Christ and the world " (Luther). (I, 1, p. 151 [172]. The Nature of the Word of God.)

2 CORINTHIANS 3$^{3-9}$ (II)
In vv. 4–18 Paul made it clear how he primarily wanted the reading of the Old Testament as a witness of the revelation of Jesus Christ to be understood by the Christian congregation. The Old Testament Scripture as such is described by Paul (v. 6) as *gramma*, i.e., as that which is simply written and indeed prescribed as holy and necessary for salvation. There is *per se* no disqualification of Scripture in this designation. Nor is there when Paul goes on to say that the *gramma* kills but the Spirit gives life. This is said in favour of the Spirit but not against Scripture, or only against a Scripture received and read without the Spirit. From this standpoint we ought calmly to reflect on Mt. 5^{17f}. ... Paul claims for himself the ministry of the new covenant (v. 6), the ministry of the Spirit (v. 8), the ministry which has an incomparably greater " glory " (v. 9). Yet he does not contest, but expressly presupposes, that even the ministry of the *gramma* as such has its " glory " (v. 9 f.). And Paul does not exclude the ministry of Scripture when he contrasts it with his own ministry, the spiritual ministry of the new covenant. On the contrary, he regards his own ministry as the true ministry of Scripture, i.e., its fulfilment. This is proved by the fact that in this very section he is commenting on Ex. 34. (I, 2, p. 514 f. Scripture as the Word of God.)

It is hardly necessary to show that this saying (v. 9b) sums up Paul's conception of service. He never understood his existence as a " slave of

Jesus Christ " otherwise than as his glory, of which he might proudly boast
should the need arise . . . No less obviously, he would not hear of any other
glory, whether for himself or others, than that of his and their service.
Paul is the classic human figure of whom we are to think when asked about
our honour or service. Yet we should not forget that he did not regard
himself as the original in this regard, but only as a copy of the original,
of the Servant of God: Phil. 2⁹. Who would think of calling the honour
of man his service, and the service of man his honour, if he were not forced
to this thought precisely from the point to which Paul and the whole of the
New Testament look? (III, 4, p. 662. Honour.)

ISAIAH 38$^{9\text{-}13,\ 17\text{-}20}$ (III)

ACTS 9$^{26\text{-}42}$ (IV)

MATTHEW 9$^{35\text{-}38}$; 10$^{1\text{-}5a}$ (V)

The expression *esplanchnisthe* is a strong one which defies adequate
translation. He was not only affected to the heart by the misery which
surrounded Him—sympathy in our modern sense is far too feeble a word
—but its went right into His heart, so that it was now His misery. It was
more His than that of those who suffered it. He took it from them and
laid it on Himself. In the last analysis it was no longer theirs at all. He
Himself suffered it in their place. The cry of those who suffered was only
an echo. Strictly speaking, it had already been superseded. It was
superfluous. Jesus had made it His own . . . He had compassion because
He saw the *ochloi*, man in the mass, the multitude, the crowd, " the
public," " everyman " . . . The crowd . . . is the pushing, moving, jostling
throng of those who all think of themselves as special cases, protesting their
different individualities and wanting to be and have something for themselves, but who in so doing merge into the sea of heads, a herd, in which
names are indifferent and distinctive figures are lost and this or that one
emerges for a moment, only to disappear again in the common mass in
which men are no longer men in any true sense . . . It is striking that Jesus
never accused or upbraided the *ochloi* as such . . . He stood with them in
an almost imperceptible but strong unity and solidarity: strong because
it was grounded in His compassion, in the fact that His only desire for
them was to take from them their misery and to take it to Himself. (IV, 2,
p. 184 f. The Royal Man.)

Cf. III, 2, p. 211.

ISAIAH 29$^{18\text{-}24}$ (VI)

THIRTEENTH SUNDAY AFTER TRINITY

LUKE 10$^{23\text{-}37}$ (I)

The scribe had answered rightly, very rightly, in respect of love to God.
But he does not ask: And who is God? That is something which he seems

to know and thinks he knows. He asks only in regard to the unperspicuous latter part of the doctrine which he has so weightily advanced. He asks only in regard . . . to the concept neighbour. It is only this concept which he wants clarified. But from the very fact that he can ask this question the physician Luke regards him as mortally ill. He thinks that the question reveals that this doctor of the Law does not actually know the second commandment at all, and therefore not the first. Luke does not, of course, express it in this way. He goes further back. He finds the real reason for the question in the fact that the man " wished to justify himself " (v. 29). The lawyer does not know that only by mercy can he live and inherit eternal life. He does not want to live by mercy. He does not even know what it is. He actually lives by something quite different from mercy, by his own intention and ability to present himself as a righteous man before God. Or he thinks that he can live in that way. He wished to justify himself. That this is the case is revealed by the question: And who is my neighbour? If a man does not know who his neighbour is, if he does not or will not know what mercy is, then obviously his intention and effort is to justify himself. . . . Why does he not go on to ask: Who is God? What is loving? above all . . .: what is the " doing " which these commandments require? . . . By asking " only " about his neighbour, he shows that he does not really know either of them (the commandments), even though he can recite them: and that is why he wants to justify himself. The converse must also be stated: that because he wants to justify himself, he does not really know the two commandments at all, although he can recite them. . . . Which is the first and basic element in his perversion? His self-righteousness, or his lack of knowledge of revelation? Who is to decide? The one certain thing is that in this man the two go hand in hand and confirm each other . . . The lawyer . . . is confronted, not by the poor wounded man with his claim for help, but by the anything but poor Samaritan who makes no claim at all but is simply helpful. It is the Samaritan who embodies what he wanted to know. This is the neighbour he did not know. (I, 2, p. 417 f. The Life of the Children of God.)

Cf. on Matthew 22³⁴⁻⁴⁰ Eighteenth Sunday After Trinity; also IV, 2, p. 811; IV, 3, p. 891.

GALATIANS 3¹⁵⁻²² (II)

1 JOHN 4⁷⁻¹⁶ (IIb)

It is not the case then . . . that we have to do a certain amount of titivation when we adopt the language of Scripture and talk of God, not in abstract terms as the " highest good " or the " absolute " or " omnipotence " or " omniscience " and the like, but personally as One who is in all these things as the knowing, willing and acting I; when in fact we take the metaphor " God is love " and as in 1 Jn. 4 understand it personally: He is the One who loves. This personal way in which Scripture speaks is not in any way childish or naive or anthropomorphic ... it corresponds absolutely and exclusively to the fact that God is not something, but someone, the One from whom man simply holds in fee the possibility of being one himself. (II, 1, p. 286. The Being of God as the One who Loves in Freedom.)

Therefore our salvation, the salvation of men and the world, takes place in Him, in His being and activity as one with us (v. 14). " God became man on thy behalf, O man " (Paul Gerhardt). He humbles Himself to our status in order to be our companion in that status, in order to share with us the assault and temptation, in order to be with us in the misery of that status with all the omnipotence of His divine mercy, in order to change that status from within, in order to turn it for good, for the very best, in order to take away the curse which rests upon us, in order to obviate the impending destruction. He comes, therefore as a helper, as a redeemer, as the one who brings another and proper order, a life which is life indeed. He comes as the kingdom of God in person. He comes to reconcile the world with God, i.e., to convert it to God. (IV, 1, p. 216. The Obedience of the Son of God.)

Cf. on 1 John 4[1-8] Twentieth Sunday After Trinity; also IV, 2, p. 776.

MATTHEW 6[1-4] (III)

What is the honour of man? It is the significance, the worth, the distinction, which he now has in the eyes of God; the value, which is now ascribed to him by the mouth and in the Word of God; the adornment, vesture and crown with which he is now clothed by God. His honour falls on him as a reflection of the honour of God Himself ... We may call honour the supreme earthly good; in it our concern is with the man himself, his soul. It may well be true that " to lose honour is to lose everything." But if honour, and with it everything, is not to be lost, it must be supremely true of it that it is secured, protected and guaranteed to man in such a way that it does not fall out of the hand of God and pass into the hands of man, to become something for him to possess, guard and administer, but that it remains in God's hand as His honour, as a gift the reality of which remains bound to the Giver and His giving, thus being genuinely guaranteed in Him and His action. This is true of the soul of man. It does not exist in and of and by itself, but by the Spirit, by the living breath of God. It is also true of the calling, justification and sanctification of man. It does not stand in virtue of the powerfulness of his existence, but of the powerfulness of the Word addressed to him. It stands in Jesus Christ. Yet thus it is no less truly given him as his own. It is really his. He lives as the creature of God, the child of his Father, and therefore in the honour and glory with which God clothes him ... The honour of man comes from the God who is alone to be admired and praised ... Where human action is deficient in this regard, where it is lacking in modesty, there results what Paul described as " vainglory " (Gal. 5²⁶; Phil. 2³). According to the context this seems to be a kind of conduct in which man, jealous of others and exalting himself above them, reaches for a " glory " which he cannot have just because he reaches for it, so that it is empty and hollow. It belongs to the very nature of the case that man will seek honour especially in recognition by others (1 Thess. 2⁶). This is apparently what those described in Mt. 6¹⁻¹⁸ had in view when they exercised their righteousness and almsgiving and prayer as far as possible with the sound of a trumpet before men, in order to be seen by them, to be lauded for their work, to appear before them in honour. Once such things are done with this intention, they lose even the reward which they might have had as good deeds. For they are no longer good and praiseworthy. They have lost the very thing sought in them, i.e., honour. (III, 4, p. 663 f., 665, 666 f. Honour.)

GENESIS 4¹⁻¹⁶ᵃ (IV)

God's holiness and righteousness seem to require a different interpretation and to be differently determined than we might have supposed from the story so far (vv. 10–12) ... In his despair Cain sees and confesses: " My punishment is greater than I can bear " (v. 13) ... Has not Cain now sought God's grace as it must be sought? Obviously, for now according to the unambiguous statement of the story he has in any event found it. " Everyone that findeth me shall slay me " (v. 14), he thinks in his despair. Yahweh answers him: Not so ... (v. 15⁻17a) ... Cain the murderer is permitted to live. It is not that he could arrange this himself, but that God wills and allows it to happen. It is not that he did not deserve death, but that God does not will the death he deserves. It is not that he does not stand under the wrath and curse of God. This has come upon Cain and he must bear it. But Cain must not be killed. The sign which God sets upon him is undoubtedly the brand of the sin which necessarily arises from his contempt of grace. It is the mark of the homicide. But this very mark is a protective sign which God has given him. In fact it is a covenantal sign by which Yahweh admits Himself to be the Avenger and Saviour of this murderer; by which—for the first time in the Bible—God binds Himself to sinful man in a kind of treaty. God is holy and righteous in such a way that He sustains the life of the one who forfeited his life before God ... God is holy and righteous to such effect that whoever is against Cain is not for but against God, the holy and righteous One, and will necessarily be the victim of an even heavier judgment. In God's patience, then, there triumphs the almighty, gracious and merciful, and therefore the holy and righteous, being of God. (II, 1, p. 412 f. The Patience and Wisdom of God.)

Cf. I, 2, p. 427; II, 2, p. 341 and 355.

MARK 12⁴¹⁻⁴⁴ (V)

Acts 6[1-7]   (VI)

Diaconate means quite simply and generally the rendering of service. Hence it does not denote only a specific action of the community but the whole breadth and depth of its action. For with its witness it always serves both God and man. It is only customarily and never unconditionally that the term has come to be used to denote a special ministry, namely, the helping of those in physical or material distress both within the community and outside. In this sense, however, it has proved to be both meaningful and useful. The origin of the diaconate in this special sense is to be found in the account in vv. 1–7 of the solemn selection and institution of seven men, whose names are given, to undertake the *diakonia* of the daily provision particularly for widows (though probably this word is meant to cover all in material want) within the circle of the infant Christian fellowship in Jerusalem . . . We hear no more of the discharge of their particular task . . . In the rest of the New Testament the word *diakonia* usually indicates quite generally the relationship of service in which especially the apostles stand, but also all other Christians, and Jesus Christ Himself at their head (Rom. 15[8]). Certainly in Rom. 12[7] (unlike the parallels in 1 Cor. 12[8f., 28f.]), *diakonia* is mentioned as one of the various *charismata*. Again, in Rom. 16[1] a woman Phoebe appears as *diakonos* of the community of Cenchrea, and deacons are mentioned with bishops in the introduction to Philippians (1[1]) and also in 1 Tim. 3[8f., 12f.] as the bearers of specific functions in the Church, though we are not told exactly what their particular tasks are. It is only in the 2nd century that the term is clearly used to link social and liturgical obligations. In the Roman Catholic sphere this is still reflected in the fact that the diaconate is the final stage in the preliminary orders which precede the sacerdotal ministry as the full spiritual office. In the older Reformed Churches the term " deacon " or " assistant " was often used to describe the second pastor in a congregation in distinction from the first, the dignified *archidiaconus* or " chief assistant " being used in the case of the Minster Church at Basel. But this is a reactionary deviation from the renewal of a social diaconate attempted in the course of the 16th-century Reformation by Bucer in Strassburg and both theoretically and practically by Calvin in Geneva. (IV, 3, p. 889 f. The Ministry of the Community.)

Cf. I, 1, p. 58; IV, 3, p. 610.

FOURTEENTH SUNDAY AFTER TRINITY

Luke 17[11-19]   (I)
Galatians 5[16-25]   (II)

But in this life even . . . the Christian is not only in Jesus, not only what he is in Him, and therefore not only free. In solidarity with all other men he is also in himself, in the flesh, in the past which is continually present . . .

To the extent that he is in the flesh and not in the spirit he is " dead in sins " (Col. 2¹³; Eph. 2¹). He is not just half-dead, or apparently dead. He is a corpse awaiting the resurrection, and we have to speak in all seriousness of his past which unfortunately is always present. He is engaged in the conflict of the Spirit against the flesh, but also of the flesh against the Spirit (v. 17), and in the last resort he will not refuse to confess with the apostle Paul " that in me (that is, in my flesh) dwelleth no good thing " (Rom. 7¹⁸). Conflict does not mean peaceful co-existence, let alone co-operation . . . No co-operation, then, between the two! For how can there be co-operation between total freedom and total bondage? How can the Spirit give assistance to the flesh, or the flesh to the Spirit? The doctrine which makes this *caveat* necessary is the Romanist doctrine of man's co-operation in the accomplishment of his justification (which as Romanists use the term includes what we call sanctification). (IV, 2, p. 496 f. The Sloth and Misery of Man.)

This is the plenitude of fruits for which (v. 22) there will have to be . . . both sowing and reaping . . . Weeds will also be found on those fields, and these will be a threat to the good seed. There will also be unskilful or wrong cultivation, a lack of seriousness in caring for the good seed. There will be curable or perhaps incurable setbacks to its growth. It will always be necessary that the good work of the Holy Spirit which has begun thus or thus should begin again at the beginning, that the man to whom a beginning has been given should not be ashamed but happy that here or there, in this way or that, he may thus take this wholly new and supremely astonishing form, that he should be thus " continued." A man is no Christian if he is not willing, ready, modest and courageous enough, so long as he lives, so long as he is given the unique opportunity, to move forward, not according to the impulses of his own heart or the fancies of his own mind, but according to the impulsion and direction of the Holy Spirit, constantly marching into a land (a small portion of the land) " that I will shew thee " (Gen. 12¹). (IV, 4, p. 39. Baptism with the Holy Spirit.)

JOHN 9¹⁻⁷, ¹³⁻¹⁷, ³³⁻³⁹ (III)

It is with man's evil existence in itself and as such that Jesus is concerned in His acts . . . He finds and sees man in the shadow of death. His miraculous action to man is to bring him out of this shadow, to free him from this prison, to remove the need and pain of his cosmic determination. He unburdens man; He releases him. He calls and causes him to live as a creature. Man can again rise up and walk, again see and hear and speak . . . He can eat and be more than satisfied. He can drink and he is given wine—good wine. He is delivered from every torment and embarrassment and he can breathe again. He can be a man again—a whole man in this elemental sense. His existence as a creature in the natural cosmos is normalised . . . There is another remarkable and almost offensive feature in the miracle stories which has been continually obscured, i.e., painted over in ethical colours, in so much well-meaning exposition (especially in the Western Church). This is that in these stories it does not seem to be of any great account that the men who suffer as creatures are above all sinful men, men who are at fault in relation to God, their neighbours and themselves, who are therefore guilty and have betrayed themselves into all kinds of trouble. No, the important thing about them in these stories is not that they are sinners but that they are sufferers. Jesus does not first look at their past, and then at their tragic present in the light of it. But from their present He creates for them a new future. He does not ask, therefore, concerning their sin. He does not hold it against them. He does not denounce them because of it. The help and blessing that He brings are quite irrespective of their sin. He acts almost (indeed exactly) in the same way as His Father in heaven, who causes His sun to shine on the good and the evil, and His rain to fall on the just and the unjust (Mt. 5[45]). The truth is obvious, and is brought out elsewhere, that the evil which afflicts mankind is in some sense a punishment; that " the wages of sin is death " (Rom. 6[23]). But there is no trace of this consideration in the miracle stories. It is, indeed, expressly excluded here (v. 2 f.). (IV, 2, p. 222 f. The Royal Man.)

Cf. IV, 2, pp. 236–240.

1 THESSALONIANS 1[2-10]   (IV)

How little natural brotherhood is to be expected between us men, i.e., how little proclamation of it as a universal, ethical truth, is shown by the story of Cain and Abel, of which there are warning reminders in Mt. 23[35] and 1 Jn. 3[12f.]. The story also has the significance of a promise. According to Heb. 11[4], by faith Abel offered a better sacrifice, by which, even though he is dead, he still speaks on behalf of the murderer. But this is not because Abel and Cain were brothers, as the sons of Adam and Eve. It is because of the new brotherhood based on the fact that his sacrifice is prophetic of Jesus Christ and His sacrifice. The first-born among many actual brethren, the true and proper brother is, therefore, Jesus Christ (Rom. 8[29]). It is only in Him and through Him that there shall be others. They are " brothers in Christ " (Col. 1[2]), because He is not ashamed to call them brethren (Heb. 2[11]) and as such to be equal to them in all things. He speaks of them as His brethren (Mk. 3[34], Mt. 28[10], Jn. 20[17]). He it is who gives this name to their mutual relationship (Mt. 23[8], Lk. 22[32]). They are brethren as " brethren beloved of God " (v. 4) . . . The name of brother in its biblical sense can only be understood christologically, i.e., from the standpoint of the resurrection and ascension of Jesus Christ. The fatherhood of God and the sonship of man is originally and properly true in Jesus Christ. It is only true for us by transference, through Him. Similarly, brotherhood and brotherliness among men are not a requisite of their humanity, but a new creation of the revelation and reconciliation of God. Brotherhood arose among men because Jesus created it between Himself and individual men, by calling them into relationship with Himself, that nearness of brothers which cannot be destroyed or doubted but is absolutely necessary and indisputable; by allowing their humanity to enter into blood relationship with His; by giving them His Father to be their Father. It is that way, in Himself and not otherwise, that He made them brethren one to another. Any confirmation of their brotherliness one to another can consist only in the fact that each recognises in the other the original and proper brother Jesus Christ and is therefore summoned to the praise of God by him, or, in the strict sense, by Jesus Christ through him. (I, 2, p. 426 f. The Life of the Children of God.)

Cf. III, 4, p. 95.

1 Samuel 2$^{1\text{-}10}$ (V)

II, 2, pp. 188–294. The Eternal Will of God in the Election of Jesus Christ.

Hebrews 13$^{1\text{-}9b}$ (VI)

It is a striking fact that only once in the New Testament is the word *gamos* used of marriage: " Marriage is to be held in honour by all " (v. 4). Elsewhere it refers only to the marriage feast, and almost always to the eschatological marriage feast of Christ the Bridegroom; and there are no other words in the New Testament for the concept of marriage which we regard as so important. It is obvious that in the New Testament community marriage can no longer be an obligation. And it can no longer be a terrible disgrace in our time to be unmarried. (III, 4, p. 143 f. Man and Woman.)

How can a man be a Christian without remembering the teachers who have spoken the Word of God to him (v. 7)? How can he be a Christian without realising that he is bound to members of the community as to brethren, that he is commonly engaged and committed with them? Nevertheless, the fact that a man becomes a Christian . . . is something which he owes, not to himself, nor to the human work of witness either of the community or of any Christian, but directly to the Lord of this people, the Master, whom the community and all its members seek to serve, and can only serve, with their witness. The Church is neither author, dispenser, nor mediator of grace and its revelation. It is the subject neither of the work of salvation nor the Word of salvation. It cannot act as such. It cannot strut about as such, as though this were its calling. Its work and action in all forms, even in the best possibilities, stands or falls with the self-attestation and self-impartation of Jesus Christ Himself, in which it can only participate as assistant and minister. (IV, 4, p. 32. The Foundation of the Christian Life.)

This saying (v. 8) sounds like a slogan ... Probably it is a fragment of one of the very early Christian hymns of which traces are to be found elsewhere in the Epistles. But in any case it is of basic importance. " Jesus Christ yesterday " is Jesus in the span of His earthly life, including the Easter period ... But this Jesus Christ yesterday is the same to-day.... But this does not mean that to-day He has become a man of yesterday ... He as one and the same is both yesterday and to-day. His time is also the time of the community, and the time of the community is also His time ... That is why the faith of the readers of the Epistle can only be a constant reproduction of the faith of those who proclaimed the Word of God to them (v. 7). But the text goes on to speak of a third dimension of time. To yesterday and to-day it adds " and for ever " (" in every conceivable future " as we may best translate it). Like to-day, every coming day will be His ... Thus v. 8 leads us to the same conclusion as Rev. 1^8 and *par*. Jesus Christ belongs not only to yesterday, or to-day, or an indefinite future. There is no time which does not belong to Him ... He is really the Lord of time. If we ask the author of Hebrews how he came to attribute to Jesus this extraordinary being in time, the only answer which he can give is to refer us to the point indicated a few verses later (v. 20; cf. also 4^{14}; 1^3; 8^1; 10^{12}; 12^2). Who is " our Lord Jesus "? Unless we are prepared to understand v. 8 in the light of these other passages, and therefore of the Easter axiom of this New Testament author too, we shall not understand it at all. (III, 2, p. 466. Jesus, Lord of Time.)

Cf. on Hebrews $13^{8,\ 9b}$ New Year's Eve.

FIFTEENTH SUNDAY AFTER TRINITY

MATTHEW 6^{24-34} (I)

In the service of the attestation of Jesus Christ the community cannot even with the best intentions serve two different lords, no matter who the second may be. It can serve Him only wholeheartedly or not at all. (IV, 3, p. 838. The Ministry of the Community.)

If we ever take the risk (and it is a risk) of preaching on this text, we at once meet with all kinds of sullen or dispirited or unwilling reprimands (expressed or unexpressed), and most of all, if we are honest, from our own hearts and minds. For how can we help taking care for our life? How can we model ourselves on the fowls of the air and the lilies of the field? How can we seek first the kingdom of God and His righteousness in the assurance that food and drink and clothes will be added to us? How can we leave the morrow and its anxieties—the storm which may mount and break, or the sun which may shine through—and confine ourselves to the troubles (and perhaps the joys) of to-day? How is all this possible? (IV, 2, p. 470. The Sloth of Man.)

The clear biblical basis for our consideration of the rest demanded of man as relaxation in his work is naturally to be found in the Sermon on the Mount, namely, in the saying that the disciples are not to be anxious ... *Merimnan* is the distress or burden or tension which man accepts as inevitable but which he really inflicts upon himself quite arbitrarily by believing that he himself has to speak the essential and decisive word in this matter by his own achievements in affirmation of his existence, that the responsibility is his and that he is the father who has to decree and regulate the future envisaged in his work, whereas the real Father, by feeding the fowls of the air and clothing the lilies of the field which cannot work, shows how graciously and mightily He cares for him, so that even as one who can work he should still exist simply as a child of his Father. This is the anxiety which must cease. And when the kingdom of God is sought first, it does cease. Work done in anxiety cannot be done aright as such. (III, 4, p. 554. The Active Life.)

Cf. on Peter 5⁵ᵇ⁻¹¹ Third Sunday After Trinity; also I, 2, p. 67 and IV, 2, p. 178.

GALATIANS 5²⁵–6¹⁰ (II)

God will not be unfaithful either to Himself or to man. He will not throw man over. He will not withdraw what He has given. But neither will He let Himself be mocked (v. 7). When man for his part is unfaithful to God and therefore to his fellows, it is inevitable, since he himself will have it so, that what God has given him should not be a means and instrument of salvation but rather of perdition. This negative operation of the good creation of God consequent upon *confusio hominum* is the truly terrifying element in the form and picture of world history. Our modern period suggests an illustration of the connexion indicated, namely, the history of modern physics in its development from atomic research to the discovery and creation of atomic weapons. All the elements of *confusio hominum* meet at this point: the good creation of God in the form of a newly discovered and glorious cosmic supply; man himself, who after a period of hesitation combines it with nothingness and places it in the service of the latter; and the recoil in which it becomes in all its glory an enemy threatening man with destruction. Robert Jungk (*Heller als tausend Sonnen*, 1956) has described this cycle in a way which is both factual and generally comprehensible. But we can see with seeing eyes, yet not perceive. Universal shrinking from the atomic death which unmistakably impends is one thing, but it is not enough to arrest the cycle. Quite another is recognition of the *confusio hominum* as such, which in this case means recognition of atomic sin. So long as this does not confront both those who advocate atomic armament in their concern either for Socialism or the " free world," and also those who oppose them, or so long as it does not do so more distinctly than is as yet the case, world history will have to proceed under this sign, though even so, to our comfort, it must still conform to the providence of God. (IV, 3, p. 700 f. The People of God in World-Occurrence.)

The one who loves God cannot be solitary. He cannot be a religious individual with his individual concerns and joys and wishes and achievements. As one who has an active part in the history of salvation he is accompanied from the very outset not merely by fellows but by brothers, by those who belong with him to the people of God, by fellow-partners in the covenant, by the " household of faith " (v. 10). (IV, 2, p. 806. The Holy Spirit and Christian Love.)

Cf. on Matthew 6^{1-4} Thirteenth Sunday After Trinity; also II, 1, p. 405.

LUKE 16^{10-12} (III)

2 THESSALONIANS 3^{6-13} (IV)
    III, 4, p. 472.

MATTHEW 19^{16-25} (V)

It is obvious that these are specific directions (v. 21; Mt. $5^{40, 42}$; $6^{19, 24, 31}$; $10^{9f.}$) given to specific men at specific times and to be specifically followed, not in a formalised or spiritualised, but a literal sense. The drift of them all is clearly that Jesus' call to discipleship challenges and indeed cuts right across the self-evident attachment to that which we possess. The man to whom the call of Jesus comes does not only think and feel but acts (here and now, in this particular encounter with his neighbour) as one who is freed from this attachment. He not only can but does let go that which is his. By doing exactly as he is commanded by Jesus he successfully makes this sortie, attesting that the kingdom of mammon is broken by the coming of the kingdom of God. (IV, 2, p. 548. The Call to Discipleship.)

Cf. II, 2, pp. 613–630; IV, 2, p. 240.

1 KINGS 17^{7-16} (VI)

SIXTEENTH SUNDAY AFTER TRINITY

LUKE 7^{11-16} (I)
    Cf. on Matthew 16^{13-20} Whit-Sunday.

EPHESIANS 3^{14-21} (II)

God alone as He who He is by Himself, and therefore as the eternal Father of His eternal Son, is properly and adequately to be called Father. From the power and dignity of this only proper name of Father there flows by grace and for faith the improper—the really improper though certainly not on that account untrue—name of Father for God as the Creator, and from this again the naming of the intracreaturely originating relation, the thing that is called fatherhood in heaven and on earth. This, too, is to be regarded as a true but improper appellation dependent on the power and dignity of God's intratrinitarian name of Father.

God's trinitarian name of Father, God's eternal fatherhood, denotes the way of being of God in which He is the Author of His other modes of being. (I, 1, p. 393 [451]. God the Father.)

No human father, but God alone, is properly, truly and primarily Father. No human father is the creator of his child, the controller of its destiny, or its saviour from sin, guilt and death. No human father is by his word the source of its temporal and eternal life. In this proper, true and primary sense God—and He alone—is Father. He is so as the Father of mercy, as the Father of His Son, of the Lord Jesus Christ ... God is the Father of whom the whole family, or all fatherhood, in heaven and on earth is named (Is. 63^{16}; Mt. 23^9; Is. 49^{15}; Ps. 27^{10}). (III, 4, p. 245. Parents and Children.)

LAMENTATIONS 3$^{22-33, 39-41}$ (III)

It is a peculiarity of the LXX that the normal translation for the Old Testament *chesed* (where we would expect *charis*) is *eleos*, of which the Old Testament equivalents are properly *chanan* and *rachan*. But in this way there is correctly suggested the affective aspect of love, peculiar, in fact, to the biblical conception of grace. The concept is, therefore, presented immediately and unmistakably in the concrete content which the biblical background implies. It is well known how often grace and mercy appear side by side in the Old Testament, the one clearly determining and elucidating the other. The New Testament terms *eleos* and *oiktirmoi* do not suggest, of course, only a feeling but an action, yet the kind of action which is determined by a feeling ... The main point is ... that God's love and grace are not just mathematical or mechanical relations, but have their true seat and origin in the movement of the heart of God ... It was quite natural that Schleiermacher should consider it impossible to ascribe to God a state of feeling specially awakened by the suffering of others and going out to assist them, and therefore that he should try to eject the idea of the mercy of God from the language of dogmatics to that of homiletics and poetry. The source of the feeling of sheer dependence has no heart. But the personal God has a heart. He can feel, and be affected. He is not impassible. He cannot be moved from outside by an extraneous power. But this does not mean that He is not capable of moving Himself. No, God is moved and stirred, yet not like ourselves in powerlessness, but in His own free power, in His innermost being; moved and touched by Himself, i.e., open, ready, inclined (*propensus*) to compassion with another's suffering and therefore to assistance, impelled to take the initiative to relieve this distress ... " His tender mercies are over all his works " (Ps. 145^9). Measured by the Lord's holiness the whole creation as such lies in need and misery and is dependent on the fact that God's mercy is new every morning (v. 23). And God does not refuse to give Himself to it. He maintains it as He has created it. He takes into account its frailty and need, giving Himself anew to it every morning. That this is all true becomes especially clear when the work of God assumes the form of His self-revelation, reconciliation and sanctification, the form of His covenant with Israel, the form of Jesus Christ. (II, 1, p. 370 f. The Mercy and Righteousness of God.)

2 CORINTHIANS 1³⁻⁷   (IV)
   Cf. on 1 Peter 4¹²⁻¹⁹ Second Sunday After Christmas.

JOHN 11¹⁻³, ¹⁷⁻²⁷   (V)
   " To fall asleep " is the characteristic New Testament term for the death which is freed from the " second " death by the death of Jesus Christ and is therefore a wholly natural thing for the Christian: v. 11; 1 Cor. 11³⁰; 15⁶; 2 Pet. 3⁴. It is noticeable that even David is now said to have fallen asleep (Acts 13³⁶). Indeed, a violent death like that of Stephen (Acts 7⁶⁰) is described almost euphemistically in these mild terms. What does this imply? It relates to the process of dying, or rather to the impression, designated, defined and shaped by faith and love, which the survivors have of what is finally perceptible in the death of a brother or sister. They see him falling asleep. What lies beyond they cannot see. For the Christians of the New Testament Jesus Christ Himself intervenes at once and absolutely on the far side of this event. His death and resurrection avail for those who have now " fallen asleep," as well as for those who survive. The hope in Him is a hope for the former too. The final thing to be said of them (apart from Jesus Christ Himself) is that they have fallen asleep ... The term " fall asleep " shows that the New Testament Christians never asked independently concerning the being or state of man in death, or tried to find an answer in the postulate of an intermediate state. They simply held fast to the confession: " I am the resurrection and life," and in the light of this hope they came to see in the visible process of dying the last conclusive symptom of a life surrounded by the peace of God. (III, 2, p. 638 f. Ending Time.)
   Dying means ... that God stands surety for man ... that this God is his hope. His only hope? Yes, his only hope. What other hope could there be? Nor is this a hope which merely flickers into being. As the command *Memento mori!* or *Memento Domini!* is unambiguously and immutably issued to man, it is already there as the hope of mortal and perishing man, and just as clear and reliable as the Word of God, as the promise given to man in Jesus Christ: v. 25 ... In place of fear of death we put hope in God as He has revealed Himself in Jesus Christ to be the hope of man. (III, 4, p. 593 f. The Unique Opportunity.)

ACTS 12$^{1-17}$ (VI)

There are passages in the Bible which seem to support the idea of guardian angels allotted to individuals. The strongest is Job 33$^{23f.}$, which unmistakably refers to the effective advocacy of an angel on behalf of a man before the throne of God. Yet even there we are not told that this one in a thousand is specifically or permanently the angel of this particular man. Again, in Acts 12^{15} we are told that when the Christians assembled in the house of Mary heard the imprisoned Peter knocking at the door, but did not realise that it was he in person, they expressed the view that it was his angel. But in this case it is an open question, as Calvin rightly observed, whether they are not merely toying with a popular notion. At all events the expression does not force us to conclude that " his " angel is his guardian angel. On the other hand, the angel who in this passage actually frees Peter and might therefore be described as his guardian angel is not described as " his angel " but simply as " the angel of the Lord." (III, 3, p. 518. The Ambassadors of God and Their Opponents; cf. also on Matthew 18$^{1-10}$ St. Michael and All Angels.)

SEVENTEENTH SUNDAY AFTER TRINITY

LUKE 14$^{1-6}$ (I)

Is it really the concern of the tradition in the stories of healings on the sabbath (Mk. 1$^{21f.}$; 3$^{1f.}$; Lk. 13$^{10f.}$; 14$^{1f.}$; Jn. 5^9; 9$^{14f.}$) merely to draw attention to the formal freedom which Jesus displayed in relation to the law of the sabbath? Can it really be the case that the cause in whose interests He made use of this freedom is a matter of indifference, the interesting thing in His attitude being simply transgression for the sake of transgression? If this seems highly improbable, we can only assume that what the tradition wishes to emphasise is that, although He did not always heal on the sabbath, He did so deliberately and gladly because His own coming meant that the seventh and last day, the great day of Yahweh, had dawned, and healing was the specific Word of God that He had come to accomplish on this day (in the name of God and in fulfilment of His own work). Thus He not only did not break the sabbath with this work but genuinely sanctified and kept it. He was free also, and particularly, to do good and not evil on the sabbath, i.e., to save life and not to destroy it (Mk. 3^4). And He looked (v. 5) " with anger, being grieved for the hardness of their hearts," on those who watched and criticised Him. We cannot understand this grief and anger, or the remarkable force with which He rejected the Pharisaic-rabbinic opposition, if we do not see that it was a matter of defending His positive freedom on the sabbath, i.e., His freedom to do on this day of His, " while it is day " (Jn. 9^4), the good and saving works of God; to cause the " light of life " (Jn. 8^{12}) to shine; or, in synoptic language, to set up the signs of the kingdom of God as the kingdom of healing and salvation. He is not angry and grieved because they are so narrow in their exposition and application of the law of the sabbath, but because they fail to recognise and therefore reject these "signs of the times" (Mt. 16³). (IV, 2, p. 226. The Royal Man.)

EPHESIANS 4¹⁻⁶ (II)

The Christian believes—and there is—only one Church. This means that it belongs to the being of the community to be a unity in the plurality of its members . . . and to be a simple unity, not having a second or third unity of the same kind side by side with it. The statement follows necessarily from all that we have seen concerning it. In all the riches of His divine being the God who reconciled the world with Himself in Jesus Christ is One. Jesus Christ, elected the Head of all men, and as such their Representative who includes them all in Himself in His crucified and risen body is One. The Holy Spirit in the fulness and diversity of His gifts is One. In the same way His community as the gathering of the men who know and confess Him can only be one. In vv. 1–7 Eph. says *in nuce* all that has to be said . . . The limit within which there can be a real plurality among those who are addressed in this way is plain. It is the plurality of these individuals within the community, corresponding to the plurality in which they are elected and reconciled in Jesus Christ and called and endowed by His Spirit. In the event their calling and endowment follows their gathering to the equally real unity of His body. They are therefore included in it once and for all—with the absolute uniqueness of the Lord whom they all know and confess. That is how the matter is stated in 1 Cor. 12⁴⁻³¹ and Rom. 12³⁻⁸. In the New Testament there can be no question of a plurality of unities. The unity is a single unity. Otherwise it is not what the New Testament knows as the *ecclesia*. (IV, 1, p. 668 f. The Being of the Community.)

Cf. on Luke 13²²⁻³⁰ Fifth Sunday After Epiphany; also IV, 3, pp. 856–859.

MATTHEW 15¹⁻¹¹ᵃ, ¹⁸⁻²⁰ (III)

It is instructive to set beside the story of the twelve-year-old Jesus the argument with the Pharisees concerning the relationship between the command of God and human tradition (vv. 3–9). The point at issue here is a Pharisaic interpretation of the Law, disputed by Jesus, which claims that preference is to be given to a supposed duty to God as against the duty to parents. When a man says to his father and mother: "That by which thou mightest have been profited by me is Corban, i.e., a sacrificial gift for the temple" (Mk. 7¹¹), then according to the tradition he no longer owes them anything. Jesus says that this abandons, rejects and makes of none effect the commandment of God. He calls those who give this teaching hypocrites, i.e., people who are concerned only in appearance about the commandment of God and the obedience due to it. He applies to them the saying of Is. 29[13]. Why? The reason is quite evident in the context. For we can see that the rule proclaimed here is of human invention, and only professedly to God's glory, by the fact that the claim of God is supposed to cancel that of the parents, to send them away emptyhanded, and thus to rescind the fifth commandment and the associated warning. But the real claim of God advanced and represented by God Himself does not do this, and cannot have such an effect. Those who teach otherwise have long since gone away from God. (III, 4, p. 250 f. Parents and Children.)

Cf. II, 2, p. 482.

1 CORINTHIANS 9[16-23] (IV)

The apostle of Jesus Christ not only can but must be a missionary (v. 16). It is not merely the formal necessity of proclaiming the Word of God, nor the humanitarian love which would rather not withhold this Word from others, that forces him to do this. The determining factor is the concrete content of the Word itself. The truth which he knows about Jesus Christ and human life compels him almost as it were automatically to speak wherever it is not yet known. It is like air rushing into a vacuum, or water downhill, or fire to more fuel. Man and his life stand under the sign of God's judgment. This is not just a religious opinion. It is a universal truth. It applies to all of us. It decides concerning every man as such. It leaps all frontiers. It is more urgent and binding than any human insight, however clear and compelling, or any convictions, however enthusiastically embraced. This truth is the driving power behind the Christian mission. Apart from it, there would be no indication where it should be pursued or not pursued. Where it is recognised it bursts all barriers. (III, 2, p. 607. Ending Time.)

Solidarity with the world means that those who are genuinely pious approach the children of the world as such, that those who are genuinely righteous are not ashamed to sit down with the unrighteous as friends, that those who are genuinely wise do not hesitate to seem to be fools among fools, and that those who are genuinely holy are not too good or irreproachable to go down " into hell " in a very secular fashion (G. Cesbron). The solidarity of the community with the world means to give as little offence as possible to Jews and Greeks as well as fellow-Christians (1 Cor. 10[32]). Even more strongly, it means to be as a Jew to Jews and as without law to those who are without law (v. 20). Or, to put it more strongly still, it means to be all things to all men (v. 22). (IV, 3, p. 774. The Community for the World.)

Cf. on Luke 17[7-10] Septuagesima; also III, 4, p. 76.

AMOS 5[4-6, 21-24] (V)

The sacrifices of the Old Testament belong to the human history of religion, but there is more to them than that. They are also a provisional and relative fulfilment of the will and commandment of God. They are a genuine element in the history of the covenant and the history of redemption. In sacrifice Israel—fallible, sinful and unfaithful Israel—is summoned to bow beneath the divine judgment, but also to hold fast to the divine grace. Of course, this living meaning of sacrifice can sometimes fade. It may become a mere religious observance. It may be understood as a *do ut des*. It may become an attempt on the part of the people to acquire power over God, to assure oneself before Him, to hide one's sin instead of acknowledging it. Instead of a terror-stricken flight to God it may become a sinful flight from him to a sacred work. When this happens, but only when this happens and as an attack upon it, the prophets (Amos $5^{21f.}$; Is. $1^{10f.}$; Jer. $7^{21f.}$) and many of the Psalms (like $40^{7f.}$; $50^{13f.}$; $51^{18f.}$) take up their well-known inflexible attitude against it. (IV, 1, p. 278. The Judge Judged in Our Place.)

Cf. on Hebrews 9^{11-15} Fifth Sunday in Lent (Judica); also II, 1, p. 386.

2 Peter 1^{3-11}

(VI)

Concrete reality is an event in Jesus Christ, an event which is both wonderful and simple, infinitely disturbing and infinitely comforting, the *communicatio gratiarum* which comes to all flesh in His flesh, the exaltation of human essence to fellowship with the " divine nature " (2 Pet. 1^4). It does actually take place in the homecoming of the Son of Man which, although it is seen and known and confessed from the opposite standpoint, is identical with the way of the Son of God into the far country. The spoil of the divine mercy, the result of the act of atonement, is exalted man: new in the power of the divine exaltation; no longer far from God but near to Him, a man who even as such and precisely as such is a man as we are; the first-born of a new humanity; the second Adam who is still our elder Brother and in whose exaltation our own has already taken place. His history is the Word of God addressed to us and to the whole world. It is the promise that we shall be like Him (1 John 3^2); that we are " predestinate to be conformed to the image of his son " (Rom. 8^{29}), " that the life also of Jesus might be made manifest in our mortal flesh " (2 Cor. 4^{11}) . . . All that we know of man's exaltation derives from what we know of the return of the Son of Man as the act that took place in and with the way of the Son of God into the far country, of the exaltation of our human essence as it is an event in Him. Our life is hidden—not yet revealed—with Him. It is not to be sought on earth, but above, in Him. But with Him it is *realiter* hidden and lifted up in God (Col. $3^{1f.}$). It is exalted to His glory and dignity and majesty. (IV, 2, p. 103. The Homecoming of the Son of Man.)

EIGHTEENTH SUNDAY AFTER TRINITY

MATTHEW 22[34-40]   (I)

To the extent that the commandment to love God refers us to our existence in the time and world which comes and remains, the commandment to love the neighbour in the time and world which now is and passes, we are in fact dealing with a first and a second commandment, a primary and a secondary, a superior and a subordinate, an eternal and a temporary. The two times and worlds are not symmetrical. They do not balance each other. The one prevails over the other. That which comes and remains has the priority and superiority over that which now is and passes. This is something which belongs to the nature and essence of both of them as they are posited and illuminated by the divine revelation. It is therefore quite right that in the text of Matthew the commandment to love God should be described not only as the first, but also as the " great " commandment. It is in fact the basic and comprehensive commandment, the greater circle which includes in itself the lesser commandment of love to the neighbour . . . And therefore love to the neighbour is undoubtedly commanded for the sake of love to God and in and with the commandment to love God. Love to God is the real cause and expository principle of love to the neighbour. Love to the neighbour is in fact the token of love to God. To that extent, as something commanded in respect of our existence which now is and passes, by its very nature it can be the erecting only of a sign, and not of a completed and eternal work. But we must be careful not to treat it arbitrarily. It is also right that the second commandment should be put alongside the " first " and " great " with the express declaration that it is " like " it. (I, 2, p. 411 f.; cf. pp. 362–454. The Life of the Children of God.)

There is just cause for the question of a Scandinavian author quoted by Soe whether love for man has increased with the obvious decrease of love for God. (III, 4, p. 49. The Holy Day.)

The command to love has reference to God, but also to the neighbour. It has the one dimension, but also the other. It finds in the Creator the One who points it to this creature, fellow-man. And it finds in this creature, fellow-man, the one who points it to the Creator. Receiving and taking seriously both these references in their different ways, it is both love for God and love for the neighbour. Thus the structure of the humanity of Jesus Himself is revealed in this twofold command. It repeats the unity of His divinity and humanity as this is achieved without admixture or change, and yet also without separation or limitation. (III, 2, p. 216 f. Jesus, Man for Other Men.)

Cf. on Luke 10[23-37] Fourteenth Sunday After Trinity; also IV, 1, pp. 105–107.

1 Corinthians 1[4-9] (II)

It is remarkable that there is no New Testament evidence for the fine saying of Luther that it is the Holy Ghost who calls man. This does not mean that the saying is not true and valid. The presence and action of the Holy Spirit are the *parousia* of Jesus Christ in the time between Easter and His final revelation. But we certainly ought to learn from this fact that in this context the Holy Spirit is not spoken of in such a way that Jesus Christ is obscured or even completely concealed as the Subject who acts in Him and through Him and therefore truly calls. Where the New Testament speaks generally of calling as the historical beginning of the Christian state, in obvious agreement with the Old it calls God Himself the great Caller. It does this explicitly in 1 Thess. 2[12] and 4[7], 1 Cor. 1[9] and 7[15] and Heb. 5[4], and implicitly in a much larger group of sayings. Yet this does not prevent Christians from being described as the called of the *Kyrios* or of Jesus Christ, as in 1 Cor. 7[17] and Rom. 1[6]. And . . . whenever the process of vocation is described as such . . . there is no question of an action of God the Father in which He in some sense by-passes or overlooks Jesus and deals with the person called simply as God. Nor is there any question of a corresponding action of the Holy Spirit . . . On the contrary, when vocation is recounted as a history, Jesus Christ is quite plainly the One who calls. If . . . God as well as Jesus Christ is described as the One who calls, this is not, of course, an indication that the New Testament knows two kinds of vocation, the one effected by God the Father, the other by Jesus Christ, and possibly a third by the Holy Spirit . . . The statements are complementary. To the question of the concrete form in which God calls, the only answer is obviously that it is Jesus who does it in all the concreteness of His humanity. And to the question how He does it, the only answer is obviously that in what this man does God is at work in His eternal mercy and omnipotence. The New Testament does not see two or three different things here, but only one thing. (IV, 3, p. 503. The Event of Vocation.)

Leviticus 19[1-3, 13-18] (III)

The people may and shall and must be " holy to me " (10[3]), i.e., enabled to worship Me, the Holy One, and therefore to attest Me as the Holy One in the world . . . The holiness of God demands and enforces the holiness of His people (19[2]). It requires that His own divine confrontation of the world and all men should find a human (and as such very inadequate, but for all its inadequacy very real) correspondence and copy in the mode of existence of this people, in and with the fact that He has made Himself the God of this people and this people His people. The imperative: " Ye shall be holy," is simply the imperative indication of the irresistible dynamic of the indicative: " I am holy," i.e., I am holy, and act among you as such, and therefore I make you holy—this is your life and norm. (IV, 2, p. 501. The Sanctification of Man.)

Why is Christian love also love for the neighbour? . . . To what extent does love for God necessarily entail love for the neighbour? . . . It is as well to state plainly and simply that this is the case. Christian love has these two dimensions and is thus love for the neighbour. The history of salvation is both a history between God and man and also a history between man and man. It is the second as and because it is the first . . . As and because it is first a history between God and a people (Yahweh and Israel in the Old Testament and Jesus Christ and His community in the New) . . . the life of this people, the common life of its members, becomes part of the event and itself the history of salvation. Because these men are together in relation to God they are among one another in a very distinctive way. As the history of salvation takes place vertically as the act of God's love and the corresponding act of human love for God, it also takes place on the horizontal plane where these men are together reached by the divine act and together engaged in the corresponding act. It takes place unavoidably that there is a definite connexion of these two men among themselves posited in and with their twofold passive and active relationship to God. This connexion is their mutual love; the love of each for his neighbour. It is their love for one another because they are those who together are loved by God and love Him in return. Since it is a matter of love on the vertical plane, how can it be anything else on the horizontal? The two planes are distinct and must not be confused. But they are also inseparable . . . The history of salvation is fundamentally this twofold history, and therefore side by side with that indicated by the first commandment, and inseparably from its fulfilment, it is also the history indicated by the second: "Thou shalt love thy neighbour as thyself." As the one who loves God you cannot do otherwise. As you love God, you will love your neighbour; the one who with you is loved by God, and loves Him in return. (IV, 2, p. 809 f. The Act of Love.)

Cf. I, 2, pp. 401–454. The Life of the Children of God, The Praise of God.

COLOSSIANS 3^{18}–4^1 (IV)

As God the Creator calls man to Himself, He also directs him to his fellow-man. The divine command affirms in particular that in the encounter of man and woman, in the relationship between parents and children . . . man may affirm, honour and enjoy the other with himself and himself with the other. (III, 4, p. 116. Freedom in Fellowship.)

The recurrent term for the description of woman's relation to man is *hypotage* (1 Cor. 14^{34}; Col. 3^{18}; Eph. 5$^{22, 24}$; 1 Tim. 2^{11}; Tit. 2^5; 1 Pet. 3^1) . . . Everything depends on the correct translation. What is here expected of women in their relation to men—and mostly, but not exclusively, of

wives towards their husbands—is in no sense to be conceived on the
analogy of the relationship between subject and prince, subordinate and
superior, or chattel and owner. Of course, the word does speak of subordination, but in such a way that the emphasis is on a mutual adaptation
and co-ordination. The authority to which woman bows in her subordination to man is not the latter's, but that of the *taxis*/order to which both are
subject. It is not saying too much to comment that in so far as man in his
sphere is obedient to the direction of the same Lord of the same *taxis* he
ipso facto subordinates himself to woman. In any case, it is nowhere said
that men should assume a position of superiority in relation to women, but
that they should love them (v. 19), that they should live together with them
according to knowledge as fellow-heirs of the grace of life (1 Pet. 3⁷).
(III, 4, p. 172. Man and Woman.)

Cf. III, 4, pp. 116–240. Man and Woman; pp. 240–285. Parents and
Children.

MATTHEW 5³⁸⁻⁴⁸   (V)
Jesus did not resist the evil (. . . in the legal and political sphere) which
He had come to root out. He was the Judge, and He did not judge:
except, perhaps, those who thought that they could be the judges; except
by causing Himself to be judged for these usurpers of judgment. His
injunction to His followers, not as a law, but as a free call to freedom, is
of a piece with this. They are not to resist evil (v. 38 f.) . . . More than
that, if they do not want to be judged, they are not to judge (7¹ᶠ·). More
still, they are to love their enemies (5⁴³ᶠ·) and pray for their persecutors,
as children of their Father in heaven who causes His sun to shine on the
good and the bad . . . and obviously as brothers of Jesus, who, when His
enemies (really the enemies of God) did their worst against Him, prayed
for them (Lk. 23³⁴) . . . It is again clear—for what political thinking can
do justice and satisfaction to this injunction and the One who gives it?
—that this involves a shaking of every human foundation; that the right
of God is in irreconcilable conflict with every human right; that the divine
state is quite incompatible not merely with the wicked totalitarian state but
with every conceivable human regime; that the new thing cannot be used
to patch or fill the old. It is evident that human order is here betrayed
into the proximity of a final and supreme menace . . . In all these dimensions
(economic, cultic, family etc.) the world is concretely violated by God
Himself in the fact that the man Jesus came into it and is now within it.
(IV, 2, p. 179. The Royal Man; cf. also Mark 2¹⁸⁻²² Second Sunday After
Epiphany.)

God therefore wills—and by His Word and Holy Spirit He creates—
that similarity between Him and us. What He is for us in His sphere as
God, Creator and Reconciler, we can be for Him in our sphere as sinful
creatures. We can therefore love. And in loving we can participate in

His perfection, v. 48. This is not a law which crushes and kills. It would be so only if we were to hear it, not from the mouth of Jesus Christ, from which it comes to us as a law fulfilled by Him, but as a human regulation, which we would have to fulfil. Heard from Him, it is indeed the Law, but the Law as the promise and form of the Gospel, the Gospel in the Law. Is there any news more glad and comforting than that God wills this similarity between Him and us and has already created it in Jesus Christ? (I, 2, p. 395 f. The Life of the Children of God.)

Cf. on 1 Corinthians 4$^{1-5}$ Third Sunday in Advent; also IV, 2, p. 548 and II, 2, p. 512.

ACTS 16$^{9-15}$ (VI)

It is thus impossible that the community . . . should pass by those who are without as the priest and Levite passed by the man who had fallen among thieves. All those who are without are waiting not only for the understanding and solidarity and participation, but for the helping action of the Christian community, for that which it alone in the whole world can do for them. Whether they are aware of it or not, their whole being and striving and existence utters the cry of the Macedonian: " Come over . . . and help us " (v. 9). To be sure, they do not realise that they await and need what the community of Jesus Christ can do and is called to do for them if God acknowledges its activity. If they did, why should they look around for so many different means with which they think they can help themselves? Yet this does not alter the objective fact that they do actually need and lack and seek and expect to find the one thing which the Christian community of all creatures is called to do for them. In spite of every appearance or subjective experience to the contrary, this is true of every man, since none can evade what God is and has done for him in Jesus Christ and what it is appointed that he, too, should know in His Word. (IV, 3, p. 778. The Community for the World; cf. p. 476.)

SEPTEMBER 29. SAINT MICHAEL AND ALL ANGELS

MATTHEW 18$^{1-10}$ (I)

As a " new creation " (2 Cor. 5^{17}) the Christian begins his life as one who is quite different, who starts again from the very first, who is in fact a little child in this sense. This is the meaning when in v. 1, replying to the question of the disciples about the greatest in the kingdom of heaven, Jesus sets a little child in the midst of them (v. 3) . . . This has nothing whatever to do with a childlike mind and character, with childlike simplicity and innocence, as sentimentally suggested by many expositors. " As little children " means in the absolute novitiate which characterises the existence of children. In Mk. 10^{15} and Lk. 18^{17} the saying . . . is preceded by the positive statement: " Of such (*toioutoon* = those engaged in an absolute beginning of this kind) is the kingdom of God." As new-born babes Christians are to drink the rational or unadulterated milk (of the word of the Lord preached to them, 1 Pet. 1[25]), that they may grow thereby to their future salvation (1 Pet. 2[2]). (IV, 4, p. 180. The Foundation of the Christian Life.)

It is certainly stated here that the heavenly Father of Jesus stands in a particular relationship to these little ones which is mediated by angels. But it does not say, as even Calvin maintained, that each of them has his own angel charged to be a guardian angel. The popularity of this concept in the Early Church and ever since is suspicious. Does it not owe more to the heathen notion of the " genius," usually accompanied even more capriciously by the " daemon," than to the biblical passages quoted in its favour (Job 33[23f.]; Acts 12[15])? Most of the older Reformed dogmaticians, in contrast to the more easy-going Lutherans, refused to take up the matter. Quite apart from any questions of disposition, it might be asked why there should not be a particular relationship between angelic reality and each individual. It not this necessarily the case? Does not the relation-ship between God and man (by the Word and Spirit of God) always have an individual character? But does this necessarily imply a permanent private angel for each private person? The most forceful, because positive, objection to this view was again brought by Calvin, who main-tained that the divine care for an individual is not committed only to one angel, but that all are concertedly (*uno consensu*) concerned about our salvation. If we do not think it sufficient that all the hosts of heaven keep watch over us, what will be the value of thinking that one angel in particular is our guardian? This is sound angelology ... In the life of each man the angels prosecute the cause of the kingdom of God, and therefore they are the best possible representatives of the cause of this man himself. (III, 3, p. 518 f. The Ambassadors of God and Their Opponents.)

LUKE 10[17-20]   (Ib)
    Cf. on Luke 10[17-20] Third Sunday After Easter (Jubilate).

REVELATION 12[7-12]   (II)
    The angelic and demonic spheres do not belong together either by nature or origin. The demons are not as it were the poor relations, or the vicious, disreputable and troublesome relations of angels. Between heaven and hell, between that which comes from above and its opposite, which meets and resists it from below and would like to be above, there is nothing in common. It is thus quite inappropriate to speak of God and the devil or angels and demons in the same breath ... The older theology was responsible for very serious confusion when it spoke about angels and demons under the title *De bonis et malis angelis*, or simply

De angelis, as though they could both be brought under the one concept " angels," like the white and black pieces at chess which are both brought out of the same box and can both be put back in it at the end of the game. To be sure, Mt. 25^{41} speaks of the devil and his angels, Rev. 12^7 of the dragon and his angels, and 2 Cor. 12^7 of the angel of Satan. Again angels are obviously to be regarded as hostile powers in the list in Rom. 8^{38}. But when these beings are brought into the same connexion with the *diabolos* or *drakon* or *satanas*, as elsewhere *angelos* is with *kurios* or *theos*, it is obvious that this is simply a manner of speech from which we cannot legitimately conclude that there is a genus " angel " and that within this genus there are two species, the angels of God and the angels of the devil. The genitive of origin and nature obviously divides the two classes of *angelos* in such a way that there can be no question of any correlation between them but only that of absolute and exclusive antithesis. Just as the word " nonsense " does not denote a particular species of sense, but that which is negated and excluded by sense, so *angeli mali* are not a particular species of angels, but the reality which is condemned, negated and excluded by the opposing angels which as such are *angeli boni*. In the few biblical passages in which angels and demons are seen together at all (including Mk. 1^{12}), they are always understood to be in radical conflict. (III, 3, p. 519 f. The Ambassadors of God and Their Opponents.)

JOHN 12$^{25-32}$ (III)

ACTS 5$^{14, 17-29}$ (IV)

A declaration ... so long as it remains theoretical, entailing no obligation or venture on the part of him who makes it, is not confession and must not be mistaken for it. It becomes confession when the word as such implies an action, making an obvious decision in which its subject is revealed and exposed as a member of the Christian community in the larger or smaller publicity of his surroundings. There are good and perhaps strong Christian words which are not confessions because they are merely spoken among the like-minded where they cost nothing and do not help to make visible the contours of the Christian community. They become confessions when they openly intrude into the sphere of false faith and there bring to light what the Christian community regards as true and untrue, as right and wrong; when he who utters them makes himself so responsible for the cause of the community that he can no longer withdraw, but for good or evil has now to answer for this cause as his own. A man confesses when with his Christian declaration he champions this cause before men, and especially before those to whom it is alien, disclosing the community and accepting the consequences of this disclosure, in his own person ... It is in confessions of this kind (vv. 29–32; c. 4$^{8-12}$), in such words of direct aggression, that the Christian community always was and is built up. (III, 4, p. 84 f. Confession.)

EXODUS 23²⁰⁻²³ (V)

The salvation or overthrow of Israel depends upon whether or not it will hearken to the voice of the angel, to the living voice of Moses and later of the prophets (in the broadest sense of this term), and therefore to the living and never utterly silent voice of God Himself. What is the use of Israel's possessing and observing the Law if it will not do this? How it sins against the Law itself—perhaps even in a literal sense, but at all events against its spirit even though its letter be strictly observed, and therefore against the meaning and the purpose in which and for which it is given—if it is not obedient to the angel, for whose voice it should have been prepared by the Law and to whose authoritative office the Law bears witness! How the Law is misused, and made an instrument of sin in the sense finally indicated by Paul, if man considers himself obedient and righteous, and himself wants to bring about the fulfilment of the promise, by keeping the Law—as though he could keep the Law in any other way but by being willing and ready to obey the voice of God who has called him to Himself in the Law, and willing and ready to be the man— the man committed to this Lord—who is marked as such by the Law! To keep the Ten Commandments is to take up the position which they outline and define, and in this—the only possible—position to wait for the specific commands of God for which the proclamation of the Law prepares us, to be constantly obedient to His call. The man who does this is righteous and will live. The man who does not transgresses all the Ten Commandments and the whole Law, however precisely his conduct keeps within the limits defined by the Ten Commandments. For without living obedience to the living God, he does not in fact stand in the place to which he is directed by the commandments. (II, 2, p. 686. The Command as the Decision of God.)

REVELATION 12¹⁻⁶, ¹³⁻¹⁷ (VI)

(HARVEST) THANKSGIVING

LUKE 12¹³⁻²¹ (I)
I, 1, p. 163 [p. 185].

2 CORINTHIANS 9⁶⁻¹⁵ (II)

The new thing that man does as he may love has the form and character of an impartation. To love is to do that which is better than " to receive " (Acts 20³⁵), namely, to give. It is because it is a matter of giving that we must insist so strongly that love cannot be a merely inward action. Dispositions and thoughts and emotions may be very lofty and profound, but their movement is inward; they are not giving. A merely inward action is not a genuine action at all. It is not one in which something happens. But according to the example of God Himself love is the action of giving, and it is therefore one in which man moves out from himself. " God loveth a cheerful giver " (v. 7). Giving is very different from keeping and taking. *Eros* takes and it then has to keep and take again. Love breaks this circle. The one who loves gives. He is marvellously freed to do this. In the power of the Holy Spirit he does this new and unexpected thing. It is not that he has not received and does not have— for how else could he give? He is most generously endowed—the wealthiest man on earth—and he is correspondingly grateful. But he does not think about this. He simply is it. And he is it, and enjoys it, only as he gives ... But it is as he does this also that, while he is not justified, yet, as the great and miserable sinner that he is as well, he is useful to God, and set in His service—a Christian. Where there is love and therefore giving, there is always this happening; and a house, if not a temple, of God is established in the midst of sinners. But giving, as we know, means self-giving—sacrifice. And in practice this includes many kinds of giving. It is not sacrifice if—to speak with brutal frankness— it does not involve the offering of money, from which not even the Christian is parted too easily. The sacrifice of time will also be required, even at the risk of becoming victims of the terrible race of " Chrono-phagi." (IV, 2, p. 786 f. The Act of Love.)

MARK 4$^{26-29}$ (III)

As I see it, not merely the parable of the seed which grows secretly but also that of the sower refers to the community existing in the last age of world history. Growth is a process which takes time ... The communion of saints shows itself to be fruitful in the mere fact that as it exists it enlarges its own circle and constituency in the world. It produces new saints by whose entry it is enlarged and increased. Of course, we are not told ... that it will become constantly greater in this way so that all living men may eventually become Christians. What we are told is that it has the supreme power to extend in this way, that it does not stand therefore under serious threat of diminution, and that as a subject which grows *per definitionem* it has an astonishing capacity even for numerical increase. (IV, 2, p. 644 f. The Growth of the Community.)

It is not for nothing that in the New Testament the picture of building is often confusingly intermingled with that of the divine planting. We have here a growth which is as little the result of human industry as the completion of the building, and a human industry which is only the effect and symptom of this growth, so that whether man sets his hands to work or folds them or even lays them in his lap he can only be a spectator and affirm that it takes place (v. 27) " he knoweth not how "—in a process which continues both when he works and also when he does not, but is perhaps, in the words of Luther, " drinking Wittenberg beer with Philip and Amsdorf." (IV, 2, p. 631 f. The True Church.)

As the community grows spiritually, there is no compulsion but it may also grow extensively and numerically. It is hard to decide formally which of these two directions . . . is denoted by the parables in vv. 26 ff. and vv. 30 ff . . . The progress of the Church—to adopt a term which has gained a peculiar currency in the ecclesiastical politics of Basel—denotes in the New Testament primarily and predominantly, although not exclusively, spiritual progress; the progress of the *sancti* in their relationship to the *sancta*. Progress means that they go forward together on their appointed way from their origin to their goal. (IV, 2, p. 650 f. The Growth of the Community.)

GENESIS 8$^{15-22}$
(IV)

Both passages (9$^{1-17}$ and 8$^{20-22}$) speak of an obligation which God imposes upon Himself. In both passages we can see a corresponding obligation on the part of man. But " man " here is not the community of tribes which is Israel but the whole of humanity after Noah. If, then, as accounts of a covenant—which they are—they stand in the same series as all the other accounts from Sinai to the covenant under Ezra, they differ from all the others in that they speak of a covenant of God with the whole of humanity before and outside Abraham, and indeed, in 9$^{10, 12, 15f.}$, with all the living creatures with which Noah escaped the Flood. If we compare this with Gen. 12 f. we find that in relation to the " covenant " there are indeed " two concentric circles " (Procksch) in which the relationship of God to man is actualised: in the Noachic covenant it is with the human race as a whole, in the covenant with Abraham only with Israel . . . The Noachic covenant . . . is already a covenant of grace in the twofold sense of the concept grace: the free and utterly unmerited self-obligation of God to the human race which had completely fallen away from Him, but which as such is still pledged to Him (as is shown by the sacrifice of Noah in 8^{20} and the divine directions in 9$^{1f.}$); and as the sign of the long-suffering of God obviously also the promise of the future divine coming which will far transcend the mere preserving of the race. (IV, 1, p. 26 f. The Covenant as the Presupposition of Reconciliation.)

At the beginning of the Bible we twice find (Gen. 6^5 and 8^{21}) the emphatic expression that God looked upon the evil of the thoughts of man's heart. In the first passage it says that in face of this fact it repented God that He had made man and that He resolved to destroy man from the face of the earth. And, conversely, in the second passage the same fact is given as the reason why God will no more curse the ground for man's sake, and will no more smite all things living. Therefore the judgment upon man as such is not annulled. On the contrary, the truth of it is the reason why the covenant of grace is established with Noah—the covenant which is announced already in the context of the first passage (6⁸). (II, 1, p. 103. The Readiness of God.)

Cf. II, 1, p. 413; I, 2, p. 47.

JOHN 4³¹⁻³⁸ (V)

Especially in John's Gospel the active life of Jesus Christ is described as an operation and work in the light of God's work, and in relationship or even identity with it: v. 34; 5¹⁷, ³⁴; 9⁴; 17⁴ . . . This central, atoning and saving operation of God is His work as the Lord of the covenant of grace, and it is this which Jesus faces, by which He sees Himself governed and determined, and which He adopts and fulfils by His own work. His life becomes an active life *par excellence* inasmuch as it is orientated to this Word of God *par excellence*. Concretely, it consists quite simply in what is constantly described in the summarised account of Acts as His proclamation of the kingdom by words and deeds. He fulfils the *kerygma*. This is the unassuming act of His life, surpassed only by the content of the *kerygma*, i.e., the coming of the kingdom as such in His suffering, death and resurrection. This simple thing is the human act in the supreme and most concrete sense. (III, 4, p. 486 f. The Active Life.)

ACTS 14⁸⁻¹⁸ (VI)

Revelation does not link up with a human religion which is already present and practised. It contradicts it, just as religion previously contradicted revelation. It displaces it, just as religion previously displaced revelation; just as faith cannot link up with a mistaken faith, but must contradict and replace it as unbelief, as an act of contradiction . . . The most remarkable development of the Old Testament judgment on idolatry (e.g., Jer. 10¹⁶; Is. 44⁹⁻²⁰) is to be found in the passages Rom. 1¹⁸⁻³²; Acts 14¹⁵⁻¹⁸; 17²²⁻³¹ . . . In the light of the self-revelation of the truth, our human being and activity is seen to be in its ultimate and profoundest reality a fight against the truth. It stands over against the truth self-revealed there at an angle of 180⁰ . . . In and with the proclamation of Christ (in Rom. 1 as well as the speeches in Acts) the men to whom this proclamation is made and who in it learn about the relationship of God and man, i.e., about God's grace, have to admit that in this opposition they have a relationship to truth, which they deny and betray by this opposition. When the grace of God is proclaimed to them in Christ, they have to concede that " God has not left himself without a witness " (v. 17). For in and with the proclamation of the grace of God in Christ there is disclosed to them the witness of God, from which they have fallen away and with which they have been brought into radical contradiction . . . In the speeches of Acts the witness which is disclosed and awakens and accuses in this way (Rom. 1²⁰) . . . is its knowledge of God as the Creator: " He did you good . . ." (v. 17). Yes, He! They come to know this afresh. And they come to know afresh that this was what they already knew ... If God is the Creator, how can there be such a thing as a mediation which we ourselves establish? How impossible all these things are! And yet how real is the struggle against the grace of revelation in favour of a capricious and arbitrary attempt to storm heaven! In this struggle against grace the known God has become an unknown one. There is no future for opposition to the truth, now that it has as such invaded us in God's revelation (Acts 17$^{24-29}$). All that really remains for us—personally—to do is " to turn from these vanities unto the living God " (Acts 14^{15}). (I, 2, pp. 303–306. The Revelation of God as the Abolition of Religion.)

Cf. on Acts 17$^{16-34}$ Third Sunday After Easter (Jubilate).

NINETEENTH SUNDAY AFTER TRINITY

MATTHEW 9$^{1-8}$ (I)

As a second general phenomenon which points in the same direction—it is the merit of K. L. Schmidt (RGG^2, Art. " Jesus Christ ") to have brought this emphatically to our attention—we may cite the fact that the New Testament tradition has presented the revealing activity of Jesus as an inextricable interrelation of word and act and indeed of word and miracle. It is a weakness of R. Bultmann's *Jesus* (1926) that he ignores this insistent demand of the texts and construes Jesus one-sidedly in terms of His sayings. The acts which invariably speak and are to be heard as well are miraculous acts. How they are connected with the central content of the words of Jesus may be seen from the story of the paralytic in Mk. 2$^{1-12}$, where to the horror of the scribes—who immediately speak of blasphemy and not unjustly from their standpoint—Jesus not only speaks of the forgiveness of sins but actually forgives sins and, to show His authority for this act-word, cures the paralytic. God's act as it takes place visibly, the totality of a gracious act on man, emphasises that the word spoken visibly, the totality of a gracious act on man, emphasises that the word spoken is God's word. This is the meaning of the miracles ascribed to Jesus (and expressly to His apostles too on the basis of the authority conferred on them by Jesus)—and it is a meaning which marks off these miracles, however we assess them materially, as at any rate something very distinctive amid the plethora of miracle stories in that whole period. Their distinctive feature, however, lies in their complete and indissoluble combination with the word of Jesus, a combination which distinguishes this word no less from mere prophesying than the miracles from mere thaumaturgy, a combination in which both word and deed in the same way give evidence of something above and beyond ethos (" history ") and physis, of a higher authority confronting the whole state of human and indeed cosmic reality. Who is the One who, obviously speaking representatively for this higher authority, can speak thus because He can act thus and act thus because He can speak thus? (I, 1, p. 400 f. [458 f.] God the Son.)

In the miracle stories of the New Testament there is only one story . . . in which there is a prior reference to the sin of the one who is healed, and even here there is no demand for repentance, but the sin is annulled unrequested and without examination, in view of the faith, not of the man himself, but of those who had brought him to Jesus, v. 2. He says this with just the same free initiative as He later says: " Arise, and take up thy bed, and go thy way into thine house " (v. 6). The obvious aim of the story is to bring out the connexion of Jesus' miracles with His proclamation. But instead of interposing a psychologico-moral dependence of the second saying on the first it is far better to see that in the immediate proximity of the second the first itself is pure, free proclamation and not a psychologico-moral encouragement. With the same free power with which the Son of Man later tells the paralytic to rise and walk He first forgives him his sins. And He does the second in order that " ye may know " that He has the power to do the first. (IV, 2, p. 223. The Royal Man.)

EPHESIANS 4²²⁻³² (II)

In conflict with their former conversation they are to put off " the old man which is corrupt according to the deceitful lusts "; to put him off as one can only discard an old coat that is obviously in rags, and to do so in a movement in which there can be no hesitation, no looking back, no halting half-way, but which can only be accomplished at once and totally because it is a matter of life and death, because everything is at stake, and would be lost if it were not accomplished at once and totally. This is what is demanded by the injunction of the apostle . . . This is the aspect of the operation of the Holy Spirit to the extent that it is correction, that it is His critical and judging and purifying work. It is with this either-or that He contends for man and therefore against him. Christians are among those who come to see this. Just because they know and proclaim the reconciliation of the world with God, they cannot come to terms with the world. Just because they know and proclaim the reconciliation of the world with God, they cannot come to terms with the world. Just because they hope for the resurrection of the flesh as it has been revealed already in the resurrection of the man Jesus, they cannot concede to its desires any authority or right. Just because they live by the forgiveness of sin, they cannot adopt it into their programme. And just because they are the house of God, it is expressly with them that judgment begins on the fleshly, sinful, worldly man (1 Pet. 4¹⁷). (IV, 2, p. 371 f. The Direction of the Son.)

The royal man of the New Testament tradition is created after " God " (v. 24). This means that as a man He exists analogously to the mode of

existence of God.   In what He thinks and wills and does, in His attitude,
there is a correspondence, a parallel in the creaturely world, to the plan
and purpose and work and attitude of God.   (IV, 2, p. 166.   The Royal
Man.)

MARK 1^{32-39} (III)

JAMES 5^{13-20} (IV)

God's communication with man . . . is so real . . . that man is not merely
permitted to hear God, to answer Him, to worship Him, and in that
worship to find comfort, peace and purity, but he may actually call upon
God in the most definite way to do for him and give him what he needs.
So real is this communication that where it occurs God positively wills
that man should call upon Him in this way, in order that He may be his
God and Helper.   We need not hesitate to say that " on the basis of the
freedom of God Himself God is conditioned by the prayer of faith " . . .
He is willing not merely to hear but to hearken to the prayer of faith; He
not only permits to faith the prayer which expects an answer but has
positively commanded it.   The Bible is completely unambiguous about
this: Prv. 15^{29}; Ps. $145^{18f.}$; 50^{15}; Jas. $5^{16f.}$; Mt. $7^{f.}$; Lk. $18^{6f.}$.   (II, 1,
p. 510 f.   The Constancy and Omnipotence of God.)
Cf. oñ Luke 18^{1-8} Twenty-fifth Sunday After Trinity.

JOHN 5^{1-18} (V)

There is only one story (Mk. $2^{1f.}$) in which there is a prior reference to
the sin of the one who is healed . . . And there is only one story again
(Jn. 5^{1-18}) where we have a subsequent reference to the sin of the one who
is healed (v. 14).   It is to be noted, however, that Jesus' initial question to
this man was simply: " Wilt thou be made whole? " (v. 6), and that the
only answer the man gave was to explain why it was that he had not so far
found the healing that he desired in the pool of Bethesda, v. 7.   There is
no question of any ethical purpose on the part of Jesus, or ethical insight
on the part of the man.   The warning tells us, of course, that there is
something worse than thirty-eight years of infirmity, i.e., to treat the grace
which has been given as though it had made no difference and to continue
in sin.   But the point of the story is not to be found in the warning . . .
And in any case . . . there is no mention of sin at all in the rest of the
stories.   It is tacitly presupposed that those who were healed were sinners
and ought not to continue in sin.   But this has no thematic significance in
the texts.   In the true sense, their transgressions are not imputed to them
by Jesus (2 Cor. 5^{19}).   What is imputed is only that they are poor and tragic
and suffering creatures.   In the strict sense, it is only as such that they are
taken seriously.   (IV, 2, p. 223 f.   The Royal Man; cf. on John 9 Fourteenth Sunday After Trinity.)
Health means capability, vigour and freedom.   It is strength for human

life. It is the integration of the organs for the exercise of psycho-physical functions ... Yet " health is not a final end in itself; it is defined and limited by the meaning of life, and the meaning of life is nothing but preparedness for devotion and sacrifice " (R. Siebeck, *Medizin in Bewegung*, 1949, p. 486). We are indeed appalled at the many people who look upon health itself as a lofty or supreme goal, and " live for their health " alone. Lovingly cherishing their bodies or even their souls, and being constantly interested in what is good, less good or even bad for them, they raise such things as sun, air and water, the power of different herbs and fruits, the beauty of a tanned skin and the dynamic strength of well-tempered muscles, and perhaps the possibilities of medical and psychological skill, to the level of beneficent demons to which they offer a devotion and credulity, and which they serve with a devotion and enthusiasm, that can only show them to be the unhealthiest persons ... Health is the strength to be as man ... Sickness is partial impotence to exercise the functions of body and soul. It hinders man in his exercise of them by burdening, hampering, troubling and threatening him, and causing him pain. But sickness as such is not necessarily impotence to be as man. The strength to be this, so long as one is still alive, can also be the strength and therefore the health of the sick man. And if health is the strength for human existence, even those who are seriously ill can will to be healthy without any optimism or illusions regarding their condition. They, too are commanded, and it is not too much to ask, that so long as they are alive they should will this, i.e., exercise the power which remains to them, in spite of every obstacle. Hence it seems to be a fundamental demand of the ethics of the sick bed that the sick person should not let himself cease to be addressed, and to address himself, in terms of health and the will which it requires rather than sickness, and above all to see that he is in an environment of health ... The command which we must always obey is the command to stand upright and not to fall. (III, 4, pp. 356–359. Respect for Life.)

Exodus 34⁴ᵇ⁻¹⁰   (VI)

The fact that God is gracious ... implies that He forgives the sinner his sin (v. 9; Num. 14¹⁹). That is, He Himself with His inclination, good will and favour intervenes on behalf of the one who has sinned against Him. His own good free will is to Him truer and more significant—infinitely more so—than the evil will of the sinner. He does not regard and treat the latter as he would have to be regarded and treated on the basis of his evil human will, but as he must be regarded and treated on the basis of the good will of God now turned towards him; because He is God, because this covering and wiping out of sin, because this unmerited, kind, and utterly different view and treatment of His creature is not merely in His power but is His right and therefore His majestic will: Ps. 103⁸, ¹⁰⁻¹²

That this should happen and be true for us is the prayer of biblical man when he cries out: " Be gracious unto me. " This is what God's inclination, good will and favour means for God Himself and for us. It is always God's turning to those who not only do not deserve this favour, but have deserved its opposite. (II, 1, p. 355 f. The Grace and Holiness of God.)

Cf. on Exodus 32¹⁵⁻²⁰, ³⁰⁻³⁴ Fifth Sunday in Lent (Judica).

TWENTIETH SUNDAY AFTER TRINITY

MATTHEW 22¹⁻¹⁴ (I)

It is an invitation, and indeed an invitation to a feast, to a marriage feast: v. 4. The epilogue (which is wrongly conjured away by many exegetes) tells us about the individual who certainly came, but came without a wedding-garment (v. 11 f.), and it shows that in the last resort it all boils down to the fact that the invitation is to a feast, and that he who does not obey and come accordingly, and therefore festively, declines and spurns the invitation no less than those who are unwilling to obey and appear at all. Reluctant obedience to God's command is not obedience, and decisivly for this reason, that in itself and as such the command of God is a festive invitation. (II, 2, p. 588. The Command as the Claim of God.)

A more difficult verse ... is v. 14. Jesus has just told the parable of the wedding-feast ... There is then added the independent saying: " Many are called, but few are chosen. " The verse forms a *crux interpretum*, sincd its most obvious meaning, in analogy to the saying quoted in Plato's *Phaedo* about the few real Bacchantes among the many Thyrsus bearers, seems to be in flat contradiction with all the other passages and to speak about a calling which has no election as its presupposition ... My own view is that we may and must agree with K. L. Schmidt (TWNT, III, p. 496; TDNT, III, p. 494) in regarding the saying as a paradox. It may thus be freely paraphrased as follows. Many are called, but there will only be few who in following the call will prove worthy of, and act in accordance with, the fact that as the called of God they are His elect, predestined from all eternity for life with Him and for His service. There will only be few who in the words of 2 Pet. 1¹⁰ are obedient to their calling and make sure, i.e., validate and confirm, their election. There will only be few who really are what they are as called, namely, elect or Christians. (IV, 3, p. 485. The Vocation of Man.)

Cf. on Revelation 3¹⁻⁶ Second Sunday in Advent; cf. also IV, 3, p. 851.

EPHESIANS 5¹⁵⁻²¹ (II)

Cf. on Colossians 3¹²⁻¹⁷ Fourth Sunday After Easter (Cantate). Cf. also I, 2, pp. 252–257.

Acts 2[41-47] (IV)

The continued existence of the Christian community implies constant " adding " of men to it (v. 41). Seen from below, this means that . . . they enter into and belong to it . . . To enter into and belong to the Christian community is to step out of blindness and neutrality into the kingdom of God. Those who carry out their decision to join declare that they are aware of the kingdom of God, not as a spectacle which they may attend as spectators, but as an action by which they themselves are summoned to action. They bear witness that it concerns them, and that it does so in such a way that they must confess its occurrence by their own existence . . . This committal includes the fact that a man does not merely bind himself privately but that in accordance with his conviction he does so publicly, allowing himself to be addressed, together with all those who are in the same position, in the words which Peter was once unwilling to accept: " And thou also wast with Jesus of Nazareth " (Mk. 14[67]). With this commitment a man fulfils the affirmation of the existence of the Christian community and thus partakes in its service. (III, 4, p. 491 f. The Active Life.)

In v. 44 f. we read of a bold attempt by the most primitive post-Pentecostal community . . . There is only one other direct mention of this attempt, in Ac. 5[1f.]. It has often been taken up since in different forms. But in whatever form can it ever have more than the significance of an attempt? It is worth pondering that the venture was at least made. And it will always be inevitable that there should be impulses in this direction wherever the Gospel of Jesus is proclaimed and heard. But it has never happened—least of all in the modern system called " Communism "—that even in smaller circles the way which leads in this direction has been trodden to the end. (IV, 2, p. 178. The Royal Man.)

Cf. IV, 2, pp. 641–660.

John 6[37-44] (V)

Cf. on John 6[37-40] New Year's Day.

1 John 4[1-8] (VI)

The love of God is . . . (3) creative, i.e., a love which causes those who are loved by Him to love . . . As it is essential to it to be (1) elective and (2) purifying love, it is also essential to it to be the basis of human love: the creative basis; not merely a rational basis . . . ; nor a purely moral basis . . . ; nor a quasi-physical basis, as though the impact of the love of God caused man to love like a ball which is set in motion . . . Love is " of God " (v. 7). But this means precisely that (as He made heaven and earth *ex nihilo*, or formed Adam from the dust of the earth according to Gen. 2[7], or can raise up from the stones children to Abraham) He can make of those who cannot and will not love (for they are sinners) men who do actually love . . . New and different men are needed in order that love may take place as a human act. And God creates these new and loving men. It is in this way that He is the basis of human love.

The statements " God is " and " God loves " . . . explain and confirm one another. It is in this way, in this identity of being and love, that God reveals Himself to us as He loves us . . . We can reverse the statement (in v. 8 and v. 16) and say that love is God. The context shows that this was the mind of the author. In v. 8 he calls the man who does not love one who does not know God, whereas in v. 7 he says of the man who loves that he does know God. Love presupposes knowledge of God, and knowledge of God results in love. The reason why this is the case is given in v. 8b: " God is love ". To know Him is to know His love as that in which He is and is God. Hence it is love again (this time the corresponding love of God) which according to v. 7b comes to man " of God. " The continuation in v. 9, which speaks of the revelation of God's love in the sending of His Son, explains how this love is known, and therefore how God is known, and therefore how man may and should love in the realisation of this knowledge. But what is revealed in this revelation and known in this knowledge is that which is formulated in v. 8b, namely, the being of God which is that of the One who first and as such is love, and by which the being of the man who knows God in this revelation must be directed. (IV, 2, p. 776 and p. 755 f. The Basis of Love.)

TWENTY-FIRST SUNDAY AFTER TRINITY

JOHN 4^{47-54}   (I)

" And so . . . we should hold His Word glorious and lofty as an almighty power. For whoso hath it hath all and can do all. Again, whoso hath it not, him naught else can or shall guard against sin, death and devil. For what our dear Lord Christ doth here with the nobleman's son, saving him from death by His almighty word and keeping him alive, that will He do for us all by His Word if we will but accept it. . . ." (Luther). (I, 1, p. 144 [165]. The Speech of God as the Act of God.)

Cf. also I, 1, pp. 232–234 [266–268].

MATTHEW 12^{22-30}   (Ib)

Cf. on Luke 11^{14-28} Third Sunday in Lent (Oculi)

EPHESIANS 6^{10-18}   (II)

For the conflict of the community is not just with flesh and blood, and definitely not just with the corruption of man both without and within, but (v. 12) with principalities and powers, with the great and generally accepted presuppositions which rule the world in the continuing darkness of this age, with the spirits of evil which seem to strive against it even from heaven itself. If it is to offer resistance in the evil day, if having done all it is to stand, it has no option but to take to itself the armour of God (v. 13). Listening to His truth, subjection to His righteousness, a readiness for His Gospel, faith in Him, the salvation which is in Him and comes from Him—this is how the equipment is described in vv. 14–17. And its last and supreme piece is " the sword of the Spirit, which is the word of God. " Finally (vv. 18–19)—as a clear reminder that in all this we have to do with God's own equipment, so that there can be no question of self-evident triumph on the part of those of God's warriors who seize it—the passage closes with a simple call to prayer and watchfulness " with all perseverance and supplication for all saints, " including himself, the apostle adds, that to him too (for it is not self-evident even in his case, or something peculiar to him) " utterance may be given, " to open his mouth boldly and joyfully to make known the mystery of the Gospel. It is with this exclusive confidence that the community looks for its preservation from the danger which engulfs it. We remember that it is in Ephesians that the glory of the community is so finely described . . . The reference is to the glory of the community as it is genuinely threatened in the world (c. 1, 2, 4$^{11-16}$). (IV, 2, p. 671 f. and cf. p. 674. The Upholding of the Community.)

The instructed Grand Inquisitor or Antichrist who can commend his evil cause, and therefore the man of sin in the full power of his work, is a sympathetic and a seriously illuminating and convincing figure, not to be confused with such unsympathetic associates as Hitler, Mussolini or Stalin, and able to count upon finding many well-disposed people to applaud and follow him. It is his perverse relationship to the truth, his marching out in armour very similar to the armour of God in Eph. 6$^{11f.}$, which makes him so sympathetic, illuminating and convincing. There are thus good reasons why his sleight of hand is so successful, why it seems to be even more successful than the prophecy of Jesus Christ which it imitates, in order to free itself the more securely from it. If it lacks solidity, the fact that falsehood is so light means that it can cover a good deal of ground. How, then, are we to differentiate it from the truth? (IV, 3, p. 438. The Falsehood and Condemnation of Man.)

Cf. IV, 3, p. 647; IV, 4, p. 7.

MATTHEW 10$^{34-39}$ (III)

Nor are brutal hostilities suggested by the saying about the sword which Jesus has come to bring, and related sayings, but a radical, yet not aggressive, but materially very serious separation of the disciple from all the prejudgments and burdensome claims which conflict with his discipleship and which spring from the fact that he is also the child of his parents. Thus the sayings are not weakened when we say that they do not clash with the commandment: " Honour thy father and thy mother, " but only with the biological and sociological conventions of the framework within which this commandment is pronounced. They limit this framework by referring to another which is not only superior, but alien to it, and which does not make inapplicable the commandment, but the natural and social conventions, valid therein. We may not go further than this in the interpretation of these sayings. (III, 4, p. 262. Parents and Children.)

The " sword " (v. 34) . . . is obviously the same sword as was to pierce through the soul of Mary (Lk. 2[35]) " that the thoughts of many hearts may be revealed " . . . The presence of the man Jesus meant the presence of this sword. He was the light of which we are told in Eph. 5[13] that all things are reproved by it. From the very first, and radically, He was the *venturus iudicare vivos et mortuos*. Already according to the reported witness of the Baptist in Mt. 3[12]: " His fan is in his hand . . ." To use the words which preface the account of His activity in Mk. 1[15], His presence meant that the time was fulfilled, and the kingdom of God was at hand, in threatening proximity to every sphere of human power and dominion. (IV, 2, p. 158. The Royal Man.)

The "sword": The context makes it quite clear that this is not a sword which the disciples have to draw but the sword which is sharpened and drawn against them, the sword which Paul mentions in Rom. 8[35], where he then goes on to quote Ps. 44[22]: " For thy sake are we killed all the day long; we are counted as sheep for the slaughter. " (IV, 3, p. 625. The Christian in Affliction.)

1 JOHN 2[12-17] (IV)

Apart from Heb. 12, the New Testament gives us only a few express directions on the theme of the relations of youth and age . . . If v. 13 f. relates also though not exclusively to earthly fathers, we see that what the author writes and has already written to the " fathers " consists in the statement: " Ye have known him that is from the beginning. " What distinguishes them from the little children and young men addressed also in the same context, and determines their relationship to the latter, is that they are those whose authority springs from their recognition of the One who was from the beginning, and is thus really the " Eldest. " But in 1 John it is plain that He who was from the beginning is Jesus Christ. Hence the fathers are His witnesses to those who follow them, the younger generation. It is surely clear that if the severe, demanding, judicial or legal character of their task does not disappear, it must certainly recede into the background in view of this foundation of their own status . . . In later Christianity . . . when Heb. 12 was read as if it offered a Christian directive, it was supposed that the task of *paideia* must be essentially understood as a legal pedagogy to be exercised with great patriarchal majesty, and therefore as the task of chastisement, i.e., as the necessary execution of judgment upon imaginations of the heart which are evil from youth (Gen. 8²¹). But it was obviously forgotten, irrespective of whether a little corporal punishment was solemnly included or later excluded, that the work and revelation of Jesus Christ necessarily signify a decisive and fundamental change in the history of pedagogy. Now that the Father, for all the sins of men young and old, has subjected the Son to the yoke of the Law, " to redeem them that were under the law " (Gal. 4⁴ᶠ·) . . . even in the relation of human fathers to their children severity and discipline, commands, judgments and punishment can have only a secondary place, and no longer assume the primary role which is apparently allotted to them in the Book of Proverbs. In the aeon inaugurated by the first *parousia* of Jesus Christ, the task of parents is not primarily and decisively to attest the Law to their children, but primarily and decisively the Gospel. (III, 4, p. 281 f. Parents and Children.)

Cf. on Hebrews 12⁴⁻¹¹ (VI).

GENESIS 32²³⁻³² (V)

This passage says of Jacob, who undoubtedly is already elected and called by God, that he wrestles with God until morning, and that God—obviously—did not overcome him. From the immanent standpoint he is and continues to be an enemy of grace. This is indicated by the new name Israel, which he acquires: " Thou hast striven with God and with men and hast prevailed "—a great distinction, but at bottom a shattering one, which reminds us of the religious history of the people whose ancestor Jacob was. The giving of this name to Jacob is a fulfilment of the judgment. But this is not the meaning and object of the history. After the conflict the sinew of Jacob's thigh is touched and dislocated by God. So, then, although he is not overcome by God, he is and continues to be a man weakened by God. Again, in his wrestling with God, Jacob will not let God go, because he desires to be blessed by Him. Again, God actually does bless this steadfast opponent of his. And finally, Jacob calls the place of this conflict with God " Peniel "; " For I have seen God face to face and my life is preserved." The place where there is knowledge of the truth of the Christian religion will have to be such a Peniel, and it can be such a Peniel only where a man stands wholly and utterly against God, and in this resistance he is marked by God, and therefore cannot make any other request than: " I will not let thee go, except thou bless me," and in this very prayer of his he is heard and blessed, and in this very blessing he sees the face of God and in it he knows the truth. (I, 2, p. 338 f. The Revelation of God as the Abolition of Religion.)

The story of this nation is only too much a repetition of the story of its tribal ancestor, who has to wrestle not only with man but with God, and though disabled by God nevertheless wrestles with this One till dawning: " I will not let thee go, except thou bless me." The nation' decline and fall seems to be God's own triumph, and this nation's salvation seems to lie exclusively in the fact that, like a drowning man, it must clutch constantly at the hand, must constantly be saved by the hand, that smites it so frightfully. Between the covenant and its fulfilment there is suffering and death for those in whom it is to be fulfilled. (I, 2, p. 87. The Time of Expectation.)

HEBREWS 12[4-11]   (VI)

The crisis which comes upon man when he encounters the righteousness of God, but in which the grace of God is secretly present and operative, is frequently described in the Bible as chastisement: Job 5[17]; Rev. 3[19]. In an apparent paradox, Ps. 62[12] grounds and recognises the mercy of God in the fact that He renders " to every man according to his work." The normative conception is that of the father who shows his fatherly love to the son by the strict exercise of his fatherly right: Prov. 3[11f.]; Heb. 12[7f.] The original form of this conception, which plainly reveals its relation to the redemptive history, is perhaps in the promise given to David in 2 Sam. 7[14f.] with respect to his son . . . The warth of God is purposeful, not purposeless and meaningless and unlimited. So little is it the latter that in contrast to the livelong and indeed eternal goodness of God its duration can be rather boldly described as only for a moment (Ps. 30[5]; Is. 54[8]). The men of the Bible do not fail to recognise its seriousness. But they boldly count upon its formal limitation: Ps. 102[14]. And they always look back to its dominion (Ps. 118[18])—this was the passage which Paul had in mind in 2 Cor. 6[9] . . . " Now no chastening for the present seemeth to be joyous, but grievous; nevertheless afterward it yieldeth the peaceable fruit of righteousness unto them that are exercised thereby " (v. 11). Where there is this fruit, there has obviously been the corresponding seed. (IV, 1, p. 537 f. The Judgment of God.)

Cf. III, 4, p. 281.

TWENTY-SECOND SUNDAY AFTER TRINITY

MATTHEW 18[21-35]   (I)
PHILIPPIANS 1[3-11]   (II)

What is the meaning of *ta diapheronta* (v. 10)? Obviously " that which is relevant in the existing situation " (W. Grundmann). But what is, in fact, relevant in the existing situation? It is certainly not a kind of necessity immanent in the situation, a kind of " law of the hour," so that the capacity for *dokimazein* and its exercise consist in a kind of divination, an uncanny sense of the demands of the time. Quite apart from the inclinations of our own fleshly nature, the existing situation as such is always ruled by all sorts of demons, and sensitiveness to it can have very little to do with sensitiveness to the will of God. The passage speaks expressly of testing the *diapheronta*, and not of an instinctive feeling for their greater or lesser necessity. The sovereign decision of God in His command stands absolutely supreme above the existing situation, although absolutely related to it. And the point at issue is the mutual relation between this, that or the other possible line of action in this situation and the divine command. *Ta diapheronta* are, then, the various possibilities of action open to us in the existing situation, and the relevant question is whether we can (and so should) adopt this or that particular possibility in the confidence that the relation between it and the divine command will be positive and therefore the action will be " good, and acceptable, and according to the purpose of God " (Rom. 12^2) ... This enquiry cannot be replaced by even the most penetrating systematic or intuitive analysis of the situation as such and the objective and subjective factors which condition it. For, obviously, this enquiry begins where an analysis of that kind leaves off. (II, 2, p. 639 f. The Sovereignty of the Divine Decision.)

Cf. IV, 3, pp. 516–518.

ISAIAH $1^{2-6,\ 18-20}$ (III)

The next thing we are unequivocally and indispensably told by the Old Testament is the particular fact that the man elected by God, the object of the divine grace, is not in any way worthy of it. From what we hear of the people of Israel and its kings, he shows by his action that he is a transgressor of the commandment imposed on him with his election, an enemy of the will of God directed and revealed to him. The God of the Old Testament rules among His enemies. He is already on the way into the far country to the extent that it is an unfaithful people to whom He gives and maintains His faithlessness ... The normal answer of Israel to the question put to it in its election (in connexion with the thought of sonship) is that the " children " of Israel are " corrupted children " (v. 2, 4; c. $30^{1,\ 9}$; Jer. $3^{21f.}$ ...). The place taken by the one Israelite Jesus according to the New Testament is, according to the Old Testament, the place of this disobedient son, this faithless people and its faithless priests and kings ... " The Word was made flesh." The Old Testament testifies pitilessly what is meant by " flesh." The Old Testament was needed to testify this because the Old Testament alone attests the election of God, and it is only in the light of God's election that we see who and what is man—his unfaithfulness, his disobedience, his fall, his sin, his enmity against God ... The being and nature of man are radically and fundamentally revealed in the human people of Israel as chosen and loved by God, in the history of that people, in Jewish flesh. From the negative standpoint that is the mystery of the Jews and their representative existence. That is what anti-Semitism old and new has constantly thundered, but without understanding that we have here a mirror held up to the men of all peoples. (IV, 1, p. 171 f. The Way of the Son of God into the Far Country.)

ROMANS 7¹⁴⁻⁸²   (IV)

Our question here concerns the man justified by God ... Is there such a man? Does he even exist? Has he ever existed? Will he ever exist? The Christian does not really need to look at the heathen and unbelieving and indifferent to be forced to ask this question. Is he himself, the Christian, the man justified by God? Does he know himself as a man who is really on the way from Rom. 7 to Rom. 8, who can take Ps. 23 sincerely on his heart and therefore legitimately on his lips in this movement and as the subject of this history? (IV, 1, p. 610. The Justification of Man.)

Towards the end vv. 21–25 are interrupted by a short but remarkable conversation which the apostle has with himself (vv. 24–25a)—a strange cry, or rather two cries, the one answering the other. Here we have to do with the little window which does at least let a glimmer of light into the prison cell. And here again we have a direct proof that in this context Paul is not speaking in recollection—or only in recollection—of an earlier period in his life, or in the assumed role of a Jewish or Gentile unbeliever. " O wretched man that I am! who shall deliver me from the body of this death? " We make Paul extremely rhetorical if we take it that his complaint is only in recollection. And he drops the assumed role of a Jewish or Gentile unbeliever when—we might almost say from the outside—he answers his own complaint: " I thank God through Jesus Christ our Lord." The two sayings are very abrupt. And they come together very abruptly. But they are meaningful together, the one pointing backwards, the other forwards. And together they fix the mathematical point at which the justification of man takes place as his transition from wrong to right, from death to life ... Living already and altogether by the answer, living already and altogether in the deliverance which has already come to him, he still has to live in and with the question. He could not do the one if he tried to refuse the other, to be only the man of the answer, not to be wholly and utterly the wretched man of the question. He can only be both at once. But not in that unhappy contradiction ... but rather in the transition, the history of justification, in that translation as it is really both at once, as indicated in the relationship of the two sayings in v. 24 and v. 25a. If we read carefully the exposition in Rom. 8 we shall soon realise that even there the " also," and therefore the " both together," has not completely disappeared, nor has the " wretched man " of Rom. 7: the beginning of justification in the very midst of man's sin. (IV, 1, pp. 588–591. The Pardon of Man.)

Cf. III, 2, p. 620 f.

MATTHEW 5²³⁻²⁶   (V)

1 JOHN 3[18-24]   (VI)

Man's love, as an imitation of God's love, is an act, and not merely an internal but an external act, the act of the whole man. A man may have many thoughts and emotions of love and yet not love or give himself by a long way. If he does love, he does not do so partially, and therefore he does not do so just inwardly or just outwardly. It is another question how much or little of his whole being is lacking when he loves. There will always be a good deal. But no deficiency in this regard can be justified theoretically by reducing the love for which he was liberated to something merely inward. He is freed by the love of God to love " in deed and in truth " (v. 18). Where there is love, there takes place something from God, but in space and time, " with hearts and hands and voices." (IV, 2, p. 786. The Act of Love.)

Cf. on 2 Corinthians 9[6-15] (Harvest) Thanksgiving; also IV, 2, p. 276.

TWENTY-THIRD SUNDAY AFTER TRINITY

MATTHEW 22[15-22]   (I)

PHILIPPIANS 3[17-21]   (II)

When our earthly tent perishes, we have a building prepared by God in heaven, an eternal house not made with hands (2 Cor. 5[1]), the better country to which men of God have always been on the way in faith (Heb. 11[16]). There in heaven is our Jerusalem: the free woman which is the mother of us all (Gal. 4[26]; Heb. 12[22]); the *polis* which will come down from thence " prepared as a bride adorned for her husband " (Rev. 3[12]; 21[2, 10]); the heavenly *politeuma* in relation to which our present status is that of colonists who live in this world but are lawful members of that which is above (Phil. 3[20]). (III, 3, p. 435. The Kingdom of Heaven.)

Cf. II, 2, p. 723.

MATTHEW 5[13-16]   (III)

Secularisation (sc. of the community) is the process by which the salt loses its savour (v. 13). It is not in any sense strange that the world is secular. This is simply to say that the world is the world. It was always secular. There is no greater error than to imagine that this was not the case in the much-vaunted Middle Ages. But when the Church becomes secular, it is the greatest conceivable misfortune both for the Church and the world. And this is what takes place when it wants to be a Church only for the world, the nation, culture, or the state—a world Church, a national Church, a cultural Church, or a state Church. It then loses its specific importance and meaning; the justification for its existence. (IV, 2, p. 668. The Upholding of the Community.)

What particular objection can the world have to a Church which understands and discharges its task in so innocuous a way? Its contradiction and opposition will usually be directed only against a community which brings out the concrete relevance of the Gospel. But if the Church does in fact make itself invisible, and the Gospel is being made or has been made timeless and irrelevant on its lips, it has to realise that it has forfeited its own true right to exist, that it cannot expect any serious respect on the part of the world, that it cannot be sure of its own cause in face of it, and above all that its vitally necessary connexion with its Lord has been hopelessly broken. As salt which has lost its savour (v. 13), it is good for nothing but to be cast out and trodden under foot of men. (IV, 2, p. 816. The Task of the Community.)

The man who believes in Jesus Christ is, as such, the lighted candle which belongs *per se* to the candlestick. His taking cognisance is also a giving ... The consequence is irresistible that where anyone believes as a Christian a history is enacted: a history of the heart which, as such, is audible and visible in world-history; an individual history which, as such, calls for impartation and communication; a secret history which, as such, has a public character and claim; a history which is not apparent ... but a history of immeasurable dynamic because it takes place in the light of the great history of God. (IV, 1, p. 776 f. The Act of Faith.)

Cf. I, 1, p. 50 [54]; III, 4, p. 487; IV, 3, p. 619.

ROMANS 13$^{1-8}$ (IV)

It is a separate question that of all human societies the Church has to understand the state, which comprehends and co-ordinates all the others, as a divinely appointed institution, as an element of the lordship of Jesus Christ, as the great human representative of His lordship over the world outside, so that in this wider sense its officials can be regarded as the " ministers of God " (v. 6). It certainly can and must confess in relation to it that it understands its own spiritual centre to be the centre of the being and constitution of the state as well. But ... it cannot try to force it to understand itself in the same way as the Church understands it; or to understand the Church in the same way as the latter understands itself. It will always find that even though the majority of citizens and many officials are good Christians the state confronts the Church as its worldly partner, and that in their mutual relationship it is always on its own presuppositions that it will think and reason and deal with it in its various laws and decrees. The most that it can ever expect from the state in practice is to be assigned a more or less exalted position and function within its own law in relation to corporations and societies.—The form in which the state regulates its connexion with the Church, i.e., the Church's assimilation into its own order within the framework of its understanding (or misunderstanding) of its nature and essence, is the law of Church and state, in which as the possessor of sovereignty in its own sphere, and the supreme guardian of all law and order established and valid within it, the state guarantees an appropriate place to the Church, but is also vigilant to see that it does not transgress the appointed limits. It does this in virtue of the fact that with many other rights it also claims a *ius circa sacra*: not *in sacra*, in an attempt to shape its will and rule its inner life; but *circa sacra*, as that which guarantees these limits on both sides. It may be the state itself which lays down the law of the Church, e.g., by definite articles of constitution and by the sanctioning of corresponding legislation in the Church. Or sometimes it is a matter for mutual arrangement in the form of concordats. The state may even grant certain privileges extending either to public recognition of the Church as a legal corporation, or even to its recognition (as everywhere in Europe once, and even yet in Spain) as the Church of the official state-religion. (IV, 2, p. 687 f. The Order of the Community.)

Cf. III, 3, p. 458 f.

1 KINGS 19$^{8-18}$ (V)

It may well be described as one of the most striking and therefore necessary experiences of our own age that this view (of Jaspers) has not been clearly demonstrated. Millions of our contemporaries have been constantly plunged from one frontier situation (in the most intense sense) to another. But what has it all meant to them in practice? Has anyone encountered the wholly other, and been changed by this encounter, as a result of taking part in the fighting in Russia or Africa or Normandy, of suffering the Hitler terror, of enduring aerial bombardment, hunger and imprisonment, of losing loved ones, of being in extreme danger of death dozens of times, and of having some sense of personal implication in the common guilt? Humanity is tough. It seems to have been largely capable of dealing with the confrontation of transcendence supposedly implied in these negations of its existence. Surely Jaspers himself noticed that it passed largely unscathed through the first world war, in retrospect of which he wrote his *Philosophie*. And if appearances do not deceive, we have also passed through the second unscathed. If any one has been changed in these years, it is certainly not in virtue of the extraordinary situations into which they have led him. According to the present trend, we may suppose that even on the morning after the Day of Judgment—if such a thing were possible—every cabaret, every night club, every newspaper firm eager for advertisements and subscribers, every nest of political fanatics, every pagan discussion group, indeed, every Christian tea-party and Church synod would resume business to the best of its ability, and with a new sense of opportunity, completely unmoved, quite uninstructed, and in no serious sense different from what it was before. Fire, drought, earthquake, war, pestilence, the darkening of the sun and similar phenomena are not the things to plunge us into real anguish, and

therefore to give us real peace. The Lord was not in the storm, the earthquake or the fire (v. 11 f.). He really was not. (III, 2, p. 114 f.
Phenomena of the Human.)

"Yet I have left me seven thousand in Israel . . ." (v. 18) . . . seven
thousand who have not conformed, who have not joined in the great
apostasy, and therefore a minority of Israel who are to be brought safely
through the fire of God's wrath and punishment. Now in the first instance
this settles the point that at any rate the prophet is not the only exception,
as he himself thinks; that he is not entirely alone with God. God has
seen to it that where he stands others also stand. But all the same we might
ask what do even these seven thousand prove for the whole, for Israel as
such? May it not be that even these seven thousand, too, only confirm
the fact that Israel as such is rejected? If we read further, however, we
see that these seven thousand . . . represent the whole, Israel as such. For
seven thousand is the number of " all the people, even all the children of
Israel " (20^{15}) in the story which immediately follows. And much later
(2 K. 24^{16}) seven thousand is also given as the number of the men of might
in Jerusalem who were carried into captivity by Nebuchadnezzar . . . It is
these seven thousand of 1 K. 19, and not the unfaithful majority, who
represent Israel as such. By " leaving " them God holds fast to Israel as
such, and it is decided that He has not rejected His people. When therefore (in the same breath with which judgment is announced on the majority)
the solitary Elijah is consoled by a reference to these seven thousand men,
he does not stand alone, but as the holder of his commission he is invisibly
surrounded by these seven thousand proved men. Even in his loneliness
he stands effectively before God for the whole of Israel, for Israel as such.
(II, 2, p. 270. The Election of the Community.)

2 THESSALONIANS 2^{1-17} (VI)

In the New Testament *mysterion* denotes an event in the world of time
and space which is directly initiated and brought to pass by God alone, so
that in distinction from all other events it is basically a mystery to human
cognition in respect of its origin and possibility. If it discloses itself to
man, this will be, not from without, but only from within, through itself,
and therefore once again only through God's revelation. The appearance
and development of certain demonic and ungodly powers, which in a
puzzling way are tolerated for a while by God, though they hasten to their
defeat and destruction, and hence to the revelation of their nothingness
and of God's sovereignty, can be called a *mysterion*, cf. the great mystery of
iniquity which precedes the final return of Jesus Christ (v. 7), or the whore
Babylon-Rome, which is drunk with the blood of the witnesses of Jesus
(Rev. 17^5). To be understood along the same lines is the partial hardening
of Israel which for the time being is simply to be noted and bewailed as a
fact (Rom. 11^{25}). As a rule, however, a *mysterion* is a form of the doing of

God's positive will, cf. Mk. 4^{11}; 1 Cor. 2^7; Col. 1^{27}; $2^{2f.}$; 1 Tim. 3^{16} etc. (IV, 4, p. 108. Baptism with Water.)

Cf. on John 20^{19-31} First Sunday After Easter (Quasimodogeniti).

REFORMATION (SUN)DAY

JOHN 2^{13-22} (I)

MATTHEW 5^{1-10} (Ib)

This poverty (Lk. 6^{20} correctly interpreted by Mt. 5^3), true and saving despair, is the gift of the Holy Spirit, the work of Jesus Christ. In this it resembles faith, of which it is a part. As the gift of the Holy Spirit and the work of Jesus Christ, it is known decisively in the knowledge of our own sin and therefore and primarily in the knowledge of the divine compassion, forgiving us our sins. Before Damascus Paul first sees and hears his Lord, then he falls to the ground, a trembling comes over him, and he is blinded. As the gift of the Holy Spirit and the work of Jesus Christ, this poverty is a reality of faith. That is, it does not consist abstractly in our own experiences of poverty, no matter how powerful. It consists concretely in the poverty of Christ as it became an event upon Golgatha. This alone is the radical and the final exposure of our poverty and in that way the ground of our riches (2 Cor. 8^9). As the gift of the Holy Spirit and the work of Jesus Christ, this poverty is a fundamental and comprehensive poverty. It is genuine despair, because it is saving despair. What is destroyed by it is not only our certainty, but also our uncertainty, and the disillusionments which lead up to it: not only our defiance but also our desperation, not only our illusions but also our complete absence of illusions, not only our good but also our bad conscience. It is despair about ourselves. Therefore it is despair about even the negative possibilities of the defining of human existence. Of course, it can and often enough—perhaps usually— does coincide with such negative possibilities. Concrete human folly, abjectness and weakness, which can be fixed and understood as such, are naturally intended . . . and on the basis of divine election they may be sanctified as signs of that laudable poverty in spirit, of that divine sorrow unto repentance of that true and saving despair . . . If they are " feelers " on man's side, it is not in any neutrality as general human possibilities. It is only as signs sanctified by divine election. It is only on the basis of a revelation which has already been enacted and received. They do not belong, then, to anything that man can know about himself from his own standpoint. Consequently they are " points of contact " newly posited by God, not present already in the nature of man. Therefore they are not the object of a natural theology under the third article. (I, 2, p. 265. The Freedom of Man for God.)

Cf. also Fourth Sunday After Easter (Cantate).

REVELATION 14⁶ᶠ. (II)
MATTHEW 10²⁴⁻³³ (III)

It was of value that the older Lutherans ... laid particular stress upon the thesis that the divine world-governance extends to all things and to each individual thing ... They were again wrestling with Democritus and Epicures, but also with Aristotle ...; with the view that some things and events are too small, too insignificant, too unimportant, indeed too futile, for us to be able to suppose that the Godhead will in any way be interested in them. *Minima non curat praetor.* Will God really concern himself with the growth of caterpillars in the grass sprouting in the province of Saxony in any given year? Or with the thread hanging from the beggar's coat? He does, they quite rightly answered, with a reference to Augustine: *Videte, quia minima non contemnit Deus; nam, si contemneret, non crearet.* (III, 3, p. 174. The Divine Ruling.)

The particular confessing, the express witness to God which His command claims, is particular because its decisive concern is undoubtedly with man's mouth, tongue and lips, with his talking and speaking. We must not try to be too spiritual at this point, or rather, too ethereal. The fact that the work of the mouth alone is not enough, that there is a mere lip confession resting on no true knowledge and therefore empty, does not alter in the slightest the fact that the confession of God which is always demanded is also a confession of the lips. It is in his spoken word that man, like God, comes out into the open, making himself clear, intelligible and in some way responsible, venturing forth and binding and committing himself. In his word man hazards himself. And it is demanded of him that in his word he shall continually hazard himself to God's glory, coming out into the open as a partisan of God ... Just as Jesus has bound Himself to speak and still speaks for men, so without doubt they on their side are bound to speak of him. If they fail to do the latter, they risk the loss of the former: v. 33. And if it is asked how what is impossible for man and is yet demanded can become an absolute necessity for him, the answer must be that He who gives man this commandment and imposes on him this obligation puts him also in the position to do what is demanded; indeed, that by His power He causes man to achieve what is demanded. (III, 4, p. 75 f. Confession.)

Cf. on Matthew 10²⁶⁻³³ June 25 Anniversary of the Augsburg Confession; also II, 2, p. 499.

GALATIANS 5¹⁻¹¹ (IV)

The Christian hopes in Jesus Christ. Can it hope in Him as the coming Judge? Yes, in Him as such, since as Judge He is the same as the One who then came in His resurrection and who is now present in the enlightening power of His Holy Spirit. Not an unknown judge of fable, but He who is well-known to the Christian comes as Judge of the quick and the dead and therefore as his Judge ... There can be no doubt that His judgment is the future of the whole world and therefore of the Christian too. There can be no doubt that the heart and mind and work of the Christian too, with all that all other men have either been or not been, done or not done, will then come truly and ultimately into the fire of a radical and incalculable testing. There can be no doubt that even among Christians many of those who are apparently first will be last and last first, and much of that which is thought to be first in the way of Christian thought and speech and action will be last and last first. Above all, there can be no doubt whose fire will burn and purify and sift, whose standard and judgment will reign and find application, who will set all men and all things, not in any light, but in His own light. There can thus be no doubt that those who know Him will look and move forward to His judgment, fire and testing, not with hesitant but with assured and unequivocally positive and therefore joyful expectation. If they wait for His grace which judges, and which cuts with pitiless severity in this judgment, they still wait for His grace. If they wait for His grace which is absolutely free, unmerited and sovereign in the execution of His judgment, they still wait for His grace. If they wait for His righteousness, as is inevitable since it is His coming which is expected, they wait for the righteousness of His grace. For this reason they are not afraid, but hope for righteousness (v. 5). In the words of *Qu.* 52 of the *Heidelberg Catechism*, the Christian finds comfort in the return of Christ to judge the quick and the dead, because with uplifted head he waits for the Judge from heaven who has already exposed Himself to the judgment of God for him, and taken away all cursing from Him, in order that He may receive him with all the elect—I omit the less satisfactory part of this fine statement—into heavenly joy and glory. (IV, 3, p. 922. The Subject of Hope and Hope.)

Cf. on Galatians 4^{22}–5^1 Fourth Sunday in Lent (Laetare); also III, 4, p. 604.

JOHN 8^{31-36} (V)

V. 34b: in the briefest of biblical formulations we have the whole doctrine of the bondage of the will. *Non potest non peccare* (not able not to sin) is what we have to say of the sinful, slothful man. His sin excludes his freedom, just as his freedom excludes his sin. There is no middle position ... The sinful, slothful man wills. He is a Hercules, the arbitrer of what he does. But he does what he does in the corruption of his will. He does not, therefore, do it *libero* but *servo arbitrio*. In a deeper sense than the poet had in mind, it is the curse of an evil deed that it inevitably gives birth to fresh evil. To be sure, the slothful man chooses—in that dreadful negation of true choosing—as he always did. But he chooses only on the path that he has entered. And on this path, however he may choose, he cannot choose as a true man (for he has turned aside from this genuine possibility) but in all his choices, having yielded to corruption, he can only act corruptly. His starting-point is the repudiation of his freedom. He cannot, therefore, do that which corresponds to his freedom. He necessarily does that which he could not do in the exercise of it. This is the bondage of the human will which is the bitterest characteristic of human misery . . . The liberation of man in Jesus is his new birth and conversion as it has taken place in Him. The freedom which man has and exercises in him is a new creation. In Him he is free from the committal of sin and for faith, obedience and gratitude. He is, therefore, genuinely free (" free indeed, " v. 36). (IV, 2, p. 495 f. The Sloth and Misery of Man.)

A first thing which characterises Christian faith is the fact that it consists in the orientation of man on Jesus Christ . . . We can say the same thing in another way. Faith is the human activity which is present and future, which is there, in the presence of the living Jesus Christ and of what has taken place in Him, with a profound spontaneity and a native freedom, but also with an inevitability in face of His actuality. The reverse is equally true: with an inevitability, but with a native freedom . . . The second thing that we have to say of faith in its relationship to Jesus Christ as its object is that, as it is related to, it is also based upon it. We do not compromise its character as a free human act if we say that as a free human act . . . it has its origin in the very point on which it is orientated. It is also the work of Jesus Christ who is its object. It is the will and decision and achievement of Jesus Christ the Son of God that it takes place as a free human act, that man is of himself ready and willing and actually begins to believe in Him. The two things are not a contradiction but belong together. If the Son makes us free, we are free indeed (v. 36). The Son makes a man free to believe in Him. Therefore faith in Him is the act of a right freedom, not although but just because it is the work of the Son. (IV, 1, p. 744 f. Faith and Its Object.)

Cf. on Galatians 4²²⁻³¹; 5¹ᵃ Fourth Sunday in Lent (Laetare).

ROMANS 3¹⁹ᵇ⁻²⁸   (VI)

The *sola fide* does not actually occur in the Pauline texts. Yet it was not an importation into the texts, but a genuine interpretation of what Paul himself said without using the word *sola*, when Luther translated v. 28: " . . . by faith alone . . . " Say what we will about the possibility and the freedom and the right and the compulsion and the practical necessity of the doing of works—the works of the law or the works of faith—according to Paul a man is not justified by the fact that he does these works, and therefore to that extent he is justified without them. And the faith by which a man is justified stands alone against this " without " even though it is not without works, even though it is a faith which " worketh by love " (Gal. 5⁶). But if he is not justified by the works of the holy Law of God, but by faith, then obviously he is justified only by faith, by faith alone, *sola fide*. (IV, 1, p. 622. Justification by Faith Alone.)

Cf. IV, 1, p. 561.

TWENTY-FOURTH SUNDAY AFTER TRINITY

MATTHEW 9[18-26]   (I)

As Jesus acts in His commission and power it is obvious that God does not will that which troubles and torments and disturbs and destroys man. He does not will the entanglement and humiliation and distress and shame that the being of man in the cosmos and as a cosmic being means for man. He does not will the destruction of man, but his salvation. And he wills this in the basic and elemental sense that he should be made whole. He does not will his death, but life. He does not negate but affirms the natural existence of man. And He does not affirm but negates that which attacks and frustrates it, the shadow of death and prison in which man is necessarily a stranger to himself. And as His affirmation is joyful to the very core, His negation is in every sense unwilling and vexed and wrathful. The sorrow which openly or secretly fills the heart of man is primarily in the heart of God. The shame which comes on man is primarily a violation of His own glory. The enemy who does not let man breathe and live, harassing him with fear and pain, is primarily His enemy. He is wrathful against His own true enemy, which is also the true enemy of man, when He is wrathful against sin. And the coming of His kingdom, His seizure of power on earth, is centrally and decisively the power and revelation of the contradiction and opposition in which, speaking and acting in His own cause, He takes the side of man and enters the field against this power of destruction in all its forms. That is why the activity of the Son of Man, as an actualisation of His Word and commentary on it, necessarily has the crucial and decisive form of liberation, redemption, restoration, normalisation. " Cast away, dear brothers free, All your woes, Wants and foes, All needs are met in Me. " He goes right past sin, beyond it and through it, directly to man himself; for His purpose is always with man. And, forgiving his sins, He tackles the needs and fears which torment him, and lifts them from him: " Go in peace, and be whole of thy plague " (Mk. 5[34]).

Why (v. 24, cf. Mk. 5[40]) was Jesus so severe? He was face to face with the cult of death. Death was something which they thought it a self-evident law of reason and custom to regard as an unassailable fact and therefore to treat with pious sentimentality as a supreme power. Jesus denied both the law and the power, cf. Mk. 5[39, 41]. The reality of God, omnipotent in His mercy, is set against the obvious reality of death. Which will prove to be the greater, the true reality? Jesus alone can see how the decision will go. He Himself stands in this decision and makes it. And

His solitary No to death, in the power of His solitary Yes to the omnipotent mercy of God, is the reason for His severity in that house of death. When He enters this house, it can no longer be a house of death. (IV, 2, pp. 225–227. The Royal Man.)

Cf. III, 4, pp. 356–374.

COLOSSIANS 1 [9-14]					(II)

The autonomy of our existence has been taken from us. He has taken it to Himself; He has not taken away our existence from us. We have not ceased to be ourselves. We are still free. But in that existence He has left us without root or soil or country, " having transferred us to the kingdom of the Son of his love " (v. 13), having Himself become our root and soil and country. From the standpoint of His incarnation and exaltation, the fact that we are translated into the kingdom of the Son of God means that as the Second Adam He has assumed human nature, that He has united it to His divine person, so that our humanity, our existence in this nature, no longer has any particularity of its own, but belongs only to Him. And from the standpoint of the reconciliation and justification effected in Him, it means that, bearing our punishment, achieving the obedience we did not achieve, and keeping the faith we did not keep, He acted once and for all in our place. We cannot, therefore, seek our own being and activity, so far as they still remain to us, in ourselves but only in Him. (I, 2, p. 391. The Life of the Children of God.)

The kingdom of darkness (v. 13) is the conclusion in disobedience (Rom. 11[32]), the unity into which the divine verdict had previously fused all men. Those who are translated by Him into the kingdom of His dear Son come out of this kingdom and leave it behind them—being delivered by " the Father of mercies and God of all comfort " (2 Cor. 1[3]). Those who have their future in the one kingdom have their past in the other. (IV, 1, p. 502.)

JOHN 11 [32-45]					(III)

" What troubled Him in the first instance (v. 33 f.) was this display of weeping, this tribute, as it were, to His opponent, death, this desire of men to grovel in their wounds, this tacit magnifying of the omnipotence of death which is really a murmuring against God. But His vexation extended beyond this to His opponent, the prince of this world, who had succeeded in reducing to such abject slavery the man who was called to bruise his head " (F. Zündel, *Jesus*, 1922, p. 236). The short statement follows very oddly in v. 35: " Jesus wept." He too? Yes, He too. We may perhaps recall at this point the Pauline: " Weep with them that weep " (Rom. 12[15]). But His weeping with them means that He is fighting for them. It is therefore misunderstood by those who rather finely said: " Behold how he loved him " (v. 36) as well as by those who more maliciously suggested: v. 37. For on the way to the grave of Lazarus, weeping with those who wept in face of the unequivocally revealed reality of death, the " participation " of Jesus is not a compromise. It is itself a resolute No to this reality. Looking this death and its death more soberly in the face than anyone else, He is already on the way to banish it from the world. (IV, 2, p. 227. The Royal Man.)

DANIEL 12¹⁻⁴ (IV)

III, 2, p. 619 and III, 3, pp. 455–457.

JOHN 5¹⁹⁻²⁹ (V)

What is hope, and what does it mean for the Christian, who, since Jesus Christ has not yet spoken His universal, generally perceptible and conclusive Word, finds himself in that dwindling and almost hopeless minority as His witness to the rest of the world? If the great Constantinian illusion is now being shattered, the question becomes the more insistent . . . What can a few Christians or a pathetic group like the Christian community really accomplish with their scattered witness to Jesus Christ? What do these men really imagine or expect to accomplish in the great market, on the battle-field or in the great prison or mad-house which human life always seems to be? (Is. 53¹). And what are we to say concerning the countless multitudes who either *ante* or *post Christum natum* have had no opportunity to hear this witness? . . . The Christian is obviously burying his head in the sand if he is not disturbed by these questions and does not find his whole ministry of witness challenged by them . . . Yet he is permitted and commanded . . . as a Christian, and therefore unambiguously and unfalteringly, to hope, i.e., in face of what seems by human reckoning to be an unreachable majority to count upon it quite unconditionally that Jesus Christ has risen for each and every one of this majority too; that His Word . . . is spoken for them as it is spoken personally and quite undeservedly for him; that the same Holy Spirit who has been incomprehensibly strong enough to enlighten his own dark heart will perhaps one day find a little less trouble with them; and decisively that when the day of the coming of Jesus Christ in consummating revelation does at last dawn it will quite definitely be that day when, not he himself, but the One whom he expects as a Christian, will know how to reach them, so that the quick and the dead, those who came and went both *ante* and *post* Christum, will hear His voice, whatever its signification for them (v. 25). (IV, 3, p. 918. The Subject of Hope and Hope.)

Cf. on Romans 13¹¹⁻¹⁴ First Sunday in Advent; on Luke 12³⁵⁻⁴⁰ New Year's Eve, and on Revelation 3¹⁴⁻²² Day of Prayer and Fasting.

REVELATION 7⁹⁻¹⁷ (VI)

Cf. on Revelation 3¹⁻⁶ Second Sunday in Advent; also IV, 4, p. 14.

TWENTY-FIFTH SUNDAY AFTER TRINITY

MATTHEW 24$^{15-28}$ (I)
1 THESSALONIANS 4$^{13-18}$ (II)

To understand the New Testament hope, we must fix our eyes firmly on three points: 1. the relationship between the crucifixion of Jesus as the event in which man's sin and guilt and consequent death are abolished and time is fulfilled, and His resurrection as the preliminary indication of this event establishing faith in Jesus as the Deliverer from death; 2. the relationship between the resurrection of Jesus as the preliminary indication inaugurating the last time and establishing the Church and its mission, and His return in glory as the conclusive, general and definitive revelation of this event; and 3. and above all, the being of man with Him which is promised to and actualised in faith in Jesus, and in virtue of which he has his own death and the dawn of the last time behind him in the death of Jesus, is born again in His resurrection to a life in God concealed throughout the last time, and will be revealed in glory as one who has this life when Jesus returns in glory as the goal of the last time. (III, 2, p. 623. Ending Time.)

The ten virgins (Matthew 25) are supposed to go out and meet the bridegroom. This is the meaning of *hyp'antesis* (v. 1) or *ap'antesis* (v. 6), and it is implied by the description in v. 10 of their going out to escort the bridegroom and accompany him to the marriage feast with their lamps alight. Exactly the same picture is given when Paul states that the community, both living and departed, will be " caught up . . . in the clouds, to meet the Lord in the air " (v. 17). With Jesus Himself, His community as such, in His service, will come and be revealed in the world in glory, and will even assist the Lord in the judgment of Israel (Mt. 19^{28}), in the judgment of the world and angels (1 Cor. 6$^{2f.}$), and in His kingly rule (1 Tim. 2^{12}; 1 Cor. 4^8; Rev. 5^{10}), so that it can be called a " royal priesthood " (1 Pet. 2^9), and it can be said that the whole creation is waiting for this revelation of the sons of God (Rom. 8^{19}). (III, 2, p. 505. Jesus, Lord of Time; cf. also on Matthew 25$^{1-13}$ Sunday Next Before Advent.)

Cf. on John 11$^{1-27}$ Sixteenth Sunday After Trinity; also III, 2, pp. 510 ff.

PHILIPPIANS 3$^{7-14}$ (IIb)

The justified man exists . . . as he hopes . . . for a final goal of his hope, for the solution of the riddle and removal of the contradiction, the revelation of the mystery of his history in all those transitions which he continually has to make. He does not grope in the dark. He knows the way on which he finds himself. He knows that he is not caught up in a futile vacillation or movement in a circle . . . He can hold to that which is promised, to the unshakeable and indestructible thing which cannot be lost, because it cannot be revoked, only in the assured but continually renewed striding, only in the joyful and confident but hazardous and laborious movement which is described by Paul in v. 12: " Not as though I had already attained, or were already made perfect . . ." (IV, 1, p. 602 f. The Justification of Man.)

We have only to think again of 1 Cor. 9$^{24f.}$ and Phil. 3$^{12f.}$ to realise and continually to remember that as the " firstfruits of his creatures " (Jas. 1^{18}) Christians are those who are called by God, reconciled and exalted to fellowship with Him in Jesus Christ, and instructed by the Holy Ghost. It is their portion as such to seek, to set their affection, to go, to run, to press on and to sacrifice. They are with the Lord and they follow and serve Him, but they are not themselves lords. He alone is the Lord. His grace is sufficient for them. (IV, 2, p. 377. The Direction of the Son; cf. also on 1 Corinthians 9$^{24-27}$ Septuagesima.)

The compulsion obeyed in conversion is not abstract; it is not blind or deaf. It is the compulsion of a permission and ability which have been granted. It is that of the free man who as such can only exercise his freedom. The omnipotence of God creates and effects in the man awakened to conversion a true ability. He who previously vegetated to death under a hellish compulsion, in a true comparison with the driftwood carried downstream, may now live wholly of himself and be a man. The coming, the opening up of this " may " is the revelation of the divine summons to halt and proceed; the power which makes his life life in conversion. Because and as he is given this permission and ability, he necessarily stands at this point. He *must* leave those things which are behind, and reach forth unto those things which are before, pressing towards the mark. (IV, 2, p. 578. The Awakening to Conversion.)

LUKE 18$^{1-8}$ (III)

On the basis of the freedom of God Himself God is conditioned by the prayer of faith . . . The living and genuinely immutable God is not an irresistible fate before which man can only keep silence, passively awaiting and accepting the benefits or blows which it ordains. There is no such thing as a Christian resignation in which we have either to submit to a fate of this kind or to come to terms with it. Resignation (whether accompanied by astrology or not) is always the disconsolate consolation of unbelief. There is, of course, a Christian patience and submission, as there is also a Christian waiting upon God. But it shows itself to be genuine by the fact that it is always accompanied by the haste and restlessness of the prayer which runs to God and beseeches Him, by the haste which rests on the knowledge that God takes our distress to heart, and expects that we for our part will take His mercy to heart and really live by it, so that in our mutual turning to one another He may be our God and therefore a Helper in our distress, allowing Himself to be moved by our entreaties. (II, 1, p. 511. The Constancy and Omnipotence of God.)

The royal Man (Jesus) shares as such the strange destiny which falls on God in His people and the world—to be the One who is ignored and forgotten and despised and discounted by men. Among other men this One who is truly exalted is not as such a great man. He has nothing of what the world counts as recognition and authority and honour and success. His place is not one of the recognised peaks on the sunnier side of human life. His kingdom has neither the pomp nor the power, the extent nor the continuance, of even the smallest of human kingdoms which all the same it overshadows and questions. His power is present to men in the form of weakness, His glory in that of lowliness, His victory in that of defeat. The final concealment is that of His suffering and death as a condemned criminal. He who alone is rich is present as the poorest of the poor. (IV, 2, p. 167. The Royal Man.)

Cf. IV, 2, p. 647.

JAMES 5$^{7-11}$ (IV)

Cf. on Matthew 25 Twenty-Sixth Sunday After Trinity and Sunday Next Before Advent; also III, 2, p. 505.

MATTHEW 12$^{38-42}$ (V)

DANIEL 5 (VI)

TWENTY-SIXTH SUNDAY AFTER TRINITY

MATTHEW 25$^{31-46}$ (I)

But what is the community that may enjoy this expectation? This has not yet been decided. It will be decided when Jesus comes again: 2 Cor. 5^{10}. And it is from this future that the parable looks back so strikingly to the present time when Jesus is still hidden. The issue will be decided by the attitude and conduct of the community to Him while He is still hidden. Then it will be known what the community will be which will stand at His right hand in this future. But where is He hidden now? With God, at the right hand of the Father? in His Word and sacraments? in the mystery of His Spirit, which bloweth where it listeth? All this is true enough, but it is presupposed in this parable, and the further point is made, on which everything depends, that He is no less present, though hidden, in all who are now hungry, thirsty, strangers, naked, sick and in prison. Wherever in this present time between the resurrection and the *parousia* one of these is waiting for help (for food, drink, lodging, clothes, a visit, assistance), Jesus Himself is waiting. Wherever help is granted or denied, it is granted or denied to Jesus Himself. For these are the least of His brethren. They represent the world for which He died and rose again, with which He made Himself supremely one, and declared Himself in solidarity. It is for them that He sits at the right hand of the Father, so that no one can know Him in His majesty, or honour and love Him as the

Son of God, unless he shows concern for these least of His brethren. No one can call God his Father in Christ's name unless he treats these least as his brethren. This is the test which at the last judgment will decide concerning the true community which will inherit the kingdom: whether in this time of God's mercy and patience, this time of its mission, it has been the community which has succoured its Lord by giving unqualified succour to them in this needy world. It will be well with it if it has obviously done this, if it has been affected by the concrete miseries of the world, not passing by on the other side with haughty disdain, but being simply and directly human, with no excuses for the contrary . . . Such is the question addressed to the community of the present by the approaching *parousia*. It is posed to all its members, to its orders and cultus and preaching and theology. What has all this had to do with the afflicted who as such are Jesus' brethren? Has the community been first and foremost human in all that it has done? (III, 2, p. 507 f. Man in His Time.)

In diaconate the community explicitly accepts solidarity with the least of little ones (v. 40, 45), with those who are in obscurity and are not seen, with those who are pushed to the margin and perhaps the very outer margin of the life of human society, with fellow-creatures who temporarily at least, and perhaps permanently, are useless and insignificant and perhaps even burdensome and destructive. In the diaconate these men are recognised to be brothers of Jesus Christ according to the significant tenor of the parable of the Last Judgment, and therefore the community confesses Jesus Christ Himself as finally the hungry, thirsty, naked, homeless, sick, imprisoned man, and the royal man as such. In the diaconate the community makes plain its witness to Him as the Samaritan service to the man who has fallen among thieves—a service fulfilled in company with Him as the true Neighbour of this lost man. In the diaconate it goes and does likewise (Luke 10[29f.]). And woe to it if it does not, if its witness is not service in this elementary sense! For if not, even though its proclamation of Christ is otherwise ever so powerful, it stands hopelessly on the left hand among the goats. If not, even though its zeal in other respects is ever so ardent, it is on the steep slope which leads to eternal punishment. Without this active solidarity with the least of little ones, without this concrete witness to Jesus the Crucified, who as such is the Neighbour of the lost, its witness may be ever so pure and full at other points, but it is all futile. (IV, 3, p. 391. The Ministry of the Community.)

Cf. I, 2, p. 429; IV, 1, p. 106.

2 Thessalonians 1[3-10]   (II)
Cf. on John 13[31-35] Fifth Sunday in Lent (Judica); also IV, 3, p. 614.

Genesis 19[12-29]   (III)
It should be understood that in faith we are not asked to look past the

God who lives for us and stare into the abyss. We have not to fear that it might again threaten us, that we might again be swallowed up by it. We apprehend by faith God's justifying and rewarding righteousness, and it is the unbelief of Lot's wife to try to look back and again reckon or even trifle with the reality or the possibility of damnation and death. For this is not a serious calculation but a wanton trifling. It can only be a false Christian earnestness which causes a man to suspend his faith as it were, to lay aside for a moment the decision about his salvation contained in God's revelation, and to place himself at the critical point where it is seen that the end of one way is eternal glory and of the other way everlasting fire ... We are clearly invited by this summons to give ourselves to the God who lives for us and saves us by His life for us. But the reference to the condemning and punishing operation of God's righteousness means ... that we are to understand God's life for us and therefore our deliverance from judgment as His mercy by which there comes to us that which we have not deserved and of which we are not worthy. (II, 1, p. 392 f. The Mercy and Righteousness of God; cf. also pp. 159–161.)

2 CORINTHIANS 5$^{1\text{-}10}$ (IV)

As I see it, we may also inquire at least whether it is really certain that this passage (vv. 1–5) speaks only of the individual anthropological *eschaton* and does not ... bear also (although not exclusively) an ecclesiological and eschatological sense. Mention is made in v. 1 of our earthly house which is a tabernacle. This house is obviously temporary and will be pulled down. But as we move towards the pulling down of this house there is already prepared for us " a building of God, an house not made with hands, eternal in the heavens." In the first house we " groan " (vv. 2–4), i.e., with reference to the transition from the first to the second. As we desire to be clothed upon, or covered, by this house from heaven, we await fearfully the moment when the first house will have gone and we are not yet surrounded and protected by the second, when we are found naked, and find ourselves " on the street." It is no good removing out of the old if there is no assurance of the new. But correction and comfort are at hand. God Himself assures us of a certain entrance into the new, and therefore a calm evacuation of the old (v. 5), by giving us the pledge of the Spirit in our hearts (cf. 1 Cor. 1^{22}). To what does all this refer? According to the verses which precede and follow there can be no doubt that it has an individual and anthropological reference to the transition from our present abode in the body ... to a corresponding abode with the Lord ... On the other hand, the " we " of whom Paul says all this are not in the last resort a plurality of individuals who, taught by the Christian religion, engage in anxious and hopeful reflection concerning their individual death and that which lies beyond. What we have here is another instance of the apostolic and ecclesiastical plural ... The concepts "building" and "house" are not anthropological terms in rabbinic Judaism. If they are to be understood as such (which is possible, but unnecessary), we shall have to appeal to Mandaean or Iranian sources. In the New Testament, however, these terms are used with a thoroughgoing ecclesiological connotation. In view of these various points it seems obvious to me that by "our earthly house, which is a tabernacle" and which is therefore doomed to perish, we have first and comprehensively to understand the community in its present form, and only then, and included in this, the present physical existence of the individual Christian as he lives in the body. Similarly, by "the house not made with hands, eternal in the heavens," we have first and comprehensively to understand the new form of the community (identical with the *politeuma* of Phil. 3^{20} and the heavenly Jerusalem of Rev. 21^2), which here and now is future and transcendent, but which is perfect and comes down from heaven, from God, upon it, and only then the specific incorruptible *oiketerion*, the eternal tabernacle (Lk. 16^9), of the individual Christian which is included in it. (IV, 2, p. 628 f. The Holy Spirit and the Upbuilding of the Christian Community.)

No matter how it comes, even for the Christian the end means thus far and no further. You have had your time and no more remains. You have been given your chances, possibilities and powers of varying degree and nature. It is now all up with them, and you can expect no more. This was your life as a witness of Jesus Christ. This was what you made of it according to the measure of your faith and love, in acceptance of the task laid upon you, in the use of the powers granted for its execution, within the limits of your obedience and faithfulness. You cannot alter anything, or improve anything, or rectify anything. With the totality of whatever you have done, of your completed life work, you must now encounter your Lord, come before His judgment throne, and pass through the fire in which it will be definitively shown who and what you are, and what you have done or not done as such. Been and done! *Non plus ultra*! "Forth thou must go, thine hour hath run its course" (Schiller). (IV, 3, p. 926. The Subject of Hope and Hope.)

Cf. II, 2, p. 654 and IV, 1, p. 728.

MATTHEW 25$^{14-30}$ (V)

The community has the task of turning the property of its Lord to profitable use. What is entrusted is His Gospel, and His Spirit. The interval between the resurrection and the *parousia* is the time of Jesus because it is the time of the community and its service. His final revelation will therefore be critical for His community because it will reveal that, entrusted with His Gospel and Spirit, it has really served Him. It will be admitted to the marriage feast only if it has increased in good and loyal service the comparatively few goods entrusted to it. The Word which belongs to it seeks new hearers; it must not cease to pass it on to others. The Spirit given to it seeks new dwelling-places and new witnesses; it must so obey the Spirit that its witness makes new dwelling-places and evolves new witnesses. This is the whole purpose of the witnessing time, the time of the community . . . The parable shows us (v. 24 f.) that the conduct of the servant who buried his talent was not merely unprofitable, but positively lazy and wicked. It was not merely a refusal of service, but rebellion against the Lord. Thus the community which in the interim period is not a missionary community, winning others by its witness according to the measure of its power, will be banished, at the return and final revelation of the Lord, into outer darkness, where there can be only weeping and gnashing of teeth instead of the promised banquet. At the end of the time between the community will be justified before the Lord, and will stand and have a share in His glory, only if in the time between it has understood and realised that all its faith and love, all its confession and works, are nothing at all without daring and aggression, without sowing in hope; only if it has understood and practised its witness as a commission. For the time between is not the time of an empty absence of the Lord, nor is it the time of a bewildering delay in His return, in which it is enough for the community to maintain and help itself as best it can. On the contrary, it is the time of God's patience and purpose, and it is therefore the business of the community to recognise the character of this time, and therefore never to think that it has plenty of time in this time, but to " buy up " this time in relation to those who are " without " (Col. 4^5; Eph. 5^{16}). It can never have enough time here and now for the fulfilment of its task. For it knows what the world does not know, and it owes it to its Lord to make it known to the world. (III, 2, p. 506 f. Man in His Time.)

Cf. III, 4, p. 603.

REVELATION 19[11-16] (VI)

What we have here is a description of the *parousia* of Christ. But we are also told in v. 14: " And the armies which were in heaven followed him . . ." They obviously have and reveal their true being as the host of heaven in the Word of God whom they follow and accompany as He comes from heaven to earth. Similarly, the picture in Rev. 4—the great heavenly doxology offered by the four and twenty elders, the seven spirits and the four living creatures gathered round the throne of God—is only as it were made actual and concrete, or at any rate explained, by that of Rev. 5, in which the Lamb slain (v. 6), the Lion of the tribe of Judah, the Root of David (v. 5), comes forward and takes the book with the seven seals (v. 8), and a corresponding doxology is offered to Him by that assembly, accompanied this time by ten thousand times ten thousand angels and thousands of thousands (v. 11). It is also of a piece with this that there is only one passage in the Bible, namely, in the account of the nativity (Lk. 2¹³), which speaks of a manifestation and function of the *plethos*, i.e., of the fulness or totality of the heavenly hosts on earth. (III, 3, p. 448 f. The Kingdom of Heaven.)

Cf. II, 2, p. 96 f.

DAY OF PRAYER AND FASTING

LUKE 13¹⁻⁹ (I)

It is for the sake of Him who is to come, for the sake of the Lamb of God who will bear away the sin of the world (Jn. 1²⁹), that the sustaining long-suffering of God (cf. Rom. 3²⁵ᶠ·) which befalls the vessels of wrath (Rom. 9²²) is possible and necessary. This bearing to an unexpected end is the secret of the history of Israel—and therefore also the secret of the continuing existence of the Synagogue alongside the Church. He not only waits for its repentance. But in so doing He wills it as a sign of His wrath and freedom which is also the abiding sign of God's mercy. "No power in the world will be able to extirpate Judaism. Indeed, not even the Jews themselves will be able to extirpate themselves so long as God's long-suffering endures this year also (Lk. 13⁸) the vessels of wrath" (E. Peterson, *Die Kirche aus Juden und Heiden*, 1933, p. 34). It may be asked whether the Church does not actually need the intrinsically so incomprehensible counterpart of this Israel which after the fulfilment of its hopes repeats its old obduracy and in so doing is carried towards its hope. It has in any case repeatedly to learn from the existence of the Synagogue, as a living commentary on the Old Testament, from what sort of "lump" (Rom. 9²¹) it has itself been taken, how it is with man who is found by God's grace, and in the reflection of this knowledge how it is with the grace of God itself, how deeply God has humiliated Himself on man's behalf in order to exalt him so highly. (II, 2, p. 226. The Judgment and the Mercy of God.)

ROMANS 2¹⁻¹² (II)

God does not renounce His government when He exercises patience. If God gives further opportunity to sinful man and grants him life, it is perhaps because, as in the case of the Ninevites (Jonah 4), he has already repented and converted. Ezekiel 18²¹ᶠ· is obviously to be understood on this presupposition . . . Or else the patience of God is exercised with the aim and intention of inducing his future repentance and conversion. Paul seems to speak of this in Romans 2⁴ when he asks the impenitent Jew whether he despises the riches of God's mercy, patience and long-suffering. The same point is made in Romans 9²²ᶠ· . . . and again in 2 Peter 3⁹. It was in this sense that in 1 Timothy 1¹⁶ Paul described himself, who later became the type of faith, as an object of the *makrothumia* of Jesus Christ. Under this heading we may also include the remarkable recapitulation of a constantly recurring situation in Israel's history at the beginning of the Book of Judges. According to this survey there is a repeated cycle of Israel's apostasy, God's wrath and Israel's deliverance to its enemies, followed by a new invitation to Israel to return to God, a new manifestation of God's help and deliverance, and then again a fresh apostasy, a fresh outburst of divine wrath and a fresh deliverance to the surrounding nations (Judges 2¹¹⁻²²).—But this raises a problem which has so often involved lax and unworthy conceptions of God's patience. What is the real aim and intention of God when He exercises patience? What is this human penitenace for the sake of which, in prospect or retrospect, God contains His anger, sometimes refusing to execute punishment, but giving men further opportunities of life, sometimes punishing only one, but leaving others the gifts of life, sometimes mightily destroying but no less mightily saving? Indeed, is there anywhere or at any time a real act of human penitence for the sake of which it is worth while to God to spare men and to give them time and life? Was the human race any better after the Flood than before it? Did it not immediately think it right to build the Tower of Babel? Was not all its penitent zeal only too much like Israel's passing cry for help in the time of the Judges? Where is there in the presentation of the Bible itself a single penitent whose existence really justifies the patience of God and therefore the preservation of the creature? Abraham, Isaac or Jacob? Moses or David? Are there any genuine exceptions to what we read in Isaiah 65¹ᶠ·....? What, then, is the meaning of the patience of God? Does it not mean that God allows Himself to be mocked? For when and where will not both the actual and the anticipated penitence prove a disappointment? (II, 1, p. 414 f. The Patience and Wisdom of God.)

MATTHEW 12³⁰⁻³⁷   (III)

When Jesus encountered men, there were those who spoke all manner of evil against the Son of Man—although this could be forgiven, because it rested on a failure to see or understand His existence and words and acts. And there could also be a very different (and unforgivable) speaking against the Holy Ghost, the denial and calumniation of the revealed and recognised secret of His existence and words and acts. The Pharisees, who saw His work but explained it as a work of the devil, thus condemning as evil the good fruits of the good tree, had need to ask themselves whether they were not guilty of this blasphemy (vv. 31–35). Either way, however, the saying in v. 30 is true and basic ... a saying which J. A. Bengel has rightly interpreted: *Non valet neutralitas in regno Dei.* (IV, 2, p. 150. The Royal Man.)

ISAIAH 5¹⁻⁷   (IV)

MATTHEW 11$^{16-24}$ (V)

" This generation " is described as angry with John the Baptist because of his asceticism . . . and with Jesus because of His freedom from asceticism . . . True wisdom is always different from what this generation has expected and desired, and therefore the latter, like the disappointed children in the market-place, believes itself to have reason to complain: v. 17. What are the representatives of wisdom to do? Should they determine their conduct accordingly, dancing when there is piping and lamenting when there is mourning? No, but as they continue to do undeviatingly in face of these complaints what as wise men they must do, it happens that wisdom is justified and justifies itself in its works, i.e., in that which the wise as such must faithfully do . . . For the true works of wisdom are the works of its representatives so long as the latter—and what else is to be expected when they are John the Baptist and Jesus?—will only remain faithful and obedient. They, too, do not need to look for any other justification for their works. They are justified as wisdom justifies itself in and by their works. (II, 1, p. 436. The Patience and Wisdom of God.)

REVELATION 3$^{14-22}$ (VI)

Time as the time of New Testament man is time ruled by the Lord who has already come but is still to be manifested . . . It is ruled and limited by Him: v. 20. The time in which men now exist is simply the time between His knocking and entering. As this " last hour " (1 Jn. 2^{18}), it is wholly His hour, even though it is also an hour of time and belongs to time as such. It should be noted how closely its beginning and end are brought together in the Gospel of John: 5$^{24, 25}$ . . . There is no identification of the beginning and end (note the future in v. 25), but it is quite evident that there can be no question of any other decision, judgment, or ruling apart from that of the One who here stands at the beginning and end on the almost imperceptible line between them. In this interval, therefore, the world can only be transitory (1 Cor. 7^{31}; 1 Jn. 2^{17}). Now that the last hour has struck, the world can only retire. Moreover, in this interval the world has neither breath nor space nor opportunity to make independent claims or to exercise influences different from and perhaps even opposed to those of the Lord. Its end, i.e., the manifestation of its end in and with that of the Lord, is too near for this (1 Cor. 10^{11}), as is also the beginning of another world, commencing with the manifestation of the Lord, of the new heaven and the new earth (2 Pet. 3^{13}). The vanishing of the night and the breaking of the day (1 Thess. 5$^{4f.}$; Rom. 13^{12}) have begun and can no longer be stopped. Because the same Lord stands at the beginning and the end, because He is the Alpha and the Omega, the One who is and as such the One who was and the One who comes, because He is at both points the *pantokrator* (Rev. 1^8), the time between, which is no longer that of His first *parousia* but not yet that of His second, is His time, the time ruled by Him. (III, 4, p. 581 f. The Unique Opportunity; cf. also on Romans 13[11-14] First Sunday in Advent and on Luke 12[35-40] New Year's Eve.)

Cf. I, 1, p. 247 [283]; II, 1, p. 54.

SUNDAY NEXT BEFORE ADVENT

MATTHEW 25[1-13]   (I)

In this chapter the community is asked whether it understands and takes seriously and turns to good account its present existence under the lordship of Jesus in the form of the Spirit as considered in relation to the future ... It is asked whether it is active in relation to the new coming of the Lord, or whether it is merely passive ... When Jesus is finally revealed, the Church of the interim will stand at His side, with its testimony to the whole world. This is the promise of the parable (vv. 1–13). But it also contains a challenge. Five virgins are wise and five foolish ... The parable is controlled by the question whether oil is available to replenish the lamps at the critical moment. If the lamps stand for the witness of the community, with which it can and should stand at the side of the returning Lord at the end of time, the oil represents something which makes this witness vital and strong not only now but then, something which is essential if it is to render this supreme service in the final revelation, because, if it does not have it, it cannot acquire it, and it will be unable to render this supreme service. The parable asks ... whether the community will have this absolutely indispensable something. It is a matter of that which will make its witness equal to the revelation of its Lord in this decisive test, even though it may have failed a thousand times in the interval. It is a matter of the harmony in which it must find itself with Him for all its human frailty and perversity if it is to stand at His side in face of the world. What is meant is clearly the self-witness of Jesus by the Holy Spirit apprehended in faith and love. This is what founded the community of the intervening time. This is the content of its witness. This alone can give its witness vitality and strength. This is the only pledge of its hope, constant in all its inconstancy. This is the vital element in virtue of which the community can be equal to its returning Lord for all its lowliness, associating itself with Him and having a place at His side in the final revelation. The parable does not ask the community concerning its witness as such. It presupposes that it will finally be there with its lamps burning and shining. It asks concerning the oil to furnish these lamps of witness at the decisive moment when its witness reaches its goal; and therefore, since the goal may be reached any moment, concerning that which makes its witness possible here and now, in the interim period. What is its attitude to the source which alone can preserve it? What is its attitude to the self-witness of Jesus now given to it by the Holy Spirit? How about its faith in Him and love to Him? If it lacks that which is necessary enough now but absolutely indispensable at the end, its hope will prove to be its judgment, its witness will be lacking when its hope is on the very brink of fulfilment, and it will be incapacitated at the very moment of its supreme service. Let the community see to it that it is wise and not foolish. Let it see to it that its relation to the Jesus Christ who was yesterday and is to-day is such that it can only encounter and serve as His community the One who will live and reign for ever. (III, 2, p. 505 f. Man in His Time.)

Cf. on Luke 12³⁴⁻⁴⁰ New Year's Eve.

2 PETER 3³⁻¹⁴ (II)

" Where hope is wanting, however clearly and elegantly we discourse of faith, it is certain we have it not. For if faith is . . . a firm persuasion of the truth of God—a persuasion that it can never be false, never deceive, never be in vain, those who have received this assurance must at the same time expect that God will perform his promises . . . Faith believes that God is true; hope expects that in due season he will manifest his truth. Faith believes that he is our Father; hope expects that he will always act the part of Father towards us. Faith believes that eternal life has been given to us; hope expects that it will one day be revealed. Faith is the foundation on which hope rests; hope nourishes and sustains faith. For as no man can expect anything from God without previously believing his promises, so, on the other hand, the weakness of our faith, which might grow weary and fall away, must be supported and cherished by patient hope and expectation. For this reason Paul justly says, ' We are saved by hope ' (Rom. 8²⁴). For while hope silently waits for the Lord, it restrains faith from hastening on with too much precipitation, confirms it when it might waver in regard to the promises of God or begin to doubt of their truth, refreshes it when it might be fatigued, extends its view to the final goal, so as not to allow it to give up in the middle of the course, or at the very outset. In short, by constantly renovating and reviving, it is ever and anon furnishing more vigour for perserverance " (Calvin, *Institutio*, III, 2, 42). How much need faith has of hope may be seen from the innumerable temptations which assail and shake those who would cling to the Word of God, from the delay of God in the fulfilment of His promises (cf. Hab. 2³), from the hiding of His face, from the *aperta indignatio* with which He can sometimes startle even His own people, from the scoffers who ask where is His coming, who argue that all things remain as they were, and who can so easily insinuate their doubts into ourselves and the world around (2 Pet. 3⁴). Only a concentrated faith which is sustained by hope, and raised up by it to the *contemplatio aeternitatis*, realising that one day is with the Lord as a thousand years, is a match for this kind of mocking question. (IV, 3, p. 913. The Subject of Hope and Hope.)

Cf. III, 2, pp. 508–511.

LUKE 12$^{35\text{-}40}$ (III)

Cf. on Romans 13$^{11\text{-}14}$ First Sunday in Advent, on Luke 12$^{35\text{-}40}$ New Year's Eve and on 1 Peter 4$^{7\text{-}11}$ Sunday After Ascension-Day (Exaudi).

REVELATION 4$^{1\text{-}8}$ (IV)

The time of Jesus is not only a time like all others; it is also different from them. For all other times are confined to the three dimensions. They begin, they endure, and they come to an end. According to the standpoint of the observer, they are future, contemporary or past.

1. Every other time begins, and therefore from the standpoint of an earlier time it is a future time. This means that it does not yet exist at this earlier time.

2. Every other time has duration, and therefore from the standpoint of the same time it is present. This means that its contemporaneity is limited to its duration, and to that of the contemporary observer.

3. Every other time comes to an end, and therefore from the standpoint of a later time it is already past. This means that it no longer exists at this time.

But these limitations of all other times—the times of all other living creatures—do not apply to the time of the man Jesus.

1. To be sure, the life of the man Jesus has a beginning, and His time was once future. Yet this does not mean that it did not then exist.

2. The life of the man Jesus has duration, and therefore it was once contemporary. Yet this does not mean that it was present only in its duration, and from the standpoint of contemporaries.

3. The life of Jesus comes to an end and therefore it becomes past. Yet this does not mean that it then ceased to be.

The removal of the limitations of its yesterday, to-day and to-morrow, of its once, now and then, is the distinctive feature of the time of the man Jesus . . . What is for all other times, the times of all other living creatures, an absolute barrier, is for Him in His time a gateway. (III, 2, p. 643 f. Jesus, Lord of Time.)

Cf. on Revelation 5$^{1\text{-}14}$ Third Sunday in Lent (Oculi).

ISAIAH 35$^{3\text{-}10}$ (V)

IV, 3, p. 339.

REVELATION 22$^{12\text{-}17,\ 20f.}$ (VI)

We may summarise in the words of Revelation 1^8: " I am he that is." The present in which there is real recollection of the man Jesus and the particular and preliminary revelation accomplished in Him, and real expectation of this man and God's final and general revelation with Him—this present " between the times " is His own time, the time of the man Jesus . . . " I am—which was. " The past to which we look back from the present of the man Jesus is, like this present and the future which lies before it, His time, the time of the man Jesus . . . " I am . . . which is to come " . . . The future to which we look forward from the present of the man Jesus is, like this present itself, and the past which lies behind it, His time, the time of the man Jesus. (III, 2, p. 468, 478, and 493. Jesus, Lord of Time.)

Can the Christianity and the Church which really derive from and are grounded in the resurrection of Jesus Christ ever be anything better than the place where, from out of and beyond all the required representations of Jesus Christ, the kingdom, the covenant, reconciliation and its fruit, men can only cry and call out: " Lord, have mercy upon us! Even so, come, Lord Jesus "? Is not perhaps the surest test of genuine Christianity and Church life whether the men united in it exist wholly in this expectation and therefore not at all in a supposed present possession of the glorious presence of their Lord? Will not His truly promised and therefore undeniable presence among them necessarily show itself in the fact that they exist as those who know an honest and basic lack, and thus hope for His conclusive appearing and revelation and their own and the whole world's redemption and consummation, looking and marching towards it in Advent in a movement from Christmas, Good Friday and especially Easter? What other time or season can or will the Church ever have but that of Advent? (IV, 3, p. 322. The Glory of the Mediator.)

SCRIPTURE REFERENCES IN
THE PREACHER'S AIDS